DATE DUE

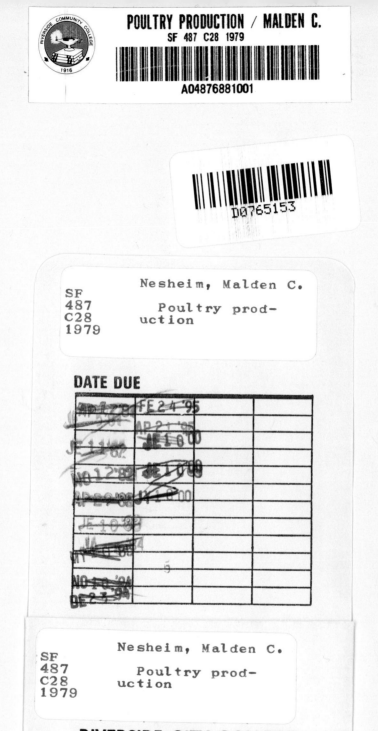

RIVERSIDE CITY COLLEGE

LIBRARY

Riverside, California

1981

Poultry Production

Poultry Production

MALDEN C. NESHEIM, Ph.D.
*Professor of Nutrition, Cornell University
Ithaca, New York*

RICHARD E. AUSTIC, Ph.D.
**Associate Professor of Animal Nutrition
Cornell University, Ithaca, New York**

LESLIE E. CARD, Ph.D.
*Professor of Animal Science, Emeritus,
University of Illinois, Urbana, Illinois*

TWELFTH EDITION

Riverside Community College
Library
4800 Magnolia Avenue
Riverside, CA 92506

Lea & Febiger • *Philadelphia 1979*

Library of Congress Cataloging in Publication Data

Nesheim, Malden C
  Poultry production.

  Eleventh ed. (1972) by L. E. Card and M. C. Nesheim.
  Includes index.
  1. Chickens.   2. Poultry.   I. Austic, Richard E., joint author.
  II. Card, Leslie Ellsworth, 1893–   Poultry production.   III. Title.
  SF487.C28   1979   636.5'08   78–31386
  ISBN   0–8121–0665–2

1st edition, 1914, by W. A. Lippincott
2nd edition, 1916, by W. A. Lippincott
3rd edition, 1921, by W. A. Lippincott
4th edition, 1927, by W. A. Lippincott
5th edition, 1934, by W. A. Lippincott and L. E. Card
6th edition, 1939, by W. A. Lippincott and L. E. Card
7th edition, 1946, by W. A. Lippincott and L. E. Card
8th edition, 1952, by L. E. Card
9th edition, 1961, by L. E. Card
10th edition, 1966, by L. E. Card and M. C. Nesheim
11th edition, 1972, by L. E. Card and M. C. Nesheim
12th edition, 1979, by M. C. Nesheim, R. E. Austic, and L. E. Card

Published in Great Britain by Bailliere Tindall, London

Printed in the United States of America

Print Number: 5   4   3   2   1

Preface

This edition of *Poultry Production* reflects a major change in authorship which interrupts a continuity that goes back over forty-five years. For the first time since 1934, Dr. Leslie E. Card has not played an active role in the revision of *Poultry Production*. The book still reflects many of Dr. Card's contributions to earlier editions, and the basic organization is not changed. Dr. Richard E. Austic has joined the authors and provides his perspective to the book, based upon his broad experience in teaching and research in poultry science.

Several chapters have been rewritten or extensively revised. We have continued to stress fundamental principles in poultry production and have not been able to provide details on all aspects of poultry production. We hope, however, that the book will present a good overview of the poultry industry and of the practices needed to insure the successful operation of a poultry business.

We are indebted to many individuals for helpful suggestions. Special mention should be given to the assistance of Bruce Calnek, Charles Ostrander, and R. K. Cole at Cornell, George Rogers and Carl Voslow at the United States Department of Agriculture (USDA), and David Crompton at Cambridge University. Mr. Rogers of the USDA has provided us with statistical data on the poultry industry and the preliminary analyses from the 1974 Agricultural Census. Several organizations have given permission to use various illustrations, and we are grateful for their help.

Ithaca, New York   M. C. NESHEIM, PH.D.
                                                        R. E. AUSTIC, PH.D.

Contents

Fig. 1–1. A modern white leghorn layer, the primary egg producer in today's poultry industry. (Courtesy Shaver Poultry Breeding Farms Ltd.)

Chapter 1

The Poultry Industry

The production of poultry in the United States and generally throughout the world is carried out by a highly specialized, efficient poultry industry that has been a leader in trends of scale and industrialization that have taken place in American agriculture over the past half century. Few other agricultural industries have shifted as rapidly and completely from small scale, nonintensive production units to a highly specialized intensive industry as has the poultry industry. Such changes have caused rapid shifts in geographical distribution, industry concentration, organization, and marketing patterns.

The total number of chickens produced in the United States annually amounts to more than 3.6 billion. These are kept for two separate purposes, the production of poultry meat and the production of table eggs (Figs. 1–1; 1–2). The organization and methods used by the two aspects of the poultry industry are different, and generally commercial table egg production and broiler production are carried out by separate enterprises.

The poultry industry, through the production of eggs, broilers, and turkeys, accounted for 7.1 billion dollars in gross farm income in 1976 in the United States.

MEAT PRODUCTION

Commercial broiler production accounts for 92% of the poultry meat produced in the United States today. This is in marked contrast to the era in poultry production when poultry meat was largely produced from spare cockerels, whose sisters became laying flock replacements, and from hens culled from the laying house. In 1934, when the U.S. Department of Agriculture (USDA) began reporting commercial broilers separately from farm-raised chickens, 4% of total chicken meat was produced as broilers. The growth of the commercial broiler industry has been spectacular as

1

→

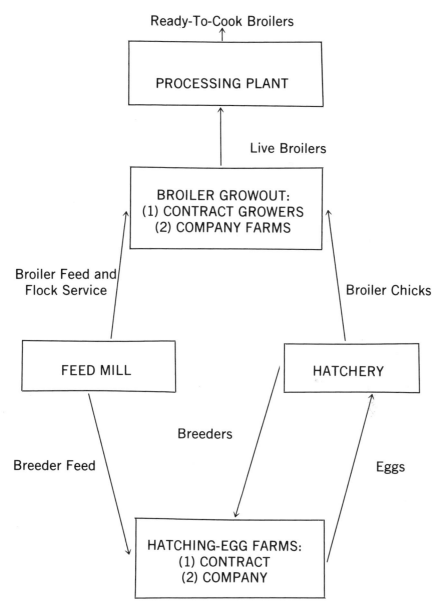

FUNCTIONS OF
A TYPICAL INTEGRATED BROILER FIRM

USDA   NEG. ERS 8235-77 (7)

Fig. 1–3. Organization of the broiler industry. (Courtesy of the U.S. Department of Agriculture.)

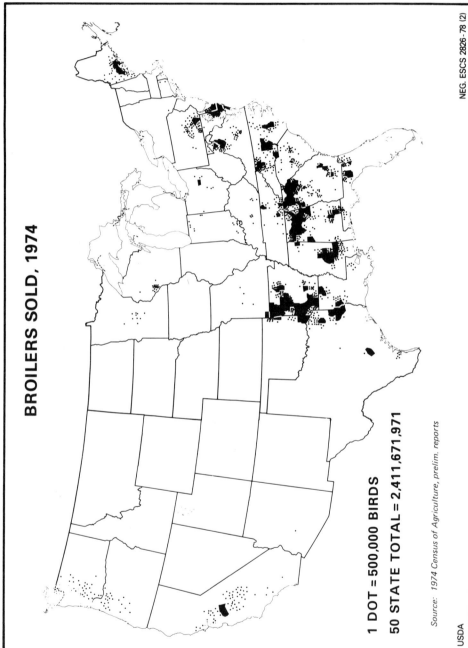

BROILERS SOLD, 1974

1 DOT = 500,000 BIRDS
50 STATE TOTAL = 2,411,671,971

Source: 1974 Census of Agriculture, prelim. reports

USDA

NEG. ESCS 2826-78 (2)

Table 1-2.   The Ten Leading States in Broiler Production, 1977

	Thousands
Arkansas	569,558
Georgia	485,879
Alabama	428,099
North Carolina	339,271
Mississippi	255,846
Maryland	198,509
Texas	185,322
Delaware	156,081
California	112,500
Virginia	98,024
Ten-state total	2,829,089
United States total	3,399,960

Data from the U.S. Department of Agriculture.

The west North Central states have declined in egg production relative to the region's needs and the South Atlantic, South Central, and Pacific regions have shifted from egg importing regions to egg exporting regions in just 20 years. The ten leading egg producing states are shown in Table 1-4. In 1955, Iowa was the major egg producing state, and only California, Pennsylvania, Indiana, Texas, and Minnesota were in the top ten states in both 1955 and 1976. Total production of eggs in the United States has changed relatively little during the past 30 years, despite an increase in the U.S. population of over 50% during that time (Table 1-5).

The number of farms producing eggs has declined rapidly over the past 20 years. There are probably about 200,000 farms in the United States with hens producing market eggs. Over 90% of these farms have less than 3,200 hens and produce only about 15% of the total supply. The USDA has estimated that 85% of the market eggs in the United States are produced by about 6% of the poultry farms or about 12,000 large commercial egg producers. There has been a trend toward the formation of large egg-producing companies that have multiple farms. According to USDA estimates, the 20 largest egg-producing companies in the United States account for about 18% of total egg production on about 1,100 farms.

The egg production phase of the poultry industry is only a component of the entire process of providing poultry products to consumers. The individual components of the egg industry are shown in Figure 1-5.

Increasingly, many of the functions involved in egg production are being consolidated so that they are carried out by an individual integrated firm or by several firms that have entered into contracts to carry out various functions of egg production. The USDA recently estimated that

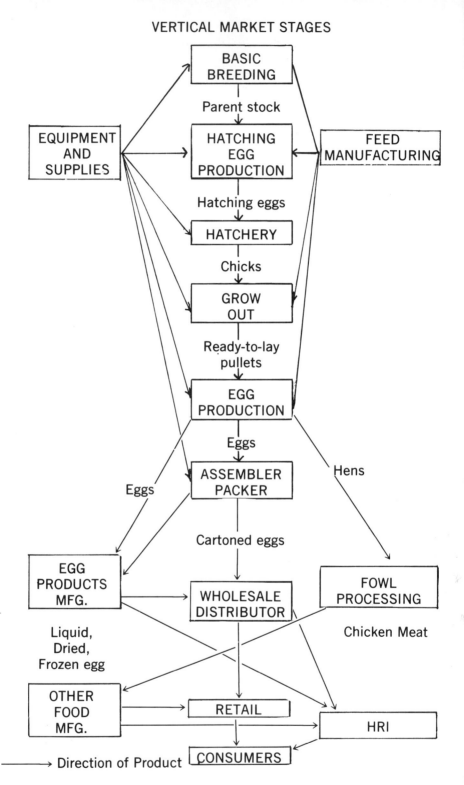

Fig. 1–5. The organization of the egg industry. (L. Schrader, O. Forker, H. Larzelere, and G. Rogers: The Egg Subsector of U.S. Agriculture. NC 117 Monograph #6, Purdue University, 1978).

Table 1–3.   Changes in Egg Production by Regions

Region	Regional Supply of Shell Eggs as Percentage of Regional Consumption 1955	1975
New England	81	104
Middle Atlantic	76	53
East North Central	98	72
West North Central	277	137
South Atlantic	63	134
South Central	78	120
Mountain	77	64
Pacific	100	129

From USDA Statistics

Table 1–4.   Ten Leading States in the Production of Eggs (1977)

	Average No. Layers during Year	Eggs Produced (millions)	Share of U.S. Output (percent)
California	36,469,000	8345	12.9
Georgia...........................	23,515,000	5535	8.6
Arkansas	16,130,000	3812	5.9
Alabama..........................	13,434,000	2998	4.6
Indiana	12,833,000	3004	4.7
Florida	12,633,000	2998	4.6
North Carolina	12,374,000	2968	4.6
Pennsylvania	12,136,000	2943	4.6
Texas	10,433,000	2380	3.7
Minnesota	8,875,000	2120	3.3
United States	274,642,000	64,540	

Table 1–5.   Egg Production in the United States, 1940–1975

Year	Average No. Hens & Pullets During Year	Rate of Laying No./Hen	Eggs Produced Millions	Gross Income $1,000
1940	392,655	134	39,695	582,211
1945	369,430	152	56,221	1,751,381
1950	339,540	174	58,954	1,772,571
1955	309,297	192	59,526	1,954,746
1960	295,284	209	61,602	1,848,389
1965	301,053	218	65,560	1,840,650
1970	312,922	218	68,282	2,223,608
1975	277,030	232	64,391	2,814,821

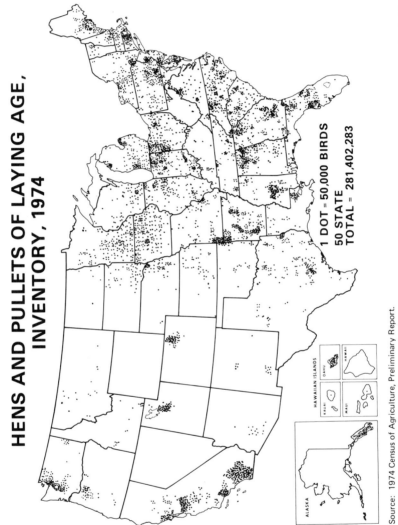

HENS AND PULLETS OF LAYING AGE, INVENTORY, 1974

1 DOT = 50,000 BIRDS
50 STATE TOTAL = 281,402,283

HAWAIIAN ISLANDS
OAHU
HAWAII
KAUAI
MAUI

ALASKA

Source: 1974 Census of Agriculture, Preliminary Report.

USDA

NEG. ESCS 2940-78 (2)

Fig. 1-6. Distribution of layers in the United States.

Table 1-6. Total Hours for Poultry Meat and Egg Production

Year	Million Hours for Farm Work for Poultry	Index of Production per Hour of Labor 1967 = 100
1940	145	17
1950	163	26
1960	82	56
1970	43	124
1975	28	187

45% of the eggs produced today involve some contract arrangement and integrated production. Individual integrated firms also are important in egg production, as more than 35% of commercial egg production is carried out by large-scale integrated operations.

The concentration of the industry has occurred for several reasons. The technology for large-scale production is readily available and quite successful. The declining per capita consumption of eggs has placed considerable economic pressure on the egg industry and has forced changes that have resulted in increased efficiency that can be achieved through changes in scale and industry organization.

The trends of increased concentration and increased scale of poultry production have resulted in considerable increases in labor productivity. The data in Table 1-6 show that in 1940, 145 million hours were spent on farm production of poultry meat and eggs, whereas in 1975, only 28 million hours were spent. This is equivalent to a reduction in labor force employed on a full-time basis from about 70,000 to about 13,000 in spite of the fact that total production of poultry meat and eggs has increased greatly since 1939. The increased labor productivity is shown by the data in Table 1-6 which indicate that labor productivity has increased more than tenfold from 1940 in the poultry industry.

ASSOCIATED INDUSTRIES

The concentration and specialization of the poultry industry have led to the development of allied industries to supply the products needed to support the technology used. Thus suppliers of housing, equipment, hatchery equipment, processing and packaging equipment, health products, and feed are needed to support the poultry industry. These represent a significant component of the total economic impact of the poultry industry.

These industries have also felt the changes in concentration in the poultry industry. There were 797 chick hatcheries in the United States in 1975 compared to 5,045 in 1957 and 2,365 in 1965. There are about 10,000 feed mills in the United States, about 50% of which probably handle some poultry feed. Four to five companies probably supply most of the equipment needs for production and marketing in the poultry industry.

RELATIONSHIP OF THE POULTRY INDUSTRY TO U.S. CROP PRODUCTION

A primary function of the poultry industry is the conversion of feed grains, by-product feeds, and protein concentrates to a form that is prized for human food. The relative importance of the poultry industry to U.S. agriculture can be seen by the statistics in Table 1–7. In 1977, 22% of all the feeds fed to livestock in the United States were fed to poultry. This included 19.5% of the corn fed to livestock and 42.6% of the high protein feeds. Of the feed grains that were produced in the United States in the 1976/77 crop year, 53% were fed to livestock, about 9% were used by the food industry and for seed, and 24% were exported. Therefore, we consume far more of the grain produced in this country in the form of livestock products than we consume as grain directly. The poultry industry by itself uses more grain than is consumed directly by people. Thus the feeding of livestock provides a major market for products produced by the farms of this country. Indeed, most of the grain exports are made to countries where they are used for livestock feed. In 1976/77 about 80% of U.S. grain exports were made to Western Europe, Japan, and the Soviet Union, where much of the grain was used to feed livestock.

The poultry industry consumed 42.6% of the high protein feeds fed to livestock in 1977, with the major proportion being soybean meal. The United States exported about 564 million bushels of soybeans in 1976/77 which were sent largely to Western Europe and Japan to supply a high

Table 1–7. Consumption of Harvested Feed by Poultry in 1977 in 1000 metric tons (USDA estimates)

	Corn	Sorghum	Other Grain	High Protein Feeds	Other By-product Feeds	Total
All livestock	107,352	13,300	17,824	21,720	17,562	177,758
Laying hens and pullets	9,369	1,375	2,067	2,667	2,122	17,600
Growing replacement stock	782	385	797	980	281	3,225
Broilers	8,483	345	348	3,867	544	13,587
Turkeys	2,227	150	358	1,740	235	4,710
Total fed to poultry	20,861	2,255	3,570	9,254	3,182	39,122
% of all feeds fed to livestock fed to poultry	19.5	16.9	20.0	42.6	18.1	22.0

protein supplement for poultry feeding. When exports are considered, poultry feeding consumes an even greater proportion of the output of U.S. farms than is shown in Table 1–7.

CONSUMPTION OF POULTRY PRODUCTS

The products of the poultry industry provide high quality human food. The trends in consumption of poultry meat and eggs in the United States since 1950 are shown in Table 1–8. Poultry meat consumption has more than doubled since 1950 while egg consumption steadily declined. Presently eggs provide about 2% of the protein, 4.7% of the iron, and about 6% of the vitamin A in the U.S. diet. Poultry meat provides U.S. consumers with about 8% of their daily protein intake.

Poultry meat and eggs represent one of the cheapest sources of protein available to the U.S. consumer. Twenty grams of protein from eggs cost 21 cents in 1976, the same as the cost of 20 grams of protein from chicken meat. In comparison, 20 grams of protein from white bread cost 18 cents, from hamburger 21 cents, turkey 26 cents, ham 43 cents, beef rib roast 59 cents, and from pork chops 65 cents. This low cost has undoubtedly been a major stimulus to the rapid expansion of poultry meat consumption over the past 20 years. In 1956, the cost of 20 grams of protein from chicken meat was 18 cents. The increase in cost over the past 20 years has been minimal compared to the increase for other meats whose cost has doubled or tripled in the same 20-year period.

Although the expanding consumption of poultry meat has been a major stimulus to the expansion of broiler production, the decline in egg consumption has been of major concern to the industry. The reasons for the reduction in egg consumption are complex. Consumer meal patterns have undoubtedly played a role. Eggs are traditionally a breakfast dish in the United States and are not used as much for lunch and dinner. Breakfast patterns have changed since more of our population has

Table 1–8. Trends in Consumption of Poultry Products and Red Meats since 1950

	Chicken lb/capita	Turkey lb/capita	Egg No./capita	Red Meats[a] lb/capita
1950	20.6	4.1	390	137.4
1955	21.3	5.3	371	152.2
1960	28.0	6.1	335	146.9
1965	33.4	7.4	314	148.3
1970	40.5	8.0	311	164.6
1976	43.3	9.2	276	167.6

[a]Beef, pork, lamb, veal.
Data from the U.S. Department of Agriculture.

become urban and less time is allocated for breakfast preparation. Egg consumption has also undoubtedly been affected by medical controversy relating fat and cholesterol intake to heart disease. Interestingly, worldwide egg consumption is increasing. Consumption in Eastern Europe has increased by 25% and in developing countries by 18%. The consumption of eggs in Israel, West Germany, and Japan is currently higher per capita than in the United States. Most of Western Europe and the Soviet Union consume more than 200 eggs per capita. Egg substitutes have had some effect on demand. There are several low-cholesterol egg substitutes on the market that provide a yolk substitute with natural egg white. Other proteins, such as soybean protein, have been used to substitute for eggs in some manufacturing processes.

The size of the egg industry in the United States will be heavily dependent upon future trends in egg consumption.

WORLDWIDE POULTRY PRODUCTION

The changes in technology that have occurred in the past 40 years in the poultry industry have also been an important stimulus to the poultry industry worldwide. Expanding incomes in many parts of the world have increased consumer demand for poultry products. The technology developed for feeding, disease control, and production management can be used nearly all over the world with relatively little modification. Thus the technological advances in poultry production have been quickly applied in many parts of the world. Accurate statistics are not easy to obtain for production in some areas. USDA estimates of egg production in various parts of the world are shown in Table 1–9.

Egg production in Canada is centered in the province of Ontario, which produces some 40% of the total Canadian production. Other leading

Table 1–9.   Egg Production in Various Regions of the World, 1976 (USDA Figures)

Region	Eggs Produced (millions)
United States	64,850
Canada	5,280
Mexico	7,665
Brazil	6,000
Argentina	2,900
Western Europe	84,670
Eastern Europe	32,522
USSR	55,100
Japan	32,500
Australia	3,248

provinces for egg production in Canada include Quebec, British Columbia, Manitoba, and Alberta. West Germany, the United Kingdom, France, and Italy have the largest poultry industries in Western Europe. Poland produces about one third of the eggs in Eastern Europe. Egg production in Japan has expanded rapidly in recent years. Although good figures are not easy to obtain, the Food and Agriculture Organization of the United Nations (FAO) data indicate that China is the second largest egg producing country in the world.

In Canada, Ontario and Quebec are the leading broiler provinces, producing about 68% of the total Canadian production. Western Europe, Latin America, Eastern Europe, and the Soviet Union have all developed important broiler industries.

United States production is primarily used for domestic consumption. In 1976, the value of poultry and poultry products exported was $207,129,000 or about 3% of the total value of U.S. poultry products marketed in 1976. Frozen chicken and turkey meat accounted for nearly 60% of the value of the exported poultry products. Hatching eggs and breeding chicks were the next largest category of exports, with a total value of about 36 million dollars. Only about 1% of U.S. table egg production moves in egg export channels.

Chapter 2

Biology of the Fowl

Chickens are probably the most numerous domestic birds in the world. From 8 to 9 billion chickens are raised in the world annually, although precise estimates of world production are difficult to obtain. Some estimates of world numbers of domestic poultry were made in 1975 by Crompton and Nesheim (Table 2–1). Zoologically the chicken belongs to the genus *Gallus* of the family *Phasianidae*. The domestic chicken is called simply *Gallus domesticus*. The wild ancestors of the domestic chicken probably originated in Southeast Asia. Four species of wild jungle fowl are still known in that area: *Gallus gallus,* the red jungle fowl; *Gallus lafayetti,* the Ceylonese jungle fowl; *Gallus sonnerati,* the grey jungle fowl; and *Gallus varius,* the black or green jungle fowl. The red jungle fowl, *Gallus gallus,* has the widest distribution of the wild species and may well be the chief ancestor of modern chickens (Fig. 2–1).

The biology of the domestic fowl is closely related to the biology of other birds. Although the chicken has been domesticated since at least 2000 B.C., and has been subjected to extensive breeding for size, color patterns, conformation, and egg-laying ability during much of its domesticated history, it still retains much in common with its wild ancestors. Knowing some of the important features of avian biology can aid immensely in understanding the factors that influence the ability of chickens to lay eggs, grow rapidly, and serve as efficient sources of human food.

ANATOMY

The Skeleton

The skeleton of the fowl is compact, light in weight, and very strong. The vertebrae of the neck and tail are movable, but the body of the

16

Table 2–1. Estimated Populations of Some Domestic Birds in the World

	Ducks	Geese	Fowls	Turkeys	Total
Africa[a]	5,189,000	4,614,000	410,364,000	1,734,000	421,901,000
Asia[a]	64,209,000	2,429,000	757,289,000	3,038,000	826,965,000
China[a,b,c]	21,060,000	3,510,000	1,119,690,000	25,740,000	1,170,000,000
Europe[a]	28,700,000	14,055,000	1,206,659,000	13,594,000	1,263,008,000
North and Central America[a]	674,000	365,000	302,481,000	8,782,000	312,302,000
Oceania[a]	1,147,000	228,000	29,882,000	717,000	31,974,000
South America[a]	9,249,000	102,000	457,992,000	4,858,000	472,201,000
U.S.A.[c,d,e]	12,508,000	1,069,000	3,387,953,000	120,085,000	3,521,615,000
U.S.S.R.[a,b,c]	10,800,000	1,800,000	574,200,000	13,200,000	600,000,000
TOTALS	153,536,000 (1.8%)	28,172,000 (0.3%)	8,246,510,000 (95.7%)	191,748,000 (2.2%)	8,619,966,000 (100%)

With permission from Crompton, D.W.T., and Nesheim, M.C.: Host-parasite relationships in the alimentary tract of birds. *In* Advances in Parasitology, Vol. 14, 95–194, 1975. Copyright by Academic Press Inc. (London) Ltd.

[a] FAO: Production Yearbook, 25, 1971.

[b] Estimates of species not given by FAO. Total numbers of domestic birds for these regions were calculated by us according to the proportions found in the world.

[c] Not included in continental location.

[d] U.S. Department of Commerce: U.S. Census of Agriculture (1964) Vol. II, Ch. 1 for ducks and geese.

[e] U.S.Department of Agriculture: Agricultural Statistics (1972) for fowls and turkeys.

Fig. 2–1. A male and female red jungle fowl *(Gallus gallus)*, probably the major wild ancestor of domestic chickens.

chicken has only one movable vertebra along its length. The body vertebrae are fused into rigid structures that give the body sufficient strength to support wings. The major bones of the chicken are shown in Figure 2–2.

Birds are distinguished by having many bones that are *pneumatic*, that is, they are hollow and are connected to the respiratory system. Bones of the skull, the humerus, the clavicle, the keel, and the lumbar and sacral vertebrae are all connected to the respiratory system. This connection is so intimate that a chicken can breathe through its cut humerus, the bone in the upper portion of the wing, if the trachea is closed off.

Many bones contain a unique type of bone called medullary bone. This bone fills the marrow cavity with fine interlacing spicules of bone that provide a readily available source of calcium for eggshell formation when calcium intake is low. Medullary bone is found in the tibia, femur, pubic bones, sternum, ribs, ulna, toes, and the scapula. Nearly 12% of the total bone of a mature pullet may be medullary bone. In the ribs, as much as 30% of the total bone is in this form. This bone is not normally found in males or in nonlaying hens but can be caused to form by administering estrogen, the female hormone. Pullets, when maturing, begin to deposit medullary bone about 10 days prior to formation of the first egg. In wild birds, this bone provides sufficient calcium for shell formation even though dietary intake of calcium during egg laying may be very low. However, calcium stores in the skeleton of the domestic hen are only sufficient to provide eggshells for relatively few eggs. About 40% of the total skeletal calcium is lost by hens after laying 6 eggs when they receive a diet containing a low amount of calcium.

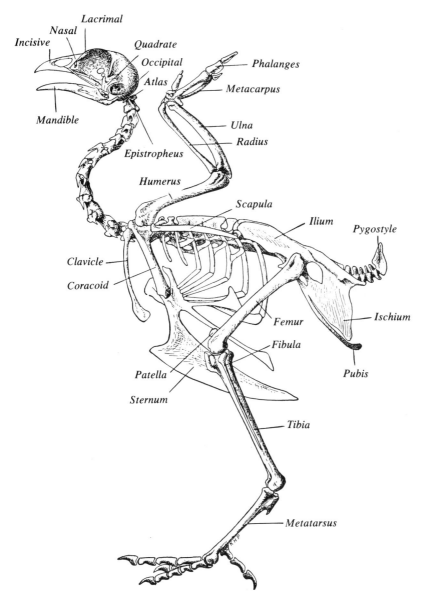

Fig. 2–2. The skeleton of a fowl.

Muscular System

Muscular tissue is the principal contractile organ of the body. It is responsible for nearly all movement in higher animals. Three principal types of muscle are present: smooth muscle, which is found in blood vessels, intestine, and other organs not under voluntary control; cardiac muscle of the heart; and skeletal muscle. Skeletal muscle is responsible for most voluntary movement and makes up most of the edible portion of the carcass of a chicken. The breast, thigh, and leg muscles are the most prominent muscle systems in the body of the bird. Because of the adaptation of birds to flight, the breast muscles make up a particularly large portion of the musculature.

Chickens and turkeys contain both red muscle and white muscle, corresponding to the dark and white meat familiar to consumers. The red muscle contains more myoglobin, an iron-containing, oxygen-carrying compound, than does white muscle. The myoglobin is similar in some respects to hemoglobin, the oxygen-carrying red pigment of blood.

Respiratory System

The respiratory system consists of the lungs, the passages leading to the lungs, and the air sacs. The lungs are closely attached to the ribs in the upper portion of the thoracic cavity. The lungs are rather rigid structures which expand and contract relatively little during respiration. It is primarily change in pressure within the air sacs that causes air to pass into and out of the lungs. Active contraction of respiratory muscles occurs during both inspiration and expiration.

The chicken has 4 pairs of air sacs, ranging in position from the neck to the abdomen, with a single median sac located in the cavity of the thorax. These sacs open into the lungs and communicate with the pneumatic bones of the body. The air sacs are delicate, thin-walled structures that are difficult to recognize when they collapse as a chicken is autopsied.

The voice of the fowl is produced in the syrinx, or lower larynx, located where the trachea divides into the two bronchi. The syrinx is the only part of the respiratory tract that is capable of producing sound; the upper larynx serves only to modulate the voice. The syrinx is essentially the same in both male and female. The normal hen does not crow because she lacks the psychological incentive to do so. If this incentive is provided experimentally, by suitable injections of the male sex hormone, hens will crow.

Respiration and Temperature Regulation in Chickens

Since warm-blooded animals constantly produce and lose heat, a complex mechanism must be used to maintain a constant body temperature. Heat loss from the body may be as sensible heat, that is, heat that can be measured in a calorimeter, and as latent heat. Latent heat is the heat required for evaporation of water, which occurs primarily in the respiratory passages. It requires 577 calories to change 1 gram of water from a liquid to water vapor at 91° F with no change in temperature.

Sensible heat losses, by radiation, convection, and conduction of heat from body surfaces, make up the major heat losses from the body at environmental temperatures below 80° F. Above 80° F loss of heat by evaporation of water from the respiratory tract becomes an increasingly important means of heat dissipation. Panting may be observed when chickens are kept under high envirnomental temperatures.

Since chickens have no sweat glands, the lungs and air sacs have been considered the most important evaporative coolers in the chicken. However, a report from Michigan State University suggests that these structures are not the major points of heat transfer. In the Michigan studies the temperature and moisture content of air were measured at the nasal passages and at various locations in the respiratory tract. The results showed that the majority of the heat and moisture transfer to the respiratory air occurs during inspiration. The mucosa from the nasal opening to the base of the trachea seems to be most important in the heat-moisture transfer. The transfer of heat from lung and air sac surfaces was considered to be small, since the inspired air was nearly at body temperature and was saturated with water before entering the lungs.

The Michigan State workers also reported that the comb and wattles have a large role in sensible heat losses. About 40% of the total sensible heat produced by the chickens was found to be lost from the head region. Since dubbing or removal of some of the comb of white leghorn hens is a common practice, one might speculate that this has some influence on the heat losses that occur in chickens, especially at low temperatures.

The Skin

Chickens have a relatively thin skin over most of the body which is free of secretory glands. The only exception is the uropygial or oil gland (preen gland), which is found on the upper portion of the tail. Numerous specialized structures are associated with the skin, such as the comb, wattles, ear lobes, scales on the legs and toes, spurs, claws, and the beak. The size and color of the comb and wattles are particularly associated with gonad development and secretion of the sex hormones.

Skin color depends on combinations of pigments in the upper and lower layers of skin. Yellow skin and shanks are due to carotenoid pigments of dietary origin in the epidermis, along with the absence of melanic pigment. Black and its variations are caused by the presence of melanic pigment in the epidermis. The darkest shank occurs when melanic pigment is present in both the dermis and the epidermis. Yellow in the dermis is obscured by black in the epidermis.

Blue or slaty blue shanks occur when the only pigment present is black in the underlying dermis. With black in the dermis and yellow in the overlying epidermis, the shank appears willow green in color. White shanks result from the complete absence of both types of pigment.

Modern broiler strains are usually selected for yellow skin and shanks, since these seem to be preferred by consumers. The yellow color desired by many markets is due to the presence of pigments obtained through the diet.

Feathers

Birds have a unique covering over much of the body. Feathers are protection for the bird, aid in keeping the body warm, and are essential for flight. The annual renewal of the feather coat constitutes a considerable physiological expense to the fowl, since the feathers make up from 4 to

Fig. 2–3. Different types of feathers. *(A)* Primary of pigeon—an important flight feather with a stiff vane. *(B)* Underwing covert of a great blue heron; downy portion overlapped by an adjoining feather. *(C)* Wing covert of owl; the downy edge makes possible the noiseless flight of this bird. *(D).* Feather of ostrich; the power of flight has been lost, and the entire vane is downy. (Beebe: *The Bird*. Courtesy of Henry Holt and Company)

9% of the empty live weight, depending on the age and sex of the individual.

Though the body surface of most birds is almost entirely covered by feathers, there are only a few species in which the feathers actually grow from the entire surface of the skin. In most species, including the fowl, the feathers are arranged in definite areas or feather tracts. Several of these tracts, or *pterylae,* are paired, as may be seen readily by examining a picked carcass.

The parts of a typical body feather are the quill, which is continuous throughout the vane of the feather as the shaft or rachis; the barbs, branching from the shaft; the barbules, branching from the barbs; and the barbicels, branching from the barbules. Except for size differences, most of the variation in the form and structure of feathers is due to differences in the mode of structure of the barbules and their branches (Fig. 2–3).

The order of formation of the shaft of the feather is strictly apicobasal, and the order of age of the barbs is naturally the same. Similarly, in each barb, the apex at the margin of the feather is the first formed, and the central end attached to the shaft is the last. Thus there are two time gradients in each feather: from the apex to the base along the shaft, and from margin to center along the barbs.

The rate of growth of the shaft is approximately uniform throughout its length, at least during the formation of the vane of the feather. The rate of growth of the barbs, on the other hand, diminishes from the apex to the

Fig. 2–4. Sex dimorphism in structure of feathers. From left to right the paired male and female feathers are from the wing bow, neck, and saddle regions. The male feathers (on the right in each pair) appear more pointed and lacier because of the large areas free from barbules toward the tip of the feathers. (Photo by Dr. W. F. Lamoreaux, Cornell University)

base of each, that is, from the margin of the feather to the shaft. This form of growth plays a large part in determining the pigmentation and general pattern of the feather. The time required to form the vane of a breast feather is approximately 20 days from the time of plucking an old feather.

The large feathers of the wings and tail are definite in number and are molted and replaced, as a rule, in a regular order. This fact can be used as a basis of estimating the length of time that certain birds have been out of production.

There are well-known differences between the sexes in the appearance of feathers in the neck, back, saddle, and tail sections (Fig. 2–4). These are among the secondary sexual differences that are characteristic of birds. In certain "hen-feathered" breeds the feathers in these sections are essentially alike in both sexes. The Campine and the Sebright bantam are examples.

Blood—The Circulatory System

In contrast to its reptilian ancestors, the chicken has a four-chambered heart, two atria and two ventricles, which allow efficient circulation to the lungs to provide sufficient exchange of O_2 and CO_2 to support a high rate of metabolism. The blood of a chicken makes up about 8% of the body weight in chicks one to two weeks of age and about 6% of the weight of a mature hen.

The heart rate of a mature small fowl, such as a white leghorn, is about 350 beats per minute. Larger breeds such as the Rhode Island red have lower heart rates averaging about 250 beats per minute. Dropping a day-old chick has been shown to increase the heart rate from 300 beats per minute to 560. The deep body temperature of a mature chicken is about 41.9° C (107.4° F).

The blood functions in transport of oxygen and carbon dioxide, transport of nutrients to body cells, in temperature regulation, and in transport of important metabolites, hormones, and waste products to appropriate places in the body. Chicken blood contains from about 2.5 to 3.5 million red blood cells per cubic millimeter depending on age and sex. The blood of adult males contains about 500,000 more red blood cells per cubic millimeter than are found in the blood of a hen. Avian red blood cells contain a nucleus, in contrast to the red blood cell of a mammal. The red blood cells contain the hemoglobin, the oxygen-carrying pigment of blood. About 30% of the volume of whole blood of a young chicken or laying hen and up to 40% in adult males is made up of cells.

The *spleen* is an organ associated with the circulatory system, found near the gizzard in the abdominal cavity, in which red and white blood cells may be formed, and which may act as a reservoir for red blood cells.

Excretory System

The excretion of water and metabolic wastes occurs largely through the kidneys. The avian kidneys are rather large elongated organs located tightly against the top of the abdominal cavity closely associated with the backbone. Each kidney is divided into three separate readily visible lobes. The kidney is made up of many small tubules or nephrons which are the main functional feature of the kidney. The cells and blood protein are filtered out of the blood as the filtrate passes into the kidney tubule. Water and compounds conserved by the body are largely reabsorbed while waste products to be eliminated are excreted in the urine. The kidney has a key role in regulating acid-base balance and maintaining osmotic balance of body fluids.

Chicken urine is a yellowish fluid containing a white pasty substance that is largely uric acid. This is the material that gives bird droppings their characteristic white appearance. Uric acid is the major end product of nitrogen metabolism in birds and is an extremely water-insoluble compound.

The urine passes out of the kidney through the ureters which end in the cloaca. This is a chamber common to the digestive, urinary, and reproductive passages which open externally at the vent. Some urine, after reaching the cloaca, enters the rectum of the chicken, where some further reabsorption of water occurs.

Digestive System

The digestive system is the passage connecting the outside environment to the metabolic world of an animal (Fig. 2–5). The development and anatomy of the alimentary tract largely determine the type of food that is nutritionally useful for a particular species. Carnivores have very short digestive tracts, whereas in herbivores the alimentary canal is relatively long. The relationship of length of body to length of digestive tract of the cat is 1:4, the dog 1:6, but in the sheep the ratio is 1:27. The chicken has a ratio of body length to length of intestinal tract of about 1:4.

The types of food most useful to chickens resemble those that are also most useful to cats and dogs, rather than to cattle and sheep. The chicken has a simple digestive system, in which there is little place for microorganisms living in the digestive system to help digest food, as in ruminants such as cattle and sheep. Thus, chickens must depend on the enzymes secreted by appropriate portions of the digestive system to break down complex food molecules to simpler substances capable of being absorbed. When food is consumed that cannot be digested by the digestive enzymes present, the food is not useful to the chicken.

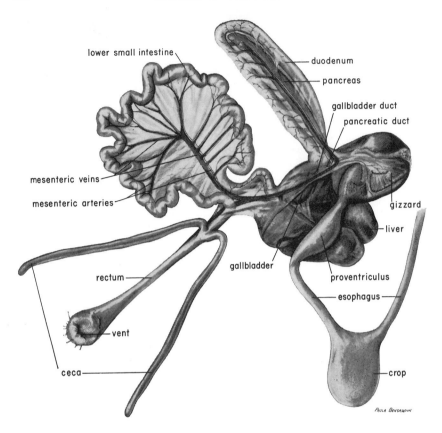

Fig. 2–5. Digestive system of the fowl, spread out to show the component parts. Note its relatively short length and the many blood vessels to transport nutrients as they are absorbed.

Mouth, Esophagus, and Crop. The distinctive character of the mouth of a bird is the absence of lips and teeth. These parts are replaced by a horny mandible on each jaw forming the beak. The tongue in fowls and turkeys is shaped like the barbed head of an arrow with the point directed forward. The barblike projections at the back of the tongue serve to force food toward the esophagus when the tongue is moved from front to back. Salivary glands are present which secrete a mucous saliva that lubricates the food as it passes down the esophagus.

The crop is a pouch formed as a specialized area of the esophagus. Little digestion occurs in the crop, and its chief function is as a storage organ. The stomach of the fowl has relatively little storage capacity.

Glandular Stomach. The true stomach (proventriculus) of a bird appears as little more than an enlargement at the end of the esophagus. Hydrochloric acid and an enzyme (pepsin) aiding in protein digestion are secreted by the wall of the proventriculus. Because the time spent by food in the proventriculus is short, digestion taking place there is probably of relatively little importance.

Gizzard. The gizzard is oval, with two openings on its upper side, one from the proventriculus and the other opening into the duodenum. It is composed of two pairs of red, thick, powerful muscles covered internally with a thick horny epithelium. The muscles of the gizzard are very strong. The muscles of a turkey gizzard for example can crush a hickory nut, which requires 75 kg mechanical pressure for crushing.

The chief function of the gizzard is to grind or crush food particles. This process is normally aided by the presence of grit or gravel taken in through the mouth. With uniformly ground rations, grinding in the gizzard is probably relatively unimportant for good digestion. With whole grains, however, grinding in the gizzard is essential before they can be properly digested. The constant action of the gizzard may be heard by holding a little chick, which has been supplied with grit, to the ear.

Pancreas. Immediately after its attachment to the gizzard, the intestine is folded in a loop called the duodenum, the sides of which are parallel and enclose the pancreas. The pancreas secretes pancreatic juice into the lower end of the duodenum through the pancreatic ducts. Pancreatic juice neutralizes the acid secretion of the proventriculus. The pancreatic secretion contains enzymes that hydrolyze proteins, starches, and fats. In the absence of pancreatic juice, little digestion of these substances occurs.

Liver. Bile is necessary for proper absorption of fats from the small intestine. The bile is produced in the liver and is conveyed to the lower end of the duodenum by two bile ducts. The one from the right lobe of the liver is enlarged to form the gallbladder in which the bile is stored and concentrated. The presence of food in the duodenum causes the gallbladder to contract and empty its bile into the intestine. The duct from the left lobe does not have an enlargement but goes directly to the small intestine, where the bile ducts enter together.

Small Intestine. The small intestine is normally considered to have two distinct parts, the duodenum and the lower small intestine. Enzymes present in the pancreatic juice act on starches, fats, and proteins while enzymes produced in the intestinal wall complete the digestive process by breaking down small fragments of protein molecules (peptides) to amino acids and by splitting disaccharides such as sucrose and maltose into simple sugars which can be absorbed. Since there is no specialized area in the digestive tract for bacterial action to aid the breakdown of foodstuffs, only feed material that can be digested by the enzymes secreted by the chicken are useful as food.

The digestion and absorption of food takes place primarily in the small intestine. The mucosa lining the small intestine is characterized by a series of folds, villi, and crypts that greatly increase the surface area of the epithelial lining (Fig. 2–6). In addition, the epithelial cells lining the villi

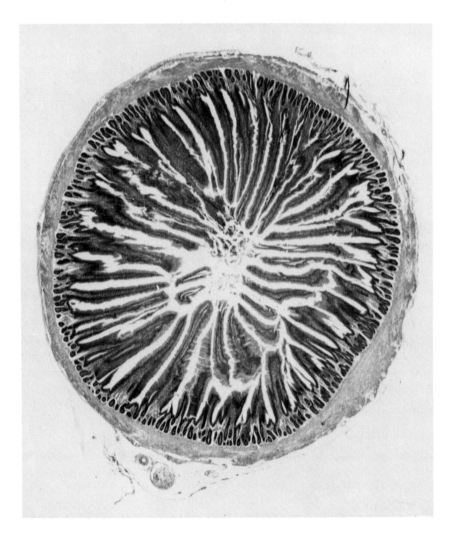

Fig. 2–6. A cross section of the small intestine of an 8-week-old chicken showing the extensive surface area of the epithelium lining the small intestine. The long projections into the center of the section are termed villi. (Courtesy of P.L. Clarke, Cambridge University.)

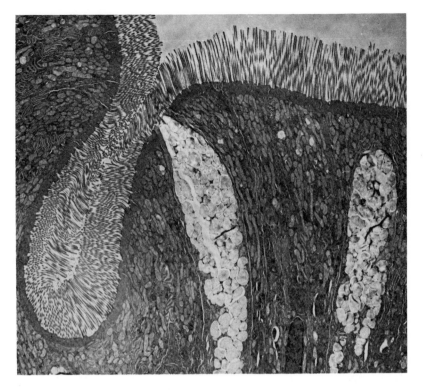

Fig. 2–7. Electron micrograph of surface of intestinal epithelium from a chicken showing the microvilli on the mucosal cell surface. The light-colored globular material is within a goblet cell, a mucous-secreting cell in the intestinal epithelium. (Courtesy of D.W.T. Crompton, Cambridge University.)

have finger-like projections (microvilli) that also increase the absorptive surface (Fig. 2–7). This extensive surface area, along with the blood flow to and from the intestine (Fig. 2–8), makes it possible for a meal to be digested and absorbed in less than 3 hours by domestic fowl (Fig. 2–9).

Ceca. At the juncture of the lower small intestine and the rectum are two blind pouches given off from either side, called ceca. These are usually 4 to 6 inches in length and are usually filled with fecal matter. With the usual modern highly digestible rations fed to poultry the ceca have little function in digestion. In adult birds fed highly fibrous rations, some digestion of fiber may take place in the ceca by action of microorganisms.

Rectum and Cloaca. The large intestine is short and consists of a short rectum leading to the cloaca. The rectum of an adult chicken is usually not more than 3 or 4 inches long. The cloaca is a chamber common to the digestive, urinary, and reproductive passages, which opens externally at the vent. The urine is discharged into the cloaca and excreted with the

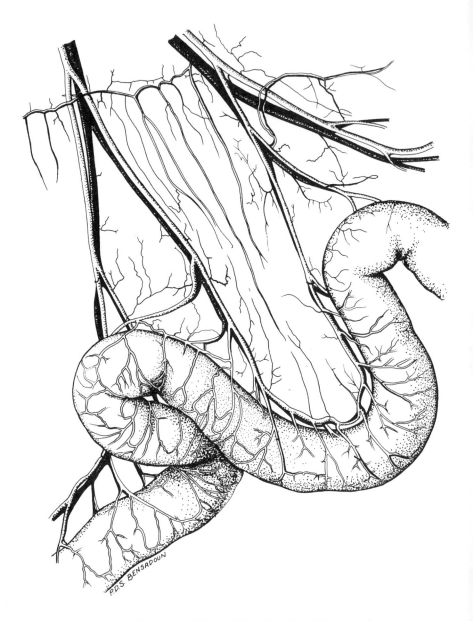

Fig. 2–8. A drawing of a section of the small intestine of a chicken showing the extensive blood supply. The white vessels are arteries and the black vessels are veins. (Courtesy of D. W. T. Crompton, Cambridge University, from Crompton, Malfunctioning of the gut. Parasitism, from digestion in the fowl. Br. Poultry Science Ltd. Edinburgh, 1976.)

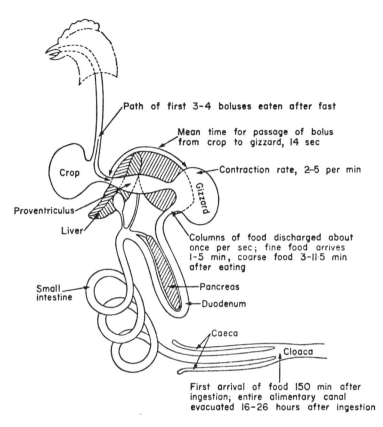

Path of first 3-4 boluses eaten after fast

Mean time for passage of bolus from crop to gizzard, 14 sec

Contraction rate, 2-5 per min

Crop

Gizzard

Proventriculus

Liver

Columns of food discharged about once per sec; fine food arrives 1-5 min, coarse food 3-11.5 min after eating

Small intestine

Pancreas

Duodenum

Caeca

Cloaca

First arrival of food 150 min after ingestion; entire alimentary canal evacuated 16-26 hours after ingestion

Fig. 2–9. Diagrammatic representation of the passage of food down the alimentary tract of the domestic fowl. (From K. M. Henry, A. J. MacDonald, and H. E. Mc Gee, J. Exp. Biol., *10*:153, 1933.)

feces. White pasty material in chicken droppings is largely uric acid that has precipitated from urine.

Nervous System

The nervous system integrates the functions of the body. Stimuli from senses are integrated and responses originate from the nervous system. The prime elements of the nervous system are the nerve cells and their processes. These cells are concentrated in the brain, the spinal cord, and certain other locations in the body called ganglia. The nerve cell processes make up the nerves of the body. Usually the nervous system is divided into two parts, the somatic or the cerebrospinal part of the central nervous system, which is responsible for the voluntary actions of the body, and the autonomic system which is responsible for the coordination of involuntary actions of organs such as intestines, blood vessels, and glands.

The chicken has a very small cerebral cortex or neocortex, which is better developed in animals considered to be of higher intelligence. The hypothalamus, which is involved in such functions as regulation of feed and water intake, regulation of secretions by the anterior pituitary and aggressive and sexual behavior, is as well developed as in many mammals.

The optic lobes of the brain are particularly well developed, suggesting that the chicken is a highly visual animal, one that uses its sense of sight to a highly developed degree. The eyes constitute a larger proportion of the head than in mammals. Apparently chickens can distinguish colors quite well.

Chickens probably are not able to recognize a specific large form but can distinguish differences in shape and size. A portion of a large figure may be used for recognition rather than the whole figure.

Hearing is a well-developed sense in birds. The hen is attracted to her chicks by their calls and there seems to be a form of communication between a hen and her chicks by means of sound signals. The ear of the chicken is well developed, although anatomically it is more like a reptilian than a mammalian ear.

The sense of smell is not highly developed in birds. Chickens have the neuroanatomical structures associated with the sense of smell, although behavioral responses to odors are difficult to demonstrate. Chickens do have the ability to discriminate between certain tastes or flavors, but taste has not been shown to be important in devising acceptable feed for poultry.

Although the chicken is not given credit for a great amount of intelligence, fowls have the ability to learn many conditioned reflexes. Perhaps readers have seen chickens, trained to perform certain types of behavior, "playing baseball, dancing," in response to some signal, and then receiving a reward of food.

Chickens kept in flocks also develop a definite social order or relationship to their flock mates. Many studies have been made of the behavioral characteristics of chickens. If a small number of unacquainted hens are placed together in a pen, a "peck order" soon develops. Fights occur between two hens until each bird has had some encounter with all the others. The winner of each encounter has the right to peck the loser without being pecked in return. In this way a social order develops with the hen in the first rank of the peck order having the right to peck all others in the group, whereas others only have the right to peck those below them in the social order. At the bottom of the peck order is a hen that can be dominated by all the rest in the group without retaliating in any way.

In males, the intensity of these initial fights is greater than among females. If a new male is placed with a group of males whose peck order is established, he may be killed before he is able to find his niche in the social order.

Some behavioral scientists have suggested that flocks should be moved as a group to new locations, and that introduction of new hens to a group should be kept to a minimum to avoid the necessity of reestablishing the social order of the flock.

Housing individual hens in cages eliminates the peck order, but a social order is established when several hens are housed in a single cage.

The existence of a peck order among chickens indicates that they are able to recognize each other as individuals; otherwise pecking would be indiscriminate. This recognition may be based on features of the head, since changing the position of the comb or removing the comb may disrupt the established position of that hen in the peck order until she can reestablish it.

Other types of behavior are seen in chickens. Common to most birds, there are definite patterns of behavior associated with sexual activity. Various types of behavior can be influenced also by breeding. Aggressiveness is a trait that apparently can be rather easily influenced by genetic selection.

The Endocrine Glands

In addition to the action of the nervous system in regulating body functions, the endocrine system is very important for controlling body processes. The control messages of the nervous system are transmitted by electrical stimuli, whereas the endocrine system acts through chemical stimulators, carried to their site of action by the blood stream. The endocrine system is made up of many glands secreting hormones that act on many organs throughout the body (Fig. 2–10).

The endocrine glands include the testes, the ovary, the pineal, the thyroid, the parathyroids, the pituitary, the adrenal, the ultimobranchial body, and the islets of Langerhans of the pancreas. Hormones are also produced in the gastrointestinal tract and in the brain.

The endocrine glands represent an ingenious system of controlling body processes (Fig. 2–11). The anterior portion of the pituitary produces hormones that regulate the secretion of other endocrine glands. These hormones include the thyroid-stimulating hormone, adrenocorticotrophic hormone, and two gonadotrophic hormones which affect the activity of the thyroid, adrenal, and sex glands, and growth hormone which regulates the growth of the whole animal.

The release of these regulating hormones from the anterior pituitary is controlled by releasing factors produced in a portion of the brain called the hypothalamus. Thus, the nervous system can interact with the endocrine system in this way.

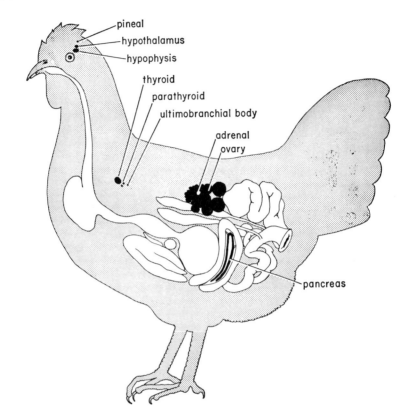

Fig. 2–10. Endocrine glands of the chicken and their location in the body.

Stimuli can be received by sensory receptors in the nervous system which can cause the release of hormone-releasing factors in the hypothalamus, which in turn cause another endocrine gland to secrete a hormone. The effect of light on the reproductive cycle of birds is a fascinating example of the interaction of the nervous system with endocrine glands. This is discussed in detail later in this chapter.

Endocrine glands have profound effects on body processes. The thyroid hormone affects metabolic rate of the animal and also affects feather growth and color. Hypothyroid chickens have characteristically long silky feathers and very poor reproductive activity (Fig. 2–12).

Secretions of the adrenal gland affect carbohydrate and mineral metabolism and also help the chicken cope with stresses. Hormones of the gastrointestinal tract regulate the secretion of digestive juices in the proventriculus and the pancreas, contraction of the gallbladder, and perhaps passage of food through the digestive system. Insulin and

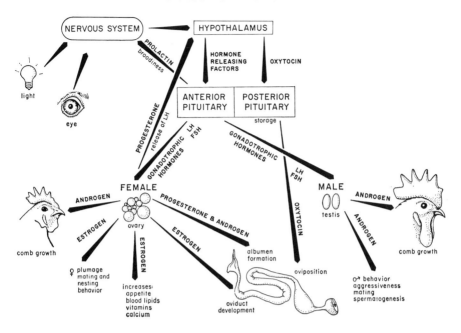

Fig. 2–11. Relationship between the nervous system, endocrine glands, and the reproductive system in male and female fowl.

Fig. 2–12. Hen on the left shows feather development typical of hypothyroidism. She is from a strain of chickens that are genetically hypothyroid. The hen on the right is a normal hen. (Courtesy of Dr. R. K. Cole, Cornell University)

Fig. 2–13. Two male chickens of the same age. The one on the right has had the anterior pituitary gland removed (hypophysectomy). The lack of several hormones can be observed. Notice the lack of secondary sex characteristics (gonadotrophic), smaller body size (growth hormone) and the long depigmented feathers. The abnormal feather development is due to absence of thyroid hormone from lack of stimulation of the thyroid by thyrotrophic hormone. (Courtesy of Dr. A. Bensadoun, Cornell University)

glucagon, produced by the islet of Langerhans and the Beta cells in the pancreas, regulate carbohydrate metabolism. The parathyroid gland and the ultimobranchial body secrete hormones that regulate calcium deposition and mobilization from bones and are undoubtedly important in producing good eggshells. Hormones from the posterior pituitary aid in regulation of blood pressure and water balance and in the actual laying of the egg (Fig. 2–13).

The hormones involved in reproduction are the most important from a poultry production standpoint, and these will be discussed in detail.

REPRODUCTION IN THE FOWL

The reproductive organs include the ovary and oviduct in the hen and the testes in the male. Although bird embryos possess two ovaries and oviducts, only the left one normally develops and becomes functional in nearly all species of birds, including the domestic fowl.

Reproductive System of the Male

The male fowl possesses two testes which are situated high up in the abdominal cavity, along the back, near the anterior ends of the kidneys

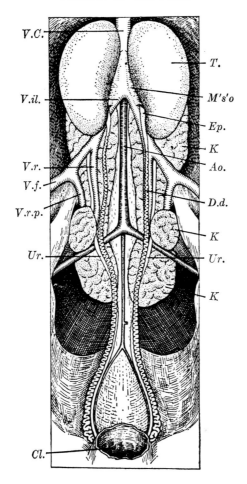

Fig. 2–14. The reproductive and urinary organs of the male fowl: *T.*, testis; *D.d.*, ductus deferens; *K.*, kidney; *Ur.*, ureter; *Cl.*, cloaca. (Courtesy of L. V. Domm.)

(Fig. 2–14). These never descend into an external scrotum, as is the case with other farm animals. In form they are more or less ellipsoid, and in color light yellow, frequently having a reddish cast caused by the numerous much-branched blood vessels on the surface.

In gross structure, the testis consists of a large number of slender, much-convoluted ducts, from the linings of which the sperm are given off. These ducts, called seminiferous tubules, appear in groups separated by delicate membranes extending inward from a membrane surrounding the organ. They all lead eventually to the ductus deferens, a tube which conducts the sperm outside the body.

Each ductus deferens opens into a small papilla, which together serve as an intromittent organ. These are located on the dorsal wall of the cloaca. The so-called rudimentary copulatory organ of the fowl has no connection with the deferent ducts and is located on the median ventral portion of one of the transverse folds of the cloaca. It is this rudimentary organ, or male process, which is used in the classification of baby chicks according to sex on the basis of cloacal examination.

The male responds to light in the same manner as the female fowl. Increasing day-length causes release of gonadotrophic hormones from the anterior pituitary. These in turn cause enlargement of the testes, androgen secretion, and semen production and stimulate mating behavior. Males used by breeders need to be lighted properly for maximum fertility. Males kept for breeding should not be lighted to stimulate gonad development until they will be used.

Ovaries

The ovary of a laying hen usually contains 5 to 6 large yellow developing egg yolks (follicles) and a large number of small white follicles which represent immature undeveloped yolks. The oviduct is the site of egg white secretion, shell membrane, and eggshell formation. Although the reproductive organs are the site of germ cell production, they are also endocrine glands. In the immature pullet the ovary and oviduct are small and undeveloped. Development of the ovarian follicles is stimulated by the *follicle-stimulating hormone* (FSH) from the anterior pituitary gland. This hormone causes the ovary to develop and follicles to increase in size. The developing ovary begins to secrete hormones. *Estrogen* from the ovary causes the oviduct to develop and also causes an increase in blood calcium, proteins, fats, vitamins, and other substances necessary for egg formation. The pubic bones spread and the vent enlarges under the influence of estrogen. The ovary also produces another hormone, *progesterone*, which acts on the hormone-releasing factors in the hypothalamus to cause the release of the *luteinizing hormone* (LH) from the anterior pituitary which causes release of a mature yolk from the ovary. Progesterone is also necessary in proper functioning of the oviduct. As the yolk passes down the oviduct the remainder of the egg is formed. The actual expulsion of the egg from the oviduct is also probably under hormonal control. Injections of extracts of the posterior pituitary will cause expulsion of an egg from the uterus. However, removing the posterior pituitary does not abolish the actual laying of the egg (oviposition). The removal of the ruptured ovarian follicle from which a yolk was released will delay the laying of an egg for one or more days. This indicates how complex the regulation of the egg-laying cycle is and also shows that its regulation is far from being completely understood.

Under the stimulation of the gonadotrophic hormones of the pituitary, the ovary of the laying hen also secretes some of the male sex hormone, *androgen*. This hormone is responsible for the red waxy comb and wattles of the normal laying hen and affects the secretion of albumen by the oviduct.

Lighting and the Laying Cycle

Although the events of the laying cycle can be attributed to the influence of several hormones, external influences can affect the cycle by action of the nervous system. Both egg laying and ovulation are subject to the external influence of light and darkness.

The lighting schedule appears to act as a cue for hormone release that causes certain events to occur. If hens are subjected to a fourteen-hour day, with lights on from 5 A.M. to 7 P.M., most eggs are laid in the morning. Ovulation occurs about 30 minutes after laying of the previous egg. This ovulation is preceded 8 hours earlier by a release of LH from the anterior pituitary. In hens on a definite lighting schedule, this release of LH normally occurs in the dark. Therefore, if an egg is laid late in the day, at 4 P.M. for example, the LH release prior to ovulation would have to be in the daytime. Under these conditions the LH release would not occur, the ovulation would be delayed, and the hen would skip a day between eggs. If the lighting schedule is shifted 12 hours, so that the light and dark periods are made exactly opposite, in a few days the flock will shift the timing of egg laying to correspond to the new lighting schedule.

Although the light and dark periods seem to cue the hen into timing ovulations, this timing does not seem to be essential for egg production. If hens are subjected to 24 hours of light, ovulations seem to be distributed evenly over the 24 hours. Thus hormone release seems to occur in the light, but when there are periods of light and dark, the release of the hormone seems to be cued by the light pattern. This is an illustration of the complexity of the nervous and hormonal influences on egg production.

Time of laying may also be influenced by feeding schedule. If hens receive no light cues by being kept under continuous light with natural daylight excluded, and are fed only from 8 A.M. to 4 P.M., most of the eggs will be laid during those hours. On the other hand, if feeding is from 8 P.M. to 4 A.M. the hens will adjust to the new schedule by laying most of their eggs during the new feeding period.

The management of lighting systems is an integral part of poultry production. Birds are extremely sensitive to photoperiod. Wild birds normally begin nest building, mating, and egg laying during the spring time when day length increases, and cease egg production and mating behavior during periods of the year when day length is decreasing. Domestic birds respond to light in the same fashion.

Growing pullets, when they reach a certain stage of sexual maturity, are stimulated by increasing day-length. Longer days cause release of factors from the hypothalamus which in turn cause release of LH and FSH from

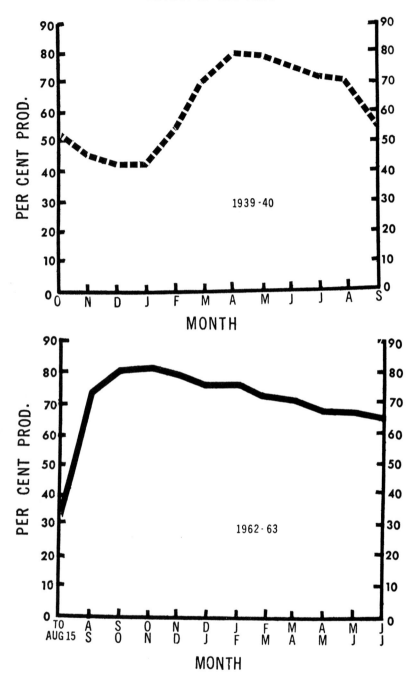

Fig. 2–15. Production pattern of hens from 1939–40 New York random sample egg laying test (top) when no artificial lights were used and from the 1962–63 test (bottom) when artificial lighting was used.

the anterior pituitary. These hormones set into motion the processes leading to sexual maturity and egg laying.

When egg laying begins at too early an age, the eggs are small and less valuable to the producer. If egg laying is delayed to a later age, the first eggs laid are larger and economically more valuable.

Thus in northern latitudes, pullets hatched in December, if reared under natural day-length, will mature at a time when the day-length is increasing. This will result in precocious maturity and resulting economic losses from marketing small eggs. If, on the other hand, pullets are hatched in late spring, they will mature when natural day-length is decreasing. They will not mature prematurely, and egg size will be more desirable at the start of lay.

Since pullets are reared throughout the year in modern poultry production systems, control of lighting during pullet rearing is important to control maturity. This is discussed in detail in Chapter 5.

Hens in lay must never be subjected to decreasing day-length. Decreasing day-length will result in lower egg production. For this reason supplemental light must be used to maintain a constant 14- to 16-hour day-length throughout the egg production year. Prior to the widespread use of artificial lighting, egg production followed marked seasonal patterns. Data in Figure 2–15 are from the 1939–40 New York Random Sample Egg Laying Test. The pattern of egg production shown illustrates the effect of season. Egg production increased during spring months of increasing light and decreased during months of decreasing light. This is in contrast to the egg production pattern in the same Random Sample Test in 1962, also shown in Figure 2–15, when artificial lights were used throughout the year. Production rose to a peak after about 2 months of production and showed a slow steady decline the remainder of the year independent of the season. This is a typical production pattern for a flock properly managed today. Although many factors differed in the two years compared, the lighting practice undoubtedly was one of the most important in the changing production pattern.

Although commercial practice has generally used artificial lights to maintain a 14- to 16-hour day-length during egg production, studies at Cornell University have shown that interruption of the night or dark period with a short period of light, can be as effective as longer continuous light exposure. When the 24-hour lighting pattern was 2L, 10D, 2L, 10D, or 2L, 12D, 2L, 8D, egg production was the same as when hens received 16L, 8D. The interruption of the dark period with a short period of light is apparently as stimulating to reproductive function as exposure to longer continuous light periods. Such lighting schemes potentially can save considerable electrical energy in lighting laying houses.

Chickens do not respond to all wavelengths of light. Orange and red lights (6,640 to 7,400 Å) are most effective. Shorter wavelengths are not effective in stimulating reproduction. Normal white incandescent bulbs give sufficient light at the effective wavelengths.

The light stimulus appears to have a threshold level of intensity beyond which further increases in brightness of light have no effect. Thus greater egg production cannot be stimulated by using very bright lights. A level of 0.5 to 0.9 foot candle of light should be provided at darkest points of exposure of the hen. Excessive light is unnecessary and is economically unsound.

The Oviduct

The oviduct of the hen is a large folded tube occupying a large part of the left side of the abdominal cavity. It has a good blood supply and has muscular walls that are in nearly continuous movement during the time egg formation takes place. In an immature pullet, the oviduct is very small. The data in Table 2–2 show the changes in size of the oviduct that occur in immature pullets, laying hens, and hens that are in a molt.

Large variations occur in size of the oviduct depending on the stage of the reproductive cycle. These size changes are dependent upon the levels of the gonadotrophic hormones being secreted by the anterior pituitary and estrogen production by the ovary.

The oviduct may be divided into five rather clearly defined regions. Beginning at the end nearest the ovary, these are: (1) the funnel or infundibulum, (2) the magnum where the thick albumen is secreted, (3) the isthmus, which secretes the shell membranes, (4) the uterus or shell gland, and (5) the vagina, the passage to the cloaca (Fig. 2–16).

Yolk Formation

The ovary of the laying hen contains numerous ova varying in size from microscopic to those visible to the unaided eye (Fig. 2–17). Over 3,000 visible ova have been counted in the ovary of a laying hen. Although many investigators have tried to find correlations between the number of

Table 2–2.   Influence of Sexual Maturity and Molting on Oviduct Weight and Length

	Oviduct	
	Weight, gm	Length, cm
4-month-old pullet	1.10	9.69
5-month-old pullet	22.00	32.21
Pullet after first egg	77.20	67.74
Hen in full molt	4.20	16.92

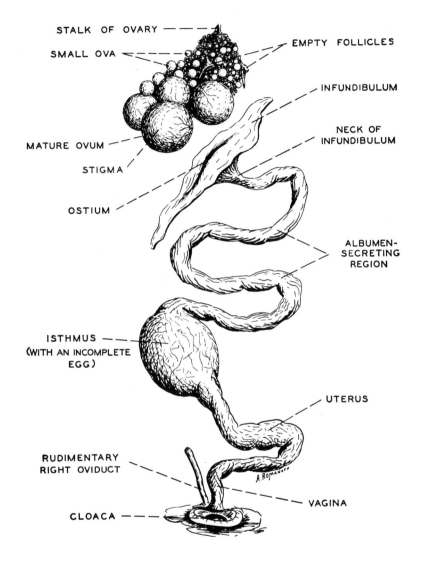

Fig. 2–16. Ovary and oviduct of a chicken. (Courtesy of A. L. Romanoff and John Wiley & Sons, Inc., New York.)

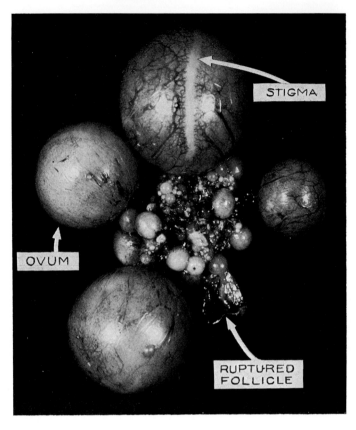

Fig. 2–17. Ovary from a hen in laying condition, showing ova of various sizes and a ruptured follicle from which an ovum was recently released. (Courtesy of Cornell University)

visible ova and egg-laying ability, none of any consequence has been found. Domestic birds, however, do have many more visible ova than wild birds.

The ova are spheres varying from those varely visible, to mature ova, the size of a normal egg yolk. About 10 days before a yolk is to be released from the ovary, it begins to grow rapidly. The diameter of the yolk may increase from 6 to 35 mm the last 6 days before ovulation and is formed in concentric layers (Fig. 2–18).

The yolk is enclosed in a membrane, termed the follicular membrane, attached to the ovary. This membrane is well supplied with blood vessels. The components of the yolk must be transferred from the blood stream across this membrane into the yolk itself. The follicular membrane possesses a readily visible streak, lacking blood vessels, called the stigma,

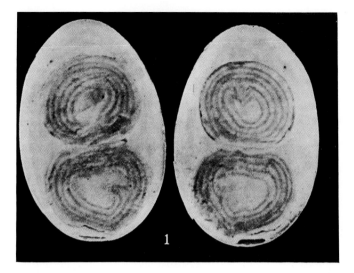

Fig. 2–18. A double-yolked egg, showing how the yolk is formed in concentric layers. The hen was fed a small amount of a fat-soluble dye (Sudan III) on each of five successive days. (After Gage and Fish)

which ruptures and releases the mature ovum or yolk at the time of ovulation. If some blood is released with the yolk, a blood spot may be formed in the egg.

The ovulated egg yolk is engulfed by a funnel-like structure of the oviduct called the *infundibulum*. Normally about 18 to 20 minutes are required to complete this process. Occasionally the infundibulum does not pick up a yolk released from the ovary. When this happens, the yolk is lost in the abdominal cavity and is eventually reabsorbed. Hens that do this routinely are called "internal layers" and appear to be in laying condition, although they never lay a completed egg. It is probable that even normal layers occasionally fail to "catch" an ovulated yolk in the infundibulum, and this yolk does not result in a completed egg.

Egg White Formation

The magnum is the longest portion of the oviduct, about 33 cm in length. In this portion the albumen, or egg white, is secreted around the yolk. Four distinct layers of albumen can be recognized in an egg: the chalaziferous layer, attached to the yolk; the inner thin albumen; the thick albumen; and the outer thin albumen. Three-fourths of the albumen is made up of the thick and outer thin albumen. The albumen as secreted in the magnum appears to be homogeneous, but the addition of water and turning and twisting of the egg later during egg formation seem to be responsible for the separation of the albumen into these four layers. The chalazae, the twisted cordlike structures extending out from the yolk, are formed as the egg is rotated in the lower portions of the oviduct. They apparently are mucin fibers arising from the inner thin white of the albumen.

Shell Membrane Formation

The shell membranes are added to the egg in the isthmus. These membranes, which are made up of many interlacing fibers (Fig. 2–19), are somewhat permeable to both water and air. Two membranes are formed, an inner and an outer shell membrane. These are rather loose-fitting membranes when first formed. Water is added to the egg in the uterus to "plump out" the egg into its final shape. The outer shell membrane is about 3 times as thick as the inner one. The outer membrane is about 0.05 mm thick, and the inner is only 0.015 mm. The membranes normally adhere to each other except at the large end of the egg, where they are separated to form the air cell. The air cell is quite small when the egg is

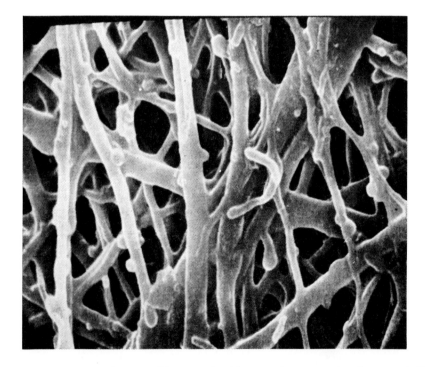

Fig. 2–19. Photograph taken with a scanning electron microscope of an inner eggshell membrane. This picture shows the interlacing fibers that make up this membrane. (Magnification 5000 times). (Courtesy of Dr. D. V. Vadehra, Cornell University)

first laid but progressively increases in size as the egg cools and as water later escapes from the contents by evaporation through the membranes and the shell.

The Eggshell

The egg remains longest in the uterus, or shell gland, where the eggshell is formed, a process requiring 19 to 20 hours. The shell is made up almost entirely of calcium carbonate deposited on an organic matrix consisting of protein and mucopolysaccharide. The shell is intimately bounded by the shell membranes on the inside. The shell is embedded in the membranes by a structure known as the basal cap, a portion of cone layer, which is the innermost part of the shell. The major portion of the shell is made up of a palisade or column layer which is penetrated by numerous pores extending through the shell. The final layer of the shell is known as the cuticle, an organic material covering the surface of the egg (Fig. 2–20). The cuticle seals the pores and is useful in reducing moisture losses and in preventing bacterial penetration of the eggshell. A diagrammatic representation of an eggshell structure is shown in Figure 2–21.

The formation of the eggshell requires an adequate supply of calcium ions to the shell gland and the presence of carbonate ions in the shell gland fluid in sufficient quantity to form the calcium carbonate of the eggshell. Some of the relationships between blood calcium, CO_2 and bicarbonate ions in the blood and shell gland are shown in Figure 2–22. This diagram suggests that the major source of the carbonate ions for shell formation is carbon dioxide derived from the blood or metabolism of the cells in the shell gland, although some authors believe that blood bicarbonate also

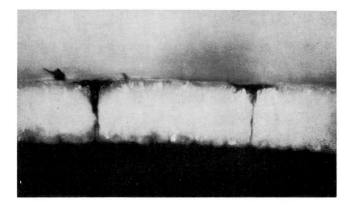

Fig. 2–20. The edge of a broken shell, showing two pores partially filled with the external cuticle or bloom (enlarged 60 times). (Courtesy of California Agricultural Experiment Station)

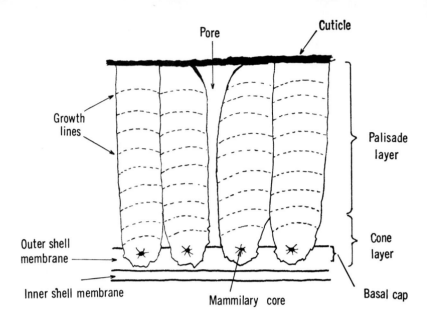

Fig. 2–21. A representation of the structure of the eggshell.

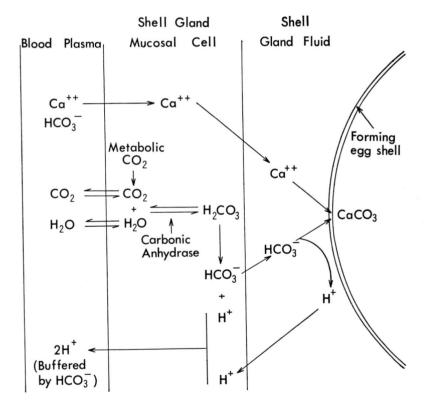

Fig. 2–22. The chemical events of eggshell formation showing the production of the carbonate portion of the eggshell.

PLATE I

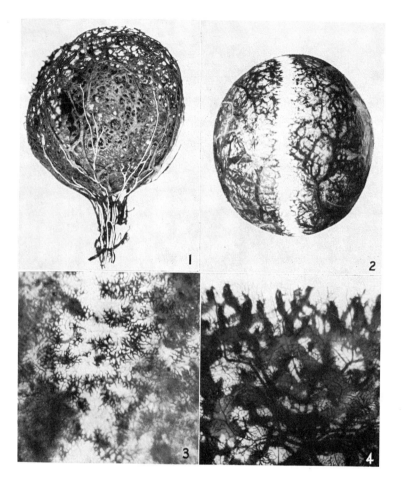

VASCULAR SYSTEM OF THE OVARIAN FOLLICLE
(After Nalbandov and James)

1. Vinylite resin cast of the vascular system of a mature follicle and its stalk. Arteries white and veins dark.

2. Injected preovulatory follicle. Note that no large blood vessels extend across the stigma.

3. View from inside a follicle showing that vascularization of the stigma consists primarily of a fine capillary network.

4. India ink injection of the vascular system of a preovulatory follicle viewed from the inside. The stigma is at the upper edge of the picture.

contributes to shell carbonate ions. The formation of the bicarbonate ion from CO_2 and H_2O is mediated by the enzyme carbonic anhydrase found in the shell gland mucosa. Factors influencing the acid-base balance of the blood may influence the process of shell formation. For example, factors that cause an excess of hydrogen ions in blood (a metabolic acidosis) interfere with the calcification process because the excess hydrogen ions may inhibit the further production of H^+ ions when $CO_3^=$ ions are formed in the shell gland fluid. When a hen pants in hot weather to increase heat loss by water evaporation from the respiratory tract, she also causes a reduction of CO_2 and HCO_3^- ions in the blood. The loss of HCO_3^- and CO_2 from the blood lowers its buffering capacity, although this may result in a metabolic alkalosis. The low HCO_3^- in the blood lowers its buffering capacity and may result in a poor buffering of the hydrogen ions produced during shell formation. This again may interfere with $CO_3^=$ production and probably explains why hens lay eggs with thin shells in hot weather.

Hens fed usual laying rations high in calcium probably obtain the majority of the eggshell calcium directly from the food, but they also may withdraw some from bones, especially during nighttime hours when they are not eating. About 2 grams of calcium are deposited in each eggshell. Thus a hen has a high requirement for dietary calcium, higher than any of the other domestic animals.

Strong eggshells are essential for profitable marketing of eggs. Breakage caused by handling eggs from farm to market is the cause of much economic loss to the poultry industry. The proper functioning of shell formation in the uterus is essential to profitable poultry production.

LEGEND FOR PLATE II

RADIOGRAPHIC VIEWS OF EGGSHELL FORMATION IN THE HEN.
(After Bradfield and Fozzard in the Journal of Experimental Biology, Vol. 28)
1. Radiograph of a hen taken 6½ hours after an egg had been laid. The new yolk has been surrounded by both the white and the shell membranes and has passed into the shell gland (uterus). The first faint outlines of the calcareous shell can barely be detected.
2. The same egg 3 hours later.
3. The same egg 12 hours after the previous egg had been laid.
4. The same egg still later, 23½ hours after the previous egg had been laid. The gradual increase in shell thickness, as shown by x-ray absorption, is clearly evident.
5. A different egg which was observed at frequent intervals during the last few hours before it was due to be laid, so that the rotation could be followed. This radiograph was taken halfway through the rotation, and the egg is therefore seen end-on. The picture was slightly blurred by the breathing movements of the hen. Note the lowered position of the egg in the body cavity. The time required for rotation is between one and two minutes.
6. The same egg shown in views 1, 2, 3, and 4, but 25½ hours after the previous egg had been laid, and one-half hour before it was itself laid. In the preceding views (1 to 4), the pointed end is caudad, but here the egg has rotated through 180° so as to bring the blunt end caudad.
7. Calcium carbonate suspensions used for comparison.

PLATE II

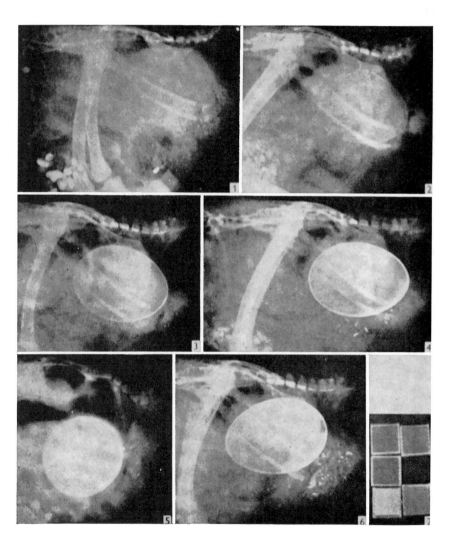

Laying of the Egg

Eggs are normally formed with the small end first as they move down the oviduct. This is true of wild birds as well as of the fowl. But curiously enough, if the hen is not disturbed in the act of laying, a large proportion of eggs are laid large end first. This fact had puzzled poultry workers for many years. Not until an English investigator used radiographic techniques and published his findings in 1951 was the series of events made clear.

As can be seen in Plate II, the fully formed egg is turned horizontally (not end-over-end) through 180 degrees just prior to laying. In order for this to happen the egg must drop from its normal position high up between the ischia to a point opposite the tips of the pubic bones. This position is necessary because the normal egg is too long to turn in a horizontal plane within the pelvic arch. The position of an egg after it has turned and is ready to be laid is shown in Figure 6 of Plate II. Rotation of the egg is accomplished in a matter of one to two minutes. Should the hen be disturbed as she raises herself slightly from the nest when the egg is about to turn, she is likely to expel it immediately and in that event it will be laid small end first. There is also some variation among hens and no doubt among breeds in the consistency with which they lay eggs large end first. It is not known whether hereditary factors are involved.

No valid reason has been advanced for the fact that eggs are formed small end caudad. As for the reversal prior to laying, it seems reasonable to assume that muscular pressure required for expelling the egg is more effectively applied to the small end.

Time Intervals in Egg Formation

Careful observations made on anesthetized birds at the Kansas Agricultural Experiment Station, together with autopsy records of hens in laying condition, have made it possible to estimate with considerable accuracy the time required to form the various parts of the egg. These time intervals are summarized in Table 2–3, along with average lengths of the various parts of the oviduct as determined on 70 white leghorn hens at the University of Illinois.

The time between laying and the next ovulation ranges from 14 to 75 minutes, and there is also some variation in the rate of passage through the different sections of the oviduct (Table 2–4). Hens with small clutches, long intervals between eggs, and low intensity also have long delays in ovulation. Poor production of low-intensity hens is caused not only by the longer period of egg formation but also by a longer delay in ovulation between clutches.

Records on 119 Rhode Island red pullets for one year at the Massachusetts Station showed an average interval of 26.5. hours between

Table 2–3. Approximate Length of Various Parts of Oviduct and Time intervals in Egg Formation

Section of Oviduct	Approximate Length (centimeters)*	Approximate Time for Yolk to Traverse (hours)†
Infundibulum (and chalaziferous region)	11.0	0.25
Magnum	33.6	3.00
Isthmus	10.6	1.25
Uterus	10.1⎫	20.75
Vagina	6.9⎭	
Interval between laying and next ovulation	. . . .	0.50

* Illinois data on 70 White Leghorns.
† Adapted from Warren and Scott (1935).

Table 2–4. Average Time Spent by Eggs in Different Parts of the Oviduct*

Item	Time for Egg Formation (hours)					
	25	26	27	28	29	30
Time from laying of one egg to entrance of isthmus by next egg	4.3	4.6	4.2	4.7	5.2	5.3
Time in uterus	18.0	18.4	19.9	19.8	20.8	21.6
Time from first indication of shell to laying of egg	13.8	14.7	15.6	16.4	17.0	17.9
Number of eggs observed	9	25	20	42	44	21

* Adapted from Warren and Scott (1935).

successive eggs in the same clutch. The shortest interval observed for any one hen was 23 hours in April, and the longest was 31.7 hours in February. The average interval for all birds was shortest in April (25.7 hours) and longest in February (27.7 hours).

Shape, Size, and Color of Eggs

The normal or characteristic shape of the egg is determined in the magnum, but the specific shape may be modified by abnormal or unusual conditions in either the isthmus or the uterus.

Eggs laid by a hen after the anterior half of her isthmus had been removed were, for the most part, more irregular in shape than eggs laid before the operation. In another hen the isthmus was torn longitudinally and then closed with catgut sutures. After the operation this hen laid eggs with characteristically wrinkled shells, suggesting that the specific shape of the shell membranes, as determined in the isthmus, has a direct influence on shell shape.

Operations on the uterus showed clearly that shape of the egg may also be affected by that portion of the oviduct. Eggs laid by a hen after cotton was placed at the sides of the uterus had a depression reaching more or less around the egg.

That there is great variability in the size of hens' eggs is well known, but the specific causes of this variation are not so well established. It is obvious that the weight of the egg is equal to the sum of the weights of its parts, and that anything affecting the weight of any of the parts may be expected to have some influence on the weight of the entire egg. The small size of eggs laid by pullets at the beginning of the laying period is due in part to the smaller size of yolks in such eggs, as well as to the lesser amounts of albumen. The shell is, of course, formed to fit the egg contents.

The position of an egg in the clutch affects its weight. The second egg of a two-egg clutch is nearly always smaller than the first egg, and in clutches of several eggs, the first egg is usually the heaviest, with a progressive decrease in the weight of the egg laid on each successive day. This decrease is almost entirely the result of a decrease in the amount of white, since yolk size appears to be nearly constant, for any given hen, for all clutch positions.

Double-yolked eggs occur when two yolks move through the oviduct together, either from simultaneous ovulations or delay in a yolk's passage through the oviduct (Fig. 2–18). Conrad and Warren concluded that 90% of double-yolked eggs were due to simultaneous ovulation of two yolks that had matured at the same time or to premature ovulation. Triple-yolked eggs are extremely rare.

Eggshells of modern breeds are white or various shades of brown. Brown eggs occur because the pigment is deposited in the shell as it is formed in the uterus. Hens normally lay eggs of the same color, but there may be considerable variation in color among hens of the same breed. Hens that lay eggs of various shades of blue or green are known in Central and South America.

On some occasions, normal oviposition does not occur and an egg remains in the shell gland for longer than the normal time. If the following ovulation occurs at approximately the normal time, another egg will be formed and will enter the shell gland along with the first egg that was held. The two eggs in the shell gland will be in contact with each other, and the second egg will have a depression at the point where the two eggs touch. Calcification occurs on the second egg at all points except where the two eggs in the shell gland touch. The first egg may eventually be laid while the second stays in the shell gland. Calcification can then occur at all points of the second egg, including the depressed point where the two eggs were touching. When this egg is laid a few hours later, it has a characteristic

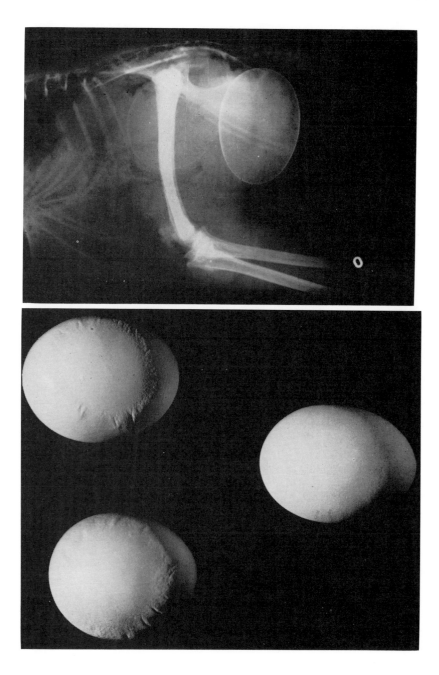

Fig. 2–23. Bottom, abnormal eggs (left) resulting from delayed oviposition which causes two eggs to be present in the uterus simultaneously (x-ray picture at top). The shell abnormality occurs where the abnormal egg touches the completed egg.

depression in the shell. Figure 2–23 shows an x-ray picture of a hen with two eggs in the shell gland and the appearance of eggs with this abnormality. When the first egg is not laid at its normal time, both eggs may be laid on the same day a few hours apart.

If both eggs are laid at the same time, or very close together, the second may be thin-shelled or a membrane egg. Under some circumstances, up to 1 to 1.5% of the eggs laid have been reported to have this abnormality.

The Completed Egg

The gross parts of an egg are shown diagrammatically in Figure 2–24. In order of their formation they are (1) the germ spot or blastoderm, (2) the yolk, (3) the white, (4) the shell membranes, and (5) the shell. The germ spot is closely associated with the yolk and represents the living portion of the egg. The blastoderm represents embryonic development in a fertile egg that has occurred prior to laying of the egg. In a nonfertile egg this structure is smaller and generally referred to as the germinal disc or blastodisc.

The chemical composition of an egg is shown in Table 2–5. The chief constituent of the egg is water. On a dry-matter basis the whole egg contains nearly equal quantities of protein, fat, and ash. Egg yolk is the most concentrated source of nutrients in the egg. It is only about 50% water and is very high in fat. In addition to the major components listed in the table, egg yolk contains a multitude of chemical compounds such as vitamins, minerals, pigments, and cholesterol. The protein and fat content of egg yolk can be altered little by the diet of the hen, but many of the other components, such as vitamins, minerals, and pigments, can be

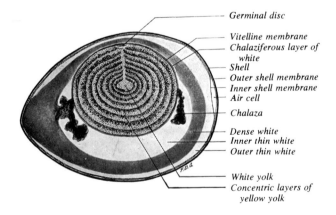

Fig. 2–24. Composite diagram showing, in vertical section, the parts of a fresh pullet egg. (Courtesy of F. B. Adamstone)

Table 2–5. Approximate Chemical Composition of the Egg and Its
Parts

	Entire Egg	Egg Contents	Yolk	White	Shell and Membranes
Water	66%	74%	48%	88%	2%
Dry matter	34	26	52	12	98
Protein	12	13	17	11	6
Fat...............	10	11	33	—	—
Carbohydrates......	1	1	1	1	—
Ash	11	1	1	—	92

altered greatly by the diet fed to the hen. The egg white is mainly protein
and water with a small amount of carbohydrate. The eggshell consists
primarily of mineral matter, nearly all of which is calcium carbonate. The
shell membranes are a combination of protein and mucopolysaccharide.

The complete egg is quite resistant to spoilage largely because of
resistance of the shell to penetration and multiplication of microorganisms. The cuticle on the eggshell tends to fill the pores of the shell and
retard moisture loss and microbial penetration. The shell membranes are
also a major line of defense against penetration by bacteria. The egg white
contains proteins, particularly one called lysozyme, that have antibacte-
rial action to help retard the spoilage of eggs.

Chapter 3

Poultry Breeding

The science of genetics deals with the mechanisms of heredity, the transmission of characteristics of parents to their offspring. The science of poultry breeding, as applied to poultry production, uses the principles of genetics to develop strains or breeds best suited for the production of poultry meat and eggs. Poultry breeding is essentially applied genetics, drawing heavily on principles of genetics to accomplish the aims of a poultry breeding program. The science of genetics is one of the most exciting and dynamic in biological science today.

The *chromosomes,* in the cell nucleus, are the carriers of genetic information. These chromosomes are duplicated in the process of cell division *(mitosis)* so that the duplicates are identical and carry the same genetic information. In normal cells, chromosomes occur in pairs; in mature germ cells the chromosomes are unpaired so that when a sperm fertilizes an egg, half of the chromosomes in the fertilized egg are from the sperm and half from the egg. In this way both parents contribute to the genetic information in the paired chromosomes of the embryo.

The unit of heredity is called the *gene.* It can be thought of as a unit of genetic information carried by an animal sufficient to affect a specific character. This character may be feather color, comb type, skin color, a specific enzyme, or an enzyme regulator in metabolism.

In recent years the molecular basis of heredity has become much better understood. The most important genetic material in cell nuclei has been shown to be deoxyribonucleic acid (DNA), a large molecular weight compound made up of repeating units of four organic bases—thymine, adenine, cytosine and guanine—associated with a sugar and phosphoric acid. The sequence of these four bases in DNA acts as a code in which information can be transferred from one cell to another during the process of cell division. The code can be translated by cells to make proteins and enzymes of specific structures that determine the basic morphology and functioning of a cell. The genetic information also controls differentiation, which is the process by which a group of cells become an organ, or which controls whether an embryo will become a chicken or a pig or a man. Basically, a gene corresponds to a sequence of organic bases in a large DNA molecule.

The science of genetics has proceeded today to the point where the code of bases in DNA is largely understood, and specific genes have been synthesized in the laboratory. Poultry geneticists must keep abreast of advances in basic genetics to keep alert for findings that may have practical application to the improvement of breeding stock.

Many geneticists feel that eventually the hereditary mechanism may be well enough understood to allow introduction of new genetic material directly into the cells of an individual to repair genetic defects or to introduce a specific character. This type of genetic engineering presents numerous moral and sociological questions that may limit these types of applications in human medicine. Indeed it may well be that animal breeding will be the place where molecular genetic engineering is most aptly applied.

GENETICALLY DETERMINED CHARACTERISTICS OF POULTRY

Basically, all characteristics of animals are genetically determined to some degree. The size, shape, color, behavior, or tissue enzyme content of an animal are all characteristics under genetic control. The expression of hereditary characters may be modified by the environment to which an individual is exposed. Some characters are affected by environment much more than others. A hen may have genes which allow her to lay 300 eggs a year, but if she is not fed properly, given good housing, or protected from disease, these genes affecting egg production may not be expressed. On the other hand, if the hen carries genes for white plumage, the environment will not modify this character.

Chromosomes and Genes

The hereditary material of a chicken is located on 39 pairs of chromosomes in the nucleus of a cell (Fig. 3–1). These chromosomes carry the *genes*, the units of heredity.

Each gene occupies a specific location or *locus* on the chromosome. Chromosomes occur in cells in pairs, one from the sire and one from the dam. Except for the sex chromosomes in females (Z and W), each chromosome of a pair is like the other in size and shape, and each carries genes for a particular trait at the same locus on the chromosome. The genes carried at this site may exist in different forms called *alleles* on each member of a pair of chromosomes.

The type of comb, for example, is a trait that is inherited in a relatively easily understood fashion. Rose comb and single comb are comb types

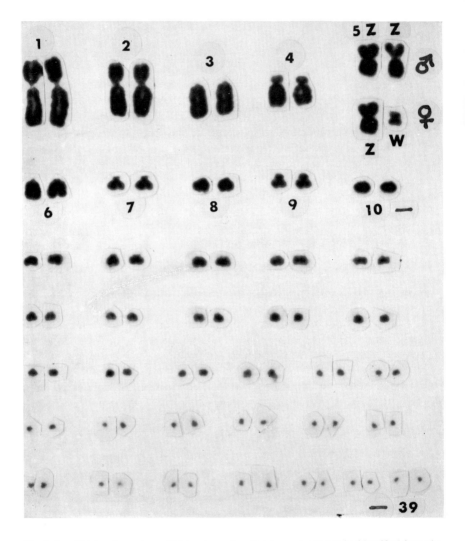

Fig. 3–1. Chicken karyotype. Thirty-nine pairs of chromosomes can be identified from the nucleus of a cell from the allantoic sac of a 4-day chick embryo with mitosis arrested in metaphase. For illustrative purposes, both the ZZ and ZW chromosome pairs are shown. In the normal cell only one of these pairs would be present. Individual members of chromosome pairs cannot be identified beyond the tenth pair because of the small size and similar appearance of these chromosomes. (Courtesy of Dr. S. E. Bloom, Cornell University)

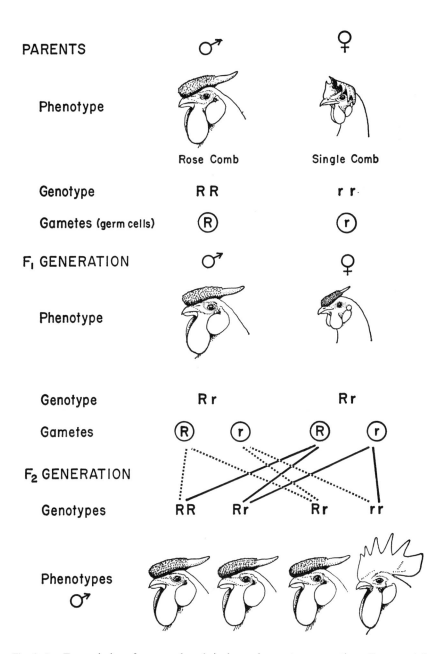

Fig. 3–2. Transmission of rose comb and single comb over two generations. Rose comb is dominant to single comb. Only the male offspring are illustrated in the F_2 generation.

commonly found in chickens. These comb types are inherited through genes located at the same loci on a pair of chromosomes. A capital R is used as a symbol for the gene for rose comb, and a lower case r is used as a symbol for single comb.

The capital R is used for the rose comb gene because it is *dominant* to the single comb gene. The single comb gene is *recessive* to rose comb. The genes R and r are called *alleles,* or alternate forms of a gene for the same character, in this case, comb type. R is said to be a dominant gene because when both the R and r gene are present on a pair of chromosomes, the individual will have a rose comb, because only the rose comb gene is expressed. It is dominant to the single comb gene. It follows that the genes present on the paired chromosomes in an individual can be RR, Rr or rr. Individuals carrying RR or rr are *homozygous* for that gene, whereas those with the Rr combination are *heterozygous.* The transmission of these genes through two generations when an RR male is mated to an rr female is shown in Figure 3–2. The *phenotypes* (appearance) of the individuals and their *genotypes* are given in the figure.

The first generation produced by crossing the two homozygous parents is called the F_1 generation or *first filial generation.* Since only one combination of germ cells is possible in the F_1 generation, all the offspring are heterozygous rose comb individuals. When two F_1 individuals are mated, two different types of germ cells are possible from each parent. Combination of these produces one RR, two Rr and one rr genotype. Thus three fourths of the progeny in the F_2 *(second filial)* generation would have rose comb and one fourth single comb. This is the familiar Mendelian 3:1 ratio for segregation in the F_2 generation when individuals homozygous for dominant and recessive characteres are crossed.

Many characteristics of poultry are inherited in a simple fashion, as in rose or single comb. White and yellow skin color constitute a pair of characters similar to rose and single comb. White skin is dominant to yellow. This character is dependent on environment, however, since yellow skin derives most of its pigment from dietary sources and is not expressed unless sufficient pigments are present in the diet. White-skinned individuals will not accumulate yellow pigments in the skin.

Plumage colors and patterns are generally characterized by simple inheritance, but several genes may be responsible for the pattern of pigment found in a particular feather. The gene for black feathers is present in many breeds of chickens, even those whose normal feather color is not black. The gene for black feathers may not be expressed, however, because of the presence of another gene. This gene is called *dominant white* and it is given the symbol I, because it inhibits the development of black pigment. This gene, in the heterozygous state, may not be completely dominant, since some black feathers may appear in adults carrying the gene for black which are heterozygous for the I gene.

This dominant white gene has been useful in developing commercial

Fig. 3–3. Frizzled fowl. The characteristic frizzled feathers of this bird are caused by a single dominant gene. Frizzled fowl have been prized by poultry fanciers for centuries. (From F. B. Hutt: J. Genetics, *22*:109–127, 1930.)

strains of broilers with white plumage. The white feathers are desired because the pin feathers are white, and lack of pigment in feather follicles makes for a better appearing dressed carcass.

There are genes for silver and/or gold plumage in all breeds of fowl. Red and blue plumage is also caused by genes affecting color of the feather. In addition, there are genes that affect the pattern of color on the plumage. In the so-called Columbian pattern of plumage, black feathers are restricted in their distribution to the neck, wings, and tail. There are also genes that affect the distribution of pigment within the feather. Thus the gene for lacing causes a black border on the feather that may have a background color of gold or silver.

Single pairs of genes also affect the structure of the feather so that "silky fowls" are known in which the feather lacks a flat feather web and has a wooly appearance. There are also genes that cause a frizzling of the feathers, in which the feathers are curled outward near their tips (Fig. 3–3). Feathers may also be present on the shanks and feet as the result of the presence of specific genes.

Because many genes affect color, pattern, shape, and distribution of the plumage, there is a tremendous variety of colors and feather patterns that have developed in the many breeds and varieties of chickens.

These are usually not seen in modern breeds used for poultry production today because of the predominance of white feathering in commercial stocks, particularly those in use in the United States. The variety of genetic changes in size, shape, color, and plumage pattern of fowl can still be seen at poultry shows at fairs where fanciers get together to exhibit their birds. Hobbyists and fanciers have preserved the genetic diversity found in poultry that has largely disappeared from commercially used varieties.

Sex Determination

One characteristic of birds that sets them apart from mammals is the manner in which sex of offspring is determined. All sperm produced by males contain a Z or sex chromosome, but females produce equal numbers of two types of ova, one containing a Z chromosome and the other a W. Thus when the fertilized egg contains two Z chromosomes the resulting chick will be a male, but, if the fertilized egg has ZW sex chromosomes, a female chick will result. Because females produce two types of ova (Z and W), they are called *heterogametic* whereas males, which produce spermatozoa with only Z chromosomes, are said to be *homogametic*. In mammals, males are exclusively heterogametic, whereas in birds, reptiles, and in most amphibia, the females are heterogametic.

Sex Linkage. Because sex is determined by the presence of two Z chromosomes in males, and ZW chromosomes in females, genes carried on the sex chromosomes may not be transmitted to both sexes in the same manner. If a hen carries a gene on her Z chromosome, that gene will not be passed to her daughters, but only to her sons, since the female has only one Z chromosome, received from the sire. When sex-linked genes produce characteristics in newly hatched chicks that are readily recognizable, these characters can be used for sex identification. The Rhode Island red × barred Plymouth Rock cross is a good example of this. The barred Plymouth Rock females carry the gene causing barring. The female chicks resulting from the cross of a non-barred male and a barred female would not be barred, since they would not receive the B gene from their mother, while the male chicks would be barred due to the dominance of the B gene received from the female. The down of the newly hatched chicks does not show barring, but those that will later develop barred feathers have a white spot on the back of the head. Thus the males will have the white spot on the head and the females will not. They can be sorted easily at hatching. The transmission of the gene in this cross is shown in Figure 3–4.

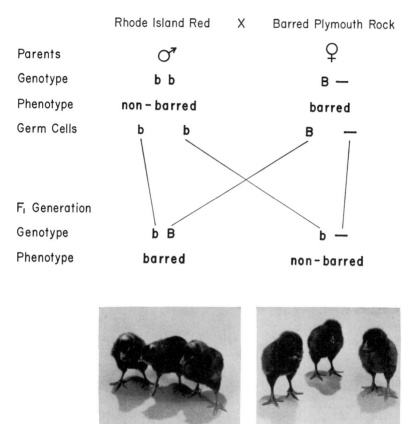

Rhode Island Red   X   Barred Plymouth Rock

Parents   ♂️   ♀️

Genotype   b b   B —

Phenotype   non - barred   barred

Germ Cells   b   b   B   —

F₁ Generation

Genotype   b B   b —

Phenotype   barred   non - barred

Fig. 3–4. Crossing of a barred Plymouth Rock female and a Rhode Island red male results in offspring that can be easily sexed at hatching. The males from this cross will be barred and this will be shown by the light-colored head spots. Those with no head spots will be non-barred and hence will be females.

Another sex-linked gene affects rate of feathering in chicks, and it can be used in the same manner. Leghorns and some other breeds are characteristically rapid feathering, whereas most of the American and other heavy breeds are slow feathering. Slow feathering is dominant to rapid feathering, and if the cross is to be used for sex identification it is necessary to mate rapid-feathering males with slow-feathering females. At hatching time the rapid-feathering female chicks from such a cross show well-developed primaries and secondaries which not only extend well beyond the down, but which are also longer than the associated wing coverts. In the slow-feathering male chicks, by contrast, the primaries are much shorter, are of about the same length as the coverts, and the secondaries are either absent or poorly developed. Later on, at about 10

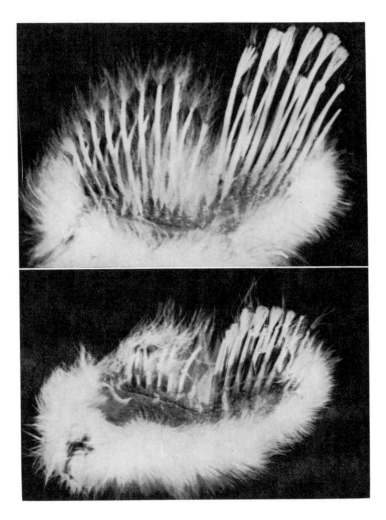

Fig. 3–5.   Slow feathering is dominant to rapid feathering and sex-linked. The difference is apparent in newly hatched chicks. In the rapid-feathering chick *(above)* the primaries and secondaries are longer than the coverts. In the slow-feathering chick *(below)* the primaries and coverts are about equal in length.

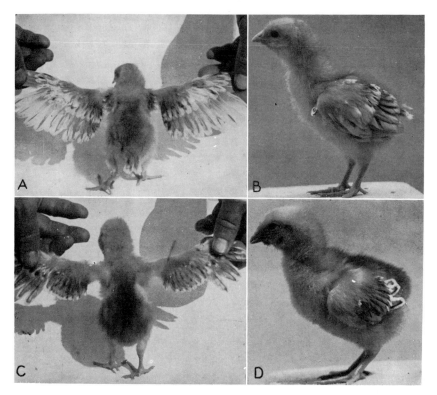

Fig. 3–6. Differences between rapid feathering *(above)* and slow feathering *(below)* at 10 days of age.

days of age, the rapid-feathering chicks show well-developed tail feathers, wing feathers extending to the tail, and a small tuft of feathers on each shoulder. The slow-feathering chicks have no tails and much shorter wings. These differences are illustrated in Figures 3–5, 3–6, and 3–7.

This characteristic is particularly useful in commercial white leghorn stocks. The slow-feathering males are normally destroyed at hatching and only the rapid-feathering female chicks are raised to maturity.

Quantitative Characters

Most of the discussion thus far has been of characters influenced by one or two pairs of genes affecting a character in a manner that can be well recognized. However, traits such as egg production, egg size, growth rate, and body conformation, which are most economically important, do not have as simple an inheritance as comb type or plumage color. These traits differ from individual to individual by almost imperceptible degrees

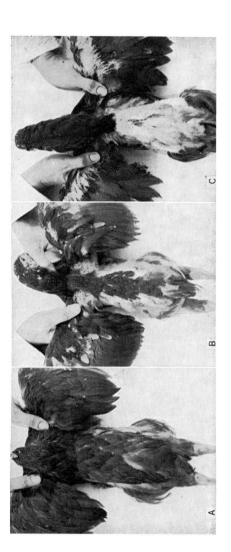

Fig. 3–7. In breeds or strains which lack the sex-linked recessive gene for rapid feathering, there is often great variation in rate of back feathering caused by autosomal genes. (Courtesy of Massachusetts Agricultural Experiment Station.)

over a wide range. Thus there is essentially a *continuous* variation among individuals in the population between the extremes. Traits that show this type of variation are known as *quantitative* characters. Often these characters are termed *polygenic* traits because many genes must affect the trait considered.

These traits are of particular interest to the poultry breeder. He must devise breeding systems that will improve the average performance of a flock in several quantitative characters at the same time.

Heritability of Quantitative Characters. Some geneticists have attempted to measure the potential improvement that can be obtained in quantitative characters by mathematical estimates of the heritability of these traits. The term *heritability* is defined as the proportion of the variation observed in a quantitative trait that is the cumulative effect of the additive genes affecting that trait. To measure heritability, statistical analysis of genetic data is conducted to attempt to separate the variation in a trait due to environment from that due to genetics. Presumably, a trait with high heritability could be improved rapidly by intensive selection, whereas less rapid improvement could be achieved by selection for traits with low heritability. Quantitative traits that seem to have relatively high heritability include body weight, feed consumption, egg weight, age at sexual maturity, egg shape, and shell color. Somewhat lower heritabilities have been reported for total egg production and feed efficiency. Traits with quite low heritability estimates include fertility and hatchability. However, in spite of an apparent low heritability, significant improvement may be made in many characters by appropriate selection techniques.

Heterosis. When animals of different inbred lines, strains, or breeds are mated, their offspring will often perform better than either of the parents. This extra vigor produced by such matings is known as heterosis, or hybrid vigor. Hybrid vigor seems to result when animals less closely related genetically are mated. Thus corn breeders recognized that when inbred lines of corn were crossed, the resulting hybrid was much more vigorous and higher yielding than either of the inbred lines. The advantages gained from hybrid vigor by plant breeders are familiar to all of us.

Hybrid vigor involves an increase in heterozygosity in a population and a decrease in homozygosity. The reason for hybrid vigor is not well understood by geneticists, but it is used to a considerable degree by poultry breeders.

An example of hybrid vigor is shown by the data in Table 3–1. Two strains of chickens, kept genetically separate for over 13 years, were crossed in experiments by Dr. R. K. Cole and Dr. F. B. Hutt at Cornell University. The offspring of the strain cross laid about 22 eggs per year more than offspring of the pure strains. In addition, the hybrids laid larger eggs, matured earlier, and had a larger body size than the pure strain hens. Many poultry breeding systems try to make use of gains to be obtained from hybrid vigor. Hybrids themselves do not breed true. To obtain the

Table 3-1.   The Change in Productivity of a Strain Cross Compared to the Pure Strains

Measurement	Change in Strain Cross Compared to Pure Strains
Eggs to 500 days of age	+22 eggs
Egg weight	+2 grams
Body weight	+130 grams
Days to first egg	−5 days

Data from Hutt and Cole: Poultry Sci. *31*:365, 1952.

benefits of hybrid vigor year after year the original lines used to make the hybrid cross must be used again each generation.

SYSTEMS USED FOR BREEDING

An animal breeder must set goals for the animal he wishes to produce, and devise breeding systems that will allow him to approach those goals. Many breeds of poultry, with their plumage color, body shape, comb type, and other distinguishing characters, represent the goal that breeders set out to meet many years ago, long before our knowledge of the genetic basis for animal breeding. Modern breeders also set goals to be achieved and use their knowledge of genetics and poultry husbandry to move toward these goals. The goals may vary to suit the objective to be reached.

Hens

Hens kept for egg production must first of all have the ability to lay large numbers of eggs. Selection of hens for rate of lay is probably the uppermost objective in the mind of the poultry breeder. However, the ability to lay large numbers of eggs is not enough. If the eggs are small, with poor shells, have watery albumen, and contain numerous blood or meat spots, the hen will not be valuable for the production of market eggs. Similarly, if a hen is highly susceptible to disease so that she has a good chance of dying before she is able to lay for a full year, the hen is not valuable. Therefore, a breeder attempting to produce a hen acceptable for production of market eggs must pay attention to many factors.

The traits considered to be of economic importance, which were measured in Random Sample Egg Laying Tests reported in the USDA combined summary of tests, included rearing mortality, laying mortality, age at 50% production, hen housed production, hen day production, feed per 24 oz. dozen of eggs, egg weight, percentage of large and extra large eggs, body weight, albumen quality, blood spots, meat spots, and shell thickness. These all must be given weight in a breeding system.

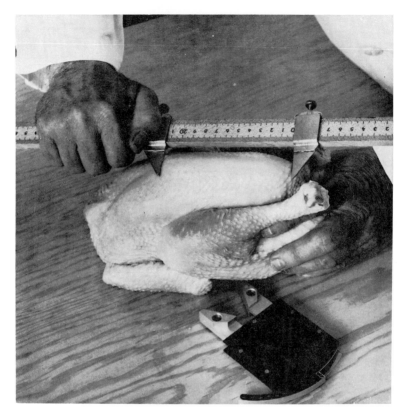

Fig. 3–8. Breeding for the improvement of broiler stock involves considering carcass conformation. This photograph shows the measurement of length of keel. The instrument lying on the table is used for measuring the angle of breast muscle. (Courtesy of Shaver Poultry Breeding Farms, Ltd.)

Broilers

A breeder producing stock for meat production has a variety of factors to consider in setting his breeding goals. A broiler must be fast growing, have acceptable body conformation (Fig. 3–8), be efficient in converting feed to meat, be free from leg weakness, be resistant to disease, and have appropriate skin and feather color. In addition to this, the parents of the broiler chick must have good reproductive characteristics in terms of fertility, hatchability, egg production, and egg size, so that broiler chicks can be produced economically.

With these complex objectives, no wonder many breeders consider poultry breeding a combination of genetics, animal husbandry, and plain good luck.

Inbreeding and Crossing Inbred Lines

Inbreeding involves the mating of closely related individuals, such as the mating of brother × sister for several successive generations. Other forms of close inbreeding involve matings of a mother × son, father × daughter, half-brother × sister, or mating cousins. Inbreeding increases homozygosity in a population. The genes carried on the chromosomes of highly inbred stock are much more uniform than if the stock is less inbred. Inbreeding generally reduces performance, since undesirable genes as well as desirable ones are concentrated in the inbred line. However, when inbred lines are crossed, heterozygosity in the resulting hybrid is greatly increased and crosses of inbred lines often show hybrid vigor. This system has been used extensively in hybrid corn production and is used for the production of some commercial stocks of chickens.

Production and maintenance of inbred lines are costly and many of them have to be discarded after trial because they do not combine well with other lines.

Crossbreeding

Breeds of poultry represent groups of individuals, related by descent, that breed true for certain characteristics which breeders agree distinguish the breed. Thus individuals within a breed of poultry, although not highly inbred, are more closely related in a number of characteristics than they would be to individuals in another breed. Thus when breeds are crossed, considerable hybrid vigor in the offspring often results.

Breed crosses are used in modern poultry breeding, more often in broiler stock than in layers. However, a useful crossbreed for production of brown eggs has been the Rhode Island red × barred Plymouth Rock. The Cornish breed is represented in most broiler strains today because of the outstanding body conformation that it gives to the broiler chick.

Strain Crosses

Within breeds there are strains that may be quite unrelated to each other that have been developed as closed flocks or have little recent common ancestry. Many of these strains represent efforts of the many small poultry breeders to select and improve their purebred stock when the poultry industry was served by large numbers of small breeders instead of relatively few large ones. Some of these strains, when crossed, give offspring that perform considerably better than the parent strain. When a particular strain in a cross nearly always gives a good result, the strain is said to have "general combining ability." In other cases, strains are useful only when crossed with another specific strain. These strains have "specific combining ability." Some strains combine well only when used as the male parent, and others must be used as the female parent to do well. To discover useful strain crosses, many strains must be tested for their combining ability. When two strains are discovered that give outstanding offspring when crossed, these strains can be maintained as parent stock for the production of the commercial strain-cross chicks. More than two strains may be useful in a cross so that the final chick produced for sale could be a three- or four-way cross. Strain crossing has been especially useful in producing commercial egg-laying stocks.

When strains are found that combine well in a strain or breed cross, the breeder is faced with several possibilities. He can maintain the parent strain as a random breeding population in an effort to retain the good combining ability of the strains. Alternatively, he can select to improve each strain in the hope that the strain cross will also be improved. In a third breeding system, individuals would be selected for mating within each strain on the basis of their ability to combine well in the strain cross. In this system, the individual strains are maintained, but selection within the strain depends on the performance of the strain cross. This breeding plan, aimed at improving the specific combining ability of strains, has been termed *reciprocal recurrent selection*.

Selection of Breeder Stock

No matter what breeding system is practiced to produce desired stock, decisions must be made as to the individuals that will be selected for breeding. To make progress toward a breeding goal, individuals that will produce superior offspring must be identified. Thus, selection of individuals for breeding is the key to making a breeding system work.

Mass Selection. Mass selection is predicated on the assumption that the appearance or performance of an individual can be taken as an indication of its breeding worth. For some characters this assumption is correct, and selection is then simple. All one need do is identify the desired individuals with respect to some reliable measure of the character in question. For many characters, however, and especially for those of economic importance which are influenced by many different genes, the assumption is so far from the truth as to be completely misleading. This arises not only because the presence of many genes makes their enumeration and recognition difficult, but because the effect of environment on the expression of the genetic character may be and frequently is great.

Mass selection, based on phenotypic performance, may be effective through the low to medium range of a given quantitative character and quite ineffective in the upper range. Egg production is a good example. There can be no doubt about the effectiveness of individual or mass selection in improving average egg production up to 160, 180, or perhaps 200 eggs per pullet per year—the exact limit depending both on the sort of stock with which one is working and on the environment under which it is kept. But continued dependence on mass selection can only lead to disappointment when it ceases to bring any further progress.

A great deal of improvement in poultry flocks has been the result of widely applied mass selection practices, particularly in the elimination of such undesirable individuals as slow growers, poor layers, and those that detract from a reasonably uniform appearance of flocks. Many flocks can still be improved by this method of selection, but as performance moves up the scale, it is necessary to use more refined selection methods or accept something less than maximum performance as the end and aim of a breeding program.

Progeny Testing. When the pedigree of breeding animals is known, it is possible to compare the egg-laying performance of the parents or sisters of individuals considered for breeding. Unfortunately, there is no guarantee that the son of a hen producing 280 eggs a year will sire daughters of equal potential. The same is true when performance of the sisters of a male are used as a means of selection of a breeding male.

A more powerful test of the breeding qualities of potential breeders is the progeny test. This involves testing the actual performance of offspring of specific matings to determine their value as breeding stock. This is a long and expensive process, since the egg-producing ability of offspring of a given mating cannot be determined until many months after the actual matings are made. The progeny must be identified and many records of their actual performance must be made. When the breeder may be interested in 8 to 10 separate characteristics of the breeding stock, the record-keeping task for progeny testing is immense. However, the outstanding proven sires and dams discovered by this procedure will make possible genetic improvement more rapid than with other less rigid means of selection. In some cases, as for broiler growth, the testing period may not be excessively long, and the outstanding matings can be chosen in a fairly short time. For egg production a partial-year production has been used successfully to predict full-year production records, thus shortening the selection process to some degree.

Selection Pressure. After the above discussion some persons may think that poultry breeding today is a simple process provided proper records are kept and summarized, and selections are made on a good scientific basis. This then would assure improvment of the stock routinely year after year. Unfortunately, breeding is not that simple. Perhaps the chief reason it cannot be that simple is that no poultry breeder can afford to be satisfied with improving a single trait such as number of eggs. His stock must be of acceptable body size and general appearance; it must live well; the chicks must grow rapidly and feather properly; and the eggs laid by surviving pullets must be of suitable size, shape, color, shell texture, and interior quality.

Suppose, for illustration, that a breeder is satisfied to use in his breeding program any sires which, on the basis of progeny test, give offspring that perform above the average of his entire flock. Only about half of all the sires tested can produce offspring above the average in any measure of egg production, for the other half must be below. Similarly, only about half can be above average in respect to egg size of progeny. But the chance for a given sire to be above average in both respects becomes 1/2 × 1/2, or 1/4. That is, only 1 in 4 can be expected to excel in both characteristics. If, now, we add a requirement that the progeny of a sire excel also in respect to suitable measures of body size, interior egg quality, and shell color, we reduce the mathematical chance of finding such a sire to 1 in 32. A small breeder may not even have a total of 32 tested sires in any one season.

There are other important characters for which selection should be practiced. For instance, no sire should be used which did not come from a family of some reasonable minimum size, and he must have a reasonable number of daughters as a basis for evaluating his own breeding worth. All will agree that choosing males that merely exceed the average in respect to the desired qualities does not constitute very rigid selection. If we say that the males chosen must be in the upper 25% of the flock in respect to five different character measurements, then instead of finding 1 in 32, we can expect by chance to find only 1 in 1,024 (namely, 1/4 × 1/4 × 1/4 × 1/4 × 1/4). And if we set the requirement at the upper 20% level, we still further reduce the chance to 1 in 3,125. At 10% it becomes 1 in 100,000. This is just another way of saying that poultry breeding is difficult and complex and that progress toward the upper physiological limit in terms of production performance is bound to be slow.

The preceding discussion should make it clear that if high average egg production is the chief aim of a breeding program, each additional character for which selection is made automatically reduces the intensity of selection which can be applied to the main objective. In the example just used, if 10% of the tested males must be used for breeding purposes, and if average egg production is the only character considered, the top 10% of the males can be chosen. But if two characters are considered, assuming no correlation between them, only about 1/10 of the males that qualify in the first character will also be in the top 10% with respect to the second. Therefore the remaining 9/10 of the males that must be saved to provide the minimum total number will fall below the desirable standard in one or both measures.

If we select for as many as five characters simultaneously, provided they are not correlated and assuming that we want the best 10% of all males as before, the intensity of selection for any one character is reduced a great deal further, actually to the equivalent of $\sqrt[5]{1/10}$. Hence it is important when making selections not to give undue weight to those characters which are of minor significance. If a breeder feels that he must select for a certain shade of plumage color, in addition to perhaps five economically important characteristics, he must accept the obvious corollary that progress toward his main objective of high average egg production will be slowed just that much more.

Fortunately, there are some short cuts. A breeder may find it wise to concentrate on one or two characters at a time. He can use production to January 1 as his measure of egg-laying ability instead of insisting on full yearly records; he can breed from pullets instead of from older hens in order to get ten generations in ten years instead of only five. All of these will help because they save time, in terms of breeding progress, and because they enable a breeder with a specified number of breeding pens to increase the selection pressure he applies to his stock. But even when all these things are taken into account, poultry breeding today is big business. It calls for extensive facilities in the way of physical equipment, large numbers of fowls, and a great deal of labor both in the keeping of detailed records and in their analysis. Some breeding operations involve more than 500 small pens for flock matings headed by individual males. The larger breeding farms make extensive use of computers in handling thousands upon thousands of individual records. Today many breeders house hens in cages and make matings by artificial insemination (Figs. 3–9, 3–10, 3–11).

Fig. 3–9. Many breeders house hens in cages and make test matings through artificial insemination. Semen collection from a male. Large numbers of males can be tested in this way without the need for large numbers of small breeding pens. (Courtesy Shaver Poultry Breeding Farms, Ltd.)

Fig. 3–10. Breeding farms must maintain large numbers of small individual breeding pens for use in testing mating combinations. (Courtesy of Shaver Poultry Breeding Farms, Ltd.)

Fig. 3–11. On breeding farms where many small matings are necessary, trap-nesting is conveniently done from a central corridor. (Courtesy of Kimber Farms, Inc., Fremont, California.)

All of this has come about, not merely as expansion and growth, but in an attempt to discover and apply more refined and precise methods of selection to the business of increasing egg production and broiler performance. As pointed out earlier, poultry breeders have come a long way by the use of a common sense approach to the problem, so that a prospective purchaser of chicks or breeding stock today can obtain at nominal cost the kind of chickens that not so many years ago were known on but few farms in the country. But because better and better performance is demanded, breeders will continue to use all means at their disposal to reach still higher goals.

Poultry Breeding Companies

The breeding companies supplying stock for commercial poultry production are far removed from the small individual breeder who was the source of chickens for the poultryman 30 years ago. These breeding companies have been able to assemble the scientific personnel and the marketing organization to generate sufficient sales to support research and breeding establishments far greater in size than was possible in the early days of scientific poultry breeding. Most of these breeding companies market on a worldwide basis.

Essentially all commercial stocks for broiler production and for laying hens are crosses of breeds, inbred lines, or strains within a breed. This has the benefit of giving hybrid vigor to the commercial chick produced, and it also provides a means for the breeder to control the stock necessary to produce the commercial chick. For example, if the mother of the commercial chick destined to be a layer is a cross between two strains, the mother will show hybrid vigor and be a good producer of commercial chicks. In addition, the mother is a hybrid, and since hybrids do not breed true, the breeder can safely send her to supply flocks throughout the world without fear that someone will be able to reproduce the stock in competition with the breeder. This is impossible without the original grandparent lines that were crossed to produce the mother of the commercial chick. These grandparent lines are safeguarded because they represent the basic product of the breeder on which he relies for the superiority of his commercial chick. Male lines may also be crosses or if pure may be safeguarded by ensuring that females necessary to reproduce the male line do not reach outsiders that may produce the male line in competition with the breeder.

The production of the commercial chick may then be done in many areas of the world through dealers and hatcheries franchised by the primary breeding company. These companies may specialize and may produce only egg-laying stock or broiler stock. In fact, in broiler breeding some breeding companies specialize in a male or female line specifically intended for crossing for the commercial broiler chick. Several large broiler firms now do their own breeding of broiler stock, so that even the breeding function is integrated into the production company.

The advent of the commercial breeding company and the superiority of modern stock produced through the efforts of these companies have reduced the number of primary poultry breeders drastically in the past several years. This has put a heavy responsibility on the remaining breeders to maintain and improve the genetic base on which the modern poultry industry rests.

BREEDS OF CHICKENS

The great variety of shapes, colors, feather patterns, body size, and other characteristics that one sees at a poultry fanciers' show attests to the many breeds and varieties of poultry that have been developed. Breeds are considered to be a group of related fowls that breed true for certain characters that breeders agree as those that distinguish the breed.

The early history of poultry breeding saw the development of many different breeds, which were characteristic of certain areas where they were developed. Well-known English breeds such as the Cornish (Fig. 3–12) or Sussex carry the name of the area where they were developed, as do the American Rhode Island reds, Plymouth Rocks, and Jersey giants. The white leghorn, originally from Italy, had many subvarieties that originated in countries of Europe and in the United States.

With the intensification of the poultry industry traditional breeds lost their commercial importance, and crossbreeding and strain crossing have

Fig. 3–12. Dark Cornish (English). The Cornish is often crossed with other breeds to produce a desirable meat-type chicken. (Courtesy of Poultry Tribune.)

Fig. 3–13. Single Comb White Leghorns (Mediterranean). (Courtesy of Poultry Tribune.)

Fig. 3–14. Barred Plymouth Rocks (American). (Courtesy of Poultry Tribune.)

Fig. 3–15. White Plymouth Rocks (American). (Courtesy of Poultry Tribune.)

Fig. 3–16.   Rose Comb Rhode Island Reds (American). (Courtesy of Poultry Tribune.)

Fig. 3–17.   New Hampshires (American). (Courtesy of Poultry Tribune.)

Fig. 3–18. An egg-type white leghorn as she would appear in the laying house. (Courtesy of Kimber Farms, Inc., Fremont, California.)

Fig. 3–19. A typical Vantress breeder male. At twenty-six weeks of age this bird weighed 11 pounds. (Courtesy of Vantress Farms, Inc., Duluth, Georgia.)

Fig. 3–20. A Hubbard meat breeder pullet. (Courtesy of Hubbard Farms, Walpole, New Hampshire.)

been used to produce the modern chicken. The white leghorn is an exception, as this breed forms the backbone of the egg industry. The characteristics preserved in breeds by early breeders have been particularly valuable to provide the plumage color, body conformation, and other features of the present commercial chickens.

Of the chickens in supply flocks tested under the National Poultry Improvement Plan in 1975, 8.9% of these tested were white leghorns, 0.6% white Plymouth Rock, 0.4% Rhode Island red, 0.2% barred Plymouth Rock, and 0.1% were New Hampshires (Figs. 3–13 through 3–18). The remaining chickens were considered to be cross-mated.

The breeders are more concerned with the characteristics of the production bird than they are with pureness of breeds (Figs. 3–19, 3–20).

Table 3–2. The More Important Characteristics of Some Representative Breeds of Chickens

Breed	Standard Weight, Pounds		Type of Comb	Color of Earlobe	Color of Skin	Color of Shank	Shanks Feathered?	Color of Egg
	Cock	Hen						
American Breeds:								
Plymouth Rock	9½	7½	Single	Red	Yellow	Yellow	No	Brown
Wyandotte	8½	6½	Rose	Red	Yellow	Yellow	No	Brown
Rhode Island red	8½	6½	Single and rose	Red	Yellow	Yellow	No	Brown
Jersey black giant	13	10	Single	Red	Yellow	Black	No	Brown
New Hampshire	8½	6½	Single	Red	Yellow	Yellow	No	Brown
Asiatic Breeds:								
Brahma (light)	12	9½	Pea	Red	Yellow	Yellow	Yes	Brown
Cochin	11	8½	Single	Red	Yellow	Yellow	Yes	Brown
Langshan (black)	9½	7½	Single	Red	White	Bluish-black	Yes	Brown
English Breeds:								
Australorp	8½	6½	Single	Red	White	Dark slate	No	Brown
Cornish (dark)	10	7½	Pea	Red	Yellow	Yellow	No	Brown
Dorking (silver-gray)	9	7	Single	Red	White	White	No	White
Orpington (buff and white)	10	8	Single	Red	White	White	No	Brown
Sussex	9	7	Single	Red	White	White	No	Brown
Mediterranean Breeds:								
Leghorn	6	4½	Single and rose	White	Yellow	Yellow	No	White
Minorca (S. C. black)	9	7½	Single	White	White	Dark slate	No	White
Ancona	6	4½	Single and rose	White	Yellow	Yellow	No	White
Andalusian (blue)	7	5½	Single	White	White	Slaty blue	No	White

The use of breed or strain crosses to introduce desired body conformation, plumage color, and heterosis is considered by commercial breeders rather than maintaining breeds *per se*.

There are nearly 200 breeds listed in the American Standard of Perfection. The more important characteristics of some of these breeds are listed in Table 3–2.

THE NATIONAL POULTRY IMPROVEMENT PLAN

The National Poultry Improvement Plan became operative July 1, 1935. It is administered in each state by an official state agency cooperating with the U. S. Department of Agriculture. Authority for an official state agency to administer the plan within the state is a memorandum of agreement between it and the U. S. Department of Agriculture. The Department of Agriculture is responsible for coordinating the program among the cooperating states.

The objectives of the plan are to improve the production and market qualities of chickens and to reduce losses from hatchery-disseminated diseases. Of the nearly 27 million birds tested for pullorum disease and fowl typhoid in 1975, only 38—a mere .0008%—proved to be reactors.

The National Turkey Improvement Plan is operated on a similar basis. Current provisions of the Plan are described in the U.S. Department of Agriculture publication, "The National Poultry and Turkey Improvement Plans" available from Official State Agencies or from the Animal Husbandry Research Division, ARS, Beltsville, Maryland 20705.

IDENTIFICATION OF HENS IN LAY

Routine culling of laying flocks is seldom practiced on commercial egg farms, simply because it is no longer economically important. When average flock egg production was no more than 200 eggs per hen, with one third or more of the individuals laying fewer than 175 eggs, a substantial saving in feed cost could be made by getting rid of the low producers as they reached the end of their laying year. But with today's better bred stock capable of laying 240 to 250 eggs a year, and with very few individuals turning out to be really poor layers, there is little to be gained by routine culling. With cage-managed flocks, culling is a simple procedure, but most operators have found that as a practical matter the removal of the few hens that are obviously out of condition is all that is necessary. The entire flock is retained for a laying period of 12 to 15 months and then replaced. However, a good poultry manager still should be able to recognize the layer from the non-layer to tell the state of production of an individual hen.

Body Changes

When laying, a hen has a large, moist vent, showing a dilated, pliable condition in contrast to the puckered hardness of the vent of a non-laying hen (Fig. 3–21). The abdominal region is enlarged in the layer, as compared with the non-layer. The pelvic bones move apart and become comparatively elastic and pliable.

In a hen that is not laying, the pelvic bones almost come together just below the vent. The same individual when in full laying may show a distance of three or even four fingers' width between them. The distance from the pelvic bone to the point of the keel (breast bone) is increased at the same time. These changes provide room for the passage of the egg, the enormous increase in the size of the ovary, with its several rapidly growing ova, and for the distention of the alimentary tract to accommodate large amounts of feed.

The rate of egg production is indicated in a measure by the relative softness and pliability of the skin and the thinness and elasticity of the pelvic bones. The subcutaneous fat of the abdomen is used up by laying, so that the abdominal skin of the heavy producer becomes velvety and the whole abdomen soft and flexible. The pelvic bones feel thin, tapering, and elastic. In the non-layer they are likely to feel thick, blunt, and stiff, and the whole abdomen is surrounded under the skin with a layer of hard fat if the bird is on full feed.

Among the most valuable indications of the heavy layer are the refinement of the head and the closeness and dryness of feathering. The wattles and earlobes fit close to the beak and are not loose and flabby. The high layer is trimmer in feathering than the poor layer, but after prolonged heavy production the oil does not keep the plumage so sleek and glossy. It becomes worn and frayed.

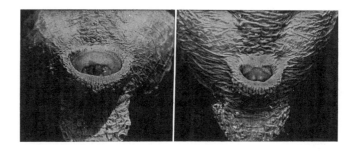

A   B

Fig. 3–21.   A, the vent of a laying hen, and B, of a non-laying hen. (Courtesy of Kansas Agricultural Experiment Station.)

There is a close correlation between the relative size of the comb and wattles and ovarian activity. If they are comparatively large, full, smooth, hard, and waxy, the hen is probably laying heavily; if the comb is limp, the bird may be laying slowly; but if it is dried, shrunken, and cold, she is not laying at all. When the comb is expanding in advance of another period of production, it often feels warm to the touch.

Pigmentation

In varieties showing yellow pigment in the subcutaneous fat, shanks, and earlobes in Mediterranean and Continental breeds, the pigment tends to disappear as laying progresses. The presence or absence of this pigment in the fowl or its eggs is directly correlated with the presence or absence in the feed of a carotenoid pigment called xanthophyll. For this reason, a hen fed on a ration devoid of such feeds as yellow corn and alfalfa meal might have the appearance of laying so far as pigment is concerned, though she had never produced an egg. The character of the feed the hen has been receiving should, therefore, always be considered in relation to her condition with reference to pigment.

When hens have feeds carrying an abundance of pigment, and the skin, shanks, and beak are not normally pale as in the English breeds, the beginning of laying diverts all the pigment received in the feed to the ovary, where it finds its way into the developing yolk. The pigment of other parts gradually disappears as a result of the natural physiological change in the structure of the skin. It is not replaced as long as the individual continues to lay.

The vent loses its pigment quickly so that a white or pink vent in a yellow-skinned variety usually indicates that the bird is laying; a yellow vent indicates that she is not laying.

The eyering formed by the inner edges of the eyelids loses it pigment a trifle more slowly than the vent. The earlobes of the Mediterranean breeds bleach out somewhat more slowly than the eyering, so that in these breeds a white earlobe on a vigorous bird usually means a longer period of continuous laying than does a bleached vent or eyelid.

The color disappears from the beak next, beginning at the base and remaining longest at the tip. The lower part loses color more rapidly than the upper. With the average yellow-skinned bird a bleached beak means that laying has been in progress for from 4 to 6 weeks.

The shanks are the last to lose their color. Bleached shanks, therefore, indicate a much longer period of production than does the bleaching of the other parts. The pigment disappears from the front of the shank first and finally from the back. A bleached shank usually indicates continued egg production for at least 15 to 20 weeks.

When laying stops, the pigment reappears in the several regions in the same order in which it disappeared. The relative rapidity of loss and regain in the various parts is probably correlated with the thickness of the skin, the pigment change being slowest where the epidermal covering is thickest. The fact that a given hen stopped laying 2 or 3 weeks back sometimes may be determined by the fact that the tip of the beak is colorless while the base is yellow.

Molting

The shedding and renewal of feathers normally occur once a year, though molting may occur in certain individuals twice in one year and, more rarely, only once in a period of two years. In the wild fowl it would have no relation whatever to egg production. Under the influence of domestication, however, the laying period has been gradually lengthened until it often overlaps the natural molting season.

Under the influence of the genes for high production, and particularly of those related to persistency and the length of the laying period, the natural tendency is for a good hen to continue to lay as late in the fall as she possibly can. The result is that she either molts late, i.e., after her long laying period is over, or molts and lays at the same time. The low-producing hen, on the other hand, stops laying in July or August well in advance of the time that growth of a new feather coat must begin in order to put the hen in condition to resist the cold weather of winter.

Fig. 3–22.   A wing showing four new primary feathers partly grown. Note the axial feather. (Courtesy of Kansas Agricultural Experiment Station.)

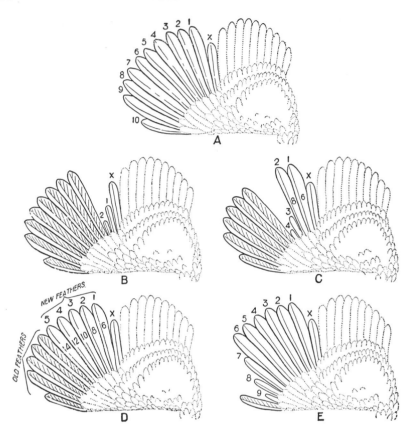

Fig. 3–23. A, a normal wing showing the primary feathers, 1 to 10. They are separated from the secondaries (shown in dotted outline) by the short axial feather, x. B, the beginning of a wing molt. 1 and 2 are new feathers growing in. C, an eight-week molt. Elapsed time in weeks is indicated on each feather. D, an unusual instance in which only five primaries were molted. E, a wing as it appears near the completion of a normal molt. (Courtesy of Kansas Agricultural Experiment Station.)

Observation of the conditions that most commonly occur in laying flocks has led many persons into two faulty conclusions with regard to molt. One is that the onset of molt is a cause of the cessation of laying, and the other is that hens never lay and molt at the same time. The facts seem to be, rather, that a hen molts late because she lays late, and that hens bred for continuous production at a high rate not only may, but often do, lay and molt at the same time. This latter condition probably does not occur except when a hen is increasing, or at least maintaining, her body weight.

The order in which the different sections of the fowl lose their feathers is fairly definite (Figs. 3–22; 3–23). The usual order is head, neck, body (including breast, back, and abdomen), wing, and tail. Not only this, but there is a high degree of regularity about the order of molt within the several sections. The wing primaries, for example, begin to drop before the secondaries. The first primary to be shed is the inside one, next to the axial feather, and the remainder are shed in succession until the last one to be dropped is the outermost primary near the tip of the wing.

The order of molt of the secondary feathers is not so regular as that of the primaries, but the most common order, when the secondaries are numbered from the axial feather toward the body, has been reported as 11, 12, 13, 14, 10, 2, 3, 4, 5, 6, 7, 8, 9,1. The axial feather is dropped at the same time as the secondary next to it.

In addition to being a late molter, the high-producing hen is also likely to be a rapid molter. Extensive observations have shown that there is no difference in the rate at which high-producing and low-producing hens grow new feathers, but that there is a decided difference in the rate at which the old feathers are shed. In no instance did an individual primary feather become completely grown in less than 6 weeks, and some feathers required 7 weeks to complete their growth. The feathers made about 20% of their growth in each of the first 3 weeks, and from 12 to 15% during each of the second 3 weeks.

The rate of laying is not materially affected by the molt, in the case of hens that lay and molt at the same time, but the rate of molt is slowed up by production. The net result is that the advantage gained by the late molter, as measured by length of the period of nonproduction, is due, not to differences in the number of feathers dropped or to the rate of growth of an individual feather, but to the fact that two jobs are performed at one and the same time.

It should be remembered also that time and rate of molt are influenced to a considerable extent by weight and physical condition of the hens and by environmental conditions, including feeding and management.

Chapter 4

Incubation and Hatchery Management

Compared to other important meat producing animals, poultry populations can be expanded at an extremely rapid rate. One broiler breeder hen, weighing 7 pounds, produces about 150 offspring in a 12-month period that may be used in the production of 600 pounds of live marketable meat. Such a rate of reproduction of offspring is a major reason for the efficiency of poultry in the production of food for humans. This reproductive capacity of chickens could not be used without artificial incubation of eggs. The use of incubators has freed the breeding hen from incubating eggs and enables her to work "full time" during the year to produce hatching eggs. This chapter will cover the important aspects of incubation and hatching to give the reader a basic understanding of the principles involved.

DEVELOPMENT OF THE CHICK

The hatching of chicks independently from any contribution by the hen is possible because the fertilized ovum never forms a connection with the mother, and embryo development essentially occurs completely outside the body of the mother. An understanding of some basic features of embryonic development is useful in understanding the incubation process.

Embryonic Development

The normal incubation period of chicken eggs is 21 days, although there is some variation in each direction. The eggs of leghorns and other light breeds commonly hatch a few hours earlier than those of the heavier breeds. It should also be remembered that in its embryonic development the bird is much more rapid than the mammal, and that this is very likely an adaptation to life within the egg. The incubation period for several birds is shown in Table 4–1.

92

Table 4–1.   Incubation Period of Eggs of Various Birds

Birds	Days
Bob white quail	24
Chicken	21
Duck (Muscovy)	35
Duck (Pekin and Mallard)	28
Goose	28
Guinea fowl	28
Japanese quail	16–19
Ostrich	42
Pheasant	24
Pigeon	17
Swan	35

Communication Between Embryos

In some species of birds, eggs in a clutch tend to hatch at about the same time in spite of the fact that some eggs have been laid earlier and thus incubated longer than other eggs. Some fascinating experiments by Dr. Margaret Vince at Cambridge University in England have shed considerable light on how synchronization of hatching can take place. These experiments have shown that embryos are able to communicate with each other in a manner that affects time of hatching. Data in Figure 4–1 from an experiment conducted at Cornell University illustrate this phenomenon. When two groups of Japanese quail eggs were set 24 hours

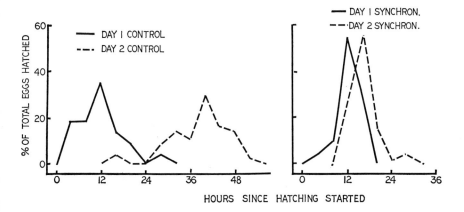

Fig. 4–1.   Effect of apparent embryo communication on time of hatch. For the control eggs, day 2 eggs were set 24 hours after day 1 eggs and incubated separately. The day 1 and day 2 synchronized eggs were also set 24 hours apart but were incubated together. In this case the eggs set 24 hours apart hatched nearly at the same time. (Unpublished data of B. J. Grieve and A. van Tienhoven, Cornell University.)

apart and maintained separately in the incubator, these groups hatched about 24 hours apart. However, when eggs from the two groups were incubated together so they were alternated and touching, both groups hatched nearly at the same time. The group set last had its hatching time accelerated by contact with the group set earlier. Apparently the synchronization of hatching is accomplished by vibrations or clicks made by movements of the embryos.

Acceleration or retardation of hatching can be caused by use of artificial clicks. In quail, stimulation with 1.5 to 60 clicks per second caused eggs to hatch early, whereas those subjected to clicks at rates of 100 to 500 per second hatched late. In chickens, artificial clicking has been shown to advance time of hatch but not to retard hatching. These experiments are a fascinating example of communication between embryos and show that nervous control of development apparently can take place.

Early Structural Development

As yolk is added during maturation of the ovum, the germ cell becomes located at the surface of the yolk beneath the vitelline membrane. Structural development begins shortly after fertilization by division of the fertilized ovum (zygote) into two daughter cells. These cells in turn divide, and a continuous proliferation of cells is inaugurated which (except for the period after laying until the egg is set) continues actively not only during incubation but throughout subsequent growth until maturity.

The first division or cleavage of the germ cell occurs about the time the egg enters the isthmus, and the second follows in about 20 minutes. The

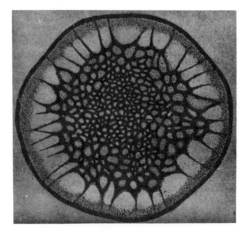

Fig. 4–2. Appearance of the blastoderm (magnified) of a hen's egg after 8 hours in the oviduct. It shows 346 cells, 34 marginal and 312 central. (After Patterson.)

third division, to form the 8-cell stage, also takes place in the isthmus, and by the time the egg is well within the uterus it has advanced to the 16-cell stage. Within the next 4 hours it advances by continued cell division to approximately the 256-cell stage.

As a result of this process of cell division while the egg is still in the oviduct, a disc-shaped layer of cells is formed. It is first a single layer of cells, but later on is several layers thick. This layer of cells, in intimate contact with the underlying yolk, constitutes the undifferentiated blastoderm as shown in magnified form in Figure 4–2.

Eventually the cells in the center of the blastoderm become detached from the surface of the yolk to form a cavity called the blastocoele. Because these cells are no longer attached to the yolk, this central area is transparent—the *area pellucida*—while the outer portion which remains in contact with the yolk is opaque—the *area opaca*. It is in the center of the area pellucida that the development of the embryo proper takes place.

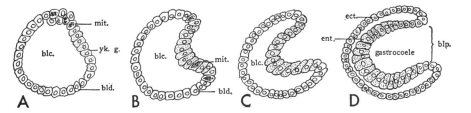

GASTRULATION IN FORM WITH ISOLECITHAL EGG HAVING ALMOST NO YOLK—AMPHIOXUS.

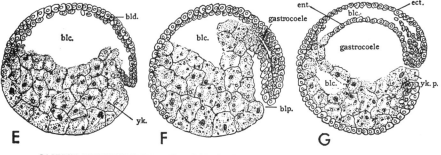

GASTRULATION IN FORM WITH TELOLECITHAL EGG CONTAINING MODERATE AMOUNT OF YOLK—AMPHIBIA.

Fig. 4–3. Schematic diagrams to show the effect of yolk on gastrulation. In the case of the chick, the still greater amount of yolk effectively prevents the formation of an open blastopore.

Abbreviations: blc., blastocoele; bld., blastoderm; blp., blastopore; ect., ectoderm; ent., entoderm; mit., cell underoing mitosis; yk., yolk; yk. g., yolk granules; yk. p., yolk plug.

(From Patten: Early Embryology of the Chick, 4th edition. By permission of The Blakiston Division, McGraw-Hill Book Co., Inc.)

Before the egg is laid, or soon thereafter, the blastoderm becomes differentiated into two layers of cells by a process referred to as gastrulation (gut formation). This involves the rapid proliferation of cells along one portion of the margin of the blastoderm, to form a second layer of cells. This second layer of cells, by its inward growth, eventually divides the cavity (blastocoele) into two. The lower cavity is the gut or gastrocoele. It is in this manner that the blastoderm becomes differentiated into two of the three germ layers—the ectoderm above and the layer of entoderm below growing into the blastocoele (Figs. 4–3; 4–4).

Shortly after incubation begins, the third germ layer, or mesoderm, originates or becomes differentiated by growing into the blastocoele between the ectoderm and the entoderm in much the same way that the entoderm earlier pushed into the blastocoele. Thus the blastoderm at this stage consists of three distinct layers of cells resting on the surface of the yolk, i.e., ectoderm, mesoderm, and entoderm. These three layers constitute the materials out of which the various organs and systems of the body are to be developed.

From the ectoderm, the skin, feathers, beak, claws, nervous system,

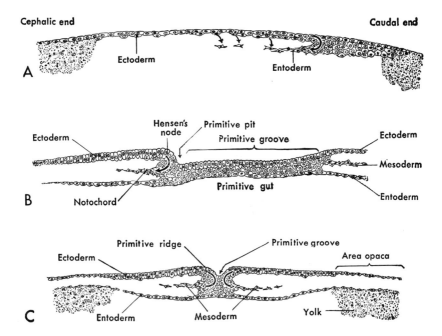

Fig. 4–4. Schematic diagrams indicating the cell movements involved in the gastrulation of chick embryos. A, Longitudinal section of the blastoderm from a pre-primitive streak chick during entoderm formation. B, Longitudinal plan of embryo of approximately seventeen hours of incubation to show the relations of the various parts. C, Cross section of an embryo in the primitive streak stage to show the turning in of cells at the primitive groove to enter the mesodermal layers. (From Patten: Early Embryology of the Chick, 4th edition. By permission of The Blakiston Division, McGraw-Hill Book Co., Inc.)

lens and retina of the eye, and the linings of the mouth and vent are developed. The bones, muscles, blood, and reproductive and excretory organs develop from the mesoderm, and the entoderm produces the linings of the digestive tract and the respiratory and secretory organs.

Gastrulation is usually, though by no means always, complete by the time the egg is laid. It seems to have been shown conclusively that the period of the gastrulation process is an exceedingly critical one, whereas the early postgastrula stage, during which most eggs are laid, is comparatively noncritical. Often, eggs that are diagnosed as infertile have in fact developed into the early stages of gastrulation. This can be determined histologically but cannot be seen by the naked eye.

The stage of embryonic development in fresh-laid fertile eggs tends to be characteristic of individual hens and appears to be correlated with hatching power. At the Massachusetts Station, pregastrula and early gastrula were the most common stages of development in eggs from low-hatching hens. Early gastrula stages were characteristic of hens with medium hatching power, and well-advanced gastrula was most commonly found in eggs from hens that gave a high percentage hatch.

Too much development at the time of laying may be as detrimental as too little. Observations made by workers in the U. S. Department of Agriculture indicate that maximum hatchability occurs when the interval between successive eggs is 27 hours, and that hatchability decreases when the interval is in excess of 28 hours.

One of the first changes in structure after the egg has begun to incubate is the appearance of the primitve streak. Simultaneously with the differentiation of the mesoderm, the primitive streak arises as two thickenings in the ectoderm, starting near the point of origin of the entoderm. The primitive streak eventually disappears completely, but it serves to mark the future longitudinal axis of the body of the embryo and its posterior extremity. Although the embryonic axis is fairly uniform, it is not absolutely fixed. It usually lies approximately at right angles to the long axis of the egg, being directed away from the observer when the small end of the egg is to the right.

The growth and development of the embryo from the cells in the area pellucida soon show a more rapid growth of cells in certain regions than in others. This uneven growth gives rise to a series of folds in which the various germ layers are involved. These folds mark off the embryo proper from the rest of the blastoderm. The first of these, the head fold, lifts the anterior end of the embryo above the remainder of the blastoderm. Later the tail fold undercuts the posterior extremity of the embryo to elevate it. Both of these join with the lateral folds which mark out the sides of the embryo. Eventually this undercutting or folding lifts the embryo well above the yolk, leaving only a narrow stalk to serve as a connection between them. Figure 4–5 is a photograph of a chick embryo after 25 to 26 hours of development.

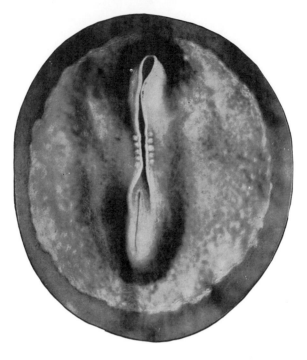

Fig. 4–5. Chick embryo of 25 to 26 hours photographed by reflected light to show its external configuration. (From Patten: Early Embryology of the Chick, 4th edition. By permission of The Blakiston Division, McGraw-Hill Book Co., Inc.)

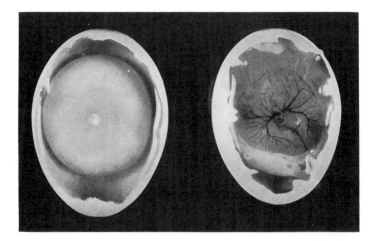

Fig. 4–6. An infertile (*left*) and a fertile egg after being held for 72 hours at a temperature of 102° F. (Courtesy of Illinois Agriculture Experiment Station.)

During the first 24 hours the head of the embryo becomes clearly defined and in it may be observed the beginnings of the central nervous system as well as the foregut, the forerunner of the alimentary tract. Blood islands appear in the area opaca outside the body of the embryo. The blastoderm enlarges considerably, embarking on the process of growth in which it ultimately surrounds the yolk.

The second day sees the embryo beginning to turn on its left side, the formation of the heart which may be observed to beat at about the thirtieth hour, the primary divisions of the brain, the beginning of the formation of the eyes, the ear pits, and the formation of the tail bud. The primary stages of organogenesis are completed within the first 3 days of incubation. After 72 hours of incubation, the eyes begin to pigment, and limb buds are clearly visible (Fig. 4–6).

The Extraembryonic Membranes

Four extraembryonic membranes are essential to the normal growth of the embryo. They are the amnion, chorion, yolk sac, and allantois.

The amnion and the chorion originate together from a fold of the extraembryonic tissue that first appears in the head region, but which eventually encircles the entire embryo. This fold, consisting of ectoderm and a layer of mesoderm, grows upward and over the embryo to fuse eventually at the top. The outer portion, with ectoderm above and mesoderm beneath, is the chorion, and the inner part of the fold with the position of the germ layers reversed is the amnion. The amnion is a transparent membranous sac filled with a colorless fluid which serves as a protection from mechanical shock and allows the embryo to move about rather freely as it develops.

A third extraembryonic membrane, the yolk sac, consists of a layer of entoderm and mesoderm growing over the surface of the yolk, with the entoderm next to the yolk. The walls of the yolk sac become lined with a special glandular and absorbing epithelium which functions in the uptake of the yolk material. Yolk material does not pass through the yolk stalk to the embryo even though a narrow opening or lumen in the stalk is still in evidence at the end of the incubation period.

At approximately 96 hours of incubation there is an outgrowth of the entoderm from the hind gut which pushes a layer of mesoderm ahead of it into the extraembryonic cavity, to form the allantois. This fourth extraembryonic membrane, the allantois, continues to enlarge until it eventually fills the entire extraembryonic cavity and thus occupies the space between the amnion and the chorion. It is a highly vascular sac which fuses with the chorion, thus bringing its capillaries in direct contact with the shell membrane. The spatial relationships of the 4-day embryo and its membranes are illustrated in Figure 4–7.

The allantois has four functions. It serves as an embryonic respiratory

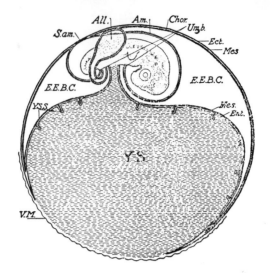

Fig. 4–7. Diagram of the chick and its embryonic membranes during the fourth day of incubation. Abbreviations used in this and also in Figure 4–9 are as follows: *Alb.*, albumen; *Alb.S.*, albumen sac; *All.*, allantois; *All.C.*, cavity of allantois; *All.I.*, inner wall of allantois; *All.S.*, stalk of allantois; *Am.*, amnion; *Am.C.*, amniotic cavity; *Chor.*, chorion; *C.T.R.*, connective tissue ring; *Ect.*, ectoderm; *E.E.B.C.*, extra-embryonic body cavity; *Ent.*, entoderm; *Mes.*, mesoderm; *S.-Am.*, sero-amniotic connection; *S.Y.S.U.*, sac of yolk sac umbilicus; *Umb.*, umbilicus; *V.M.*, vitelline membrane; *Y.S.*, yolk sac; *Y.S.S.*, yolk sac septa. (After Lillie.)

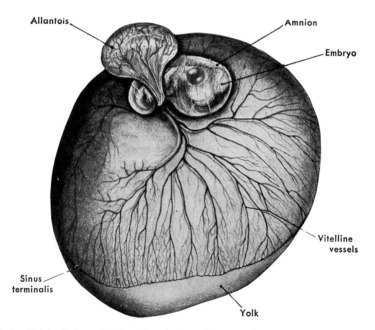

Fig. 4–8. Chick of about 5½ days' incubation taken out of the shell with the yolk intact. The chorion and the white of the egg have been removed to expose the embryo lying within the amnion, and the allantois has been displaced upward in order to show the allantoic stalk. (Modified from Kerr. From Patten: Early Embryology of the Chick, 4th edition. By permission of The Blakiston Division, McGraw-Hill Book Co., Inc.)

100

organ, exchanging gases at the undersurface of the shell; it receives the excretions of the embryonic kidneys; it absorbs albumen which serves as nutriment for the embryo; and it absorbs calcium from the shell for the structural needs of the embryo.

The growth of the amnion constricts the opening from the intestine to the yolk sac, thereby forming what is called the yolk stalk. It also brings the yolk stalk into close contact with the allantoic stalk (Fig. 4–8). These with their blood vessels are included in an extension of the embryonic body wall to form the umbilical cord.

Later Structural Development

Up to the sixth or seventh day there is nothing about the chick embryo which would help one to distinguish it from the embryo of other familiar animals. On the fourth day, the limb buds, which eventually give rise to the legs and wings, can be observed. By the sixth day the digits can be observed. The body, which has been small in proportion to the head, begins to develop more rapidly. Movement may be noticed if the egg is opened, which probably is a result of contraction of the amnion. Spontaneous movements of the legs and wings begin at about 11 days.

During the eighth day the feather germs appear in definite tracts and on the ninth the contour of the embryo becomes quite birdlike. There is a chalky deposit about the mouth opening which is the beginning of the horny beak. By this time the allantois nearly surrounds the embryo,

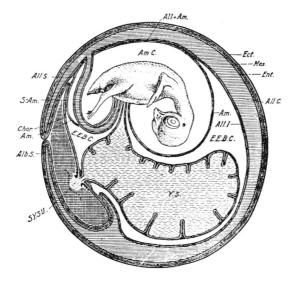

Fig. 4–9. Diagram of the chick and its membranes during the twelfth day of incubation. For the designation of parts see legend of Figure 4–7. (After Lillie.)

amnion, and yolk. A diagrammatic representation of the 12-day embryo is shown in Figure 4–9.

By the thirteenth day the down is distributed over the body, and its color may be seen through the thin walls of the sacs which still enclose the individual down feathers. On this day the scales and nails appear on the legs and feet. By the sixteenth day they are quite firm and horny, as is also the beak.

By the fourteenth day the embryo has accommodated itself to the form of the egg, so as to lie parallel to the long axis.

On the seventeenth day the amniotic fluid begins to decrease. On the nineteenth the yolk begins to enter the body through the umbilicus, apparently forced by the muscular tension of the amnion. The beak usually pierces the air cell, and the lungs begin to function, though it is not until the shell is pipped, generally on the twentieth day, that full pulmonary respiration becomes a fact, and the allantoic circulation and respiration cease.

Fig. 4–10.   Chicks hatching from pedigreed eggs. Several eggs show evidence of pipping, the first sign of hatching. (Courtesy of Babcock Industries Inc.)

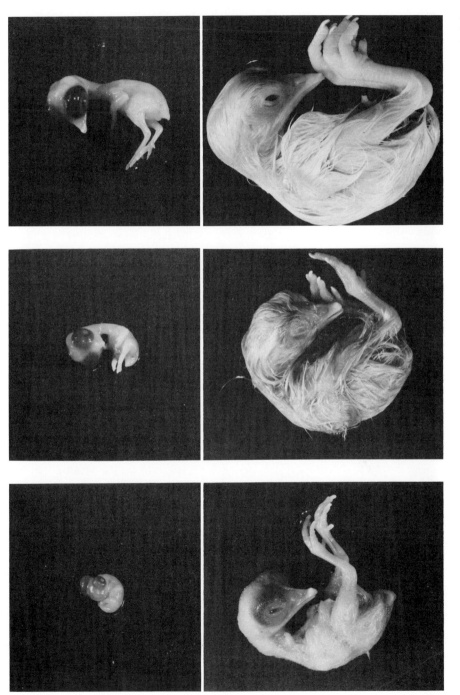

Fig. 4-11. Chick embryos at various stages of incubation. Top, left to right: 5, 7, and 9 days of incubation. Bottom, left to right: 12, 15, and 20 days.

When fully formed, the chick is normally placed with the forepart of the body toward the large end of the egg, its head bent forward beneath the right wing and the legs brought up toward the head. The end of the upper mandible of the beak is equipped with a horny cap which bears a sharp point. By means of this, while slowly revolving in the shell, a circular path is chipped around the large end of the egg, the shell membranes being cut at the same time. When the shell is nearly cut around, a final convulsion finishes the break, and the chick can emerge (Fig. 4–10). The appearance of the chick embryo at various stages during the course of its development is shown in Figure 4–11.

EXPERIMENTAL EMBRYOLOGY

The chick embryo has been a prize subject for teaching and research in embryology. This is largely due to the ease with which large numbers of embryos can be produced at any desired stage of incubation and to the special advantages of embryonic development, which occurs externally rather than *in utero,* as in the case with most mammals. Chick embryos are used for purposes too numerous to detail herein. They serve as vehicles for virus production in the preparation of specific antisera against human and animal diseases and have been used experimentally in the

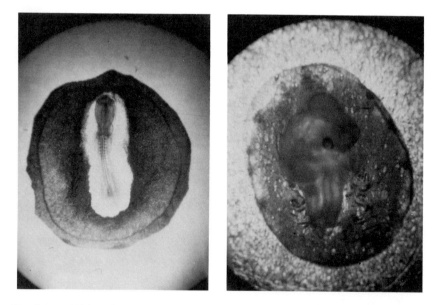

Fig. 4–12. Chick embryos cultured on nutrient agar. Left, chick embryo which has been explanted to agar at the 11 to 13 somite stage. Right, explanted chick embryo after 72 hours of culture. (From Klein, N. W., McConnell, E., and Riquier, D. J.: Enhanced growth and survival of explanted chick embryos cultured under high levels of oxygen. Dev. Biol., *10*:25, 1964.)

studies of cellular differentiation, development of organ systems, role of nutrition in development, and in the investigation of the mutagenic or teratogenic effects of chemical substances. Chick embryos are surprisingly resistant to alterations in their environment.

Some investigators have developed sophisticated techniques for embryo culture. One of these involves removal of the embryo along with its membranes to a Petri dish containing nutrient agar medium, where it may survive and grow for a period of days (Fig. 4–12). Another technique developed at the University of California involves removal of yolk from the intact egg and replacing it with culture media (Fig. 4–13). Using the latter system, investigators have studied the influence of amino acid deficiencies on the young embryo. This cannot be done with intact eggs from amino acid-deficient hens, as such hens produce fewer eggs of normal composition, or no eggs at all. By these techniques, scientists hope to elucidate the role of the egg constituents in embryo development and to extend their capabilities to study the intricate processes of development.

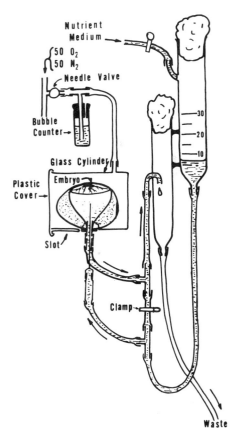

Fig. 4–13. Perfused chick embryo. Nutrient medium flows from the calibrated tube in the direction of the arrows, through a hypodermic needle into the space bounded by the vitelline membrane and yolk sac. Displaced fluid passes out of the egg through a metal sleeve around the hypodermic needle. (From Grau, C. R.: Avian embryo nutrition. Fed. Proc., 27:188, 1968.)

ARTIFICIAL INCUBATION

Artificial incubation refers to the use of mechanical equipment to replace the brooding hen for incubation of eggs. This is the foundation of the modern poultry industry allowing large numbers of newly hatched chicks to be produced on demand by the poultry producer. The production of hatching eggs that will provide strong viable chicks is a key factor in a successful hatchery operation. Many factors can affect hatching. These include fertility, storage conditions, egg size, nutrition of the dam, condition of the eggshell, genetic constitution of the embryo, incubation temperature, humidity, and gaseous environment. Since most of these are under some control of the person managing a hatchery, the control that can be exercised must be understood.

Selection of Hatching Eggs

The successful production of high quality chicks begins with the breeder. Chicks that will be used for production of eggs or poultry meat should be derived from breeding flocks selected on the basis of desired characteristics of egg or meat production. Breeders should be disease-free, fed an adequate diet, and maintained under conditions that are conducive to successful mating.

Unfortunately there is no way of telling if an egg is fertile or not prior to incubation, without opening it. Thus, if fertility is not high, many eggs will be set that do not develop embryos, and many eggs are wasted because the infertile, incubated eggs are not marketable. Many people have tried to develop methods of detecting fertile eggs prior to incubating them but without success.

Fertility of good eggs produced by breeder flocks should be in excess of 90% for white leghorn strains and 85% for broiler breeders for most of the laying year. Fertility is subject to fewer environmental influences than hatchability, but some factors are important. Males must be light-stimulated to be sexually active and to produce good semen. Males stimulated for long periods of time often lose fertility and must be periodically rested. Good management practices require that a sufficient number of males should be used. In commercial practice most breeders use from 7 to 10 cocks for each 100 hens.

Fertility is under genetic control and breeders must be aware of this in selection of breeding stock. Flocks in high egg production usually have a higher level of fertility than flocks laying less intensively. Thus, breeding performance is usually best in flocks that are in a high rate of egg production.

Not all eggs laid by a breeding flock are set. Eggs that are cracked, dirty, or misshapen are usually not used for hatching. Very small or very large eggs do not hatch as well as eggs in the middle size range. Large eggs require a few hours longer to hatch than smaller eggs, and, if maximum hatchability of large eggs is needed, they should be set about 12 hours ahead of smaller eggs.

Eggs with thin or very porous shells are not likely to hatch well because of excessive losses of water during incubation. Losses of weight during incubation usually are negatively correlated with percentage of hatch. Proper humidity in the incubator can alleviate the problem of excessive weight loss to some degree, but not completely.

Storage of Hatching Eggs

In normal hatchery operation, eggs cannot be set immediately after they are laid, although storage time is usually short. Many hatcheries will set eggs from their breeder supply flocks several times a week. Small hatcheries may set twice a week, and large hatcheries for broiler chicks may set 4 to 6 times a week to even out the work load. Under these circumstances eggs may not be stored long before they are set, and the holding conditions needed in commercial hatcheries may differ from conditions needed for storage of hatching eggs for long periods of time.

In commercial practice, hatcheries may have an egg holding room in which temperature is maintained at 65 to 70° F and 75% relative humidity. Prior to setting, eggs must be brought into the setting room and allowed to reach room temperature to eliminate sweating before they are set.

Although hatching eggs can be kept for short periods after they are laid with little effect on hatchability, prolonged storage will result in continued decline in hatchability. Proper storage conditions can do much to alleviate the effects of storage on hatchability, but eggs cannot be stored more than a week or ten days without some loss in percentage of hatch even under the best conditions.

If hatching eggs are stored up to one week, the optimum storage temperature is probably from 59 to 60° F, whereas if the eggs are kept for longer periods of storage the temperature should be from 50 to 55° F. The hatchability of eggs kept at low storage temperatures can be improved if they are prewarmed for 18 hours prior to setting at a temperature of 55 to 60° F. When storage temperatures are too low, eggs do not hatch well. For this reason eggs for market and for hatching usually are not held under the same storage conditions.

Stored hatching eggs should also be kept under relatively high humidity for best results. A relative humidity of 75 to 80% seems to be superior to lower levels in preserving hatching eggs. Presumably, low relative humidity promotes loss of water from the egg during storage.

A good argument can often be generated among hatcherymen as to the proper position of eggs during storage. If eggs are to be stored up to a week, there probably is relatively little influence of storage position on hatchability. Traditionally, hatching eggs have been stored in a large end-up position to maintain the air cell in the proper position. Eggs stored in this position will hatch better if they are turned daily when stored longer than 2 weeks. This prevents contact of the embryo with the shell membrane which may cause dehydration or physical damage.

Some recent studies at the Canadian Department of Agriculture have suggested that hatching eggs stored small end up hatch better than eggs stored large end up. In these studies, turning was not beneficial for hatching eggs stored small end up for periods up to 4 weeks.

Under some conditions, prolonged storage of hatching eggs may be necessary. Recent studies at Washington State University and the Canadian Department of Agriculture have demonstrated that prolonged storage of hatching eggs can be aided by the use of plastic film enclosures and altered gaseous atmosphere around the stored egg.

Eggs stored up to 3 to 4 weeks in packs enclosed in a sealed film of thin plastic, flushed with nitrogen, hatched better than control eggs stored unwrapped at the same temperatures. The plastic film used was relatively impervious to passage of gases. Flushing the package with oxygen was very detrimental to the hatchability of the stored eggs.

Incubators

One of the impressive aspects of today's commercial hatchery is the number of chicks that can be hatched with relative ease from incubators equipped with sophisticated controls to maintain optimum conditions for hatchability. Incubators with capacities of 100,000 eggs are not uncommon, and yet maximum hatchability is expected and routinely obtained from such equipment.

The design of a modern incubator is essentially an engineering solution to the biological parameters of temperature, humidity, air supply, and movement that have been obtained by research in incubation technique. We should not feel, however, that modern technology has been the impetus for artificial incubation of chicken eggs. Although today's incubators are marvels of good control of conditions needed to nurture a biological process, the practice of artificial incubation and construction of incubators is very old. Literature on the practice of incubation goes back to 200 to 300 years B.C. in China, and incubators were known in pre-Christian times in Egypt. Dr. Walter Landauer has traced the history of the incubation of chicken eggs in a monograph entitled, *The Hatchability of Chicken Eggs as Influenced by Heredity and Environment,* from the Storrs Agricultural Experiment Station at the University of Connecticut.

Temperature

Control of temperature is probably the most critical single factor for the successful hatching of chickens. Developing embryos are extremely sensitive to temperature of the environment.

Some eggs will hatch if eggs are continuously maintained at a temperature between 95 and 104° F. Beyond these points, essentially no eggs can be expected to hatch. The optimum temperature appears to be between 98.6 and 100.4°F in forced-draft incubators, and about 1° higher in still-air incubators.

The "physiological zero" point is the minimum temperature at which embryonic development occurs. Although it is difficult to define this point precisely, it probably is about 70° F. Embryos in newly laid eggs can be stored for some time below this physiological zero and maintain viability. However, as the embryo develops, it loses this ability to withstand periods of suspended development. Embryos are most resistant to some chilling during the earliest stages of incubation and are most susceptible to low temperatures during the last 3 days prior to hatching.

Low temperatures slow up the development process as embryos are not completely homeothermic even by hatching time. Thus lowering environmental temperature also lowers the embryo's temperature. Some data on the effect of temperature on the length of the incubation period are shown in Figure 4–14.

Suboptimal incubation temperatures that are above physiological zero seem to slow up some phases of embryonic development to a greater extent than others. This delay results in abnormal development.

Short periods of moderate cooling of eggs in incubators may not be detrimental to hatching. This is the situation often occurring in natural incubation when the hen leaves the nest for short periods to feed. In

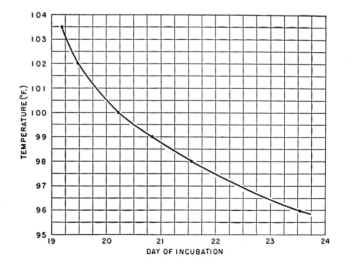

Fig. 4–14. Effect of temperature on total incubation time. As the incubation temperature is decreased from 103.5° to 96° F, the number of days from the beginning of incubation to hatching increases from slightly more than 19 to 23½. (Courtesy of U. S. Department of Agriculture.)

modern hatchery practice, this may simulate the situation occurring when power failures cause temporary cooling of incubators. Although the hatch may not be significantly affected by such events, often an increase in the number of deformed or weak chicks may result. Modern hatcheries have standby power generators to run incubators if power failures should occur.

Embryos are sensitive to temperature only slightly above the optimal incubation temperature. Even periods as short as 3 hours at 106° F during normal incubation may increase embryo mortality. A continuous incubation temperature above the optimum temperature results in mortality, and an increase in crippled and deformed chicks. Today most incubators have alarm systems that sound when incubator temperatures rise above the optimum.

Relative Humidity

The capacity of air to absorb and hold moisture increases rapidly as its temperature rises, and the drier the air in an incubator, the more moisture it will take up from the eggs. Control of relative humidity is therefore important in artificial incubation.

There is a relationship between relative humidity and temperature. With three forced draft incubators operating at the same dry bulb temperature (99° F) there was a spread of 48 hours in time of hatching when they were operated at wet bulb temperatures of 75°, 85°, and 90° F, respectively. These correspond to relative humidities of 33, 56, and 70%. When the temperature in the low humidity machine was adjusted to 100° F, and that in the high humidity machine to 98° F, all three machines hatched chicks in the normal period of 21 days. The inference seems clear that, at least in the forced-draft type of incubator, as the humidity is increased, the temperature requirement is decreased.

Barott, at the Beltsville Research Center, found that with the temperature held constant at 100° F, the oxygen content kept at 20%, the CO_2 content kept below 0.5%, and the rate of air movement at 12 cm per minute the best hatches were obtained at a relative humidity of 61%. The true optimum might easily be slightly above or below this figure, and a variation of 5, or even 10, points either way would not be seriously detrimental to hatching results.

That high humidity may be important in ways other than its effect on the hatching percentage is well illustrated by experiments conducted at the Kansas Station which showed that the maintenance of a wet bulb reading of 95° F in a forced-draft incubator at hatching time practically eliminated the spread of pullorum disease from infected chicks to noninfected chicks hatching in the same machine.

The mortality to two weeks of age among chicks hatched from eggs laid by nonreactor hens, and hatched in the same machine with eggs from reactor hens, was 29, 15, and 6% when the wet bulb readings at hatching time were 75°, 85°, and 95° F, respectively. At the same time the mortality among healthy control chicks was 5%.

Oxygen and Carbon Dioxide

Embryos use oxygen in their metabolism and give off carbon dioxide. The concentration of these gases in the air has a significant effect on hatchability. Air contains 21% oxygen, and this seems to be the optimum concentration for the developing embryo. Any fall in oxygen below this level results in a lowered percentage of hatch. In studies at the USDA Research Center at Beltsville, hatchability fell about 5 percentage units for each 1 percentage unit drop in oxygen concentration of the incubator air. Oxygen concentrations above 21% also reduce hatchability, but embryos seem more tolerant to excesses of oxygen than to a deficiency.

Proper oxygen concentration is not difficult to maintain in incubators provided with proper air circulation systems.

When eggs are incubated at relatively high altitudes, the lowered partial pressure of oxygen in air may cause reduction in hatchability. In work reported from three experiment stations in the western United States, eggs were hatched at 240, 3,950, and 7,160 feet above sea level. The percentage hatch obtained was 85, 74, and 64%, respectively, for the three locations. There are reports that increasing the concentration of oxygen in incubators at high altitude will improve the percentage of eggs that hatch.

Carbon dioxide concentration in air surrounding incubating eggs also affects hatchability. High concentrations of CO_2 are detrimental, with 5% CO_2 in the air resulting in zero hatchability. Effects on hatchability may be observed when the CO_2 concentration is above 0.5% and certainly above 2% a striking fall in hatchability occurs.

Since the normal oxygen and CO_2 concentrations in air seem to represent an optimum gaseous environment for incubating eggs, no special provisions to control these gases in incubators are necessary other than to maintain an adequate circulation of fresh air at the proper temperature and humidity.

Position of Hatching Eggs

Eggs are normally incubated large end up. Under these conditions, the head of the embryo develops at the large end of the egg near the air cell. When eggs are incubated small end up the majority of embryos develop with their heads in the small end of the egg, and frequently these embryos do not hatch. If eggs are left in a single position throughout the incubation period, they hatch poorly, whereas turning eggs during the incubation period improves the hatch compared to that of unturned eggs. A hen

Fig. 4–15. Trays of hatching eggs being wheeled into a large "room type" incubator. (Courtesy Chickmaster Incubator Corporation.)

sitting on her nest turns eggs frequently, using her body as she settles on the eggs and using her beak as she reaches under her body.

Modern incubators are equipped with turning devices that are able to rotate egg trays through an angle of 90°. These are controlled by a timing mechanism, and usually eggs are turned every hour. This is probably more turning than is required for optimum hatchability, since 6 to 8 times daily is probably sufficient.

There is wide variation in incubation design and construction. Some examples are shown in Figures 4–15 through 4–18.

Fig. 4–16. Setting trays of eggs in a room size incubator. (Courtesy of Chickmaster Incubator Corporation.)

Temperature and Humidity in Hatchers

In commercial hatchery practice chicks are not hatched in the "setters" used for the bulk of the incubation period. Separate incubators usually called "hatchers" are used to complete the incubation process.

There are several reasons for using separate setters and hatchers. The two types of machines are kept in different rooms, so the hatching process is kept separate from the incubation. When eggs hatch, much down, egg debris, and many microorganisms are released. This can be isolated from

Fig. 4–17.   Egg trays being placed in an incubator with a "drum" type tray holding system. (Courtesy of Robbins Incubator Company.)

other eggs in the incubator room. The hatchers can be easily cleaned, disinfected, and fumigated between hatches without disturbing the remaining eggs incubating in the setters. Hatchers are kept under slightly different temperature and humidity conditions from those of the setters. Eggs are usually transferred to the hatcher on the nineteenth day of incubation. The temperature is lowered to 98° F, and humidity is maintained the same as in the setter until hatching begins. At this point the humidity may be raised until the hatch is removed. There is some evidence that the hatch may be slightly improved by the lower incubation temperature in the hatcher. Hatcheries also use special chick-holding trays in which eggs must be placed for hatching (Fig. 4–19). Turning is not required in the hatcher.

Testing

In commercial practice, incubating eggs are seldom tested for progress of development prior to hatching. This would require considerable labor, and the relatively few eggs removed from the incubator would not add

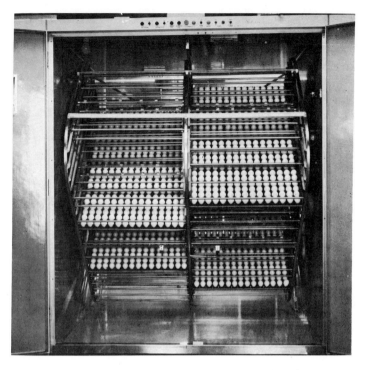

Fig. 4–18. A partially loaded incubator showing the drum tilted in the forward position. The drum is tilted to turn the eggs over an angle of 90°. (Courtesy of the Robbins Incubator Company.)

much incubation space. However, under some circumstances, it may be desirable to test incubating eggs to check fertility or embryo mortality. This can be done readily by candling the eggs.

Two classes of eggs can be removed on the basis of an early test—"infertiles" and "early dead." In a technical sense the term *infertile* refers to an egg that has never been fertilized, but practically it includes those that have started to develop but have died at such an early age that they cannot readily be distinguished by candling. Dead embryos are relatively easy to distinguish. Often the egg contains an enlarged clear space, and the embryo appears to have settled in the bottom of the egg. The clear space lacks the pink cast and large blood vessels that are characteristic of the live embryo.

The so-called infertile egg appears to be clear save for a floating shadow, which is easily distinguished as the yolk.

The live embryo is spider-like in appearance during the first few days, the body of the embryo representing the body of the spider and the radiating blood vessels its legs. The live embryo floats about freely in the contents of the egg when the egg is rotated before the candling lamp.

Fig. 4–19. Chicks ready to be removed from a hatcher. (Courtesy of Chickmaster Incubator Corporation.)

The early dead may be recognized by the absence of the blood vessels, by its adhering to the shell, or by the quite typical pink ring, called the blood ring, surrounding it.

A second test may be made after 14 to 16 days of incubation. If the first has been accurately done, there will be only dead embryos to test out. The live embryo at this time appears nearly to fill the egg. In the one or two light spaces that are usually present, blood vessels will be noticed and the chick embryo will frequently be seen to move when the egg is rotated.

If suitable equipment is used, infertile eggs may be detected with a high degree of accuracy after 15 to 18 hours of incubation. A 75-watt blue bulb is used. In each fertile egg there can be seen on the surface of the yolk a small spot about the size of a dime. This is the tiny embryo. No such spot can be seen in an infertile egg.

Even 15 hours of incubation will cause a marked deterioration in the market quality of infertile eggs. Eggs of AA quality, after 15 hours at incubation temperature, may grade no better than B quality.

FACTORS IN HATCHABILITY

We have discussed several factors that influence hatching of eggs, such as preincubation storage and incubation conditions. In addition, factors such as egg size, shell quality, and age and productivity of breeders have been shown to affect hatchability. Apart from these, other factors can have a considerable influence on the ability of eggs to hatch. These include nutrition of the breeding hen, genetic constitution of the embryo, and disease.

Nutrition

Although nutrition will be considered in detail in later chapters, the importance of nutrition of the dam in hatchability must be stressed here. The egg must contain all the nutrients needed by the embryo when it is laid by the hen. There is no further contact with the mother once the egg is completed. Therefore, breeder hens must be fed rations that will supply adequate quantities of the nutrients needed for embryo development. Since it is difficult to affect the protein, fat, and carbohydrate content of an egg by dietary means, the nutrients most susceptible to diet changes are the vitamins and trace elements.

Nutrient deficiencies can reduce hatchability, and often malformed embryos grow as a result of the nutrient deficiency. It is rather difficult, however, to identify the nutrient deficiency responsible for poor hatchability by examination of the embryo. The time of embryo mortality and the deficiency observed often depend on the degree of deficiency of the nutrient involved. This is illustrated by the data in Table 4–2. Various levels of pantothenic acid were added to a basal diet for hens which was nearly devoid of pantothenic acid. After 25 weeks of feeding these diets, no chicks hatched from eggs laid by hens fed the diet containing no added pantothenic acid and nearly none from the diet with 1 mg/kg added. One peak of embryo mortality occurred from 1 to 4 days in all treatments, but the later peaks changed as the amount of pantothenic acid in the diet was altered.

Two major peaks of embryo mortality are usually observed, even in normal hatches. These are during the first 2 to 4 days of incubation, and then at 19 to 21 days, just at hatching time. As illustrated in Table 4–2, the embryo mortality peaks shifted, depending on the degree of nutritional deficiency. The hatchability of eggs from hens fed 2 mg of pantothenic

Table 4-2. Effect of Pantothenic Acid Deficiency on Hatchability and Chick Mortality

Pantothenic Acid Added to Basal Diet for Breeders mg/kg diet	% Egg Production of Breeders	% Hatchability	Peaks of Embryo Mortality Days of Incubation	Chick Mortality 1st 24 hrs after Hatch %
none	56	0	1–4 11–17	—
1	68	2.6	1–4 17–22	—
2	65	85	1–4 19–22	35
4	62	93	1–4 21–22	0
8	65	90	1–4 19–22	0

Adapted from Beer et al., Br. Poultry Sci., 4:243 (1963).

acid per kg of diet was slightly lower than eggs from hens fed higher levels. However, even though these chicks hatched, they were weak and many died during the first 24 hours after hatching. This early mortality could be prevented if newly hatched chicks were injected with pantothenic acid at hatching. High early mortality has been observed in commercial hatchery operations, and some of this may have been due to a pantothenic acid deficiency in breeder diets. The data in this table also show that hens can produce eggs when fed a dietary level of pantothenic acid that will not allow the eggs to hatch.

Nearly all the water-soluble vitamins affect hatchability in a manner similar to the examples shown for pantothenic acid. Under practical conditions, the nutrients that may reach levels low enough to cause hatchability problems are riboflavin, manganese, pantothenic acid, and vitamin B_{12} unless some special supplements of these are used. In later chapters, breeder rations will be discussed in more detail.

Genetic Factors

Genetic factors play a definite role in hatchability of eggs. Inbreeding has been shown to lower hatchability. Some inbred lines are affected to a greater extent than others by inbreeding, but this is one of the difficulties of producing and maintaining inbred lines of poultry.

Landauer, in his monograph The Hatchability of Chicken Eggs as Influenced by Environment and Heredity from the Storrs Agricultural Experiment Station of the University of Connecticut, describes about 30 lethal genes that are known in poultry. These genes are those that may cause death of the developing chick before the end of incubation. Many of these lethal genes are associated with specific morphological features recognizable in the embryo. Some of the malformed embryos may hatch, but they may not be able to survive. These mutations, when present, may affect hatchability of eggs from a breeder flock. Since several factors, including egg structure and genetic constitution of the embryo, affect hatchability, it is not surprising that improvements can be made by selection.

Diseases

Diseases caused by Salmonella organisms such as pullorum disease are the major group of bacterial infections that influence hatchability. Salmonella organisms may be passed from infected dams into eggs. The infected eggs do not hatch as well as noninfected ones. Although other disease organisms may not pass into the egg and affect the embryo directly, they may influence the characteristics of the egg and thus indirectly affect its hatchability. Newcastle disease and infectious bronchitis, for example, may affect egg shape and shell porosity. Eggs from hens affected by these diseases frequently do not hatch well because the eggs lose excessive amounts of moisture during incubation. Therefore, hatching eggs from healthy flocks are more likely to produce the most chicks.

HATCHERY PRACTICES AND SERVICES

The business management of hatcheries is beyond the scope of this chapter, but there are aspects of hatchery operation that are integral parts of the process of producing chicks to grow as broilers or replacement pullets. These will be discussed here briefly.

Sanitation Practices

It is difficult for an "outsider" to gain access to a modern hatchery for a hatchery tour today. This is a reflection of the importance of disease control in the hatchery. Healthy chicks placed in clean surroundings are likely to develop into good productive chickens. The hatchery is a particularly important link in producing mycoplasma-free chickens. The efforts necessary to produce mycoplasma-free hatching eggs are wasted if the chicks are infected at the hatchery.

Some important sanitation practices often used in hatcheries are as follows.

Eggs used for hatching should be clean and should be collected and stored in clean equipment and containers. Washing hatching eggs may introduce microorganisms into the egg and is not a recommended practice. Clean hatching eggs should be fumigated with formaldehyde gas as soon as possible after collection.

Hatcheries should be so designed that egg receiving, incubation, hatching, chick holding, and waste disposal can be carried out in separate rooms that can be cleaned and disinfected. Wastes should be promptly disposed of and containers should be sterilized.

Eggs are often fumigated with formaldehyde gas during the first 12 hours of incubation and some time in the eighteenth to twentieth day of incubation. Eggs in incubators should not be fumigated between the twelfth and eighty-fourth hour of incubation because embryo damage may result. Empty hatchers should be thoroughly washed, disinfected, and fumigated prior to each transfer of eggs from setters.

The potential introduction of infection by employees and visitors must be controlled. This often means showers and clothing changes for employees and the banning of all visitors to the hatchery.

Disposal of hatchery waste may be a problem and unless properly done can be a major source of infection in the hatchery. Incineration of wastes is an effective means of disposal, but hatchery waste when properly cooked, dried, and ground can be made into a useful feed ingredient called poultry hatchery by-product meal. This material, composed of infertile eggs, dead embryos, weak or unsalable chicks, as well as shells and membranes, is high in protein and calcium. It must be cooked to kill potential infective agents it may contain. In hatcheries producing replacement pullets, disposal of surplus cockerels is often a problem. Some hatcheries are able to supply these for feeding mink or send them to rendering plants for use in meat meal or fertilizer.

Sexing Chicks

Although sex-linked genes for rate of feathering or color pattern are being used by breeders to facilitate sexing when chicks are a day old, sexing by cloacal identification is widely used by hatcheries to sex newly hatched chicks. The identification of the rudimentary copulatory organ or male process in the cloaca of male chicks at hatching can be used to identify sexes. It takes considerable skill to be accurate with this method of chick sexing. So many chick sexers of Japanese origin use this method that it is often referred to as the "Japanese Method" (Fig. 4–20).

By use of a special instrument, a proctoscope, it is possible to see the testes of male chicks through the intestinal wall of day-old chicks. This method has been used successfully for day-old chicks and has the advantage of requiring less training and skill than the Japanese method. Chick sexing is considered to be a hatchery service that must be routinely offered.

Fig. 4–20.   Sexing chicks by cloacal examinations, the "Japanese method." (Courtesy of Babcock Industries Inc.)

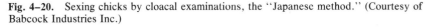

Debeaking and Dubbing

Hatcheries may also offer services such as debeaking of day-old chicks (Fig. 4–21) or removing a portion of the comb of single comb white leghorn chicks. Beaks properly cut at hatching will usually not regrow to the point where picking can be serious during the broiler growing period. Replacement pullets, if debeaked at hatching, will usually need to be debeaked again if cannibalism is to be controlled during the development and laying period.

The large combs of the single comb white leghorn hens most used for egg production sometimes are injured, particularly when the hens are housed in cages. This injury can be prevented by removing a large portion of the comb from day-old chicks. This procedure, called dubbing, is relatively harmless at that age, and the comb that develops will be smaller and less likely to be injured when the hen is an adult.

Vaccination

Most vaccines are administered after chicks have left the hatchery. Immunity passed to chicks through the egg protects the chick in the first

Fig. 4–21. An electric debeaker in use. Many thousands of chicks are debeaked when only one day old. (Courtesy of Hatchery and Feed.)

days of life and often makes vaccination ineffective. However, today most hatcheries are vaccinating day-old chicks for Marek's disease (Fig. 4–22). This is particularly true for chicks intended as replacement pullets.

Delivery

A newly hatched chick retains a substantial amount of yolk in its abdominal cavity which is sufficient to nourish it for a few days after hatching. Therefore chicks can be shipped by mail or other means that may take up to 3 days after they hatch, before they receive food and water at their destination. Provided they are not overheated or chilled during shipment, they may be expected to arrive in good condition. Most hatcheries of broiler chicks, however, attempt to deliver chicks and to

Fig. 4–22. Vaccination of day-old chicks against Marek's disease. The proper dose of vaccine is injected automatically. (Courtesy of Babcock Industries Inc.)

provide them with feed and water as soon as possible after the hatch has been taken from the hatchers. This practice has been shown to reduce some early mortality and result in a better start by the broiler chick.

HATCHERY OPERATIONS

The hatching of chicks as a business has long been an important part of the poultry industry in the United States, but the type of operation being carried on today is different from that of even 10 years ago. Some of the changes are indicated by the following tabulation reported by the U. S. Department of Agriculture.

Year	Number of Hatcheries	Total Egg Capacity	Average Egg Capacity
1934	11,405	276,287,000	24,000
1943	10,112	504,640,000	50,000
1953	8,233	616,976,000	80,000
1959	4,939	575,601,000	116,000
1965	2,365	471,318,000	199,000
1971	1,209	445,000,000	368,000
1973	989	436,286,000	441,000
1977	651	420,000,000	645,000

Table 4–3.   Commercial Chick Production, by Months, for Selected Years, as Reported by the U. S. Department of Agriculture

	1959		1976	
	Broiler-type	Egg-type	Broiler-type	Egg-type
		Millions		
January	154	36	278	36
February	150	62	268	39
March	183	118	309	49
April	180	130	310	51
May	175	86	320	48
June	169	27	308	42
July	166	14	302	38
August	150	13	294	38
September	122	14	270	37
October	122	14	267	36
November	130	13	267	36
December	142	14	282	36
Total	1,843	541	3,474	486

The fall in number of hatcheries has been dramatic. Almost half the hatcheries in business in 1971 were no longer in operation in 1977, a period of only 6 years. Of those that remained, hatcheries with more than 500,000 egg capacity accounted for over 68% of the total capacity. The hatcheries in the United States produced nearly 4 billion chicks in 1976, 88% of which were broiler chicks. There are few independent hatcheries today. Many are integral parts of broiler firms, which hatch broiler chicks to be placed with contract growers. Others are franchised hatcheries producing egg-type chicks for a major poultry breeding company.

The hatchery output in the United States is relatively constant the year round. Placements of both broiler and egg-type chicks are relatively

Fig. 4–23.   A modern hatchery is often part of a completely integrated production complex. In this case a hatchery and a feed mill are on the same site. (Courtesy of Chickmaster Incubator Corporation.)

constant to ensure a constant year-round supply of both eggs and poultry meat. This has changed somewhat in the past 20 years, particularly with respect to egg-type chicks which used to be hatched primarily in the spring. The data in Table 4–3 illustrate this trend.

These changes have altered the former position of the hatcheryman, who was in effect a manufacturer who bought his raw materials from and sold his finished product to the poultry producer. He is still rendering an essential service, but often as a part of a large integrated organization instead of as an independent operator (Fig. 4–23). His supply flocks are much larger and fewer in number than before, just as his customers may be fewer and individual chick orders much larger than in the early days of the hatchery business.

Chapter 5

Brooding and Rearing

Brooding refers to the early period of growth when young chicks are unable to maintain body temperature without the aid of supplemental heat. Rearing encompasses brooding and the subsequent growing period until sexual maturity. These are critical phases of any poultry business, as the ultimate productivity of the laying hen or performance of the broiler or roaster depends on the proper development during early stages of growth.

Systems of brooding and rearing vary greatly among poultry farms. No single method is most desirable. The growth or egg production obtained by an individual depends on its inherited ability, its food supply, and such environmental factors as temperature, air supply, and protection from parasites and diseases. Any system that satisfies the basic requirements for comfort and good health can be used successfully to produce individuals with a high potential for performance.

BROODING REQUIREMENTS

The requirements of brooding appear to be essentially those of housing, with the addition of temperature regulation. A complete brooder is simply a special form of house designed for the purpose of keeping chicks comfortable. To be commercially practical, brooding equipment must also be reasonably low in cost.

Temperature

There is no general agreement among poultrymen as to what constitutes exactly the proper hover temperature for chicks just out of the incubator or at succeeding ages. There is no cumulative experimental evidence determining definitely what these temperatures should be.

Ideal temperature conditions probably exist when there is a range in temperature always available to the chicks, from a maximum of not less than 100° F to a minimum of 60° or 70° F. When they have a choice, chicks soon learn to find the temperature that is most comfortable to them. Trouble comes not so much from temporary exposure to low or to variable temperatures, as from continuous exposure to temperatures that are too high or too low, with no opportunity for the chicks to move at will to more comfortable temperatures.

Careful tests have shown that, with the temperature taken 2.5 inches above the litter, baby chicks are apparently comfortable at all temperatures in the range from 80° to 110° F. Not until the air temperature is some five degrees above or below this range is there definite indication of discomfort and of a tendency to avoid such areas. On the other hand, extensive tests at the Beltsville Agricultural Research Center, involving 72 experiments with 30 chicks each, showed a maximum growth response during the first 9 days after hatching when the average temperature was 91° F, dropping from 94° on the first day to 88° on the ninth. In a later series of 53 similar experiments, best results were obtained when the temperature was reduced uniformly from 94° on the first day to 80° on the eighteenth. Variation in controlled relative humidity from 35% to 75% made no appreciable difference in growth to 18 days of age.

In other tests by Ota and McNally at Beltsville, broiler-type chickens were grown to 9 weeks of age in calorimeters which permitted accurate control of temperature, air movement, and relative humidity. After initial brooding temperatures of 85° to 94° F, various lots were subjected to continuous temperatures of 41°, 50°, 59°, 68°, 77°, and 86° F (5°, 10°, 15°, 20°, 25°, and 30° C). Because the calorimeters were not very large, it was necessary to reduce the number of chickens from 100 at the start to 15 in each lot at the end of a 9-week test. Air flow in the calorimeters was 10 to 11 cubic feet per minute for 100-day-old chicks, and was gradually increased to as high as 25 cubic feet per minute for 15 broilers at 8 or 9 weeks. Relative humidity was maintained near 75%.

The final live weight and feed conversion data, as related to the different environmental temperatures, are of particular interest. The results are shown in Figure 5–1. Environmental temperatures can be either too high or too low, when maintained at a constant level. The best growth occurred at a constant temperature of 68° F. Efficiency of feed conversion increased steadily throughout the experimental temperature range of 41° to 86° F.

These results should not be taken to mean that temperatures in commercial broiler houses can safely be reduced to 68° during the early brooding period. Higher brooding temperatures are necessary, especially in winter, to offset the cold wall surfaces and possible drafts, and to make certain that there is always opportunity for chicks to move to a warm area if they wish.

Effects of Chilling and Overheating. When a chick becomes uncomfortably cold under conditions of artificial brooding, and is unable to locate

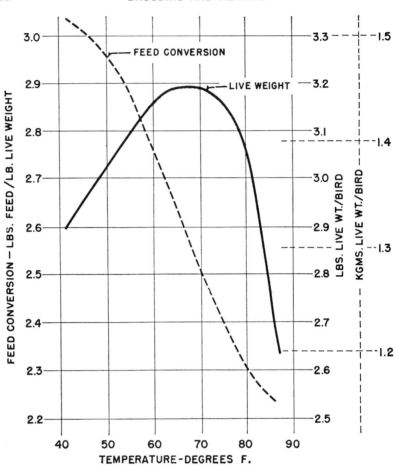

Fig. 5–1. Nine-week average live weight and feed conversion data for Athens randombred broilers grown at various environmental temperatures. (After Ota and McNally.)

heat enough to warm him quickly, he seems to obey the instinct that tells him to get his back against the mother hen. The result is that he tries to crawl under the other chicks. This action, taken up by more and more chicks, results in bunching and crowding with the accompanying evils of smothered chicks and a diminution of thrift on the part of the entire flock.

Lethal Temperature. Upper and lower lethal temperatures are those internal body temperatures above or below which an animal cannot survive. The low lethal body temperature has been studied by several workers, and ranges from 62° F on the day of hatch to about 67° at 2 weeks of age, with a gradual increase to about 73° at maturity. Maryland workers found that 2-day-old chicks could stand 35 minutes exposure at −10° F, and that at 20 days of age they could stand 75 minutes exposure at this temperature before half of them succumbed. The high lethal body temperature for the chick is the same as that for older fowls, 117° F. This body temperature is reached in about 10 minutes when chicks are exposed to an air temperature of 160° F.

Overheating occurs comparatively seldom, because chicks instinctively move away from the source of heat when too warm. If confined under a hover when the temperature runs up, they die rather quickly either from heat prostration or piling up of chicks around the perimeter of the brooding area. At room temperatures of 100° F, death losses among day-old chicks in sealed summer-sized fiberboard chick boxes were found by Wilson at the California Station to range from 20 to 50%. New Hampshire chicks were more susceptible to overheating than were white leghorns.

Ventilation

Proper ventilation is important in all phases of poultry production. Constant renewal of air in the poultry house is essential not only for supplying oxygen, but also for removal of products of metabolism such as carbon dioxide, ammonia, moisture, and heat. In fact, the removal of moisture and heat is usually most important in determining ventilation rates.

The main problem in a cold environment is removal of moisture. Chicken feces contain approximately 75 to 80% moisture, and considerable air exchange is required to keep the brooding or rearing area dry. Early studies at the California Experiment Station showed that as much as 0.04 cubic feet of air per minute (cfm) per chick when chicks were 3 weeks old would not keep the area dry under electric brooders. The American Society of Agricultural Engineers has suggested that 0.1 cfm per chick is sufficient for the purpose.

As ventilation is increased to remove the greater amounts of moisture produced by broilers as they grow in size, more cold air is drawn in from outside, and some supplementary heat should be provided to heat this extra volume of cold air. Experience of broiler growers in many parts of the country supports the theoretical calculation that an indoor temperature of 70° to 75° F should be maintained, even when the broilers are near market weight.

Ventilation needs vary with different kinds of housing, bird density, and environmental conditions. Methods of estimating ventilation rates for specific conditions are presented in Chapter 6.

Workers at the University of Idaho have used the following heat and moisture output data as a basis for determining ventilation requirements. For cold winter weather and high precipitation conditions in the Northwest they recommend insulated houses with an "R" value of 10 in the walls and 14 or 15 in the ceilings. See Chapter 6 for a discussion of R value.

Heat and Moisture Output of Broilers of Indicated Weights

Age	Average Weight (pounds)	Heat Output in Btu per 1,000 Broilers per Hour	Water Output in Pounds per 1,000 Broilers per Day
1 day	0.10	1,200	15
1 week	0.17	2,100	60
2 weeks	0.35	4,200	110
3 weeks	0.70	7,950	150
4 weeks	1.20	13,200	200
5 weeks	1.65	18,000	240
6 weeks	2.20	24,000	280
7 weeks	2.80	30,100	310
8 weeks	3.40	36,100	350

Hover and Floor Space

Well-fed chicks grow rapidly, often doubling their weight as many as five successive times in the first 6 weeks. As they grow, their need for supplementary heat becomes less, with the result that floor space in the brooder house is more likely to become critical than heated hover space. Furthermore, the optimum floor area for greatest biological efficiency may not coincide with the optimum for greatest economic efficiency. In the rearing of replacement pullets it is considered sound practice to provide 7 square inches of brooder space under the hovers for each chick started and 0.5 square foot of total brooder house floor area. For chicks reared in confinement, this will be adequate for the first 4 to 6 weeks, but only about half enough for the succeeding 4 to 6 weeks. Two square feet per bird are needed after 12 weeks.

Broilers should be allowed approximately 7 square inches of space under the brooder during the first 3 weeks and then 0.75 to 1.0 square foot of floor space after the brooding period. Actual floor space requirements may vary depending on climate and ventilation capacity.

Floor Brooding Equipment

Portable brooders are made in a number of different styles and sizes, but in commercial use the gas-heated types have largely replaced the once-popular coal stoves. Oil-heated brooders are also used in some areas. Commercial broiler growers often use hot water or hot air types with a central heating system. Several of the kinds of equipment in use today are shown in Figures 5–2, 5–3, and 5–4.

In cold weather, a guard of corrugated paper, metal, or wallboard should be placed around or along the hover, 2 to 3 feet from its edge to

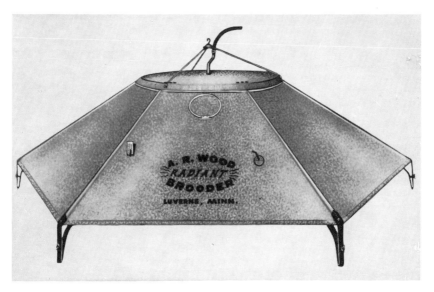

Fig. 5–2. Gas-heated brooders are widely used in broiler production. (Courtesy of A. R. Wood Manufacturing Company.)

Fig. 5–3. A convenient arrangement for keeping chicks or poults close to the hover for the first few days. (Courtesy of Big Dutchman, a division of U. S. Industries, Inc.)

Fig. 5–4. Two rows of hovers in a long brooder house. The Chain-O-Matic feeding system can be seen at the left. (Courtesy of Big Dutchman, a division of U. S. Industries, Inc.)

prevent floor drafts and to keep chicks from straying too far from the source of heat until they learn to find it easily (Fig. 5–3). In warm weather wire may be used. The guard can be removed at the end of the first week.

A decision must be made as to how many chicks to place under a single hover or heating unit, even with several units in one large house. Large flocks mean some saving in labor and equipment, but for rapid growth and low mortality it is wise to think in terms of 400 to 500 chicks when brooding replacement stock and perhaps 600 to 1,000 for broilers.

Litter

Many materials are suitable as litter. The primary requirements are that they be inexpensive, nontoxic, and highly absorbent. Dried cane fiber, wood shaving, sawdust, and corncobs are commonly used. A 2-inch layer is required at the start of brooding, and more will usually be added as the chicks grow. Wet litter must be avoided, as it is conducive to the development of many disease organisms and adds to the stress of chicks subjected to a cold environment.

Floor Rearing

If pullet chicks are being grown as replacements and are to be floor-housed as adults, low roosts should be installed when the chicks are about 4 weeks of age. A sloping platform with small roosts is usually best. If the frame is covered with hardware cloth, it provides natural and easy access to the roosts. Necessary roosting space is 4 to 5 inches per chick. If the layers are to be placed in cages, roosts during the growing period are optional.

Except for small flocks, not many replacement pullets are grown on range, but when they are so grown, roosting sheds or range shelters of some sort are necessary. These are simply light frame sheds provided with a tight roof and wire sides. They commonly have wire floors. The only interior equipment needed is roosts, because feed is supplied in large outdoor hoppers.

Cage Brooding and Rearing

Many thousands of replacement pullets are grown on wire floors not only for convenience, but also because there is no later problem of

Fig. 5–5. Many thousands of replacement pullets are grown on wire floors. Building paper covers the hover area during the first few days. (J. C. Allen and Son Photo.)

Fig. 5–6.   Some poultrymen prefer slatted floors for brooder houses.

adjustment to the wire floors of laying cages (Fig. 5–5). Some poultrymen use floors of wood slats (Fig. 5–6). In some cases, brooding is done on the floor, using the systems described, and pullets are transferred to cages for the remainder of the growing period. It is becoming more popular, however, to brood in cages as well. When this is done, central heating maintains the house at brooding temperatures, or a brooding environment is maintained in the cages by steam or hot water pipes or by electric lamps.

REARING REPLACEMENT PULLETS

Irrespective of its genetic constitution, the physical condition of the pullet at the time of sexual maturity may determine its productivity during the laying year. Most pullets are grown by the egg producer. This method allows the producer to plan the periodic replacement of his laying stock with pullets that have been raised under his standards of housing and management (Fig. 5–7). Some poultrymen specialize in the growing of replacement pullets. In most cases these operators contract with egg producers to provide replacement stock for the egg producer at specified times of the year.

Fig. 5–7.   These pullets are approaching the time when they will be moved to layer cages.
(Courtesy of California Agricultural Extension Service.)

Pullets are reared under a variety of conditions of housing and management. Rearing pullets on range was the traditional practice until the middle of this century when housing of pullets in confinement began to gain acceptance. Pullets are reared almost exclusively today in confinement on litter, wire floors, or slats and in cages. Cages are particularly effective as a means of increasing the concentration of birds and reducing labor costs associated with pullet rearing.

The nutritional requirements of pullets are outlined in Chapter 9. In general, pullets of light breeds perform well during the laying year when their requirements for energy and all other nutrients have been met during the growing period. Pullets of heavy breeds tend to accumulate excessive amounts of body fat. It is common practice to restrict food intake of these birds to produce pullets with leaner carcasses at the time of sexual maturity. This is beneficial not only from the standpoint of producing a healthier pullet but also in reducing feed costs during the rearing period.

Research shows that there may be an advantage in restricting food intake for light as well as heavy breeds during the pullet rearing period, and many producers have adopted this practice. Restriction of light breeds has resulted in slightly higher mortality during the rearing period but quite consistently lower mortality and higher egg production during the laying year. Most restriction is begun at 9 to 12 weeks of age.

The skip-a-day method involves feeding pullets on alternate days only, from 9 weeks to sexual maturity. Under these conditions pullets consume more feed on the days that feed is available than they would normally consume on a daily basis. They are unable, however, to consume enough feed in one day to satisfy their total energy requirements for 2 days. Thus growth and body fat content are reduced. Another scheme involves the use of standards of feed consumption. Under these conditions, the producer determines the amount of feed that would normally be consumed by his pullets each day and provides them with a fraction of that amount on a daily basis. Often this fraction is 75 to 85% of the amount of feed that would be consumed on a free choice basis. Typical growth and food consumption of pullets given free access to feed is shown in Table 5–1.

Another form of restriction involves the use of bulky, low-energy diets during the perod of 12 to 20 weeks of age. These diets are formulated to be adequate in all nutrients, but are sufficiently low in energy that pullets cannot consume enough of the diet to satisfy their energy needs for maximal growth. Using such a diet, it is possible to restrict growth of young pullets by 10 to 15%, an amount comparable to the growth depression with the skip-a-day and daily restriction schemes. The biological basis for the beneficial effects of feed restrictions is not known, but it may be similar to the phenomenon observed in laboratory animals where restriction during early life seems to produce healthier, longer-lived adults.

Disease Control

Disease can reduce productivity and cause permanent losses of egg production through mortality or permanent physiological impairment of

Table 5–1. Growth and Food Consumption of Growing White Leghorn Pullets

		Food Consumption	
Age Wk	Average Weight lb	Previous 2 Weeks lb	Cumulative lb
2	0.3	0.3	0.3
4	0.6	0.8	1.1
6	1.0	1.1	2.2
8	1.4	1.4	3.6
10	1.8	1.7	5.2
12	2.1	1.9	7.1
14	2.4	1.9	9.0
16	2.7	2.0	11.0
18	2.9	2.0	13.0
20	3.1	2.1	15.1
22	3.3	2.1	17.2

the pullet. Some of the more common diseases of poultry are outlined in Chapter 10. Marek's disease and two highly contagious respiratory diseases of poultry, infectious bronchitis and Newcastle disease, are normally controlled by programmed multiple vaccination during the rearing and laying period. Vaccination against other viral diseases such as laryngotracheitis and avian encephalomyelitis may be desirable if recent outbreaks have occurred on the producer's farm or in areas nearby. Coccidiosis is commonly encountered in poultry units. Measures for its control, as well as for prevention and control of a variety of other diseases, are presented in Chapter 10. Pullets grown on litter usually develop an immunity to coccidiosis; those grown in cages do not have access to droppings infested with the organism and therefore do not develop immunity. Cage-reared pullets should not be transferred to floor pens, as these birds lack immunity to coccidiosis and may develop an outbreak during the laying year.

Disease problems may be minimized by vaccination programs, avoiding stressful environmental conditions which weaken the flock's natural resistance to infection, avoiding contact with other populations of poultry or other birds, proper disposal of dead or infected birds, and maintaining a constant vigil for signs of lack of thrift or discomfort in the pullet or laying flock.

Lighting for Replacement Pullets

Several programs have been suggested for lighting growing pullets to prevent precocious sexual maturity. They are based on the principle that constant or decreasing day-length tends to delay sexual maturity, whereas increasing day-length will stimulate sexual maturity. Four examples will be given here to illustrate different systems that can be used.

The so-called step-down, step-up system does not require a lighttight house. In this system pullets, maturing in increasing day-length, are provided initially with artificial light of a long enough period so that the light can be reduced by 40 minutes to 1 hour every 2 weeks until pullets reach 22 weeks of age. After 22 weeks, the light can be increased in a similar fashion until the total day-length is 14 to 16 hours (Fig. 5–8). Under this system pullets maturing when natural daylight is decreasing would be reared under natural light.

A modified step-down, step-up system has been proposed in which a windowless lighttight house is used. Chicks are started with 20 to 21 hours of light. Light is decreased 45 minutes each week until chicks are 12 weeks of age. At this point the light is reduced to 7 hours per day until chickens are 21 to 22 weeks of age. At 22 weeks of age the light is increased to 12 to 13 hours per day and increased by an hour every month or two until 16 hours of light are attained.

A system developed at Washington State University uses a constant light system to control maturity of pullets. Chicks are started with 14

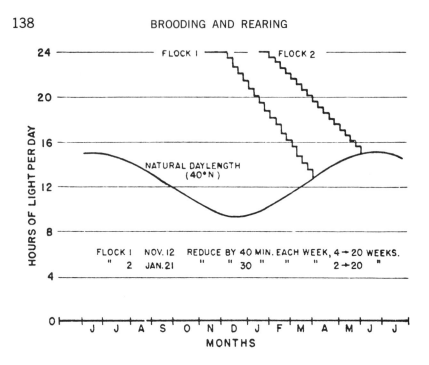

Fig. 5–8. Examples of light patterns that can be used to delay sexual maturity when pullets are grown at 40° north latitude. (Courtesy of T. R. Morris.)

hours of light and kept at this level until they are 12 to 14 weeks of age. At this time, light is lowered to 9 hours per day until chickens are 20 weeks of age. At 20 weeks the light is raised to 14 hours and may be increased to 16 hours later if desired. This system also requires a lighttight house.

Another form of a constant light system has been developed at Auburn University in Alabama. The chicks are kept at 6 to 8 hours of light from hatching to 20 weeks of age. After this, light is gradually increased (18 minutes per week) until 16 hours are reached, then held constant.

All of these systems recognize that increasing length of day tends to stimulate sexual maturity in growing pullets and that decreasing or constant day-length delays sexual maturity. The lighting system used depends on the type of housing available and the convenience to the grower.

RAISING BROILERS

The housing and management of the broiler flock are distinctly different from that of pullets which serve as replacements for the laying flock.

Chickens used for the production of meat have the inherited ability to grow rapidly and attain market weight quickly. This growth results in higher nutritional requirements than for lighter breeds, and greater feeder,

Table 5–2. Body Weight and Feed Consumption of Growing Broilers

Age wk	Body Weight Male (lb)	Body Weight Female (lb)	Cumulative Feed Consumption Male (lb)	Cumulative Feed Consumption Female (lb)	Feed Conversion* Feed/ Body Wt. (lb/lb)	Feed Conversion* Feed/ Wt. Gain (lb/lb†)
1	0.26	0.25	0.15	0.15	0.59	—
2	0.55	0.53	0.58	0.55	1.05	1.46
3	1.05	0.92	1.35	1.20	1.29	1.61
4	1.63	1.43	2.44	2.15	1.50	1.89
5	2.20	1.98	3.72	3.32	1.66	2.08
6	3.05	2.62	5.34	4.79	1.78	2.14
7	3.90	3.31	7.15	6.40	1.88	2.32
8	4.62	3.87	9.25	7.93	2.02	2.83
9	5.35	4.20	11.40	9.30	2.17	3.26
10	5.99	4.38	13.77	10.46	2.34	4.42

* Average, sexes combined.
† For each period.

floor space, and ventilation requirements. Males grow faster than females and attain market weight sooner. This difference has prompted some broiler growers to house the sexes separately rather than together, in order to have greater uniformity of body weights at the time of processing. Typical growth for both sexes is shown in Table 5–2.

While the broiler of the 1950's reached 4 pounds at 13 weeks of age and consumed 13 pounds of feed, today's broiler attains the same weight within 8 weeks on approximately 2 pounds of feed per pound of live weight. The rapid growth saves not only labor and feed but also allows the producer to raise many groups of broilers annually in his houses, thereby minimizing many of the fixed costs of production. With the usual 2 to 3 weeks' empty time between groups, this represents 5 cycles of production annually. A typical broiler flock is shown in Figure 5–9.

Food is a major item of cost in any animal product. The potential for rapid growth is expressed only when sufficient food of high nutritional quality is readily available. The principles of good nutrition are outlined in Chapters 7, 8, and 9. Ready access to food is critical in maximizing the growth.

Feeding equipment that is suited to a 6-week-old flock will not do for day-old chicks, and special means must be used to make sure that chicks learn to eat when they are first placed in the brooder. Today's commercial broiler chicks have an inherited capacity for growth that is fantastic by comparison with that of their counterparts of 30 years ago, but they still have to learn to eat and drink, and this calls for the simple but important application of good husbandry on the part of a caretaker.

Feed should be provided in shallow feeders or flat paper or cardboard surfaces, such as chick-box lids or filler flats, for the first few days. After

Fig. 5–9. Broilers approaching market age in a mechanically ventilated broiler house.

the chicks have learned to eat, the flats may be replaced by conventional feeders. Many kinds of feeders are available; the actual feeder space allotments vary according to type. Trough feeders used primarily in smaller flocks should provide approximately 1 inch of linear space per chick, increasing to 3 inches after 3 weeks. Only 1 inch of automatic feeder space is required after 3 weeks. The USDA has suggested that approximately fifteen 15-inch diameter hanging cylindrical feeders are adequate for 1,000 broiler chicks.

The importance of an adequate supply of cool clean drinking water cannot be overemphasized. Water constitutes approximately two thirds of the growing tissue of the young broiler. It is essential in digestion and metabolism and has a central role in temperature regulation at high environmental temperatures. Approximately one 1-gallon waterer per 100 chicks is recommended for newly hatched chicks. Automatic waterers allowing 0.5 inch per chick are usually adequate after 2 to 3 weeks. Supplementary waterers may be needed in hot weather.

A broiler starter diet is generally fed for the first 6 weeks and then is followed by a finishing diet. The latter, containing increased levels of fat and xanthophyll pigments, aids in the development of the uniform yellow skin color desired by American consumers.

Lighting for Broilers

Many operators like to use dim all-night lights, about 15 watts to each 200 square feet of floor area. In windowless houses some flock owners prefer to use red bulbs and grow their chicks in semidarkness. This keeps the chicks quiet, prevents cannibalism, and may have a slight effect on feed efficiency because of lessened activity.

Another practical system for windowless broiler houses is to start with 24 hours of light at a fairly high level, perhaps with a 40-watt bulb for each 25 square feet. The amount of light is then reduced each week, first by turning out part of the bulbs, and later by substituting 25-watt bulbs for the 40-watt size, and finally dropping as low as one 7½-watt bulb for each 75 square feet. This system avoids any necessity for completely light-proofing the house. It may be advisable to raise lighting levels for the last 24 to 36 hours prior to marketing, as broilers raised under low-light conditions are not easily driven into catching crates.

CAPON PRODUCTION

The purpose of caponizing is to improve the quality of poultry meat. Farmers regularly castrate calves, pigs, and lambs, but usually consider caponizing a much more difficult operation because it requires opening the abdominal cavity. Actually, the operation is simple, and the method can be learned quickly by almost anyone.

A small flock of capons could be raised to advantage on many farms, either for family use or for sale to local customers. Larger flocks often compete seriously with laying hens and pullets for house room, which is one important reason why they are not often found on general farms. Unless they can be kept for 2 to 4 months beyond the time at which the cockerels would normally be sold as roasters, it is not worth while to take the trouble to caponize.

Selection of Cockerels to Caponize

The size and condition of young cockerels to be caponized are more important than their age or variety. Males from any of the rapidly growing broiler strains will make excellent capons, as will crosses among such breeds as Plymouth Rocks, Rhode Island reds and Cornish. Leghorn cockerels make satisfactory small capons, but they are not likely to be commercially grown because of relatively high feed cost per pound of gain.

It is important that the operation be performed before the cockerels become too large, and the preferred weight is 1 to 1.5 pounds. They can be caponized when no more than 2 or 3 weeks old if suitable equipment is available. Operating on half-grown birds is likely to result in high mortality and more "slips" or incompletely castrated individuals.

Preparation for the Operation

It is always desirable to withhold feed for 18 hours and water for the last 12 hours prior to the operation, in order that the intestines may become empty and thus permit better vision into the body cavity. There is also much less danger of puncturing the intestines during the operation.

Performing the Operation

A first requirement for successful caponizing is good light. Bright daylight, preferably not in direct sunshine, is ideal. Artificial light may be used, if necessary.

The instruments needed are a sharp knife or scalpel, a small probe with a tearing hook on one end, a spreader for holding the ribs apart after the incision has been made, and a remover for taking out the testicles (Fig. 5–10). Several different types of removers are available, but a forceps type is preferred by most operators.

Some means of restraining the birds in a convenient position must be provided. The usual procedure is to fasten the wings and legs by straps or cords so that sufficient tension can be applied to hold the bird well stretched out. If both testicles are to be removed through one incision, the bird should be placed on its left side.

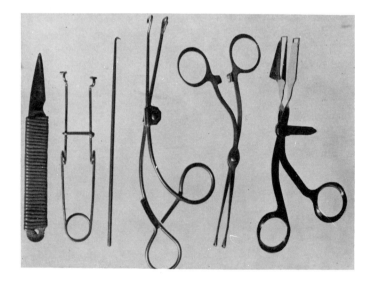

Fig. 5–10.   Instruments used for caponizing. Left to right: knife, spreader, tearing hook and probe, forceps for removal of the gonads, small forceps for operating on two-week old cockerels, and an all-in-one instrument. (Courtesy of Kansas Agricultural Experiment Station.)

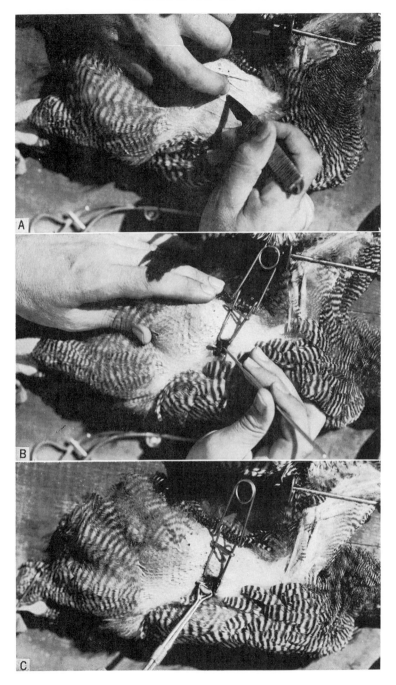

Fig. 5–11. Caponizing. *A*, Skin and thigh muscle being drawn back preparatory to making the incision; *B*, tearing the peritoneal membrane after inserting a spreader to hold the ribs apart; *C*, removing the testicle. (Courtesy of Kansas Agricultural Experiment Station.)

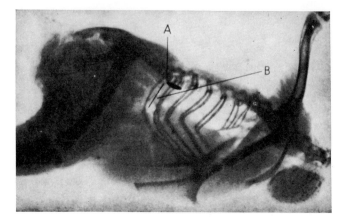

Fig. 5–12.   Radiograph of a living cockerel. The right testicle has been sketched in at *A*. The line of incision is indicated at B.

Making the Incision

It is usually necessary to pluck a few feathers from the area through which the incision is to be made. A little cold water may be used to moisten the surrounding feathers so that they will lie down out of the way. Next, with the fingers of the left hand find the last two ribs; slide the skin upward and backward toward the thigh, making sure that the underlying thigh muscles are out of the way; force the knife through the skin and flesh between the last two ribs; lengthen the incision to about 1 inch, keeping it centered between the ribs and not too near the back; and insert the spreader so as to hold the ribs about 0.5 inch apart (Fig. 5–11). If the knife has not severed the peritoneal membranes, they should be torn with the hook so as to expose the testicles to the view of the operator. The position of the testicles in the body cavity is illustrated in Figure 5–12.

Removing the Testicles

The lower or left testicle should be removed first. It is not visible, as a rule, and must be lifted into view by the forceps before it can be grasped. The entire organ and the connecting portion of the spermatic duct must be taken out in order to prevent the bird from becoming a "slip." Care must be taken, however, not to rupture any of the primary blood vessels, or internal hemorrhage will result in death before the bird is removed from the operating table.

The remover is carefully worked over the testicle and so manipulated as to enclose the entire organ. It is then drawn out with a slight twisting motion. The same procedure is followed with the upper testicle. As soon as the spreader is removed, and the tension on the bird is released, the skin and thigh muscles slip back over the incision, affording natural protection.

Because of the relatively high body temperature of chickens, it is possible to perform this sort of operation with little danger of infection. Ordinary cleanliness is all that is required.

Care After the Operation

No special care of young capons is necessary, other than to give them a clean pen or a range area where they do not have to compete with other chickens. Any good growing ration will be satisfactory.

Wind puffs often develop because air escapes from within the abdominal cavity before the incision between the ribs is healed, and becomes trapped beneath the skin. It is sometimes necessary to puncture these puffs four or five times on alternate days following the operation.

Slips result when some portion of the testicle is left in the body cavity. Occasionally a testicle is dropped inside the body after having been torn loose. If it is not removed, the bird will become a slip and will have all the external appearance of a normal cockerel. This is because the testicle, or in other cases a small portion of it, becomes attached to the inner abdominal wall and continues to secrete the male sex hormone in sufficient quantity to cause enlargement of the comb and wattles and later toughening of the flesh.

Marketing Capons

Persons who have once enjoyed roast capon of top quality are likely to be repeat customers year after year, and there is undoubtedly a potential market for capons which has never been explored. Common practice, however, has been to produce capons largely for local consumption. A few persons have developed a nice business in the sale of started capons, operated on at 3 weeks of age and sold at 5 or 6 weeks to customers who grow them to market age.

Chapter 6

Houses and Equipment

Housing serves two major functions for the poultryman. First, it permits the organization and concentration of the flock into a manageable unit and, secondly and more importantly, provides a physical environment that is conducive to optimal egg or poultry meat production. In general the chicken that is comfortable and free from stress is most likely to perform at its maximum potential. A successful poultry house will protect its occupants from extremes of temperature and other unfavorable weather conditions.

In mild climates the housing of poultry is simple, but when winter temperatures average below 10° F, with average relative humidity above 80% and with sunshine amounting to less than 5 hours a day, or when the environment is hot and moist with average daily temperatures above 95° F, the proper housing of highly productive flocks becomes a difficult problem. To understand the complicated nature of the problem and the means by which it can be solved, it is necessary to look at poultry housing from three viewpoints: (1) as a problem in biology, (2) as a problem in engineering, and (3) as a problem in economics, as each is related to the matter of "weather" control in the hen house. This means that we need to know the ideal conditions of temperature, humidity, and air change for maximum egg production, the engineering design that will make it possible to control these conditions for a flock of a given size, and the range or tolerance above and below the optimum that may be permitted for each factor without seriously interfering with production, so that we may decide what variations are permissible while still keeping construction costs within reasonable limits.

Aside from such matters as light, floor space, litter materials, and the kind and amount of essential equipment, housing requirements for hens can be stated only in terms of temperature, relative humidity, and the number of air changes to maintain the necessary minimum amount of oxygen and the maximum permissible amount of carbon dioxide. These

146

conditions are difficult to determine. It may be even more difficult to maintain any specified set of conditions.

TEMPERATURE

Chickens, like all other warm-blooded animals, produce heat, moisture, and carbon dioxide as by-products of their biological activity. The entire

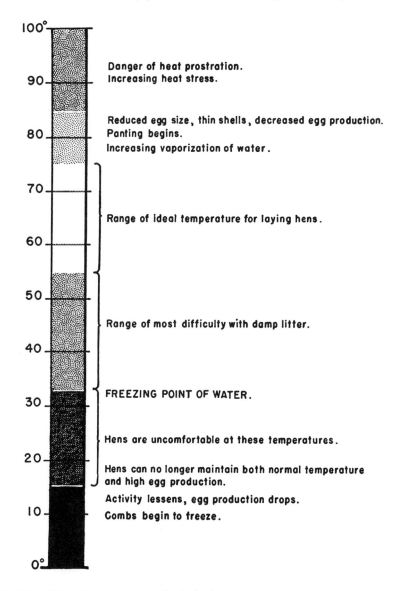

Fig. 6–1. Effect of temperature on the laying hen.

process operates to maintain body temperatures at about 106.5° F (range from 104 to 109). Since this is nearly always above the air temperature in the poultry house by from 10 to as many as 80 degrees, the hen is constantly losing heat to her surroundings. Unless energy is available to replace this heat, body temperature will fall and the hen cannot long survive.

Although the laying hen may produce eggs at a maximal rate over the temperature range of 55 to 75° F, the optimal temperature is probably closer to 75° F (Fig. 6–1). Researchers in England reported that egg production increased at each 5° C increment in ambient temperature from 15° C (59° F) to 30° C (86° F) provided the relative humidity at the highest temperature was 50% or less. The efficiency of food conversion (kg feed/doz eggs) was improved by 20% at the highest temperature, reflecting the lower amount of food energy required to maintain body temperature. Egg size and eggshell thickness tended to be reduced at the highest temperature. In practice, the producer must decide on an ambient temperature that is economically feasible. It is usually less expensive in the winter time, for example, to settle for reduced efficiency of feed conversion at cooler ambient temperatures than to provide supplementary heat in the laying house.

Heat Production versus Heat Loss

If the rate of heat loss is increased for any reason, as during a period of cold weather, heat production must be increased by a corresponding amount. Similarly, if heat production is increased, as by increased activity with no change in the surrounding air temperature, there must be an immediate increase in heat loss to prevent the body temperature from rising. Many different factors affect the rate of heat loss and the rate of heat production. The more important ones are shown in Figure 6–2.

Heat loss will be greater in winter than in summer because of the greater difference in temperature between the hen and her surroundings. If hens are exposed to wind, the increased volume of air moving past them, picking up heat as it goes, results in an increased rate of heat loss. Low wall or floor temperatures can result in greatly increased heat loss so that hens may be uncomfortable in a building with cold walls, even though the air temperature, as indicated by a thermometer, is not unreasonably low. High humidity makes air a better conductor, and moist air on a cold day will therefore absorb more heat from the hens than will dry air.

An increase in heat loss from any of the foregoing causes calls for increased heat production simply to maintain a balance and to keep the body temperature near normal. But heat production may vary independently of the demand caused by varying heat loss. Physical activity will increase heat production because energy is incompletely used in doing work and the wasted energy appears as heat. Increased feed consumption

Heat loss *increased* by:	Heat production *increased* by:
Low air temperature	Physical activity
Increased air movement	Increased feed consumption
Low wall or floor temperature	Unbalanced rations
High humidity on cold days	"Chemical regulation" of body temperature when environmental temperature falls below the critical point
Loss of feathers (molting)	
"Physical regulation" of body temperature	

HEAT LOSS *in Balance with* HEAT PRODUCTION

Heat loss *decreased* by:	Heat production *decreased* by:
High air temperature	Decreased activity
Decreased air movement	Decreased feed intake
High wall or floor temperature	(No way of decreasing heat production when profitable egg yields are required. Feed a well-balanced ration to keep heat production at a minimum for the expected production and activity.)
Heavy feather coat	
Insulation of hen houses, with consequent increase in air and wall temperatures	

Fig. 6–2.   Factors influencing heat loss and heat production in the fowl.

will increase heat production because the feed energy is not completely used, and heat is released in the process. The feeding of unbalanced rations, which leave excess nutrients to be oxidized and eliminated, will increase the total heat production. At environmental temperatures below the point at which physical regulation of body temperature is no longer effective, the so-called chemical regulation of heat production comes into play, causing an increase in heat production in order to maintain the normal body temperature as long as possible (Fig. 6–3).

Conversely, heat loss from the body will be decreased by higher environmental temperatures, by decreased air movement, and by high wall and floor temperatures. As explained later, high humidity on hot days interferes with necessary heat loss.

Heat production will be lowered by decreased activity and by decreased feed intake, but since profitable egg yields are dependent on

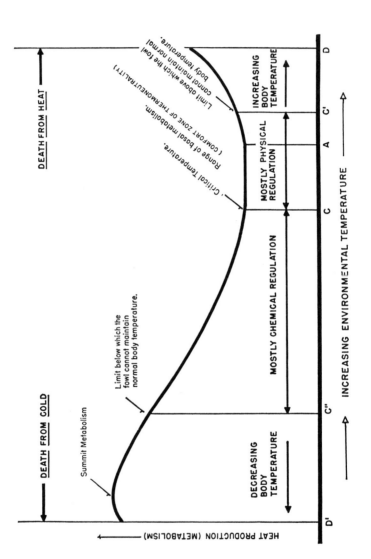

Fig. 6–3. Effect of environmental temperature on heat production and body temperature in the fowl. (Adapted from Brody.)

maximum feed consumption, there is no way to make practical use of this relationship except to feed rations that are reasonably well balanced, thereby keeping heat production at a minimum for the expected production and activity. The minimum heat production for hens at rest occurs at about 70° F.

Calculation of Heat Production

The heat production of a fasting hen at rest is about 2.75 gram calories per hour per gram of live weight. For a 4-pound (1,818 gram) hen this amounts to 5,000 gram calories (5 kilogram calories)* or 20 Btu per hour. Normal activity will cause an increase in heat production, and feed consumption will cause an additional increase proportional to the amount of dry matter consumed. The activity increment is usually estimated at about half the basal heat production, though for hens in cages it may be no more than one third. This would add approximately 7 Btu per hour for hens in cages in this example. For hens laying at a high rate—75 to 80% and consuming about 22 pounds of feed per 100 hens per day, the increase in heat production due to feeding would be about 10 Btu per hen per hour. This calculation assumes 91% dry matter in the feed and a heating effect of 68 kilocalories per 100 grams of dry matter consumed. Adding the three values (20 + 7 + 10) brings the total heat production of such hens to 37 Btu per hour. For hens in floor housing we would have (20 + 10 + 10) = 40 Btu per hour.

This calculation is of necessity an approximation because of the variation in activity and feed consumption among individual hens, because of the regular diurnal variation in basal heat production with a minimum at about 8 P.M. and a maximum at 8 A.M., and because of reduced heat production due to lower activity during the dark period. Furthermore, a reduction must be made to allow for the latent heat of vaporization because of moisture in the expired air, which is not available for warming the air of the poultry house. At winter temperatures of 30° to 40° F this is about 20% of the total heat production. Deducting this from 37 leaves a figure of 30 Btu per hen per hour, which will be used in the examples to follow.

MOISTURE

Of more practical concern to many poultrymen is the moisture given off by hens incidental to their use of feed. It often creates a real problem during cold weather. Unless it is removed by adequate ventilation or by the use of artificial heat, both the litter and the walls of the hen house may become soaking wet with condensed water vapor.

---

* Hereafter referred to as kilocalories (kcal). 1 kcal is equivalent to 3.968 Btu.

A complete water balance equation would have to take into account the fountain water consumed, water in the feed, the metabolic water released in connection with the digestion and metabolism of feed, as well as water removed in the eggs produced. In practice, however, the important components are the amount of water voided in the droppings and released to the air, the water vaporized by the hens, and the amount of water brought into the poultry house by incoming air on damp days. These will be considered in some detail.

Water Voided in Droppings

Poultry feces, as voided, contain a high percentage of water. Reported figures range from 70 to 80%, depending on whether they are based on hourly or 24-hour samples, and on the kind of feed consumed. Not all this moisture is lost to the air. Manure separated from poultry house litter under air dry conditions contains about 16% moisture, equivalent to about 4% of the original weight, but the moisture content of manure allowed to accumulate beneath cages or roosts seldom drops below 70%. Lowering this level by forced ventilation will reduce odors and help prevent the development of fly larvae.

The weight of manure voided will be from 20 to 30% greater than the weight of feed consumed. Under some conditions it may be less than this, and if bulky, low-energy feeds are fed, it will be much greater—as much as 75% greater than the weight of feed consumed. The total feed intake of a flock of a hundred 4½-pound hens laying 75 to 80 eggs a day, and fed a typical high-energy ration, will be about 23 to 25 pounds. The corresponding amount of manure voided will therefore be from 28 to 32 pounds. If 20% of this is to become free water in the hen house, there will be about 6 pounds of water a day from each 100 hens to create dampness in the house unless it is removed by adequate ventilation.

The moisture problem is one reason why more and more poultrymen are using mechanical cleaning systems for frequent removal of manure from poultry houses. Even twice-a-week removal will greatly reduce the moisture. Such a schedule will also help to keep flies at a minimum during warm weather. Some installations provide for daily removal of manure.

It should be clear that the moisture problem results from the presence of the hens and from their consumption of feed and water. In tests at the New Hampshire station it was found that litter samples taken from empty houses in January and February contained about 15% moisture, and those from pens filled with laying hens averaged about 35% for insulated houses and ranged up to more than 60% in uninsulated houses.

For broilers, the moisture content of fecal material is about 80% or slightly higher. When broilers approach market weight, the weight of fecal material excreted daily will be about half the sum of water and feed consumed.

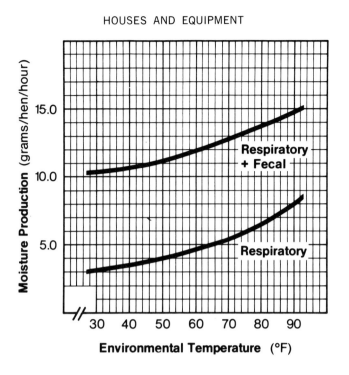

Fig. 6–4. Relationships of respiratory and fecal water to environmental temperature. (Adapted from H. Ota: The physical control of environment for growing and laying birds. In *Environmental Control in Poultry Production* edited by T. C. Carter. Edinburgh, Oliver and Boyd, 1967.)

Vaporized Water and Heat Loss

In addition to the water excreted in the droppings, a considerable amount of water leaves the body by vaporization from the lungs. Since fowls have no sweat glands, there is little opportunity for heat loss by evaporation from the skin. The amount vaporized from the lungs and air sacs varies widely with environmental temperature and humidity (Fig. 6–4). It may also be influenced indirectly by the kind of feed. Substitution of corn for all of the oats and half of the wheat middlings in a standard low-energy ration reduced litter moisture significantly in tests at the Storrs station.

Vaporization of water removes heat,* and variation in the quantity vaporized (indicated in the fowl by the rate of panting) is therefore an important means of varying the necessary heat loss from the body. At

---

* Each quart of water vaporized at body temperature dissipates about 2,150 Btu of heat. Btu means British thermal unit—the amount of heat required to raise the temperature of 1 pound of water 1° F. Water vapor is commonly measured in grains. One grain is equal to 0.0648 gram or 1/7,000 of a pound.

high air temperatures—approaching the normal body temperature—it is the only means by which the fowl can lose a substantial amount of heat. At low air temperatures, on the other hand, only a small fraction of the total heat loss is of this character—at 40° F about 20% and at 20° no more than 15%.

Increased heat production, from whatever cause, increases the amount of heat lost as heat of vaporization. At high temperatures, especially when relative humidity is also high, fowls soon reach the limit of normal physical regulation and must resort to panting to facilitate vaporization of water as the only means of losing heat rapidly enough to keep the body temperature from rising. This condition exists whenever the surrounding air temperature equals or exceeds the skin temperature so that heat can no longer be dissipated by radiation. If the air temperature rises still higher, vaporization must also serve to rid the body of heat absorbed from the hot environment. This obviously cannot continue for long, and the fowl dies from heat exhaustion. Panting is nothing but a considerable increase in the respiration rate as the fowl attempts to get rid of more and more heat by this means. The amount of water vaporized increases slowly at temperatures of 75° to 80° F, and rapidly thereafter, provided the humidity of the inspired air is low enough to permit. With inspired air at low relative humidity but at temperatures of 105° F or above, some records indicate a short-time evaporative moisture loss of 25 to 30 grams per hen per hour, along with watery droppings. If the inspired air is both warm and saturated, the hen is completely unable to avoid collapse and death. The difficulty of eliminating excess heat while maintaining other body processes begins to show at air temperatures of about 85° F. Egg size decreases, eggshells become thinner, and production is reduced.

Death losses from heat prostration are often severe in the humid sections of the country, and they are also a serious problem in hot, dry areas where maximum daily temperatures range from 105° to 115° F or higher. Survival under such conditions is closely related to the availability of drinking water and to the persistence with which fowls consume it. Figure 6–5 illustrates the relationships between ambient temperature, body temperature, and water consumption of leghorn pullets. Losses can also be reduced by intermittent spraying of the fowls and the interior of the houses. Fine mist sprayers are especially helpful in dry areas. The amount of water used is low, about 1 gallon per hour for each nozzle, and the fine mist promotes evaporative cooling. When humidity is high, cold water can be used to lower the body temperature by contact. Tests at the Beltsville Research Center showed that when no method of cooling was provided, hens were able to survive a temperature of 90° F, provided the relative humidity did not exceed 75%. At 95° they survived at humidities below 60%, but at 100° F they survived only if the humidity was 30% or lower. Very fat hens succumbed first, perhaps because the air sacs were

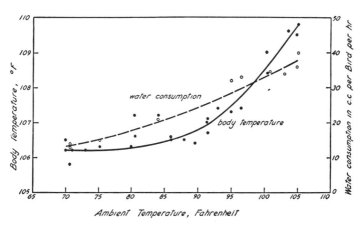

Fig. 6–5. Effects of ambient temperature on body temperature and water consumption of white leghorn pullets. (After Wilson.)

constricted and therefore unable to function efficiently in evaporating water from the body tissues.

At low temperatures, on the other hand, the heat loss from vaporization of water changes little from normal. Most of the heat loss is then in the form of sensible heat, by radiation and convection, and it is therefore available for warming the air in the hen house. When laying hens are on full feed, the excess heat available for maintaining the normal body temperature is adequate for air temperatures above 40° F. When such hens are active, as during the day, and are producing additional heat because of muscular activity, the critical temperature is lowered to about 20° or perhaps even to 15° F.

At temperatures below 15° or 20° F hens must draw on stored or food nutrients for the heat energy necessary to maintain normal body temperature, and egg production will therefore be lowered. Combs begin to freeze at about 6° above zero in dry air, and at 9° to 10° above zero in moist air.

It is clear that the compensatory range above the "comfort zone" of thermoneutrality (in which the animal feels neither hot nor cold) is much less than the range below and that fowls, like other farm animals, have more defenses against cold than against heat. They are, however, handicapped by their small size, because they have more body surface per unit of weight. The effects of a sudden drop in temperature are therefore more severe than with larger animals. In a 5-pound hen about 95% of the total body tissue is within ¾ inch of the surface of the body. By contrast, in a 1,000-pound steer only about 25% of the total body tissue is so exposed.

VENTILATION

The total air breathed by fowls at rest in a comfortable environment is about 1.6 cubic foot per hen per hour—slightly less for small hens and slightly more for large ones. For one thousand 4-pound hens this would be about 38,000 cubic feet every 24 hours. Measured by air change in the average hen house, built for the convenience of the caretaker and not simply to accommodate the hens, this is a very small requirement. It is entirely overshadowed by the rate of air change necessary to remove moisture from a tightly built house. In most instances, if ventilation is adequate to keep the house dry, it will more than meet the air requirements of the fowls. Under conditions of heat stress, that is, when both air temperature and relative humidity are high, the respiration rate is very rapid and the total volume of air breathed may be eight or ten times normal.

The amount of air that must be moved through a poultry house to carry out excess moisture will depend upon the inside and outside temperatures and the difference between them, and on the relative humidity of the inside and outside air. Raising the temperature increases the capacity of air to hold moisture. In the range of 30° to 75° F, each rise of 1° in temperature means an increase of about 5% in moisture-holding capacity of the air. The amount of water vapor in a pound of saturated air at 5° F is doubled at 20°, and redoubled successively at about 36°, 55°, 76°, and 99°. For every grain or gram or pound of water vapor the air can hold at 5° F, it can hold 32 times as much at 99°.

A typical house 40 feet wide, 380 feet long, with 8 foot ceilings may contain 30,000 four-lb laying hens. Let us assume, for example, that the outside temperature is 15° F, the outside air has a relative humidity of 70%, the inside temperature is 60°, and one wishes to maintain the relative humidity in the house at or below 75%. The required ventilation rate can be calculated as follows. Using Figure 6–4, the respiratory moisture will be approximately 5 grams per hen per hour. This amounts to 3,600,000 grams, or 55,600,000 grains per 24 hours for the entire flock. If moisture released from the droppings is taken as 5.5 grams per hen per hour, only 20% of which becomes vaporized, the droppings contribute approximately 12,200,000 grains of moisture to the total of 67,800,000 grains of moisture released into the air in the house. The outside air contains 0.7 grains of moisture per cubic foot (Fig. 6–6). When warmed to 60° F within the house, its moisture holding capacity at 75% relative humidity is 4.4 grains per cubic foot. Therefore, air passing through the house can remove 3.7 grains of moisture per cubic foot, and a ventilation rate of approximately 25.5 cubic feet per hen per hour or 6.3 complete changes of air in the structure per hour, will be required to maintain the relative humidity inside the house at no greater than 75%. This is a moderate rate of air movement. In tightly constructed, windowless houses with pressur-

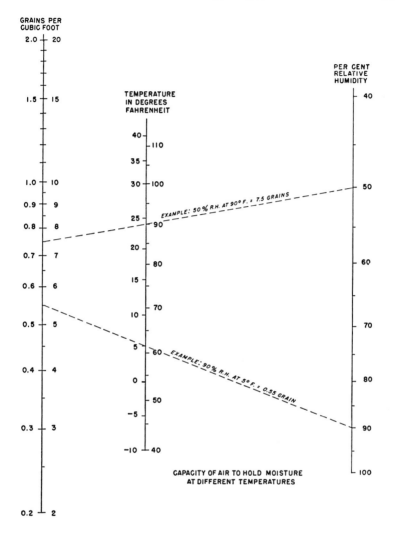

Fig. 6-6. Chart for quick determination of the amount of moisture air can hold at different temperatures and relative humidities.

ized ventilation systems, it is not unusual to provide as much as 6 or 8 cubic feet of air change per hen per minute. The hens in such houses are usually in cages, and the total air space per layer may be no more than 8 cubic feet. With pressurized ventilation there is no evidence of drafts inside the house.

Forced ventilation of the outside air through the building will remove the excess moisture whenever the humidity of the outside air is lower than that of the inside air at the same temperature. But if the relative humidity of both the inside and the outside air is the same, no amount of air change will do any good. Either the temperature of the outside air must rise so that it can hold more moisture, or its humidity must drop, if mere air circulation through the house is to remove any moisture. This state of near equilibrium between inside and outside humidity, often with an excess on the outside, is common in many poultry houses during mild winter weather, often for several days in succession. Since no change can be effected in the outside air, dampness in the house can be reduced only by (1) providing some means of absorbing moisture, such as built-up litter, (2) raising the inside air temperature by a small amount of artificial heat, or (3) providing sufficient insulation to retain the heat the hens themselves produce.

Inadequate removal of moisture in cold weather can lead to condensation of moisture on the inner surfaces of the poultry house. When such a condition persists over a period of time, moisture may damage the wall and ceiling surfaces and cause reduced insulating value if the moisture permeates the wall and ceiling insulation. Figure 6–7 relates temperature, humidity, and insulating value to predict condensation of moisture within the poultry house. The heat loss factor is the rate of heat transfer through

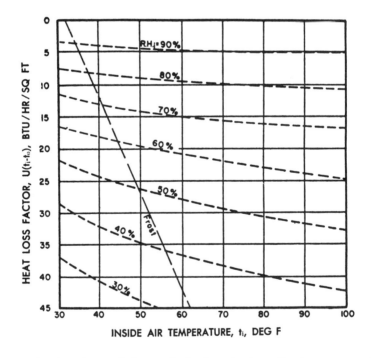

Fig. 6–7. Condensation prediction graph. Condensation is predicted to occur at relative humidities equal to, or above the point on the graph representing the heat loss factor and temperature within the house. The condensation will occur as frost if the point lies to the left of the line labeled "frost."

the wall of the house. This factor is computed as the average coefficient of heat transfer for the structure (U in Btu/hr–sq ft–deg F) times the temperature differential between the air inside and outside the house.

It is not uncommon for a metal-clad poultry house constructed with 3½ and 7 inches of fiberglass in the walls and ceiling, respectively, having R values of 15 and 20, to have a coefficient of heat transfer equivalent to 18. Using the previous example, we can determine whether moisture will condense on the inner surfaces of the house. The U value (reciprocal of R) of the wall is 6.01. We determine from Figure 6–7 that a relative humidity greater than 90% would be required in order to cause condensation. A similar house with no fiberglass insulation in the side walls may have a U value of 0.31. Under these conditions, assuming temperature of 60° F within the house, the heat loss factor becomes 14, and condensation is predicted to occur at 75% relative humidity. A house with such low insulating value will likely maintain a temperature lower than 60° under the environmental conditions presented above, thereby exacerbating the moisture problem.

INSULATION

In modern poultry houses with high densities of layers or broilers, the ventilation requirements affect greatly the amount of insulation required in the poultry house. By ignoring the contribution of ventilation for the moment, we can understand the principle of heat loss through the walls and ceiling of the structure. Let us consider, for example, the poultry house 40 feet × 380 feet × 8 feet containing 30,000 hens. This house contains 21,900 sq ft of surface area or approximately 0.73 sq ft of surface per hen. The heat production per unit of surface area equals (30 Btu/hen ÷ 0.73 =) 41 Btu per hr per sq ft of surface area. If walls and roof consist of a single layer of siding and roll roofing, the insulating value is about 2. By definition, this means that with a difference in temperature between inside and outside air of only 2° F, and with no direct ventilation, that is, with the house tightly closed, the heat loss will be 1 Btu per hour through each square foot of exposed area. A population of 30,000 hens on full feed could therefore maintain the inside air temperature of such a house at (2 × 41 =) 82° F, above that of the outside air. Assuming a tightly closed house with no ventilation, this would provide a comfortable temperature in the house with outside temperatures below 0° F. If one wished to maintain a temperature of 55° in such a house when outside temperatures dropped to −10° F, an insulation value of (65/41 =) 1.6 will be needed.

With lower densities of poultry, more insulation will be required. If the house in the previous example contained floor-housed hens having a floor density of 1.5 sq ft per bird, the house would accommodate 10,000 hens. The wall and ceiling surface area per hen is 2.2 sq ft and the heat production will be (33 Btu per hen per hour ÷ 2.2=) 15 Btu per sq ft of surface area per hr. An insulation value of (65/15 =) 4.3 will be needed to protect this flock against a drop in outside temperature to −10° F.

In practice, of course, the housing is not airtight. Minimal ventilation, even in the coldest weather, contributes to the loss of heat from the poultry house.

POULTRY HOUSE DESIGN

To combine the data on heat production, moisture removal, and insulation for the purpose of hen house design, it is necessary to include at least one other factor, namely, the amount of heat required to warm the outside air used for ventilation. At temperatures in the 35° to 40° range, it will take 1 Btu per degree of rise for each 50 cubic feet of air. Hence, if the volume of air moved through a hen house in one hour is 50,000 cubic feet, and if the difference in temperature between inside and outside air is 10° F, there must be sufficient heat available to permit 10,000 Btu per hour to be used in warming the outside air, or the inside air will soon drop to the same temperature as the incoming air.

It is possible to combine all the foregoing related factors into a heat balance equation or formula as follows:

Let H − the heat available, in this case the Btu of sensible heat produced per hen per hour
    D = the difference between inside and outside air temperature in degrees Farenheit
    A = the combined wall and ceiling area exposed to heat loss, in square feet per hen, with due allowance for glass area
    R = the insulating value of the walls and ceiling (or roof)
    V = the volume of air change in cubic feet per hen per hour
    50 = the cubic feet of air warmed 1 degree F by 1 Btu

For balanced conditions, the sum of VD/50 and AD/R must not exceed the value of H. Hence, H = VD/50 + AD/R, or H/D = V/50 + AR. Note that VD/50 and AD/R constitute the losses of heat due to ventilation and heat transfer through the surfaces of the structure, respectively.

Since the unknown factor is often the amount of air change permissible for a given temperature difference, the formula can be transformed to read V = 50(H/D − A/R). In our example of 30,000 hens in cages in a 40 × 380-foot house 8 feet high, assuming an insulating value (R value) of 18 and a temperature difference of 25°, we would have V = 50 (30/25 − 0.73/18), or 58 cubic feet of air per hen per hour. The total volume of air in the house amounts to 4.0 cubic feet per hen, and therefore (58/4 =) 14.5 changes per hour can take place without decreasing the specified 25° difference in temperature. Since we have already found that 6.3 changes, or 25.5 cubic feet per hen per hour, will be sufficient to remove the calculated amount of moisture, no further computations are necessary.

If, however, we should decide to put 10,000 hens on the floor in the same house, allowing 1.5 square feet of floor area per hen, most of the figures will change. Respiratory moisture will decrease to 18,500,000 grains in 24 hours, and moisture from the droppings will also decrease to 4,100,000 grains, making a total of 22,600,000 grains. At 3.7 grains per cubic foot, 2.1 changes per hour or 254,000 cubic feet per hour will be needed to remove the water vapor. Note that this is still 25.5 cubic feet per hen per hour. In the heat balance equation we will have $V = 50 (33/25 - 2.2/18)$, or a maximum of 60 cubic feet of air per hen per hour which can be drawn from the outside without lowering the air temperature inside the house. The volume of air per hen is now 12.2 cubic feet, permitting 4.9 changes per hour.

The heat balance equation can be used in other ways. Suppose, for example, that the house used in the previous examples has an overall R value of 18, and that we want to know what temperature can be maintained inside by a flock of 30,000 four-pound hens when the outside temperature falls to 0° F. Our transformed equation will be $D = H/(V/50 + A/R)$. Using the values already calculated, we can substitute them in the equation so that it will read $D = 30 (25.5/50 + 0.73/18)$. Solving this gives 54.5° as the answer we were after.

Similarly, we might want to determine the required R value under some assumed set of conditions. For a specific example, assume that we wish to house 10,000 four-pound hens in the building described above, and that we want to be able to maintain indoor temperatures in winter at 40° F above the outdoor temperature. Using the values that we have previously calculated for the 4-pound hen, we will set up the equation in the form $R = A/(H/D - V/50)$. When we substitute known values it will read $R = 2.2/(30/40 - 25.5/50)$. Solving this, we arrive at an R value of 9.2.

Metric Units

To see what some of these relationships look like when expressed in metric units, assume a small flock of 400 1.8-kilogram hens in a windowless house that is 10 × 10 meters and 2.4 meters high. The volume of air would be 240 cubic meters, or 0.6 cubic meter per hen. The floor area would be 0.25 square meter per hen, and the total area exposed to heat loss would be 196 square meters, or 0.49 square meter per hen. Call it 0.5 for easy calculation.

Total feed intake of a flock of 400 1.8-kilogram hens laying at the rate of 75 to 80%, and fed a typical high-energy ration, will be about 40 kilograms a day. The amount of manure voided will therefore be about 48 to 52 kilograms. If we use the midpoint between these two values and assume that 20% will become free water in the hen house, there will be about 10 kilograms of water a day to create dampness.

Total air breathed by fowls at rest in a comfortable environment is about 45 cubic decimeters (0.045 cubic meter) per hen per hour. For 400 1.8-kilogram hens this would be about 440 cubic meters every 24 hours.

The respiratory moisture given off by such a flock, calculated at 5 grams per hen per hour, will amount to 48,000 grams in 24 hours. If moisture from the droppings is taken as 10 kilograms and added to the respiratory moisture, there will be a total of 49,000 grams to be removed. At 8.5 grams per cubic meter (the equivalent of 3.7 grain per cubic foot which we used previously), it will require 240 cubic meters per hour, equal to 0.6 cubic meter per hen per hour, or 1 complete change of air per hour, to remove the water vapor.

The heat production of fasting hens at rest is about 2.75 gram calories* per hour per gram of live weight. For a 1.8-kilogram hen this amounts to 4,950 gram calories per hour. Adding 50% for normal activity and 2,575 gram calories for the heating effect of feed (assuming 91% dry matter in the feed and a heating effect of 68 kilogram-calories for each 100 grams of dry matter consumed), brings the total for each hen to 10,000 gram calories per hour. Subtracting 20% for latent heat in the expired air leaves 8,000 gram calories per hen per hour. For our 400-hen flock this will amount to approximately 77,000 kilogram calories per day.

To adapt the heat balance equation to metric units we will have:

H = heat available in kilogram calories of sensible heat per hen per hour (8.0).

D = difference between inside and outside temperature in degrees Centigrade (specified at 15 in this example).

A = combined wall and ceiling area exposed to heat loss, expressed as square meters per hen (0.5).

R = insulating value. When expressed as the temperature difference in degrees Centigrade that will just permit a heat loss of 1 kilogram calorie per hour through each square meter of exposed surface, our previous value of 9.2 in British thermal units becomes 6.1 in metric units.

V = volume of air change in cubic meters per hen per hour. 50 cubic feet of air warmed 1° F by 1 Btu are equivalent to 3.125 cubic meters of air warmed 1° C by 1 kilogram calorie.

Instead of $V = 50(H/D - A/R)$ we will have $V = 3.125(H/D - A/R)$. After substituting the new values we will have $V = 3.125(8.0/15 - 0.5/6.1)$ which gives 1.4 for the value of V. Since the total volume of air in the house is (240/400 =) 0.6 cubic meter per hen, we will have (1.4/0.6 =) 2.3 changes of air per hour that can occur with no reduction in the 15-degree difference specified as a minimum. This is well above the change per hour required to remove the calculated amount of water vapor.

The application of the foregoing discussion to practical conditions may be summed up in the following recommendations for procedures that will aid in keeping hens comfortable in cold weather without the use of artificial heat. They are listed in their approximate order of importance.

---

* The SI unit is joule (0.24 cal); 1 millijoule = 0.24 kilocalories.

1. Build large houses rather than small and thereby reduce total exposed area per hen subject to heat loss.
2. Insulate the ceiling or roof in order to reduce heat loss in winter and lessen the absorption of solar heat in summer. In a large single-story house, the ceiling or roof represents a much higher percentage of the total area exposed to heat loss than it does in a small house.
3. Control ventilation so that heat is conserved during the period of low night temperatures while the hens are relatively inactive. Humidity will rise, but it can be corrected during the daytime when the sun's heat will help dry out the house.

The aim of the foregoing procedures is to maintain hen house temperatures above freezing at all times, and to maintain a minimum temperature in the house within the ideal range (Fig. 6–1). A secondary consideration is to keep the relative humidity down to 80 to 75%, and the moisture content of the litter down to 40%. These latter conditions are more important from the standpoint of preventing dirty eggs than from their effect on egg production. The housing problem is quite different in hot climates where insulation serves to reduce the uptake of solar heat, and ventilation must dissipate the sensible heat (Fig. 6–8) and large amounts of moisture (latent heat) produced by the flock by respiration. In hot environments where winter temperatures seldom drop below freezing, open-sided houses with roll-up curtains are satisfactory. Evaporative cooling in combination with insulated housing has been used successfully in some arid areas.

HOUSE CONSTRUCTION

The purpose in building a poultry house is to furnish the greatest possible comfort to the flock at the least possible cost per bird. Just where the law of diminishing returns comes in with reference to the grade of lumber and the class of skilled labor employed for the construction is a matter of judgment in individual cases.

It is, of course, possible to err in creating an unjustifiable overhead by building an expensive house, as is not infrequently done. Just as possible and as frequent is an overeagerness to save money on first costs by using poor material and unskilled labor which is usually followed by an undue depreciation and an unsatisfactory house. Examples of poultry houses are shown in Figures 6–9 through 6–13.

Factory-built Houses

The easiest way to acquire a poultry house is to purchase one, complete with insulation, a ventilating system, and all equipment, and have it

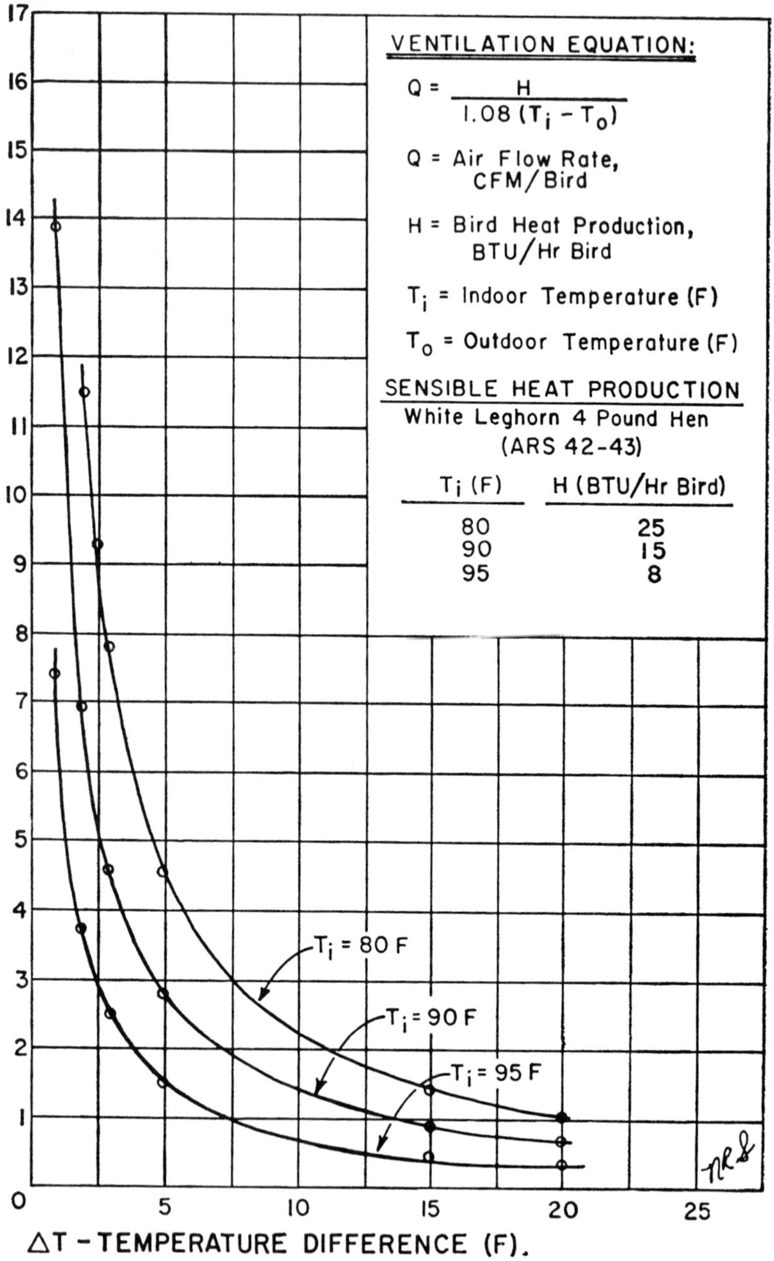

VENTILATION EQUATION:
Q = H / 1.08 (Ti - To)
Q = Air Flow Rate, CFM/Bird
H = Bird Heat Production, BTU/Hr Bird
Ti = Indoor Temperature (F)
To = Outdoor Temperature (F)
SENSIBLE HEAT PRODUCTION
White Leghorn 4 Pound Hen
(ARS 42-43)
Ti (F) H (BTU/Hr Bird)
80 25
90 15
95 8
Ti = 80 F
Ti = 90 F
Ti = 95 F
0
5
10
15
20
25
1
2
3
4
5
6
7
8
9
10
11
12
13
14
15
16
17
ΔT - TEMPERATURE DIFFERENCE (F).

Fig. 6–8. Effect of air flow on the removal of heat produced by laying hens in summer. (New York State College of Agriculture Extension Bulletin 1140).

Fig. 6–9. A two-story hen house with a 6-inch fill of wood shavings for insulation in side walls and roof. When outside temperatures ranged from 0° to 20° F, the inside temperature was maintained at 45° to 55°. (Courtesy of Minnesota Agricultural Experiment Station.)

Fig. 6–10. A custom-built windowless, pressure-ventilated house for 70,000 broilers. (Courtesy of Bill Brown Company, Rogers, Arkansas.)

Fig. 6–11. A typical broiler house widely used in Georgia. (Courtesy of Till M. Huston.)

Fig. 6–12. One-story house for layers, with bulk feed tanks conveniently located. (Courtesy of Creighton Brothers, Warsaw, Indiana.)

Fig. 6–13. This two-story windowless house with aluminum siding accommodates 40,000 layers. (Courtesy of New York State College of Agriculture at Cornell University.)

erected by the manufacturer. This is one of the recent developments in egg farming, especially in parts of the country where complete control of environment is essential to successful flock management. It is also becoming a common practice in some broiler areas.

One important reason for the growing interest in such plans is that a flock owner can be sure of the full cost in advance instead of having to depend on his own or a contractor's estimate. A second reason, important to many operators, is that financing is often easier to arrange because the entire transaction is carried out with one supplier. This can also be an advantage to the buyer when something goes wrong within the guarantee period. Furthermore, the factory-built house is likely to go up in less time than one built by a local contractor. The cost of such a house will vary with the size as well as with the type and amount of equipment included.

Many poultrymen, however, prefer to build their own houses and to select and install the necessary equipment. Some of the important considerations in poultry house construction will therefore be presented briefly.

Foundations

A good foundation must be solid enough to support the building, deep enough to prevent heaving by frost, and high enough above grade to keep out surface water. In order to leave room for the opening and shutting of doors when a deep litter is used, the top of the foundation must be at least 6 inches above the floor level. This brings the tops of the door sills 8 or more inches above the floor. If for some reason it is necessary to locate the house where the texture of the ground is such that it tends to hold moisture, a tile placed even with the bottom and just at the outside of the foundation and furnished with a suitable outlet is a necessary precaution if the house is to be dry.

Floors

The hen house floor must be moisture proof, free from cracks, and easily cleaned. It should be rat-proof and durable. A board floor, if properly laid, is free from cracks and is easily cleaned and disinfected. It is not a durable floor when compared with concrete, and it is not rat-proof unless raised well off the ground. Although the air space below such a floor effectively stops capillary moisture, there are many times during the year when circulation of cold air beneath the house may make the floor so cold as to cause condensation of moisture from the warmer air inside the house. This "sweating" of the floor is a common cause of wet litter.

Concrete floors are dry if properly constructed. They are sanitary, durable, and rat-proof. They are not cold when properly bedded with litter. In many parts of the country they have a valuable equalizing effect on the temperature inside the poultry house. The temperature of a wood floor remains within about 2° F of the outside air temperature, for a temperature range of 25° to 95° F. A concrete floor, on the other hand, may be from 5° to 7° warmer than the air at low temperatures, and as much as 15° cooler than the air temperature when the latter is 90° to 95° F. This is a point of considerable importance in keeping fowls comfortable during hot weather.

The slat floor has been popular in some sections of the country. Slats may be used for the entire floor area, or they may cover only about half

Fig. 6–14.   Slatted floor house on the farm of Franklin Steury, Berne, Indiana. (J. C. Allen and Son Photo.)

Fig. 6–15.   Part litter and part slatted floor is another common arrangement. (Courtesy of Automatic Poultry Feeder Company.)

Fig. 6–16. Interior arrangement of a 70- × 360-foot slat floor house for 25,000 layers, as used by Creighton Brothers, Warsaw, Indiana. (Courtesy of Chore-Time Equipment, Inc.)

the floor, usually a strip down the center of a long house (Figs. 6–14, 6–15, 6–16). In any case the slat portion is raised high enough above a subfloor to provide a pit for the accumulation of manure. Such pits are often equipped with mechanical scrapers for periodic removal of manure. In some of the larger installations they are deep enough to permit removal of manure by the use of a tractor with scraper blade.

Dirt floors and deep litter are sometimes used in broiler houses. They are much less expensive than other types of floors, and many growers have been well satisfied with them. The entire accumulation of litter and manure is removed after each lot of broilers is sold or, in some instances, only after three or four lots have been grown.

Walls and Partitions

The walls and partitions must be solid enough to support the roof and withstand heavy winds. Wide variation is possible in the use of construc-

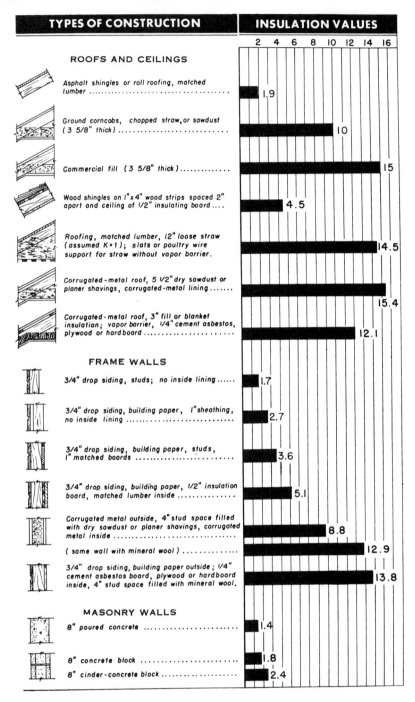

Fig. 6–17. Insulation values (R values) for some common types of wall and ceiling construction. (Prepared by the U. S. Department of Agriculture.)

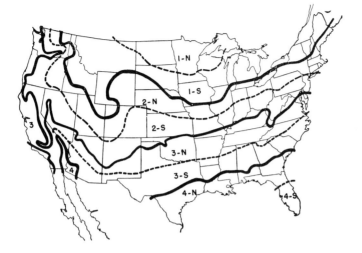

Fig. 6–18. Temperature zones as related to poultry house construction. Average January temperature in Zone 1, below 20° F; in Zone 2, 20° to 35°; in Zone 3, 35° to 50°; in Zone 4, above 50° F. Based on data from the U. S. Department of Agriculture.

tion materials, depending on availability, cost, and the insulating value desired. The recent trend has been to eliminate partitions in many of the larger houses, thereby making larger pens. This makes it necessary to give particular attention to strength of the overall structure in order to avoid danger of collapse from heavy snow loads or in windstorms.

It has become common practice to use some type of insulation in the construction of houses built for flocks of commercial size. Roof insulation helps in both summer and winter. Wall insulation is added in the colder parts of the country, the kind and amount depending on the length of the winter season and the expected minimum temperatures. Insulation values for various types of wall and roof construction are shown in Figure 6–17. The numerical values refer to the difference in degrees Fahrenheit which can exist between the warm and cold sides of a wall while permitting just 1 Btu of heat to pass through an area of one square foot in one hour. This is commonly referred to as the "R" value, for resistance to heat loss, and some types of insulating material are stamped by the manufacturer to show the R value. For technical purposes, engineers commonly use what is known as the "U" value, or coefficient of heat transfer. It is the reciprocal of the R value. R values of 2, 4, 8, and 12 are equivalent to U values of 0.5, 0.25, 0.125 and 0.0833, respectively. R values commonly recommended in the several temperature zones shown in Figure 6–18 are:

Zone	Walls	Ceiling
1-N	15	20
1-S	10	15
2-N & S	8	12
3-N & S	2–3	8
4-N & S	1	4

Vapor Barriers

Condensation of moisture within an insulated wall greatly reduces the insulating value, and may permanently injure certain types of insulating material. It is therefore important to use a vapor barrier of some sort on the inner or warm side of the insulation in order to prevent condensation at such times as the temperature falls below the dew point. This may consist of lightweight roll roofing, aluminum foil, polyethylene film and asphalt-coated paper, or two coats of asphalt or aluminum-flake paint. Some types of commercial insulating material are made with a vapor barrier surface on one side. It is important that these be installed with the vapor barrier on the inside (warm side) of the wall or ceiling, and that the barrier not be torn or damaged during application.

Ventilators

Most commercial poultrymen today use ventilating fans to insure adequate air circulation during warm weather and to control the rate of air change in cold weather. The capacity of fans should be sufficient to supply 6 or 7 cubic feet of air per minute per hen at ⅛-inch static pressure. It is easy to make the mistake of installing fans that are too small. A common type in use in large houses is 36 inches in diameter with direct drive. Another popular type is a 24-inch turnabout fan rated at 4,000 cfm at ⅛-inch static pressure. Motors should be totally enclosed, and they should be equipped with thermal-overload circuit breakers. A static pressure regulator is shown in Figure 6–19.

Both pressurized and exhaust ventilation systems are satisfactory. With a pressurized system, fans are commonly located in an attic so that they force air into the main part of the house through holes distributed over the ceiling. Exhaust fans, on the other hand, are commonly located in the side walls of the house, usually near the ceiling. It is important to keep exhaust fans free of dust and feathers. This caution applies not only to the motor housing and blades but also to the screened opening. Intake fans are less of a problem in this respect, and this is one reason why pressurized systems are preferred by many flock owners.

Standby generators, either self-powered or tractor-driven, provide excellent insurance against costly drops in egg production resulting from power failure. It is particularly important that ventilation systems in

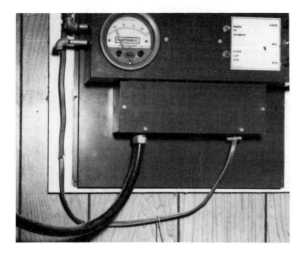

Fig. 6–19. A static pressure controller regulates air inlets to maintain a constant pressure differential between the inside and outside of the poultry house.

windowless houses continue to operate without interruption. In modern cage units with high bird density, lack of ventilation can cause suffocation of an entire flock in less than an hour. Standby generator units can also be used to keep lighting systems, automatic feeders, water systems, and egg collection belts in operation. Any standby generator should be checked regularly to make sure that it will function properly if a power failure occurs.

Windows

Windows at one time served the dual purpose of providing light and ventilation for the poultry flock. With controlled artificial lighting and high densities of poultry, windows are neither desired for lighting nor adequate as a means of ventilation. Most modern houses in the northern latitudes are windowless. Special precautions are usually taken to ensure that the houses are "lighttight" in order to ensure complete control over the intensity and duration of lighting within the house. Ventilation fans are a potential source of light. The passage of light through these units can be prevented by construction of baffled boxes over the fan opening on the exterior of the house (Fig. 6–20).

Roofs

Composition roll roofing is the material most commonly used for poultry-house roofs. It is draft and moisture proof, is easy to apply, and is

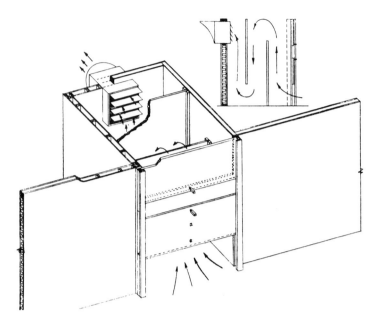

Fig. 6–20.   A double baffle for intake or exhaust fans prevents entry of light in environmentally controlled laying house.

relatively inexpensive. It must be properly laid, and it needs regular attention and occasional recoating, if it is to last more than a few years. It makes a house extremely hot in summer unless the roof is insulated or the roofing is coated with a reflecting-type paint.

Aluminum roof coatings, including exterior type aluminum foil, are being successfully used to reduce interior summer temperatures. Differences of 5° or 6° become important when exterior temperatures are high.

Built-up roofs, which consist of several layers of roofing paper cemented down with hot asphalt, are popular in some parts of the country, especially for roofs which have a very slight pitch.

Metal roofs are increasing in popularity because of their lasting quality. Less lumber is needed to support a metal roof than for composition roofing. It is advisable to use insulation under a metal roof in order to make the house cooler in summer and to prevent moisture condensation in winter.

Remodeling

It is often more economical to remodel an existing barn or other building than to build a new hen house, and some of the most practical hen houses for both farm and commerical flocks are of this sort. If the remodeled building meets the requirements stated earlier in this chapter it may be just as satisfactory as a new house, and much less expensive.

POULTRY-HOUSE EQUIPMENT

A poultry house is not complete without the accessory equipment or features that make it suitable for the particular kind of production for which it is intended. Pieces of equipment that are built in as a part of the house should be simple, few in number, adequate in size, removable for cleaning, and conveniently and systematically placed so that their care will take a minimum of labor.

Nests

The desirable qualities of a nest are that it be roomy, easily cleaned and sprayed, dark, cool and well ventilated, and conveniently located. Dark nests are preferred because the hen likes seclusion for laying. Dark nests also reduce the likelihood of egg eating. Some arrangement for shutting the fowls out at night prevents them from roosting in the nests and fouling them. This they are prone to do, especially at molting time, in order to escape being crowded by other birds on the perch.

Some poultrymen like the "community" type of nest, which is really a covered box about 2 feet wide and 6 feet long (Fig. 6–21). It has no partitions, and there is an opening at each end through which the hens may enter and leave. A sloping cover is hinged for convenience in gathering the eggs. Such nests are often built on legs so that the entire unit can be moved out from the wall for better ventilation during hot weather. Each community nest will replace 10 or 12 individual open nests.

Community-type nests are available as commercial units about 4 feet long, with wire mesh floors. At least one manufacturer provides an automatic device for closing the nests in late afternoon, gently pushing out any hens that may be occupying the nests as roosting quarters.

Trap Nests. These differ from open nests in that each one is provided with a trap door by means of which a hen shuts herself in when she enters. They are the accepted means of securing accurate individual egg records and are an essential part of the equipment for pedigree breeding where more than one female is continuously mated with one male.

They are of many different styles. First in importance is their dependability as to accuracy, though it is hardly less important that they be comfortable and attractive, if floor eggs are to be avoided.

No trap nest is a comfortable place in extremely hot weather unless every effort has been made to have it abundantly ventilated. This may even require nest floors of hardware cloth and the discarding of the use of nest bedding for a time, allowing the birds to lay on the bare wire. There should be one trap nest for every 3 hens.

Fig. 6–21. Community-type nest with egg conveyor located along the front. The system can be extended to a complete loop in a 350-foot house. Note the panel which is time-clock controlled to close the nests in late afternoon. (Courtesy of Storm Industries, Inc., Dassel, Minnesota.)

In the absence of adequate nest space, when automatic egg collecting devices are not used, excessive accumulation of eggs in the nest will result in increased breakage and dirty eggs. Regardless of the collection device, insufficient nest space will result in more eggs being laid on the floor of the laying house. In cool, damp climates litter is prone to accumulate moisture, particularly when bird density is high. Fecal material from wet litter is easily transferred on the feet and feathers of the laying hen from the floor to the nesting areas, increasing the incidence of dirty eggs.

Perches

To ensure comfort the perches should allow from 8 to 10 inches of room for each bird and be 15 to 18 inches apart. The most common material for perches is 2- by 3- or 2- by 4-inch lumber. This may be laid on the side or placed on edge. In either case it is well to round the upper edge.

Feeding Equipment

The design of feeding equipment varies considerably on different farms and in different parts of the country. No matter what style of construction is used, the feeding devices should be easy to fill, easy to clean, built to avoid waste, so arranged that the fowls cannot roost on them, and constructed in such a manner that so long as they contain any feed at all the fowls will be able to reach it. From the standpoint of practical results it is essential that ample feeding space be provided. A safe rule to follow is to have 1 foot of hopper feeding space for every 5 hens.

Automatic or mechanical feeders are standard equipment on large commercial egg and broiler farms. They save a great deal of labor and keep fresh feed available to the fowls at all times. Uninterrupted service is as important with feeders as with lights and ventilating fans, and some sort of standby generating equipment should be provided for use in the event of power failures.

Watering Devices

A perfect watering device should keep the water clean and cool in warm weather, and be of such construction that it may be easily cleaned and that freezing will not destroy its usefulness. To keep water clean the watering equipment should be high enough so that litter will not be scratched into it and so located that the fowls cannot contaminate it with droppings.

In houses lacking sufficient insulation to prevent freezing, soil heating cable may be used to protect water pipes. A thermostat should be used to shut off the current at some predetermined point, say 35° F, to prevent needless use of electric current. Proper installation, with suitable ground connections, is highly important from a safety standpoint.

Automatic watering devices are important from the standpoint of saving labor. Shallow V-shaped troughs running the entire length of the hen house and carrying a constant flow of water are satisfactory for large flocks.

Many cage installations for layers are equipped with either drip-type or small-cup waterers that minimize cleaning problems as well as spillage.

Laying Cages

The use of metal or plastic cages for laying hens has become standard practice in recent years (Figs. 6–22, 6–23). Some installations provide a single cage for each hen. Others are designed for two, three or perhaps four layers per cage. A few are the community-cage type, with as many

Fig. 6–22. This type of equipment increases labor efficiency in large cage houses. (Courtesy of Big Dutchman, a division of U. S. Industries, Inc.)

Fig. 6–23. A closer view of the electrically powered two-speed tramway shown in Fig. 6–22. Most of the work of looking after the layers is done from this overhead tramway. (Courtesy of Big Dutchman, a division of U. S. Industries, Inc.)

Table 6-1. Some Density Guidelines for Leghorn Hens in Cages

Cage Dimension		Number of Hens
Minimum	Maximum	
10″ × 12″	16″ × 20″	3
18″ × 18″	20″ × 20″	5
24″ × 24″	24″ × 30″	10
36″ × 48″	—	25

as 25 layers in each cage. A decision as to which type to use is often based on economic considerations, as costs and returns per square foot of house capacity may be more important than costs and returns per hen (Table 6-1).

In some houses there is a single tier or deck of cages over the entire floor; in others the cages are two or three decks high. Automatic watering equipment is essential, but feeding may be either automatic or manual. Eggs commonly roll to the front of the cages where they are collected by hand or, more often, by moving belts that convey them to a grading and packing room (Fig. 6-24).

Cage Density. An important question to be answered for every layer cage operation is "How many layers per cage?" Or to put it another way, "At what cage density will maximum return per layer most nearly coincide with maximum return per cage?" Numerous field tests have shown that five layers in a 12-inch × 18-inch (30-cm × 45-cm) cage will result in lower production and lower feed efficiency, whereas two layers per cage will always mean lower return per cage in spite of higher production per layer.

Results of a two-year test with leghorn layers at Cornell University indicate that under most conditions four layers per cage will give maximum returns per cage. At the costs existing when the tests were run, eggs would have had to sell for 40 cents a dozen, or better, to make it practical to use a density of five layers per cage. Some of the details are given in Table 6-2.

With single-deck installations, manure accumulates on the floor and is removed at regular intervals. Tiered cages may be provided with belts for conveying manure to one end of the house, or with platforms that can be cleaned with mechanical scrapers. Examples of manure collecting devices are shown in Figures 6-25, 6-26, and 6-27.

In some parts of southern California, where freezing temperatures are the exception and little protection from cold is needed, outdoor laying cages have become popular. As many as one-fourth of all layers in some areas are housed in this manner.

Fig. 6–24. Egg collection belts in a single-deck installation in California. (Courtesy of Jamesway Division, Butler Manufacturing Co.)

Table 6–2. Effect of Density in Cages on Egg Production, Feed Efficiency, and Returns Above Costs

	Density—Layers per Cage			
	2	3	4	5
Hen-day egg production per layer	230	229	221	204
% production—305 days	74.7	74.1	71.8	66.3
Mortality—%	9.6	8.2	14.8	22.5
Pounds of feed per dozen eggs	4.0	4.1	4.4	4.7
Results per 100 feet of cages:				
Number of layers	200	300	400	500
Dozens of eggs	3,833	5,713	7,367	8,500
Income @ 30 cents a dozen	$1,150	$1,714	$2,210	$2,550
Estimated costs	$1,136	$1,585	$2,072	$2,511
Net return above costs	$ 14	$ 129	$ 138	$ 39

Data from Ostrander and Young, Cornell University.

All that is necessary in the way of construction is a roof over the cages and some kind of framework to hold the cages off the ground (Fig. 6–28). Many variations in watering and feeding arrangements are possible, but most are aimed at making it possible to do the necessary labor of caring for the hens and gathering the eggs in a minimum amount of time.

Certain management problems, such as cannibalism, damp litter, and trap-nesting, are completely solved by the use of individual laying cages. On the other hand, there are certain new problems to meet. The percentage of cracked eggs is sometimes rather high. There will be few very dirty eggs, but a large number may be slightly soiled.

Protection from excessive heat is often a problem when outdoor cages are used, and rather elaborate sprinkling systems are sometimes necessary to prevent serious death losses when summer temperatures often range from 95° to 105° F in the middle of the day (Fig. 6–29).

CARE OF THE HOUSE

A successful poultry house must be clean, reasonably dry, well ventilated, and, above all, comfortable for the hens. Good management aimed at maintaining these conditions will pay dividends in sustained production.

Types of Litter

An important point in maintaining comfortable conditions for floor-housed poultry is the right kind of litter. Many different materials are used for this purpose, depending largely on what is locally available. Among

Fig. 6–25. Mechanical removal of droppings helps to reduce moisture in a large hen house. Creighton Brothers Poultry Farm, Warsaw, Indiana. (J. C. Allen and Son Photo).

Fig. 6–26. Three-wheel manure cleaning machine used under cages by Willis Hollowell, Ramona, California. (Courtesy of Pacific Poultryman.)

Fig. 6–27. Machine used by Ray Fisher, Lathrop, California, for cleaning under double-deck cages. (Courtesy of Pacific Poultryman.)

Fig. 6–28.   Shade is provided by a lattice connecting the eaves of two 34- × 228-foot cage houses in California. (Courtesy of Pacific Poultryman.)

Fig. 6–29.   Pipe with foggers rests on gravel between two cage houses in California. Such equipment is very important for keeping layers comfortable during hot weather. (Courtesy of Pacific Poultryman.)

the materials in common use in different sections of the country are straw, shavings, ground corn cobs, peat moss, shredded corn stalks, shredded sugar cane, oat hulls, and sawdust. Ground corn cobs head the list of desirable farm-produced litters.

In a series of tests at the Delaware station, in which more than 66,000 broilers were used, sawdust was consistently lowest in cost per 1,000 broilers, of the twelve litter materials tested. It was readily available in the area—an important practical consideration—but its moisture content frequently was too high at the time of purchase to make it wholly satisfactory. Peanut shells, ground corn cobs, peat moss, and sugar cane fiber were all ranked above sawdust except for cost. Pens containing mineral-type litters were often dusty.

Built-up Litter

When all grain is hopper-fed it is important to have a litter that does not pack readily. Ground or crushed cobs, shavings, and sawdust meet this requirement and are well adapted to use as deep or built-up litter. Built-up litter provides a warm floor. For this reason it is especially well adapted for use in the northern sections of the country. If kept in good condition, it will absorb considerable moisture on days when the humidity is high and release it on following dry days. Maintaining deep litter takes much less labor, in spite of necessary stirring, than is required to renew shallow litter at frequent intervals in order to keep it reasonably dry. Finally, there is some advantage to be gained by the fact that fowls can pick up from the litter some products of intestinal synthesis which may simplify the feeding problem. Such built-up litter need not be cleaned out oftener than once a year, and some poultrymen continue to use it for 2 years or longer.

The usual procedure with deep litter is to start in the fall with 2 to 4 inches of dry litter and add to this gradually until the floor is covered 8 to 10 inches deep by about the first of December. After that no more litter is added, but the old litter is stirred occasionally to keep it in good condition. It may be removed and replaced with clean, shallow litter in the late spring, or it may be left in until the regular fall cleaning.

Adding hydrated lime to deep litter will help to keep it in workable condition so that it is less likely to pack down. The amount of lime used varies from 15 to 25 pounds each 100 square feet of floor area. It should be distributed evenly and then worked into the litter by stirring. Additional applications can be made from time to time as necessary.

Old built-up litter, whether limed or unlimed, contains fewer yeasts, molds, and bacteria than comparatively new litter. This is probably because of its increased alkalinity, pH of 8.0 or more.

Manure Handling and Disposal

Since poultry manure contains not only the feces but also the secretion of the kidneys, it is much richer in nitrogen than that of other domestic

Table 6–3.　Plant Food Value of Chicken Manure as Affected by Quick Drying as Reported by California Agricultural Extension Service

Kind of Manure	Water Content (%)	Solid Material (%)	Weight per Cubic Yard (pounds)	Approximate Percentage of Plant Food by Weight (Multiply by 20 to get pounds per ton.)				
				Nitrogen	Phosphorus		Potassium	
				N	P	(P_2O_5)	K	(K_2O)
Fresh	75	25	1750	1.0	0.6	1.3	0.6	0.7
Partially dried	50	50	—	2.0	1.1	2.6	1.1	1.4
Dry manure	25	75	800*	3.0	1.7	3.9	1.7	2.1
Completely dry	0	100	—	4.0	2.3	5.2	2.3	2.8

*The volume-weight relationship may vary considerably at the lower moisture content due to handling, compaction and biological decomposition.

Fig. 6–30. This 2,000-gallon vacuum tank can be filled with liquid manure in four minutes. Such equipment must have a full-opening, non-restricted slide valve. In the field, the load is blown out against a baffle to spread a strip 16 to 20 feet wide. (Courtesy of New York State College of Agriculture at Cornell University.)

Fig. 6–31. This spinner-type sprayer has an auger in the bottom. When used with a tractor and power take-off, it will handle either liquid or semi-liquid manure, spreading a strip 20 feet wide. (Courtesy of New York State College of Agriculture at Cornell University.)

animals. Analyses of the urine obtained from catheterized chickens show that as much as 80% of the urinary nitrogen is present as uric acid. Unless the manure is properly handled so that putrefaction is prevented, much of the uric acid will be changed to ammonium carbonate, with consequent loss of fertilizing value.

An egg farm with 100,000 layers will produce 12 tons of manure a day, well over 4,000 tons a year. The best method of disposal, when conditions permit, is to spread it on crop land. Typical spreading equipment is shown in Figures 6–25, 6–30, and 6–31. But with an operation involving a million hens at one location, and 120 tons or more a day, manure disposal can easily become the number one problem of the whole enterprise. Solutions will vary, depending on such factors as climate, and opportunity for marketing the final product as fertilizer. A plan that works well in the semiarid southwest may not be at all suitable for the north central or southeastern states.

Lagoons have been tried with varying degrees of success, but there may be serious odor problems, and final disposition may still require spreading on crop land. Oxidation ditches work nicely for small to medium-size operations, but they are relatively expensive to install and do not solve the problem of final disposal of the treated manure.

Fig. 6–32.   This equipment is useful for stirring poultry manure during air drying in areas of low rainfall. (Courtesy of California Agricultural Extension Service.)

Fig. 6–33. Poultry manure is composted in this insulated steel drum 100 feet long and 10 feet in diamter, with a capacity of 250,000 pounds of material. The drum revolves slowly, completing the composting in five to seven days, with an end-product that contains about 3 per cent nitrogen, 6 per cent phosphoric acid and 2 per cent potash. (Courtesy of Pacific Poultryman.)

Fig. 6–34. This drum-type dryer will handle the manure from as many as 100,000 layers. Other models are available for layer capacity up to 1,000,000. (Courtesy of Arnold Dryer Co., a subsidiary of The Heil Company.)

Some operators, even with as many as a million layers, have found it practicable to collect the manure in water-filled trenches under laying cages, and haul the liquid to nearby fields for spreading on pasture or crop land.

The present trend in the industry seems to be toward drying the manure by (1) piling it outdoors and stirring frequently (in dry climates, Fig. 6–32); (2) blowing air over the manure at floor level, followed by weekly or biweekly clean-out; or (3) using an artificial dryer (Figs. 6–33, 6–34). No matter what method is used, it is important that poultry houses be designed for easy removal of manure.

Not all poultrymen have crop land available, either on their own farms or on those of neighbors, and so have turned to other possible uses of the product. Tests have shown that it can serve as a useful feed for ruminants. Microorganisms in the rumen can convert the nitrogen in uric acid to amino acids, thus providing protein that can be utilized by cattle or sheep. Broiler litter, when it is made from a plant source, has also proved useful in experimental feeding. This practice is not widespread, however, since additives such as coccidiostats, antibiotics, or arsenicals that are subject to control by the Food and Drug Administration are often used in poultry feeds and may result in illegal residues in the carcasses of the animals fed such waste.

Some research has been done on recycling poultry waste by feeding it back to layers or broilers. There was no unfavorable effect on flavor of the eggs or meat so produced, but chickens cannot make efficient use of such nutrients as remain in the waste, and feces production by chickens so fed is increased. Such recycling reduces the disposal problem by no more than 25%, with no noticeable further reduction after repeated recycling.

Chapter 7

The Principles of Poultry Nutrition

The poultry industry converts about 14% of the feed grains and 40% of the high protein concentrates available annually in the United States to poultry meat and eggs. These products are preferred by consumers to the grains and protein concentrates, and therefore they are willing to support economically the industry that converts these plant products to human food. The cost of 20 grams of protein in the form of poultry meat has increased only 22% from 1956 to 1976, and the price of 20 grams of protein from eggs increased only 40%. During a similar period the price of protein from hamburger increased 133% and the price of pork chops 140%. The relative stability in poultry meat and egg prices is largely a reflection of improvements in efficiency of production. This has been due to a combination of improvements in poultry breeding and in feeding practices. Poultry feeding is currently based on a well-developed knowledge of the principles of poultry nutrition that has been put into extensive practice. This chapter discusses the principles of nutrition on which modern feeding practice is based.

NUTRIENTS

Many microorganisms have simple nutrient requirements. If they are given several inorganic elements, water, a source of nitrogen, and a simple source of energy, they can synthesize all the chemical compounds they require for growth and reproduction. Chickens, as is the case with all higher animals, have much more complex nutrient needs. More than 40 specific chemical compounds or chemical elements are nutrients that need to be present in the diet to support life, growth, and reproduction. These nutrients can be divided into six classes, somewhat according to their function and chemical nature: (1) carbohydrates, (2) fats, (3) proteins, (4) vitamins, (5) minerals, and (6) water.

191

The carbohydrates and fats are required primarily as sources of energy in the body. Energy is needed to maintain body temperature and essential body functions for body movement and for chemical reactions involved in synthesis of body tissue and the elimination of wastes.

Most of the nutrients are absolutely essential for life. A ration must supply every known essential nutrient in the proper amounts. A ration containing all the nutrients except one will not support life. If an insufficient amount of the nutrient is present, the ration may support life, but only slow growth in the young, or not support reproduction in the adult.

The same nutrients found in a ration are also found in the body tissues and eggs of the fowl. There is not, however, a direct transfer of nutrients from the feed to the animal tissue. The nutrients must be digested, absorbed, and rebuilt into the characteristic tissue of the animal. Poultry feeds are characteristically high in carbohydrates and relatively much lower in protein and fats. Body tissue and eggs, however, are composed chiefly of protein and fat with only small amounts of carbohydrate. Thus, the nutrients supplied in feed must undergo extensive processes of digestion and metabolism in the animal body.

Energy

Animals use much of their food to gain energy to maintain their body functions and to drive synthetic reactions of the body. Energy is measured in terms of heat units or calories. A gram calorie is defined as the amount of heat required to raise the temperature of 1 gram of water from 14.5 to 15.5° C. In nutrition, the kilogram calorie or kilocalorie, which is the heat equivalent to 1,000 gram calories, is the unit most often used along with the megacalorie, 1,000 kilocalories.

In Europe, the use of the joule is becoming more common, as it has been adopted by international bodies as the international unit of energy measurement. One kilocalorie is equal to 4,184 joules or 4.184 kilojoules. It is likely to be some time before the joule replaces the calorie as a measure of energy in applied animal nutrition, at least in the United States.

When an animal metabolizes an organic compound in its food, the end products of the metabolism are carbon dioxide, water, and energy. These are the same end products produced when the compound is burned in a flame. A basic law of animal energetics is the law of Hess, which states that the total amount of heat produced or consumed when a chemical system changes from one state to another is independent of the steps by which this change is brought about. Thus the potential energy available to an animal in a compound can be measured by burning it in a calorimeter and measuring the heat produced. This will give a valid estimate of the energy released to the animal when the compound is metabolized to

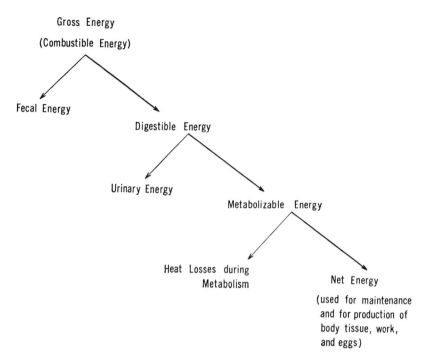

Fig. 7–1. Schematic representation of energy losses that occur when animals consume food.

carbon dioxide and water, even though the steps required to oxidize the compound are much more complex in animals than in a flame.

Although the potential or *gross energy* in feeds can be estimated in a calorimeter, the actual usefulness of a diet to animals requires further measurements because a feed must be digested, absorbed, and metabolized by animals before its energy can be released (Fig. 7–1). Therefore in some feeds a considerable portion of the gross energy may be lost before an animal has an opportunity to obtain net energy from it. The losses occur in undigested residues in feces, in nonmetabolized compounds excreted in the urine, and in losses as heat when food nutrients are being metabolized.

Measurements of the *metabolizable energy* value of individual poultry feed ingredients are most commonly used as an overall estimate of their nutritional value in feeding poultry. These energy measurements provide estimates of the ability of these feed ingredients to provide the energy needed by poultry to grow and produce eggs.

The metabolizable energy value of a pure carbohydrate such as starch and of a typical protein is about 4 kcal/g, whereas fats have a metabolizable energy value of about 9 kcal/g. The usefulness of these measurements of energy value of feed ingredients for poultry will be discussed in more detail in Chapter 9.

Carbohydrates

The basic units of carbohydrates are the simple sugars, called hexoses because each molecule contains 6 carbon atoms. Glucose, fructose, galactose, and mannose are the primary hexoses found in nature, with glucose being by far the most plentiful. Little free hexose is found in plants; mostly the hexoses are found in disaccharides, a combination of 2 hexose sugars, or in polysaccharides, polymers of many hexose molecules. The most important disaccharides found in nature are sucrose and lactose. Lactose is the sugar found in milk, and of course sucrose occurs in large amounts in such plants as the sugarcane or sugar beets. Maltose is a disaccharide produced during breakdown of starch but is not usually found free in large amounts.

The polysaccharides of major importance are starch, cellulose, pentosans, and several other more complex carbohydrates. Cellulose is the most abundant organic compound in nature; nearly 50% of the organic matter in plants probably consists of cellulose. Although cellulose and starch are both polysaccharides composed of glucose units, chickens possess only enzymes that can hydrolyze starch. Cellulose, therefore, is completely indigestible.

The carbohydrates useful to chickens are hexose sugars, sucrose, maltose, and starch. Lactose cannot be used by chickens because their digestive secretions do not contain the enzyme lactase that is necessary to digest this sugar. Feeds that are best sources of energy for chickens contain the types of carbohydrates that can be readily digested. Forages and fibrous feeds that contain large amounts of cellulose or other complex carbohydrates are of little value in feeding poultry.

The main function of carbohydrates in the diet is to provide energy to the animal. However, if all the carbohydrate is excluded from the diet, it is possible to produce a carbohydrate deficiency that is manifested primarily by poor growth. This carbohydrate deficiency can be produced only with special highly purified experimental diets.

Fats

True fats are glycerol esters of long-chain fatty acids. These are compounds of carbon, hydrogen, and oxygen, but they contain a much lower percentage of oxygen than carbohydrates. Because of this and their high content of hydrogen, fats have over twice as much energy value per unit weight as do carbohydrates. They are the most concentrated sources of dietary energy used in poultry feeding.

Table 7–1. Fatty Acids Commonly Found in Feed and Tissue Fats

Name	Designation*	Melting Point °C	Remarks
Saturated fatty acids:			
Lauric	12:0	43.6	Found in nature in large amounts in coconut fat
Myristic	14:0	53.8	—
Palmitic	16:0	62.9 ⎱	Most common saturated
Stearic	18:0	69.9 ⎰	fatty acids in animal tissue
Unsaturated fatty acids:			
Palmitoleic	16:1	1.5	
Oleic	18:1	14.0	Most common unsaturated fatty acid in animal tissue
Linoleic	18:2	—5.0	A dietary essential not synthesized by animals
Linolenic	18:3	—14.4	—
Arachidonic	20:4	—49.5	An essential fatty acid which can be synthesized from linoleic acid

* The first number indicates the number of carbon atoms; the number to the right of the colon refers to the number of double bonds.

The primary fatty acids found in feed and animal fats are shown in Table 7–1. These fatty acids vary in the number of carbon atoms they contain and in the number of double bonds. The fats that contain high percentages of saturated fatty acids (those with no double bonds), such as palmitic and stearic acid, are usually solids at room temperature. Fats such as beef tallow and lard are in this category. Other fats containing a high percentage of unsaturated fatty acids are liquid at room temperature and are usually called oils. Vegetable oils such as corn oil, soybean oil, and cottonseed oil are in this category.

Fat makes up over 40% of the dry egg contents and about 17% of the dry weight of a market broiler. Feeds are much lower in fats, most feed ingredients containing only 2 to 5% fat. Fats may be an economical source of energy for poultry rations and are frequently added to broiler and laying feeds today.

Fat is the form in which energy is stored in the body and in the egg. The percentage of fat seldom falls below 6 in the very lean animal, and it may rise as high as 40 in the very fat animal.

Other compounds are frequently found associated with fats in feeds and in the body. These include steroids, waxes, and phospholipids. Several vitamins fall in this category. Only the true fats, however, are good sources of energy for animals.

Most of the fatty acids in fats can be synthesized by the animal body. However, one fatty acid cannot be synthesized by body tissue. This fatty acid, linoleic acid, must be present in the diet of young growing chicks or they will grow poorly, have an accumulation of liver fat, and be more susceptible to respiratory infection. Laying hens fed diets severely deficient in linoleic acid will lay very small eggs that will not hatch well. Arachidonic acid, which can be synthesized from linoleic acid, can alleviate these deficiency symptoms if it is included in the diet. Linoleic and arachidonic acid are considered essential fatty acids because at least one of them must be present in the diet. The best sources of essential fatty acids are vegetable oils such as corn oil, soybean oil, or safflower oil. Rations based primarily on corn as the grain usually contain sufficient linoleic acid. However, if they are high in barley, milo, or wheat, some deficiency may be encountered in practical rations.

Proteins

Proteins are complex organic compounds containing carbon, hydrogen, oxygen, nitrogen, and sulfur. They are made up of more than 20 individual organic compounds called amino acids. A protein molecule can be visualized as a long chain or several chains of amino acids joined together by linkages termed peptide bonds. Since an average protein contains about 16% nitrogen, the protein content of a feed or carcass can be estimated by multiplying the nitrogen content by 6.25. Protein determined in this manner is referred to as crude protein.

The properties of a protein molecule are determined by the number, kind, and arrangement of the amino acids that make up the protein. With over 20 amino acids normally found in proteins, the possible arrangements into specific proteins are almost infinite. Proteins are also found combined with carbohydrates, fats, minerals, and other compounds that help to add to the complexity of proteins found in nature.

In feeding poultry, the products produced consist mainly of protein. On a dry-weight basis the carcass of an 8-week-old broiler is more than 65% protein, and the egg contents are about 50% protein. Typical broiler rations will contain from 22 to 24% protein, and a laying feed about 16 to 17%. There is a concentration of protein from diet to product in poultry feeding.

From the standpoint of nutrition, the amino acids that make up the protein are really the essential nutrients rather than the protein molecule itself. During digestion, dietary protein is broken down into individual amino acids, which are then absorbed and rearranged into specific proteins found in body tissues or in egg proteins. Body and egg proteins are made up of the same amino acids as found in dietary proteins, although the proportion of the amino acids in tissue proteins may be quite different from that in the diet.

The tissues of the chicken have the ability to synthesize some of the amino acids found in proteins, provided they have a satisfactory source of dietary nitrogen. Many of the amino acids cannot be synthesized by body

Table 7–2. The Amino Acids Required by the Growing Chick, and Their Classification as Dietary Essentials

Essential	Nonessential
Arginine	Alanine
Cystine	Aspartic acid
Histidine	Glutamic acid
Isoleucine	Glycine
Leucine	Hydroxyproline
Lysine	Proline
Methionine	Serine
Phenylalanine	
Threonine	
Tryptophan	
Tyrosine	
Valine	

tissues and must be provided in the diet. The amino acids that must be provided in the diet are often referred to as *essential* amino acids; those that can be synthesized are termed *nonessential*. This terminology refers only to their dietary essentiality because all are needed to make body and egg protein. The essential and nonessential amino acids are listed in Table 7–2. Two of the amino acids listed as essential can actually be synthesized by body tissue. Cystine can be synthesized from methionine, and tyrosine from phenylalanine. However, they cannot come from simpler compounds.

Certain other amino acids can be shown to be dietary essentials, under special conditions. Glycine, for example, can be synthesized, but not at a rate rapid enough to support maximum growth of a young chick. When a dietary protein low in glycine is fed to young chicks, their growth is improved if more glycine is added to the diet. When a highly purified diet that contains no protein and only essential amino acids is fed, glutamic acid must be added to supply nitrogen in the best form for synthesis of nonessential amino acids. Under similar conditions dietary proline may be helpful because the rate of synthesis may be too slow.

The amino acid requirements of growing chickens and laying hens are met in practice by proteins from plant and animal sources. The quality of a protein for animal feeding is determined by how closely the amino acid composition of that protein meets the dietary amino acid requirements of the animal. Usually it is necessary to choose more than one source of dietary protein and combine them in such a way that the amino acid composition of the mixture meets the dietary requirements of the animal.

The amino acids most difficult to supply in proper amounts from feed proteins are lysine, methionine, cystine, and tryptophan. They are sometimes referred to as critical amino acids because special attention must be given to meeting the requirements when formulating rations.

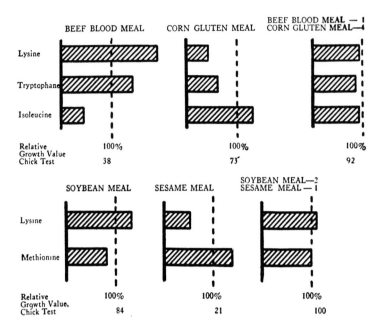

Fig. 7–2. Careful combination of protein sources will help to provide proper amino acid balance. (After Almquist. Courtesy of U.S. Industrial Chemicals, Inc.)

Although cereal grains are low in protein, they make up a large proportion of a usual poultry ration. Their proteins are particularly deficient in lysine and often in tryptophan. Protein sources to be used with cereal grains must be chosen so that they make up the deficiency of lysine and tryptophan in grain proteins.

Two examples of supplementary action between different proteins are shown in Figure 7–2. Beef blood meal is a rare example of a protein deficient in isoleucine, although it contains lysine and tryptophan in appreciable amounts. Corn gluten meal, on the other hand, contains a surplus of isoleucine, but a deficiency of both lysine and tryptophan. When the two are combined in the ratio of 1 part of blood meal to 4 parts of corn gluten meal, the mixture is nicely balanced with respect to all three amino acids, and in feeding tests it has proved to be much more effective in promoting chick growth than either blood meal or corn gluten meal alone. The second example involves lysine and methionine, as provided by soybean meal and sesame meal.

When formulating poultry rations the diet must supply all the essential amino acids in ample amounts, and sufficient total nitrogen for the chicken to synthesize the other amino acids needed.

An amino acid deficiency always is accompanied by slow growth or poor egg production. Feathering is often poor, and usually fat makes up a

Fig. 7–3. Arginine deficiency in a chick four weeks of age resulting in poor feathering and subnormal growth.

larger proportion of the carcass than in an adequately nourished chick (Fig. 7–3). Many amino acids are used for other purposes in the body in addition to being a component of protein. Tryptophan can be used to form the vitamin, nicotinic acid; tyrosine is needed for synthesis of the hormones, thyroxine and adrenalin, and formation of melanic pigments. Methionine is a methylating agent and can replace some of the dietary choline.

Vitamins

Unlike the other classes of nutrients discussed, vitamins as a group have few chemical characteristics common to all members. The classification of a substance as a vitamin is usually based on several criteria. Vitamins are organic compounds, usually not synthesized by body tissue, that are required in very small amounts in the diet. They are not major structural components of the body and most commonly function as coenzymes or regulators of metabolism. The 13 vitamins required by poultry are usually classified as fat-soluble or water-soluble. The fat-soluble vitamins include vitamins A, D, E, and K, and the water-soluble vitamins are thiamin, riboflavin, nicotinic acid, folacin, biotin, pantothenic acid, pyridoxine, vitamin B_{12}, and choline. Poultry do not require vitamin C in their diet because their body tissues can synthesize this vitamin.

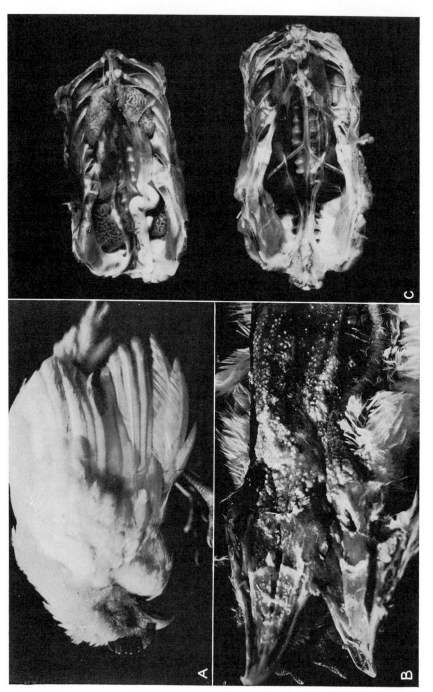

Fig. 7–4. Effects of vitamin A deficiency. A, An advanced stage. Note the exudate from the eye and the general ruffled appearance. B, The pharynx and esophagus are studded with pustules. C, Whitish urate deposits in the kidneys and the enlarged ureter of the upper specimen are compared with the normal condition below. (Courtesy of the National Research Council.)

All these vitamins are essential for life and must be provided in proper amounts for chickens to grow and reproduce. The egg normally contains sufficient vitamins to supply needs of the developing embryo. For this reason, eggs are one of the best animal sources of vitamins for the human diet.

In the following paragraphs some of the important characteristics of the individual vitamins will be discussed, together with symptoms of deficiency.

Vitamin A (Retinol). All animals require some dietary source of vitamin A or one of its precursors. Vitamin A is probably concerned with the synthesis of an important constituent of the epithelial tissues of the body. The visual pigments in the eye contain vitamin A, and most of us have learned that vitamin A helps to protect against night blindness. Deficiency symptoms in chicks include muscular incoordination, uric acid deposits in the ureters and kidneys, and general unthriftiness. Hens receiving insufficient vitamin A produce fewer eggs and eggs produced frequently do not hatch (Fig. 7–4).

Vitamin A is found in large amounts in fish liver oils, but the major sources found in nature are the plant precursors.

Chickens, like other animals, are able to transform the carotenes in plant tissues (fresh green forage, alfalfa meal, and the like) into vitamin A. They can also make similar use of the pigment cryptoxanthin in yellow corn. However, young chicks are rather inefficient in the conversion of vitamin A precursors to vitamin A. Vitamin A can now be readily produced by chemical synthesis. Vitamin A and its precursors are chemically unstable and can be readily oxidized to inactive compounds during storage of feeds or ingredients. It is a common practice to add commercially produced stabilized forms of vitamin A to rations for all classes of poultry to prevent vitamin A deficiency.

Vitamin D (Cholecalciferol). This vitamin is needed by animals for absorption and deposition of calcium. The effects of a deficiency of vitamin D are particularly severe in the young animal. Chicks receiving rations lacking or low in vitamin D soon develop rickets similar to that resulting from a deficiency of calcium or phosphorus. Growing bones fail to calcify normally and chicks are retarded in growth, unthrifty, and often unable to walk (Fig. 7–5).

Hens fed diets deficient in vitamin D lay eggs with progressively thinner shells until production ceases. Embryo development in such eggs is incomplete, probably because the embryo cannot efficiently use calcium from the eggshell.

If animals are exposed to ultraviolet light from sunlight or even from fluorescent lights, they will not develop vitamin D deficiency, even though they are receiving none in their diet. A steroid precursor of vitamin D present in secretions of the skin is converted to vitamin D by the ultraviolet radiation on the surface of the skin and is then reabsorbed

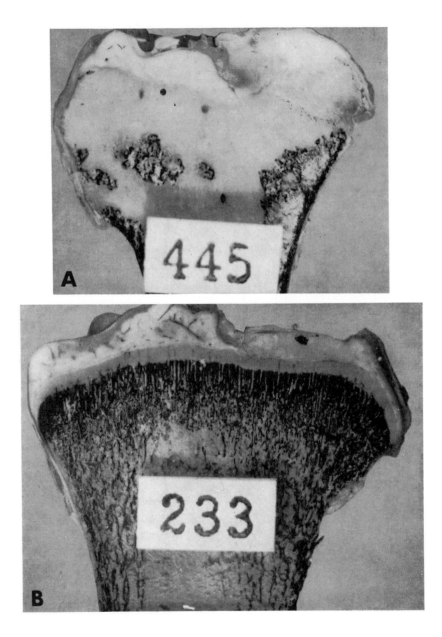

Fig. 7–5. Section of tibia of vitamin D-deficient chick (A) and a normal chick (B) after staining with silver nitrate and exposure to light. The bone from the rachitic chick has large areas of uncalcified cartilage.

through the skin or taken in by mouth as the chicken preens. Not over 0.1% of the sun's radiant energy in many parts of the country has antirachitic value, but even this small amount need be available to chicks for only 10 minutes daily to provide them with sufficient vitamin D.

Vitamin D occurs in several different chemical forms, the most common of which have been designated D_2 and D_3. Vitamin D_2 (ergocalciferol) is formed from the irradiation of ergosterol, a steroid found in plants; D_3 (cholecalciferol) is formed by irradiation of 7-dehydro-cholesterol, a steroid found in animal tissues. Vitamin D_3 is more than 30 times as efficient as vitamin D_2 for preventing rickets in chickens. Sources of vitamin D used in poultry feeding should be those whose potency has been assayed in chick experiments.

Vitamin D is now considered a hormone precursor, since in metabolism vitamin D_3 (cholecalciferol) is converted to the compound 1,25-hydroxycholecalciferol by action of enzymes in the liver and kidney. This compound is the active form of vitamin D which is transported in the blood to the intestine and bone where it affects calcium absorption and deposition.

Present-day poultry rations are supplemented with sources of vitamin D of known potency such as irradiated animal sterols, fish liver oils, or vitamin A and D feeding oils. Even though sunlight can provide vitamin D to chickens, present practices of brooding, rearing, and housing of laying hens, or broilers, make exposure of chickens to direct sunlight relatively rare.

Vitamin E (Tocopherols). A deficiency of vitamin E manifests itself in a wide variety of ways, primarily because several other dietary factors can affect the requirement of vitamin E.

In growing chicks, a deficiency can result in (1) encephalomalacia or "crazy chick disease," (2) exudative diathesis, an edema caused by excessive capillary permeability, or (3) muscular dystrophy. Encephalomalacia occurs when the diet contains unsaturated fats that are susceptible to rancidity (Fig. 7–6). Several antioxidant compounds, in addition to vitamin E, are also effective against encephalomalacia. Exudative diathesis is prevented by dietary selenium, and muscular dystrophy is a complex disease influenced by vitamin E, selenium, and the amino acids methionine and cystine. Encephalomalacia and exudative diathesis have been observed in commercial poultry flocks in many parts of the world.

Poor hatchability of fertile eggs is sometimes noted when rations for breeding hens are deficient in vitamin E. To prevent possible vitamin E deficiency, rations for growing chicks and breeding hens are usually supplemented with a source of vitamin E or a suitable antioxidant. Vitamin E can be chemically synthesized or isolated from vegetable oils. Supplements of vitamin E of guaranteed potency are available for feed supplementation. The most potent natural sources of vitamin E are whole grains and dried alfalfa meal.

Fig. 7–6.   Chick with encephalomalacia caused by vitamin E deficiency.

Vitamin K (Phytylmenaquinone; Prenylmenaquinone-4). Vitamin K is required by animals for the liver to produce certain blood proteins that are essential for the clotting of blood. Chicks fed a ration deficient in this vitamin are likely to have severe hemorrhages following a bruise or injury to any part of the body and may bleed to death from such minor injuries as those incidental to wingbanding. Mature fowls are not so easily affected, but when breeding hens are fed rations deficient in vitamin K, the chicks hatched from their eggs have very low reserves of the vitamin and are therefore susceptible to severe bleeding because of greatly prolonged blood-clotting time.

Although vitamin K is usually abundant in alfalfa meal, meat scraps, and fish meal, vitamin K deficiency has occasionally been observed under field conditions. Some modern poultry rations may have rather low levels of alfalfa meal and fish products and may contain certain feed additives that increase vitamin K requirements. Vitamin K is usually added to rations for growing chicks and breeding hens as a synthetic water-soluble form of vitamin K.

Riboflavin. This water-soluble vitamin is the one most likely to be deficient in rations made up of ingredients normally found in poultry feeds. For this reason all poultry rations should be supplemented with a

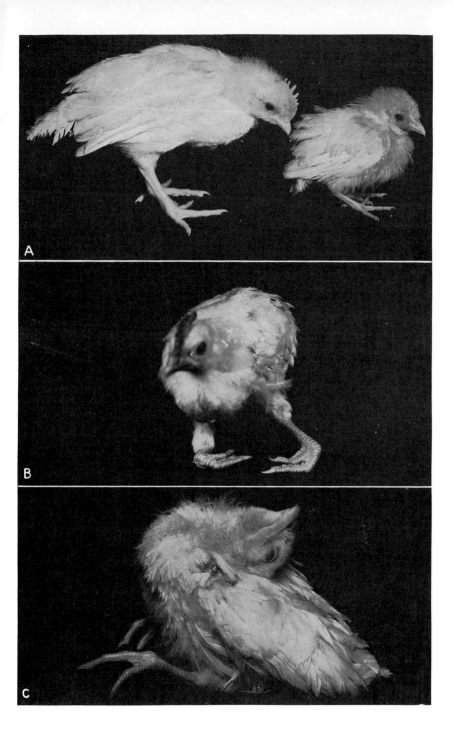

Fig. 7–7. Effects of vitamin deficiencies. A, Effect of nicotinic acid deficiency on chick growth. B, Riboflavin deficiency in a young chick. Note the curled toes and the tendency to squat on the hocks. C, Head retraction caused by a deficiency of thiamine. (Courtesy of the National Research Council.)

205

source of riboflavin. Chicks receiving rations deficient in this vitamin grow poorly and often have a peculiar lameness called curled-toe paralysis (Fig. 7–7B). Breeding hens need supplements of riboflavin in their rations, or their eggs will not hatch properly.

Riboflavin is chemically synthesized or produced during the production of antibiotics or other compounds by industrial fermentation processes. Concentrates of riboflavin from these sources can be used to supplement poultry rations. The most potent food sources of riboflavin are milk products, green forages, and fermentation by-products.

Thiamine. This is the vitamin formerly designated as B or B_1. A ration deficient in thiamine is inadequate for growth and brings on nervous disorders in both young and old birds, culminating in paralysis of the peripheral nerves (polyneuritis) (Fig. 7–7C).

The chick has a rather high requirement for this vitamin, but since it is found in abundance in whole grains which make up the major part of most poultry rations, the effects of a deficiency are not observed under practical conditions. Special sources of this vitamin are not normally added to a poultry ration.

Nicotinic Acid. This vitamin is essential for the normal growth and development of the chick (Fig. 7–7A). Since corn contains very little nicotinic acid, rations containing high percentages of corn may be deficient in this vitamin. Corn is also low in tryptophan, so there is little opportunity for conversion of this amino acid into nicotinic acid. A deficiency of the vitamin in young chicks results primarily in poor growth, an enlargement of the hock joint, and perosis. There are also a dark inflammation of the tongue and mouth cavity, loss of appetite, and poor feathering, and the chicks become nervous and irritable. With lowered feed consumption, growth is greatly retarded. Chemically synthesized nicotinic acid is generally added to rations for starting chicks and breeding hens. Among feed products, good sources of nicotinic acid include liver, yeast, wheat bran and middlings, fermentation by-products, and most grasses.

Pantothenic Acid. Young chicks fed a ration deficient in pantothenic acid show slow growth and extremely ragged feathering. Scabby lesions appear at the corners of the mouth, on the edges of the eyelid, and around the vent. In severe cases, they also are seen on the feet (Fig. 7–8B). A deficiency in the ration of breeding flocks results in lowered hatchability, and chicks that hatch frequently have high early mortality. Pure calcium pantothenate is often added to rations for starting chicks and breeding hens. In feeds the best sources are brewer's yeast, alfalfa, fermentation residues, and milk products.

Vitamin B_6 (Pyridoxine). This term is now used to include pyridoxol, pyridoxal, and pyridoxamine, all of which serve essentially the same function in metabolism. A severe deficiency results in jerky movements and aimless running about, followed by convulsions, complete exhaus-

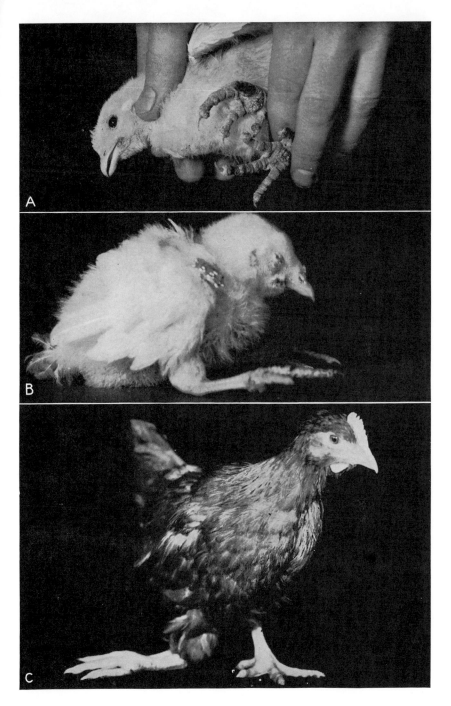

Fig. 7–8. Effect of vitamin deficiencies. A, Biotin deficiency. Note severe lesions on the bottoms of the feet, and the lesions at the corner of the mouth. B, Advanced stage of pantothenic acid deficiency. Note the lesions at the corner of the mouth, and on the eyelids and feet. C, Perosis or slipped tendon resulting from a deficiency of manganese. This condition may also be caused by a deficiency of choline, biotin, nicotinic acid or folacin. (Courtesy of the National Research Council.)

207

tion, and death. In mature fowls there is loss of appetite, followed by rapid loss of weight and death. Partial deficiency causes lowered egg production and poor hatchability

Since grains, wheat and rice by-products, milk products, meat and fish products, alfalfa, and many other feeds contain appreciable quantities of pyridoxine, a deficiency in ordinary rations is very unlikely.

Biotin. A deficiency of biotin in the ration of young chicks results in skin lesions similar to those observed in pantothenic acid deficiency (Fig. 7–8A). The feet become rough and calloused and later crack open and become hemorrhagic. Eventually, similar lesions appear at the corners of the mouth, and the eyelids may become granular.

When chicks are fed raw egg white, they develop biotin deficiency because biotin is inactivated by avidin, one of the proteins in egg white. An excess of biotin must be supplied under such conditions. Cooked egg white has no such unfavorable effect.

Biotin is also involved in the prevention of perosis, and is essential for good hatchability of eggs. The amount needed for good health and egg production in mature hens is apparently very small.

Biotin is rather widely distributed, and deficiencies are not likely to occur in chicks under practical feeding conditions. However, biotin deficiency has been observed in turkeys, and turkey rations arc often supplemented with this vitamin. Among the good sources are grains and their by-products, dried yeast, alfalfa meal, milk products, and green pasture grasses.

Choline. Along with manganese, folic acid, nicotinic acid, and biotin, choline is necessary for the prevention of perosis (slipped tendon) in young chicks (Fig. 7–8C). It is required in much larger amounts than other vitamins, but it is present in many commonly used feed ingredients. A lack of choline in rations for young chicks results in retarded growth, poor feed utilization, and perosis. Hens seem to be able to synthesize most of the choline they require. Along with methionine it serves as an important source of methyl groups which are necessary in metabolism. Rations for starting chicks may contain marginal amounts of choline, and choline concentrates are often added, especially for broilers. Good sources of choline include fish solubles, fish meal, soybean meal, and distillers' solubles. It is also present in appreciable amounts in meat scrap and dried milk.

Folacin (Pteroylmonoglutamic Acid). Folacin (folic acid) must also be included in any complete list of vitamins needed by the chicken. When young chicks are deprived of it they show retarded growth, poor feathering, and perosis. Colored plumage will be lacking in normal pigmentation. A characteristic anemia is also present. Practical rations are rarely, if ever, lacking in adequate amounts of folacin.

Vitamin B_{12} (Cyanocobalamin). Although the needs of the growing chick and the breeding hen are most critical, vitamin B_{12} is required by all classes of poultry. It is found in nature only in animal products or products of bacterial fermentation and is not found in plants. Therefore, rations containing only small amounts of animal products, such as fish meal or meat scrap, will be low in vitamin B_{12}. This vitamin is usually included in rations for starting chicks and breeding hens in the form of a commercially available vitamin B_{12} concentrate, especially if the ration is low in animal protein products.

Vitamin B_{12} contains cobalt and is the only form in which cobalt is useful in the rations of nonruminant animals. Ruminants are able to produce their own B_{12} by the action of microorganisms in the rumen, provided some source of cobalt is included in the ration.

Minerals

In addition to the carbon, hydrogen, nitrogen, and sulfur found in the organic constituents of an animal body, many other chemical elements are required nutrients. These are usually designated as minerals. The elements known to be required in the diet of poultry are calcium, phosphorus, sodium, potassium, magnesium, chlorine, iodine, iron, manganese, copper, molybdenum, zinc, and selenium. Cobalt is required only as a constituent of vitamin B_{12}. Nonruminant animals cannot synthesize vitamin B_{12} using an inorganic source of cobalt.

Calcium, phosphorus, sodium, potassium, magnesium, and chlorine are usually designated as the major elements required, since they must be present in the diet in relatively large quantities. Calcium, for example, is required in amounts up to 1% of the diet for growing chickens and over 3% for laying hens, whereas magnesium is needed at about 0.03 to 0.05% of the diet. The remaining elements are needed in only trace amounts, and requirements for them are usually expressed in parts per million or milligrams per pound of diet. Although they are required in small amounts, the lack of a trace element in the diet can be just as detrimental to an animal as a lack of one of the major elements.

Some evidence now suggests that the elements chromium, nickel, silicon, and vanadium may also be required trace elements. When steps are taken to meticulously exclude these elements from diets and the environment, some physiological responses can be observed when they are included in diets for rats or chicks. This list of required trace elements may continue to grow as experimental techniques are improved.

Calcium, Phosphorus, and Magnesium. These elements are important constituents of bone. The ash of a bone contains about 25% calcium, 12% phosphorus, and 0.5% magnesium. Lack of enough dietary calcium or phosphorus results in poor mineralization of bone. Deficient chicks have soft, easily bent bones that fracture readily. Marked deformity of the skeleton can be produced. This condition is called rickets in growing animals and can result from a deficiency of either calcium or phosphorus.

The shell of a large egg contains about 2 grams of calcium in the form of calcium carbonate. For this reason, calcium needs of laying hens are higher than for any other animal species. Lack of sufficient calcium in the diet of laying hens results in soft-shelled eggs and cessation of egg production.

In addition to the need for calcium and phosphorus as structural constituents, they also have other important functions. Phosphorus is essential in energy metabolism as a constituent of nucleic acids and for the activity of several enzyme systems. Calcium is also important in blood clotting and muscle contraction. Much of the body magnesium is found in bones, but it is also important as an activator of a large number of enzyme systems, particularly those involved in energy metabolism.

Sodium, Potassium, and Chlorine. These elements are the principal inorganic ions of body fluids. Sodium is found chiefly in fluids outside cells, such as blood, lymph, and extracellular fluid. Potassium is found chiefly inside the cells. These elements are important in maintaining acid-base and fluid balance of body tissues. Chlorine is also a constituent of the hydrochloric acid secreted by the proventriculus. A deficiency of any of these elements results in poor growth, dehydration of the body, and usually death, if the deficiency is sufficiently severe.

Trace Minerals. Trace minerals are required in small amounts by animals. Requirements for these are usually measured in parts per million or parts per billion in the diet. These elements often function as components or activators of enzymes. Some enzymes require a particular element as a part of the protein structure; others require that an inorganic ion be present for activity.

Deficiencies of trace elements produce some characteristic deficiency diseases. Iron is a constituent of hemoglobin, the oxygen carrier in blood, and is also a constituent of related compounds found in muscle and in oxidative enzyme systems. Iron deficiency causes an anemia. Iron is also needed for feather pigmentation in red feathered breeds. Zinc deficiency causes enlargement of the hock joint, shortening of the bones, and poor feather development (Fig. 7–9). Manganese deficiency leads to a twisting of the leg known as perosis and results in poor hatchability and embryo deformations in breeding hens (Fig. 7–8C).

Selenium deficiency results in exudative diathesis and degeneration of the pancreas in chicks and dystrophy of the gizzard and heart muscles in turkeys. Soils in the United States vary considerably in their selenium content. The soils of the Great Plains west of the Mississippi River generally have a good supply of selenium, and crops grown there contain adequate amounts of selenium. However, in the northwest and eastern United States, soils may be low in selenium, and crops produced on these soils contain low quantities of this element. Selenium deficiency has been observed in areas where soil levels are low.

Iodine deficiency also is an area problem. Soils around the Great Lakes

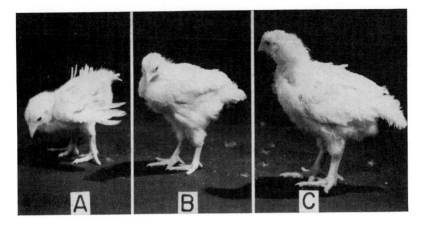

Fig. 7–9. Zinc deficiency. Chick A received a diet very deficient in zinc; chick B, a diet only slightly deficient; and chick C, a normal diet. A severe nutrient deficiency may result in characteristic deficiency symptoms; a milder deficiency may cause only slightly impaired growth rate.

are particularly low in iodine, and crops grown on these soils will be low in iodine. Lack of iodine can cause an enlargement of the thyroid gland called "goiter." Severe copper deficiency results in rupture of the aorta and severe hemorrhage in growing chicks as well as causing abnormalities of bone growth.

A deficiency of any one of several trace elements in the diet of a breeding hen affects hatchability of eggs and often results in characteristic abnormalities of the developing embryo.

Mineral Sources. In feeding poultry, special attention must be given to supplying sufficient calcium, phosphorus, sodium, chlorine, iodine, manganese and zinc in rations. The rest of the required minerals are usually widely distributed in ingredients used in poultry feeds so that no special supplements of these are needed. Calcium may be furnished as calcium carbonate in the form of limestone or marine shells. Phosphorus can be obtained from inorganic phosphorus sources such as dicalcium phosphate or by using ingredients high in phosphorus, such as meat and bone scraps or fish meal. Sodium and chlorine can be supplied by common salt (sodium chloride), zinc oxide or carbonate is the usual source of zinc, and manganese sulfate or oxide is the usual source of manganese. Precise amounts of the required nutrients can be added to poultry feeds.

Water

The internal environment of an animal is basically a water medium in which transport of nutrients occurs, metabolic reactions take place, and from which wastes can be eliminated. Water makes up from 55 to 75% of the body of chickens, depending on maturity. Young chickens contain more water as a percentage of their body weight than do older ones. Eggs are made up of about 65% water.

Because water makes up such a large proportion of the body, it is essential for life. Nutrients are transported, wastes are eliminated, and body temperature is maintained with the help of the water in the body. The evaporation of water from the lungs is one of the main methods chickens have of getting rid of excess body heat. Chickens must consume about 2 to 2.5 grams of water for every gram of feed consumed during the starting and growing period and from 1.5 to 2.0 grams of water per gram of feed as laying hens. Since an average poultry ration contains no more than 10% water, a good supply of clean drinking water is essential for poultry and egg production.

Feed Additives

Poultry feeds often contain substances that are added for purposes not directly concerned with nutrient requirements of the animal. An antioxidant, for example, may be used to prevent rancidity of the fat in the diet or to protect nutrients from being destroyed by oxidation. A large number of poultry diseases may be treated or prevented by including certain medications in the feed.

Some feed additives are used to stimulate growth rate of young chickens, although these substances are not nutrients. The most important growth-stimulating compounds used are the antibiotics.

Antibiotics are used widely in human medicine, as well as in the treatment of certain animal diseases. It has been demonstrated many times, however, that their addition to diets for poultry will often improve the rate of gain and feed efficiency of young growing chicks. The growth response obtained from antibiotics appears to be related to the control of unidentified, weakly pathogenic bacteria that reside primarily in the digestive tract. For this reason, the influence of the antibiotic is often referred to as a disease level effect. When chicks are grown in clean quarters in which chicks have not been housed before or under germ-free conditions in the laboratory, the usual growth improvements from the use of antibiotics are not obtained.

The growth-stimulating levels of antibiotics are usually considered to be from 5 to 10 grams of an antibiotic per ton of feed. Use of additives in poultry feeds is closely regulated in the United States by the Food and Drug Administration of the Department of Health, Education, and Welfare. In other countries comparable regulatory agencies exist. The various feed additives, as well as the conditions under which they may be used, are closely monitored, and care must be taken that they are used properly. Other compounds that affect the disease level of the organism are also used as growth stimulants; the most widely used of these are certain arsenic compounds.

DIGESTION

Before animals can use any of the nutrients found in food, the food must undergo a process of digestion. This is primarily the splitting of large molecules, such as proteins, fats, and carbohydrates, into simpler components by chemical processes involving the addition of a molecule of water to the bonds that are broken when simpler substances are released. Digestion is therefore essentially a process of hydrolysis.

Digestion is accomplished by enzymes that are found in the intestinal tract. Digestive enzymes are remarkable in that they are able to bring about, at body temperatures in dilute solutions and neutral pH, reactions requiring much more strenuous conditions to accomplish in the laboratory. To hydrolyze protein in the laboratory requires several hours of boiling with strong acids, yet the digestive enzymes accomplish it in the body in a very short time.

The digestive enzymes found in the intestinal tract are listed in Table 7–3, along with their locations and substrates.

The major part of all digestion in the chicken occurs in the small intestine. Starch digestion begins in the mouth, continues in the crop, and is completed in the small intestine. Glucose, the end product of starch digestion, is absorbed in the small intestine. The disaccharides, maltose and sucrose, can also be digested to simple sugars in the small intestine.

Table 7–3. The Digestive Enzymes of the Chicken

Where Found	Substrate	End Product
Mouth		
Amylase	Starch	Glucose, maltose, dextrins
Proventriculus		
Pepsin	Protein	Peptides
Small intestine		
Produced by pancreas		
Amylase	Starch	Glucose, maltose, dextrins
Lipase	Fat	Fatty acids, monoglycerides
Trypsin		
Chymotrypsin	Proteins	Amino acids, small peptides
Elastase		
Carboxypeptidase		
Produced by intestinal mucosa		
Oligo-1,6-glucosidase	Dextrins	Glucose
Maltase	Maltose	Glucose
Sucrase	Sucrose	Glucose and fructose
Amino peptidase,		
dipeptidases	Peptides	Amino acids

Fats also are digested in the small intestine. Fat digestion requires the presence of bile salts produced by the liver and stored in the gallbladder. The bile is released when the gallbladder is stimulated by the presence of food in the intestine. Pancreatic lipase digests triglycerides into fatty acids and monoglycerides. These interact with bile salts to form minute particles termed *micelles* which solubilize the products of fat digestion so they can be absorbed.

More enzymes are needed for protein digestion than for the other nutrients because each enzyme is specialized to hydrolyze certain linkages in protein molecules. The combined action of all these enzymes first degrades protein molecules to smaller fragments called peptides and then to amino acids. The amino acids are the products of digestion that are absorbed by the animal.

The vitamins and minerals normally do not require digestion as such, although some bound forms of vitamins are released from food during digestion.

The products of digestion are absorbed in the small intestine. They are transported across the intestinal cell membranes by specialized transport systems that ensure rapid and complete absorption of digested nutrients.

Bacterial Digestion

Ruminant animals such as cattle and sheep have a specialized portion of the digestive tract (rumen) where digestion by enzymes produced by microorganisms can take place. Thus ruminants, through the action of these microorganisms, are able to digest cellulose and other complex carbohydrates that are essentially undigested by the chicken. Chickens do not possess a specialized portion of their digestive tract where bacterial digestion of food components can take place efficiently. The passage of food through the digestive system of the chicken is rapid, and the only location where bacterial digestion can occur to any extent is in the ceca. There are many bacteria in the ceca and some digestion of cellulose and other complex carbohydrates and foods can occur in this organ. However, only a relatively small amount of the total food consumed by the animal actually enters the ceca, and digestion in that organ is of little importance in the fowl.

Metabolism

Animals consume food to obtain compounds needed to produce energy or to gain substrates for synthesis of important body components. Thus, all absorbed nutrients must undergo reactions mediated by body enzymes that are directed toward these ends (Fig. 7–10).

When 1 mole of glucose is metabolized by an animal to CO_2 and H_2O, 673 kilocalories of energy are made available to the animal to maintain

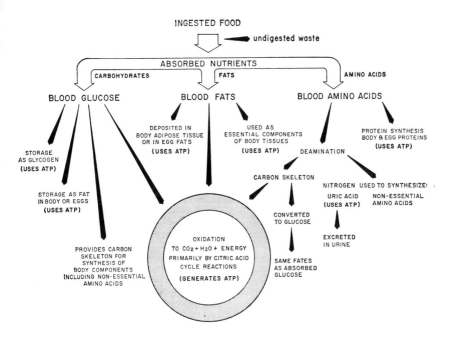

Fig. 7–10. The major fates of absorbed nutrients in metabolism.

body temperature, to use for synthetic reactions, or to provide energy for muscular work. This energy from glucose is not released all at one time as would be the case if glucose were burned in fire. Energy is released in metabolism stepwise as glucose undergoes a series of reactions, which at any one time release a small amount of the energy of the glucose molecule. In the conversion of glucose to CO_2 and H_2O about 17 compounds are formed as intermediates.

Much of the energy released in the metabolism of glucose is converted to heat, which, if not needed to keep the animal warm, is largely wasted. About 45% of the energy released during glucose oxidation can be captured by the animal as chemical energy trapped in the high energy phosphate compound, adenosine triphosphate (ATP). The ATP can provide energy needed for synthetic reactions, such as fat and protein synthesis, or immediate energy needed for muscle contractions. In this way metabolism couples reactions in which energy is released from nutrients with reactions that require energy. Animals are quite efficient in using energy released by metabolism for synthesis of body tissue.

Enzymes in the body can also release energy from fats and portions of amino acid molecules. In fact, the final metabolism of proteins, fats, and carbohydrates to CO_2 and H_2O and energy occurs largely through a common series of reactions known as the citric acid cycle.

Fate of Absorbed Carbohydrates

The end products of carbohydrate digestion are monosaccharides, mainly glucose, fructose, mannose, and some galactose. These sugars are all converted to glucose for metabolism.

Relatively little glucose is present in the body at any one time. Blood of chickens contains about 200 to 250 mg of glucose per 100 ml of blood. Glucose can be stored as glycogen in muscle and liver, but the body can store only small amounts of this "animal starch." When energy intake in the form of carbohydrate exceeds the needs of the animal for immediate energy or for storage as glycogen, it can be converted to fat and stored in body adipose tissue. In chickens, fatty acids are synthesized from carbohydrates only in the liver from which they must be transported to adipose tissue or the ovary. Carbohydrates also are a major source of the carbon "skeletons" used to synthesize the many organic compounds that make up the body. The fates of absorbed carbohydrates in the body are summarized in Figure 7–10.

Fate of Absorbed Fat

Fats can be readily oxidized to CO_2, H_2O, and energy by animals. Fats are concentrated sources of energy, with about 2.25 times as much potential energy to be released during their metabolism as carbohydrates. Absorbed fats also can be stored directly in adipose tissue or transferred to egg fat. For this reason the fatty acid composition of body and egg fats reflects the composition of the dietary fat, especially when high levels of fat are included in the diet of chickens. When low levels of dietary fat are ingested, tissue fat that is synthesized has a composition characteristic of the species. In chickens, depot fat synthesized from carbohydrate is relatively soft, containing high quantities of oleic acid. Fats are also important constituents of the body structure. Fatty acids are important components of most cell membranes. The major fates of absorbed fats are shown in Figure 7–10.

Fate of Absorbed Amino Acids

Amino acids absorbed from the intestine are used primarily for protein synthesis. If the dietary mixture of amino acids has a composition similar to that of the protein being synthesized, the synthesis of body and egg protein can be efficient. However, if the dietary protein has a different amino acid composition from that of the tissue protein to be synthesized, considerable metabolic rearrangement of the dietary nitrogen must occur. The nitrogen from excesses of essential amino acids can be removed and used to synthesize nonessential amino acids, or it can be used to synthesize uric acid and be excreted in the urine. If the amino acid mixture absorbed is deficient in an essential amino acid, little protein synthesis can occur. The amino acids are degraded, with the nitrogen excreted as uric acid, and the carbon in the amino acids is oxidized to CO_2, H_2O, and energy or converted to glucose or fat. This is a wasteful process. Diets deficient in amino acids are used inefficiently by growing chicks and laying hens. The general fates of absorbed amino acids are indicated in Figure 7–10.

Chapter 8

The Feed Ingredients

The unprecedented spread of intensive poultry production over the world has been an accompaniment of other striking changes in world agriculture. The so-called green revolution has led to tremendous increases in agricultural production of grains and oil seed crops throughout the world. This has made feed crops available to form the basis of poultry rations so that these crops can be transformed into eggs and poultry meat, two prized forms of animal protein in economically developed and developing areas of the world. The United States is particularly fortunate in the wide variety and quality of feed ingredients that are available to support its large poultry industry.

Rations must be designed to furnish the nutrients needed by poultry to grow and lay eggs. These rations are composed of ingredients whose components can be digested and absorbed by poultry so that the nutrients they contain can be useful.

In general the major sources of nutrients in poultry feeds are grains, oil seed meals, meat packing by-products, fish meals, and by-products of the processing of grains for human consumption, such as wheat, rice, and corn-milling by-products. In addition, many other products available in lesser quantities are useful. Yeast, distillery by-products, milk-processing by-products, and alfalfa meals are useful in poultry rations. For nutrients difficult to supply with natural ingredients, synthetic sources are available.

Ingredient Composition Tables

The value of an ingredient for feeding poultry can be estimated by its metabolizable energy value, obtained by appropriate energy balance experiments, and by the content of important nutrients determined by chemical analysis.

218

Many analytical data for potential feed ingredients have been accumulated which can be summarized in tables of nutrient composition. These tables list average nutrient composition of an ingredient. Since it is not possible to analyze completely each lot of a feed ingredient to be used in a ration, nutrient composition tables provide the basic information on which to base ration formulation. Such a listing of nutrient composition is given in Table 8–1.

The analytical data are shown for the protein, energy, calcium, available phosphorus, critical amino acids, fat, and fiber content of some 40 common poultry feed ingredients. Other nutrients such as vitamins and trace elements are routinely supplemented in poultry feeds, and levels of these nutrients are not always calculated from ingredient composition.

Cereal Grains and By-products

Grains represent the major sources of energy in poultry feeds. They are high in starches that can be readily digested by poultry. Grains are relatively low in protein and are deficient in the amino acids lysine and tryptophan. They are low in minerals, particularly sodium, calcium, and available phosphorus. The characteristics of the grains used in poultry feeding are summarized in Table 8–2.

Corn and milo are by far the most common grains used in poultry rations in the United States. Corn is highest in metabolizable energy value of the cereal grains, but milo is only slightly lower. The choice of grains to be used is based primarily on relative cost per unit of metabolizable energy provided.

Corn as an energy source in poultry rations has certain specific advantages. In addition to its high energy content, yellow corn is a good source of xanthophyll pigments that cause yellow coloration of shanks and skin of broilers and yolks of eggs. In addition, some of these pigments can be converted to vitamin A by the intestinal mucosa of animals. Corn contains about 4% fat which is 50% linoleic acid, making it a good source of this essential fatty acid in poultry rations.

Corn is graded in commerce from No. 1 corn, the best grade, to No. 5, plus a grade termed sample grade—the lowest grade. The grades of corn vary depending on the moisture content, the number of cracked, moldy, soft, or broken kernels, and the amount of foreign material present. The data in most composition tables refer to No. 2 corn, the most common grade in commerce.

Although corn protein is deficient in lysine, plant breeders have found that corn carrying the gene termed "opaque-2" has a much higher lysine and tryptophan content than normal corn. If commercial hybrids can be produced carrying this gene, the quality of corn protein can be greatly increased.

Milo is widely used in poultry rations and can replace corn provided the

Table 8–1.　Composition of Selected Poultry Feed Ingredients

Feedstuffs	Protein %	Metabolizable Energy kcal/lb	Metabolizable Energy kcal/kg	Fat %	Crude Fiber %	Calcium %	Available Phosphorus %	Methionine %	Cystine %	Lysine %	Tryptophan %	Arginine %
Alfalfa meal, dehydrated	17	720	1580	3	24	1.3	0.24	0.28	0.32	0.65	0.23	0.6
Bakery product, dehydrated	11	1700	3740	10	1	0.05	0.15	0.14	0.17	0.25	0.12	0.52
Barley, irrigated, or adequate rainfall	11.5	1250	2750	1.9	6	0.08	0.17	0.18	0.18	0.5	0.18	0.53
Blood meal	80	1300	2850	1.6	1	0.28	0.22	0.9	1.4	6.9	1.1	3.5
Brewer's dried grains	26	800	1760	6.2	15	0.27	0.15	0.4	0.3	0.9	0.4	1.3
Cassava flour	1.8	1350	2970	1.3	1.8	0.3	0.12	—	—	—	—	—
Coconut oil meal (copra meal)	21	700	1540	1.8	15	0.2	0.2	0.29	0.3	0.6	0.2	2.7
Corn, dent, No. 2, yellow	8.7	1560	3430	3.9	2	0.02	0.1	0.18	0.18	0.2	0.1	0.5
Corn gluten feed	22	760	1670	2	9	0.2	0.2	0.3	0.32	0.4	0.2	0.8
Corn gluten meal, 60%	60	1750	3850	3	2	—	0.2	1.6	0.9	1.4	0.3	2.2
Cottonseed meal, solvent	41	830	1820	1.9	13	0.2	0.4	0.6	1.0	1.6	0.5	4.4
Distillers' dried solubles (corn)	27	1320	2810	9	4	0.4	1.25	0.6	0.3	0.9	0.2	1.0
Fats, stabilized:												
Animal tallow		3200	7010	100								
Lard		3900	8600	100								
Fat product (hydrolyzed and intact vegetable oils and animal fats)		3700	8180	100								
Vegetable oils, stabilized: Corn, soybean, peanut, sunflower, rice bran, olive, safflower, and sesame oils		4050	8950	100								

					1.5	0.2	0.6	0.5	3.00	1.5	0.5	5.6
Coconut oil		3900	8600	100								
Vegetable refinery lipid (acid-ulated soapstock)		3500	7720	100								
Feathers, hydrolyzed poultry	84	1050	2310	2.5								
Fish meals:												
Anchovetta	65	1200	2640	4	1	4	2.8	1.8	1.0	5.2	0.8	3.4
Herring	72	1450	3190	10	1	2.9	2.2	2.0	1.2	6.4	0.9	6.8
Menhaden	60	1350	2970	8	1	5.5	2.8	1.8	0.94	5.0	0.8	3.8
Meat and bone meal, 50%	51	900	1980	10	2	10.6	5.1	0.65	0.6	3.5	0.3	3.5
Milo (and other sorghum grains)	11	1480	3250	2.8	2	0.03	0.1	0.13	0.4	0.2	0.12	0.36
Oats, 34 lb. bushel weight	12	1190	2620	4.5	11	0.1	0.15	0.18	0.5	0.5	0.16	0.8
Peanut meal, solvent	42	1000	2200	1.9	17	0.2	0.2	0.38	0.6	1.5	0.41	4.2
Poultry by-product meal	58	1325	2910	13	2.5	3.6	2.2	1.1	1.0	2.6	0.46	3.8
Rapeseed meal	35	1000	2200	7	12	0.9	0.35	0.66	—	1.9	0.45	2.0
Rice bran	13	740	1630	13	12	0.12	0.21	0.29	0.4	0.8	0.1	1.4
Safflower meal, decorticated	42	770	1690	1.5	9	0.4	0.3	0.63	0.67	1.3	0.58	3.6
Sesame meal	48	1180	2600	5	5	2	0.3	1.4	0.6	1.3	0.78	4.8
Soybean meal, 44%	45	1020	2240	0.9	6	0.32	0.29	0.65	0.67	2.9	0.6	3.2
Soybean meal, dehulled	49	1150	2530	0.8	3	0.26	0.24	0.73	0.8	3.2	0.65	3.8
Sunflower seed meal, solvent	43	800	1760	2.8	14	0.4	0.3	1.65	0.4	1.7	0.5	3.5
Wheat, hard, northern US & Canada	14	1480	3250	2.2	2.5	0.04	0.13	0.2	0.25	0.45	0.18	0.7
Wheat, soft, east and west US	10	1480	3250	2	2.5	0.05	0.13	0.13	0.2	0.3	0.12	0.4
Wheat bran	15	590	1300	4	10	0.14	0.33	0.17	0.2	0.5	0.27	0.8
Wheat middlings, midwest US	17	820	1800	4.6	8	0.15	0.23	0.17	0.2	0.6	0.2	0.9
Whey, dried	13	870	1910	0.8	0	0.9	0.8	0.15	0.3	0.9	0.15	0.4
Yeast, brewers dried	45	840	1850	5	3	0.13	0.5	0.75	0.55	3.1	0.5	2.3

Table 8-2.   Characteristics of Grains Used in Poultry Feeding

Grain	Bushel Weight lb	Metabolizable Energy kcal/lb	Metabolizable Energy kcal/kg	Protein %	Comments
Corn	56	1560	3430	8.7	Good source of vitamin A precursors, xanthophyll pigments, and linoleic acid
Milo	56	1480	3250	11	May replace corn but lacks xanthophyll pigments and is lower in linoleic acid
Wheat	60	1480	3250	10–17	Protein content varies as to area grown. Protein content of wheat used must be known
Barley	48	1250	2750	11.5	Barley grown in western dry-farming areas may be improved by water or enzyme treatment
Oats	32	1190	2620	12	Normally too low in energy for use in poultry feeds except when low-energy high-fiber feeds are desired

differences in amino acid composition, linoleic acid content, and pigmentation value are taken into consideration. Barley is a widely used grain in poultry feeding in parts of the world where corn and sorghums are not readily available. Barley is considerably lower in metabolizable energy than corn, and for this reason the price of barley ordinarily must be considerably below that of corn before its use is economical. The nutritional value of barley grown in dry-farming areas of the northwestern United States has been shown to be improved by water soaking or by certain enzyme treatments. Such effects are not observed in barley grown in other parts of the United States.

Oats are ordinarily too low in energy value to be an economical ingredient in poultry rations. However, if feeds low in energy value are desired, oats often serve as a useful ingredient.

Considerable wheat may be used in poultry rations when it is economically priced. Wheat is variable in protein content, depending on the type and the area in which it is grown. Hard midwestern or Canadian wheat may run as high as 17% protein, while that produced in eastern states may contain from 10 to 13% protein. When wheat is used, fine grinding should be avoided to prevent the wheat flour from sticking to beaks.

When wheat is milled in the course of flour manufacture, several fractions of the wheat are produced that are widely used in animal feeds. Although the energy value of these products is low compared to that of the grains, in some areas their price is often low enough that appreciable quantities may be used economically in poultry rations. These products include wheat bran, wheat mill run, wheat middlings, wheat shorts, and wheat red dog. Wheat red dog is high in energy value and when available is often an economical source of energy in poultry feeds. Wheat middlings is often found as an ingredient in poultry rations that are rather low in metabolizable energy content.

By-products of corn milling include hominy feed, corn germ meal, and corn gluten feed. Corn gluten meal is high in protein and will be discussed under protein sources. Hominy feed is a mixture of corn bran, corn germ, and part of the starchy portion of corn kernels as produced in the manufacture of pearly hominy, corn grits, or table corn meal. It must contain at least 5% crude fat. Hominy feed is often one of the most economical sources of linoleic acid in feeds, and its price occasionally makes it an economical energy source.

Fats

Considerable quantities of fats are used in poultry feeding, primarily as potent sources of energy. Fats normally contain two to three times as much metabolizable energy per unit of weight as grains. The main limitation on the use of fats in feeding, other than cost, is the physical nature of the ration containing fat. Rations high in fat tend to cake and do not flow readily. The usual practical limit for adding fats is 3 to 5% of the diet, although with special techniques pelleted diets may contain as high as 7 or 8% added fat. The major fats available for feeding are the animal fats produced as by-products of meat packing. Those that are based primarily on fat obtained from slaughter of cattle are tallows, whereas those containing considerable quantities of softer fats such as lard are termed greases. Various other fats available for animal feeding come from the processing procedures commonly used in production of edible fats or soap. These are often described as hydrolyzed animal fat or animal and vegetable fats. Various vegetable oils available for animal feeding are normally more expensive than animal fat. They are somewhat more digestible than animal fats and have a slightly higher metabolizable energy value.

Fats containing unsaturated fatty acids may not be stable. They may undergo oxidative rancidity which can result in the destruction of vitamins A, D, and E. This may be prevented by stabilizing the fats with antioxidants.

In addition to their primary importance as sources of energy, fats are also sources of linoleic acid. Vegetable oils, lard, or mixtures of animal and vegetable fats are the best sources of this fatty acid, whereas tallow is a poor source.

Table 8–3. Common Protein Sources Used in Poultry Feeding

Ingredients	Protein usual %	Metabolizable Energy kcal/lb	Metabolizable Energy kcal/kg	Limiting Amino Acids	Comments
Meat and bone meal	50	900	1980	Methionine, cystine	Good source of calcium and phosphorus. Protein quality is variable
Poultry by-product meal	58	1325	2910	None	Excellent protein if properly prepared
Fish meal	60–70	1200–1450	2640–3190	None	Good source of protein of variable quality. Contains Ca and P. Use limited to about 10% of diet to avoid fishy flavors
Hydrolyzed feather meal	84	1050	2310	Methionine, lysine, histidine, tryptophan	Poor quality protein. Limited use in poultry ration
Blood meal	80	1300	2850	Isoleucine	Often used as source of supplemental lysine
Cottonseed meal	41	830	1820	Lysine, methionine	Contains gossypol. Limited use in layer rations
Soybean meal, 44% protein	45	1020	2240	Methionine	Soybean meals must be properly heat-treated to destroy inhibitory factors
Soybean meal, dehulled	49	1150	2530	Methionine	This dehulled meal most commonly used in poultry rations
Peanut meal	42	1000	2200	Methionine, lysine	Should be checked for aflatoxin contamination, particularly when produced in semitropical humid areas
Corn gluten meal	60	1750	3850	Lysine, tryptophan	Used extensively to supply xanthophyll pigments to broiler finishing rations
Sesame meal	48	1180	2600	Lysine	Good plant source of methionine
Sunflower meal	43	800	1760	Lysine, methionine	Variable depending on maturity of seed at harvest
Safflower meal, decorticated	42	770	1690	Lysine, methionine	Must have hulls removed during processing
Rapeseed meal	35	855	1880	Lysine	Some varieties possess cyanogenic glucosides and goitrogenic compounds that limit levels that can be used
Coconut meal	21	700	1540	Lysine, methionine	In tropical areas often mold contaminated

Protein Sources

Since all grains and grain by-products are deficient in both amount and quality of protein, it is necessary to supply protein to poultry rations from other sources. The common ingredients for this purpose are the oil seed meals and certain animal protein concentrates (Table 8–3). The relative importance of the various high protein feeds is shown by the following figures for total consumption in the United States by all livestock, excluding work animals, for the years 1954, 1958, 1965, 1970, and 1976. The choice of a specific protein supplement used in a feed will depend upon its relative cost and its amino acid composition.

	1954	1958	1965	1970	1976
			1,000 Tons		
Soybean cake and meal	5,428	8,938	10,274	13,467	14,000
Cottonseed cake and meal	2,405	2,198	2,563	1,693	1,600
Tankage and meat meal	1,339	1,484	1,961	2,039	2,200
Corn gluten feed and meal	1,034	1,044	1,481	1,236	1,300
Fish meal and solubles	395	512	627	609	450
Linseed cake and meal	488	417	284	258	250
Copra cake and meal	182	148	109	99	—
Peanut cake and meal	18	75	108	173	200

These figures show the relative importance of soybean meal compared to other protein sources. The use of meat meals, fish meals, and corn-processing by-products has also increased during this period while the use of cottonseed meal and linseed meal has declined to some extent.

The sources of animal protein most commonly used in poultry feeding in the United States are meat-packing by-products, fish meals, and by-products of poultry processing. The plant sources of protein are obtained chiefly from certain oil-bearing seeds such as cottonseed, peanut, and soybean, as well as from by-products of corn milling such as corn gluten meal.

In some parts of the world, sunflower meal, sesame meal, safflower meal, and rapeseed meal represent important sources of protein for poultry feeding.

Meat Scrap. Meat meal or meat scrap consists of dry rendered residue from animal tissues. It should not contain more than traces of hair, hoof, horn, hide trimmings, blood meal, manure, or stomach content. If a meat meal contains more than 4.4% of phosphorus, it is designated either meat and bone meal, or meat and bone scrap. The usual meat product in poultry feeding is meat and bone scrap containing about 50% protein.

The proteins of meat products are good sources of lysine but are somewhat deficient in methionine, cystine, and tryptophan. Because of a high content of mineral matter, meat and bone scrap is relatively low in energy. However, rations for growing chicks containing fairly high amounts of meat and bone scrap often need little further supplementation of calcium and phosphorus. Meat and bone scrap can be used in poultry feeds at levels up to 8 or 9% of the ration. Higher levels should be avoided because the calcium and phosphorus content of the ration would become too high and the protein quality of meat meals is often variable.

Fish Meal. Fish meal is made from the tissues of undecomposed whole fish or fish cuttings which may or may not have had some of the fish oil removed. Fish meals usually contain 60 to 70% of proteins that are good sources of lysine and methionine. They supplement proteins from cereal grains particularly well, and provide considerable calcium and phosphorus in a ration. The metabolizable energy value of good quality fish meal is higher than that of most other common protein sources.

More than 4 million tons of fish meal are produced in the world annually, with the highest production in Peru and Chile in South America. In these countries, anchovetta meal containing about 65% protein is the principal product. In the United States, menhaden fish meal is the commonest meal produced on the Atlantic Coast and the Gulf of Mexico. Herring meals produced in Scandinavia, Iceland, and the east and west coasts of Canada are also important sources of fish meal.

When fish oil is present in the diet of poultry at levels greater than 1% of the diet, fishy flavors may develop in meat and eggs. Since most fish meals contain about 10% fish oil, fish meal should be limited to no more than 10% of the diet.

Poultry By-Product Meal. The official definition describes this product as the "ground dry rendered clean wholesome parts of the carcass of slaughtered poultry, such as heads, feet, undeveloped eggs and intestines, exclusive of feathers except in such trace amounts as might occur unavoidably in good factory practice. It should contain not more than 16% ash and not more than 4% acid insoluble ash." Considerable quantities of this material are now available for poultry feeding. It contains about 55% protein and is a good source of tryptophan and lysine. Poultry by-product meal can also be a good source of calcium and phosphorus.

Hydrolyzed Poultry Feathers. This product is the result of treating, under stream pressure, clean undecomposed feathers from slaughtered poultry. Not less than 80% of its crude protein content must consist of "digestible protein."

Feathers are indigestible unless processed prior to feeding. Feather meal does not have a balanced amino acid pattern for feeding poultry, since it is deficient in lysine, methionine, histidine, and tryptophan. This means that feather meal can be used only in limited amounts in poultry feeds.

Blood Meal. Ground dried blood is available in limited amounts as a source of protein. Its chief advantage is as a source of lysine, since its protein is high in lysine, provided the blood has not been overheated in the drying process. Blood proteins are unusual in that they are low in the amino acid isoleucine.

Other Animal Protein Sources. In addition to the main sources of animal proteins, a number of other animal products are available to a limited extent as protein sources in animal feeds. These include poultry hatchery by-product meal, whale meal, crab meal, liver and glandular meal, tankage, and certain milk products. The use of some of these animal products is limited because of the protein quality, amount available, or relative cost compared with the major sources of protein discussed.

Cottonseed Meal. This is the high protein residue remaining after extraction of the oil from cottonseed. Its use in feeding poultry is limited by the presence of a compound called gossypol, which can depress growth rate of young chicks or cause a characteristic discoloration of yolks laid by hens fed cottonseed meal. Low gossypol cottonseed meals (in which the gossypol has been inactivated or bound) are now available. Varieties of cotton are available with seeds nearly free of pigment glands that contain the gossypol. Meal made from this gossypol-free seed is an excellent source of protein for poultry feeding. Unfortunately this type of cottonseed meal is not being produced in quantity at this time.

The cottonseed meal used in poultry feeding normally contains 41 to 43% protein, relatively low in the essential amino acid lysine. If appreciable amounts are used, another protein source rich in lysine must be used to provide sufficient quantities of this essential amino acid in the ration.

Peanut Meal. This is the residue remaining after removal of most of the oil from peanut kernels by a mechanical or solvent extraction process. Expeller-processed peanut meal usually contains approximately 45% protein, whereas solvent-extracted meals may contain up to 50% protein, depending on the efficiency of the dehulling process. The protein in peanut meal is somewhat low in the essential amino acids methionine and lysine, and if it is used in poultry rations, other proteins or sources of these amino acids must be provided to properly balance the amino acid composition of the final protein mixture.

In some tropical countries where peanut meal is often produced, molds, particularly *Aspergillus flavus,* may grow on the peanut following harvest. This mold produces potent toxins that can cause high mortality, particularly when these meals are included in diets for ducks and turkeys. For this reason, care should be taken that peanut meals do not contain these aflatoxins.

Soybean Meal. This is by far the most important protein source used in poultry feeding today. It is produced by removing the oil from soybeans by a solvent extraction process. If soybean meal contains most of the soybean hull, it usually contains 44% protein, whereas dehulled soybean meal normally contains 49% protein. The dehulled meal is most commonly used in poultry feeding because it has a higher energy value than the meal containing 44% protein. Soybean meal is unique among major plant protein sources in that it is a good source of lysine. For this reason, soybean meal can be used in combination with cereal proteins to provide a high quality protein mixture for animal feeding. It is somewhat low in methionine and cystine, and rations composed mainly of corn and soybean meal often must be supplemented with methionine.

Soybean meal contains a number of substances that inhibit growth unless the meal is properly heat-treated. Heat treatment is a standard practice in the commercial production of soybean meal, to ensure a satisfactory source of protein for animal feeding.

Corn Gluten Meal. This is a by-product of the manufacture of corn starch or syrup by a wet milling process. It is the portion of the corn grain remaining after extraction of most of the starch and germ and removal of the bran. Corn gluten meal is now marketed in the United States primarily in the form of a meal containing 60% protein, although corn gluten meals with 41 to 43% protein also are produced. Proteins in corn gluten meal are deficient in lysine and tryptophan but are good sources of methionine. The use of this protein source is limited in rations already containing considerable protein from grains. Much of the pigment in the corn grain is concentrated in corn gluten meal. Large amounts of this ingredient are used as a source of yellow pigment for broiler skin and legs and for egg yolks.

Sunflower Meal, Sesame Meal, and Safflower Meal. In some parts of the world these oil seed residues represent important sources of protein. Sunflower seed, according to FAO statistics, is the second most important source of vegetable oil in the world, after soybeans. In 1976, 10,004,000 metric tons of sunflower meal was produced in the world, about one sixth as much as world soybean production. Eastern Europe and the USSR produced about 65% of the world total.

All of these protein sources are lysine-deficient, but sesame meal is a particularly good source of methionine. All of these meals may be rather high in fiber and low in metabolizable energy value unless special processing procedures are used to remove the seed hull from the meal.

Coconut Meal. In tropical countries coconut meal represents one of the most important available protein sources. It is not high in protein, averaging only 20%, and is rather low in energy. Mold growth often is a problem in tropical areas where coconut meal is produced. The quality of coconut meal can be improved if it is treated with sodium propionate. Provided the lysine and methionine deficiencies of coconut meal are corrected, and other good energy sources are available, coconut meal can provide useful protein for poultry.

Other Protein Sources. As world population pressures increase, the demand for good quality protein for both human and animal food increases. One source that may eventually be an important protein is derived from growing yeast on a wide variety of substances. Yeasts can grow on energy sources such as molasses, pentose sugars from paper processing wastes, and even from certain fractions of petroleum. Protein from yeast grown on petroleum fractions is already being produced for animal feeding in Europe in new plants constructed for this purpose. Yeast proteins are of generally good quality, although they are deficient in methionine. They are good sources of lysine. Because yeast contains fairly high levels of nonprotein nitrogen compounds, multiplying the nitrogen content of yeast by 6.25 often overestimates its true protein content.

Amino Acids

In addition to using protein supplements, it is possible to include amino acids in poultry feed as the individual chemical compounds. Lysine and methionine are both available to supplement poultry rations. Methionine may be used either in the form of DL-methionine or as methionine hydroxy analog.

Mineral Supplements

The mineral elements most likely to be deficient in rations for poultry are calcium, phosphorus, sodium, chlorine, manganese, and zinc. Rations composed of normal feed ingredients may be deficient in these elements unless special sources are supplied.

Calcium and Phosphorus Supplements. The most commonly used sources of calcium in a poultry ration are ground limestone and marine shells. Both of these are primarily calcium carbonate. Limestone especially intended for animal feeding should be used instead of agricultural lime. Certain limestones contain impurities that may prove detrimental when consumed in large amounts. Magnesium, present in large quantities in dolomitic limestone, is the major impurity found in limestone deposits.

Another widely fed source of calcium carbonate for laying hens is oyster shell, although other marine shells of similar composition are equally valuable. Often, both of these calcium supplements are used: ground limestone included in a laying feed to supply part of the calcium needed by the hen, and particles of oyster shell to supply the remainder of the calcium required. The oyster shell particles are retained by the gizzard and release calcium continually, even at night when lights are out and hens are not feeding.

The most important phosphorus sources in poultry feeding are dicalcium phosphate, defluorinated rock phosphate, and steamed bone meal. All are calcium phosphates which can supply both calcium and phosphorus. The calcium and phosphorus content of these supplements is shown in Table 8–4.

Table 8–4.   Calcium and Phosphorus Sources Available for Poultry Feeding

Mineral Sources	Calcium %	Phosphorus %
Bone meal, special steamed	29	14
Bone meal, steamed	24	12
Bone charcoal	27	13
Calcium carbonate	40	—
Calcium phosphates:		
Monocalcium phosphate, $CaH_4(PO_4)_2 \cdot H_2O$	16.9	24.6
Dicalcium phosphate, $CaHPO_4 \cdot 2H_2O$	23.3	18
Tricalcium phosphate, $Ca_3(PO_4)_2$	38.8	20
Dicalcium phosphate, feed grade	24–28	18–21
Curaçao Island phosphate	35	15
Defluorinated rock phosphate	33	18
Soft (colloidal) phosphate	15–18	9
Sodium phosphate monobasic, $NaH_2PO_4 \cdot H_2O$	—	21.8
Limestone	33–38	—
Oyster shell	37–39	—
Phosphoric acid, feed grade 76% pure	—	24

Sodium Chloride. Plant materials used in animal feeding are usually low in sodium and chlorine. Rations for nearly all farm animals are supplemented with a source of these elements. Sodium chloride, added as common salt, is usually included in poultry feeds at 0.25 to 0.50% of the diet. Feed ingredients grown in certain areas of the United States will contain relatively low amounts of iodine; a possible deficiency of iodine can be avoided by the use of iodized salt.

Trace Mineral Supplements. The elements manganese and zinc are normally supplied as manganese sulfate or manganese oxide and zinc carbonate or oxide. It has become common practice to supplement rations for all classes of poultry with these two trace elements. Other trace minerals required by poultry are not likely to be deficient in rations made up of the usual feed ingredients.

Vitamin Supplements

All the vitamins that may be deficient in poultry feeds can be added to the diet as chemically synthesized vitamins, or vitamins produced by fermentation processes. The vitamins are commercially available in pure form or as vitamin concentrates at relatively low cost, and they can be added to a poultry feed by means of a premix which supplies specified amounts of each vitamin.

Certain ingredients available for poultry feeding are potent sources of vitamins. These include yeasts, fish solubles, distillers' solubles, liver meal, alfalfa meal, and milk by-products.

Unidentified Growth Factors

When all the known nutrients are included in highly purified form in diets for young chicks or poults, some investigators have still reported improvements in the growth rate of animals fed certain complex feed ingredients. Those that will improve growth rate under these conditions are usually called sources of unidentified growth factors. It is a common practice to include sources of unidentified growth factors in rations for starting chicks, broilers, and breeding hens. These sources include distillers' dried solubles, condensed fish solubles, various fermentation by-products, dried whey, and dried yeast.

Dried Poultry Waste

The use of dried excreta from caged layers as a feed ingredient for poultry has been suggested by some as a means of disposal of poultry waste. Generally, dried poultry waste is high in calcium and phosphorus, contains 8 to 10% true protein, considerable non-protein nitrogen and has a low metabolizable energy value (300 to 500 kcal/lb). Treated as any other low energy ingredient, it can be used in poultry rations without detrimental effects. When dried poultry waste is fed to laying hens, about 70% of the dry matter from the waste consumed is excreted in the feces. For this reason, feeding poultry waste is not a good method of poultry waste disposal.

Chapter 9

The Nutrient Requirements of Poultry

Nutrient requirements are known more precisely for poultry than for any other species of animal. This has come about because of the economic importance of the poultry industry and also because a chick is an excellent experimental subject for nutrition studies. Proper poultry rations can be devised only by application of the nutritional information known about the class of poultry to be fed. The application of this information to poultry feeding requires knowledge of the nutrients, the feedstuffs available to supply these nutrients, and the amount of nutrient needed for the particular productive purpose. In this chapter the requirements of the nutrients will be considered, particularly their application in formulating rations.

The system of measurements used in the practical applications of nutrition research is inconsistent in the United States. Feed mills mix and sell feed using pounds and tons (2000 pounds) as the basic units. However, most research results are published in the metric system, using grams and kilograms as units of weight. Requirements for vitamins and trace minerals are usually not stated in ounces or grains per pound or ton. In practical situations, grams per ton or milligrams per pound are often used. Energy values are expressed in kilocalories per pound and not in British thermal units per pound. Thus the measuring system in use in the United States is hopelessly mixed up between the metric and English systems. Such confusion will be evident in the units used in this chapter. To eliminate as much confusion as possible, we will use both pounds and kilograms in tables listing nutrient requirements. We will discuss protein needs of laying hens in terms of grams of protein required per hen per day, but the energy levels will be listed both in kilocalories per pound and kilocalories per kilogram of ration. Perhaps one day the metric system will be universal and such hybrid measuring systems will no longer be used.

THE REQUIREMENTS FOR ENERGY

The largest single dietary need of an animal is for a source of energy. Energy is required for all physiological processes in the animal—movement, respiration, circulation, absorption, excretion, the nervous system, reproduction, temperature regulation—in short, all the processes of life.

Energy Requirements for Maintenance

Animals kept for productive purposes must be fed to maintain life whether they are producing or not. A considerable part of the feed consumed by all classes of poultry must be used for maintenance.

The maintenance requirement for energy includes the need for basal metabolism and normal activity. The basal metabolism is the minimum energy expenditure or heat production under conditions when the influence of feed, environmental temperature, and voluntary activity are removed. The basal heat production varies with the size of the animal, and in general, as size increases, basal heat production per unit of body weight decreases. The minimum heat production of day-old chicks is about 5.5 small calories per gram of live weight per hour, whereas the figure for adult hens is about half of this. As an extreme example, the resting metabolism of a hummingbird expressed as oxygen consumption is 15 ml per gram of live weight per hour. The corresponding figure for an elephant is 0.15 ml.

The energy required for activity can vary considerably but is usually estimated as about 50% of the basal metabolism. This is probably influenced by housing conditions as well as breed of chicken used. Housing in cages where activity is greatly restricted may result in lower energy expenditure for activity compared with the less restricted conditions prevailing in floor pens.

In spite of the fact that larger animals require less energy per unit size for maintenance, the total energy required by larger animals is more than by smaller ones. From the practical standpoint, this means that the smallest body size for a laying hen consistent with good production, egg size, and livability will be the most efficient for converting feed to product due to a low energy expenditure for maintenance. For broiler production the animal that reaches market weight in the shortest possible time is the most efficient in converting feed to product because the longer an animal must be fed to reach market weight, the greater the maintenance cost.

The data in Table 9–1 illustrate the effect of body weight and rate of egg production on feed required by laying hens. The feed required to maintain a non-laying hen is more than half that needed for full production. The feed needed to maintain a 4-pound hen is considerably less than for a 5- or 6-pound hen. In terms of amount of feed required to produce a dozen

Table 9–1. Estimated Feed Required per Day and per Dozen Eggs by 100 Hens of Different Weights and Egg Production (pounds)

	Feed Consumed					
	4-pound Hens		5-pound Hens		6-pound Hens	
Eggs/100 hens/day	per day	per doz. eggs	per day	per doz. eggs	per day	per doz. eggs
0	15.8	—	18.6	—	21.2	—
10	16.7	20.1	19.6	23.6	22.1	26.6
20	17.6	10.5	20.4	12.2	22.9	13.7
30	18.4	7.4	21.3	8.5	23.9	9.6
40	19.3	5.8	22.2	6.7	24.7	7.4
50	20.2	4.8	23.1	5.5	25.6	6.1
60	21.1	4.2	24.0	4.8	26.5	5.3
70	22.0	3.8	24.9	4.3	27.5	4.7
80	22.9	3.4	25.8	3.9	28.1	4.2
90	23.8	3.2	26.7	3.6	29.2	3.9
100	24.7	3.0	27.6	3.3	30.1	3.6

Feed assumed to contain 1,350 kilocalories of metabolizable energy per pound.

eggs, high production is more efficient than low production because the maintenance feed is spread over more eggs.

The same principle applies to broiler production. Broilers that reach market weight in 8 weeks require considerably less feed per unit weight than those requiring 12 weeks to reach the same weight. Each increment of growth must be maintained longer in slow-growing birds.

Effect of Temperature. Because of the ability of warm-blooded animals to maintain a constant body temperature that is normally several degrees above the environmental temperature, the animal is constantly losing heat to its surroundings. This loss of heat means a loss of energy that must be supplied in the feed. Heat production must equal heat loss if the animal is to maintain its normal temperature, and this means that there is a rapid increase in the metabolic rate whenever the environmental temperature falls below the critical point. Thus, the maintenance energy required at low environmental temperature is greater than that required at a more comfortable temperature.

The minimum rate of heat production in day-old male chicks occurs in an environmental temperature of 95° F. Heat output is more than doubled at a temperature of 75° F, in order to compensate for increased heat loss. For the adult hen the minimal basal heat production occurs over a range of about 10°, between 65° and 75° F. These values are for fasting chickens at rest. Feeding an animal will increase its heat production, and the higher the level of feeding the more heat is produced during the assimilation of the feed. A flock of hens on full feed will be better able to withstand the effects of cold weather than will a flock that is being restricted in its feed intake. There are also other adaptive mechanisms, such as greater feather cover, which may help in resistance to cold weather. However, when the temperature of a laying house falls much below 55° F, considerable food energy must be converted to heat to maintain body temperature. This can affect efficiency of conversion of feed to product during the cold winter months.

Effect of Gravity. Results of experiments at the University of California on the effects of gravity on the maintenance requirements of chickens are interesting. These observations were made during long-term experiments investigating the influence of gravity on living organisms. Male chickens were exposed for prolonged periods of time (up to 800 days) to forces of gravity up to 3 times normal by maintaining them in cages rotated by large centrifuges (up to 18 feet in diameter). The gravitational force was adjusted by varying the rotational speed of the centrifuge.

These experiments made it possible to estimate that up to 25% of the maintenance requirement of chickens was due to the muscular effort needed to resist the force of gravity. The chickens increased their energy intake greatly as the gravitational field was increased up to about 2.5 G.

One might speculate from such experiments that poultry production in the low gravity of the moon would be highly efficient, but on Saturn, feed efficiency would be so poor that future space voyages would be unlikely to use that planet as a poultry farm colony!

Energy Requirement and Food Intake

Most egg-type laying hens and growing broilers are allowed to consume as much feed as they wish. The amount of feed that poultry will consume under these conditions is primarily related to the energy requirements of the animal at the time. When other nutrients are present in adequate amounts, the amount of feed consumed is determined primarily by the energy level of the ration. Energy consumption measured in terms of kilocalories of metabolizable energy (ME) consumed per day is more likely to be constant than total feed consumption, if rations containing different amounts of metabolizable energy per unit of ration are fed. This is clearly illustrated by some data from experiments conducted at the University of Arizona, which are shown in Table 9–2. In these experiments five rations containing from 1,060 to 1,550 kilocalories of metabolizable energy per pound of diet were fed to laying hens for a total of 336 days. When feed consumption was measured in terms of kilocalories of metabolizable energy consumed, the energy consumption per hen, averaged for the whole experiment, was abour 300 kcal per day for all diets. The effect of temperature of the environment on energy consumption is also shown by this experiment. The calories consumed per hen per day for the 112 hottest days, which had an average temperature of 86° F, was more than 100 kilocalories less than the mean energy consumption for the

Table 9-2.   The Effect of Metabolizable Energy Content of the Diet and Environmental Temperature on Energy Consumption, Feed Intake, and Feed per Dozen Eggs

Metabolizable Energy per Pound of Diet kcal	Average Total Eggs hen	Feed Consumed/ 100 hens/ day lb	Feed/ Dozen Eggs Laid lb	Metabolizable Energy consumed hen/day kcal	Protein Consumed/ 100 hens/day lb
Entire experiment (336 days)					
1,060	216	30.3	5.66	321	4.8
1,200	215	25.0	4.69	300	4.0
1,350	223	22.3	4.03	301	3.6
1,450	218	20.7	3.83	300	3.3
1,550	197	18.9	3.87	293	3.0
112 coolest days (maximum 69° F, mean 55° F)					
1,060	81	35.5	5.90	377	5.7
1,200	84	29.5	4.73	354	4.7
1,350	84	25.6	4.10	346	4.1
1,450	83	24.1	3.90	350	3.9
1,550	77	22.2	3.88	345	3.6
112 hottest days (maximum 98° F, mean 86° F)					
1,060	64	24.5	5.14	260	3.9
1,200	61	19.8	4.37	238	3.2
1,350	64	18.0	3.79	243	2.9
1,450	63	16.7	3.56	242	2.7
1,550	55	15.2	3.73	237	2.4

Adapted from Heywang, B. W., and Vavich, M. G.: Poult. Sci., *41*:1389, 1962.

112 coolest days during which the temperature averaged 55° F. Even though the energy consumption for the hot days and cool days was markedly different, within each of these periods the energy consumption per hen per day was nearly the same regardless of the level of metabolizable energy contained in the diets. This experiment demonstrates that laying hens do not regulate feed consumption according to the total amount of feed they are able to consume. Hens on the lowest energy ration consumed nearly 50% more feed than hens fed the highest energy ration. These data also show that a high energy ration is more efficient in terms of feed consumed per dozen eggs produced. Less total feed is needed to provide the energy needs of the laying hen.

All the rations fed contained 16% protein. There was a wide variation in protein consumed per 100 hens per day under the various conditions shown. As will be discussed later, protein requirements must be related to expected feed consumption.

The same general principle applies to growing chicks, i.e., a young chick tends to regulate feed consumption to consume a given quantity of energy.

The data shown in Table 9-3 are from an experiment conducted at Cornell University by L. M. Dansky and F. W. Hill in 1954. This was one

Table 9–3.   The Effect of Feeding Diets of Varying Energy Level to Chicks

	Metabolizable Energy Content of Diet kcal/lb	Average Weight 11 wk lb	Food Intake per Chick lb	Metabolizable Energy Intake kcal/ME	Fat in Carcass %	Feed/gain
Basal	1,436	3.28	9.61	13,800	26.8	2.92
10% Oat hulls	1,292	3.26	9.69	12,519	23.2	2.97
20% Oat hulls	1,149	3.35	10.82	12,432	21.1	3.23
30% Oat hulls	1,005	3.22	11.23	11,286	18.1	3.49
40% Oat hulls	862	3.21	12.00	10,344	16.1	3.74

Data adapted from Dansky, L. M., and Hill, F. W.: Poult. Sci., *33*:112, 1954.

of the early experiments to demonstrate that the usable energy content of a diet had a marked effect on feed consumption of growing chicks. The results shown here were assembled from their data.

The energy content of a diet for growing chicks was varied by adding quantities of oat hulls to a basal ration to prepare a series of diets ranging from 1,436 to 862 kilocalories of metabolizable energy per pound. Oat hulls are essentially completely indigestible by chickens and provide no usable energy. When these diets were fed to growing chicks, weight gains up to 11 weeks of age were similar with all diets. Feed intake increased as the energy content of the diet was decreased. This resulted in more feed required for each pound of gain. The chicks were unable to compensate completely for the reduction in energy content of the diet by increased feed consumption. As the energy content of the diet was reduced, total energy intake was also reduced. Chicks fed the ration containing 862 kcal of metabolizable energy per lb gained the same amount of body weight as those fed the basal ration, even though they consumed nearly 3,500 kcal less of metabolizable energy. This difference in energy consumption was reflected in the composition of the carcass. The chicks fed the high energy ration had 26.8% fat in their carcasses, whereas those fed the diluted rations had progressively less fat. The fat in the carcasses of the chicks fed the low-energy diet was replaced by water.

These data are illustrative of what can be expected when rations of varying energy content are fed to growing chickens. Chicks tend to adjust feed consumption to consume a constant quantity of metabolizable energy when they are fed rations of varying energy content. They are unable to completely adjust food intake to these ration variations, however. Therefore, chicks fed rations high in energy will tend to consume slightly more energy and have somewhat fatter carcasses than comparable chickens consuming rations lower in energy. Chicks fed high-energy rations will require less total feed per unit of gain.

The chicks used by Dansky and Hill in the above studies were not from a rapidly growing strain comparable to today's broilers. It is likely that growth rate of broiler chicks would be reduced by reducing the dietary energy content from 1,436 to 862 kilocalories per pound in contrast to the example shown.

Energy Requirements for Growth

Energy requirements cannot be stated as precisely as amino acid, vitamin, and mineral requirements. Good growth rate can be achieved with a wide range of energy levels because of the ability of the chick to adjust the amount of feed consumed to maintain a fairly constant energy intake. Generally, maximum growth rate will not be achieved with rations for starting chicks containing below 1,200 kilocalories of metabolizable energy per pound. Broilers are usually fed rations higher in energy content than are replacement pullets. In broiler production, maximum growth rate is usually essential so that broilers can reach market weight in the shortest time; with replacement pullets rapid growth rate is less critical. In practice, rations for starting chicks intended as replacement pullets usually contain from 1,250 to 1,350 kilocalories of metabolizable energy per pound of diet whereas broiler starter rations contain higher levels of energy, ranging from 1,400 to 1,550 kilocalories per pound.

Energy Requirements for Egg Production

The net energy required by a high producing hen consists of energy expended for the basal metabolic rate, activity requirements, and energy stored in the egg. If the basal metabolic rate is estimated as 68 kilocalories per kg of body weight raised to the 0.75 power, the activity increment is considered as 50% of the basal metabolism, and a large egg contains 90 kilocalories of energy. A 4-pound (1.8-kg) hen in a comfortable environment, producing an egg a day, would have a net requirement of 250 kilocalories of energy per day. The efficiency of using dietary metabolizable energy for these purposes is probably about 75%, so that the metabolizable energy intake required to supply the energy needed would be about 330 kilocalories of metabolizable energy per day. This would require an intake of about 0.24 pounds of feed containing 1,350 kilocalories of metabolizable energy per pound. These assumptions form the basis for the estimates of feed consumption in Table 9–1. When a hen produces an egg only 8 out of every 10 days, the energy put into an egg will be reduced to 72 kilocalories per day and correspondingly less for lower rates of production.

Available evidence suggests that pullets coming into peak production, with a body weight between 3.5 and 4 pounds and housed in a comfortable environment, will consume about 300 kilocalories of metabolizable energy per day. As their body weight increases to slightly over 4 pounds and egg size improves, similar hens in good production probably consume from 310 to 320 kilocalories per day. Environmental factors, as discussed earlier, may alter these estimates greatly.

Because of the capacity of hens to alter consumption of feed in response to the energy content of a ration, the energy requirement of hens cannot be expressed in terms of a specific number of kilocalories of metabolizable energy per pound of ration. However, the minimum level of energy in a laying ration should not be below 1,200 kilocalories of metabolizable energy per pound to ensure maximum rate of production. When hens are subjected to a cold environment, the level of energy should not fall below 1,250 kilocalories of metabolizable energy per pound. The level of energy actually used in a ration will depend to a large degree on price of feed ingredients available.

PROTEIN REQUIREMENT

Protein needs for maintenance are relatively low, and therefore the requirement depends primarily on the amounts needed for productive purposes. To meet the protein requirement, the essential amino acids must be supplied in the proper amounts, and the total level of nitrogen in the diet must be high enough and in the proper form to permit synthesis of the nonessential amino acids.

Once the minimum amount of protein required to support maximum growth rate or egg production is supplied, additional protein is oxidized for energy. Protein is not stored in the body in appreciable amounts. Since protein is usually the most expensive component of a ration, it is not economical to feed excess protein to animals. For this reason, protein levels in rations for animals are usually kept closer to the minimum requirement than are other nutrients.

Protein Requirement for Growth

Protein and amino acid requirements for young growing chicks are particularly critical. The largest portion of the dry matter increase with growth is protein. Deficiency of either total protein or an essential amino acid will reduce growth rate. Protein synthesis requires that all the amino acids needed to make up the protein be present in the body at nearly the same time. When an essential amino acid is absent, no protein is synthesized. Incomplete proteins cannot be made. Amino acids that cannot be efficiently used for protein synthesis are converted to carbohydrates or fat that can be readily oxidized for immediate energy needs or stored in adipose tissue. The carcasses of animals fed rations deficient in protein or amino acids usually contain more fat than those from animals fed adequate amounts of a well-balanced protein.

Much of our present-day knowledge of amino acid requirements of growing chicks has been obtained from experiments in which individual crystalline amino acids have been used to formulate amino acid mixtures adequate to support rapid growth. Highly purified diets containing mixtures of crystalline amino acids have been developed that will support rates of chick growth that are nearly the same as those obtained from diets containing good-quality intact protein.

An estimate of the amino acid requirements of starting and finishing broilers is given in Table 9–4. Many factors influence amino acid requirements when they are stated as percentages of the diet, and no such table of requirements can be considered constant for all conditions.

The most important consideration in expressing amino acid requirements is the amount of feed consumed. A fixed amount of total dietary protein and essential amino acids is needed to support a given rate of gain of body tissue of constant composition. However, when the protein requirements is expressed as a constant percentage of the diet, the absolute daily intake of protein will depend upon feed consumption. Energy level in the diet is probably the most important consideration in determining food intake. For this reason, requirements expressed as a percentage of the diet are usually related to the energy content of the diet.

The data in Table 9–5 provide the information needed to calculate the protein required by growing male broilers at any level of energy in the diet. The average weight of male broilers at intervals of 2 to 8 weeks is

Table 9–4.   Amino Acid Requirements of Chicks and Laying Hens[a]

Amino Acids	Starting Broilers		Finishing Broilers	Laying and Breeding Hens	
	% of Protein	% of Diet	% of Diet	% of Protein	% of Diet
Arginine	5.0	1.16	1.02	5.0	0.85
Histidine	2.0	0.47	0.41	2.0	0.34
Isoleucine	4.0	0.87	0.82	5.0	0.85
Leucine	7.0	1.63	1.43	7.5	1.28
Lysine	5.0	1.16	1.02	4.2	0.72
Methionine	2.0	0.47	0.41	2.0	0.36
Cystine	1.6	0.37	0.33	1.6	0.27
Phenylalanine	3.5	0.82	0.72	4.6	0.78
Tyrosine	3.5	0.70	0.62	2.0	0.34
Threonine	3.5	0.82	0.72	3.7	0.63
Tryptophan	1.0	0.23	0.21	1.0	0.17
Valine	4.3	1.00	0.88	4.3	0.73
Applicable protein level		23.3	20.5		17.0

[a] These recommendations for amino acid requirements are from the National Research Council and from Scott, M. L., Nesheim, M. C., and Young, R. J.: Nutrition of the Chicken. Ithaca, N. Y., M. L. Scott and Associates, Publishers, 1976.

Table 9–5.   Estimated Gains, Metabolizable Energy Needs, and
Protein Required per Broiler per Day during Growth

Week	Average Weight of Male Broilers gm	lb	Metabolizable Energy Required kcal/broiler/day	Protein Required gm/day/broiler	gm/100 kcal ME
2	250	0.55	83	6.17	7.43
3	460	1.01	150	10.94	7.29
4	700	1.54	200	14.25	7.12
5	960	2.11	247	16.95	6.86
6	1,300	2.86	320	20.19	6.30
7	1,670	3.68	380	23.37	6.15
8	2,060	4.54	445	25.48	5.72

Estimates taken from Scott, M. L., Nesheim, M. C., and Young, R. J.: Nutrition of the Chicken. Ithaca, N. Y., M. L. Scott and Associates, Publishers, 1976.

shown along with estimated daily metabolizable energy and protein requirements. As broilers grow they require increasing amounts of energy and protein. However, as the energy needed for maintenance increases as the broiler grows, less protein is required per unit of energy in the diet. This results in a steady reduction in the grams of protein required per 100 kilocalories of metabolizable energy. The protein required as a percentage of a diet for any stage of growth can be calculated from these data if the energy content of the diet is known. Assume, for example, that a broiler starting ration contains 3,200 kcal of ME/kg (1450 kcal/lb). The protein needed for 2-week-old male broilers is 7.43 gm/100 kcal of ME. Therefore the ration must contain 7.43 × 32 = 238 gm of protein per kg of diet, or 23.8%. To obtain 83 kcal of ME (the daily energy required), a 2-week-old broiler would need to consume 26 grams of this feed. If the feed contained 23.8% protein, 6.2 grams would be consumed. This is the daily protein required. If, however, the ration contained only 2,900 kcal/kg, the broiler would need to consume 28.6 gm of feed to take in 83 kcal. Thus the protein content of the diet would have to be only 21.6% to achieve the required protein intake of 6.17 grams. Relating dietary protein to the energy content of the diet is a key principle that must be used in formulating poultry rations.

The illustration given for protein requirements of growing chickens applies equally to amino acid requirements. The amount of an amino acid required as a percentage of the diet varies with the energy content of the diet and the age of the growing animal. In Table 9–4 the amino acid requirements are expressed as percentages of the dietary protein. This is one way of ensuring an adequate amino acid intake in diets of varying energy level. Amino acid requirements are often expressed as amounts required per unit of energy. For example, the methionine requirement of growing chicks can be stated as 3.36 pounds per 1000 megacalories of metabolizable energy in the diet, as well as stating that it should be 2% of the dietary protein.

The data in Table 9–5 show that protein required per unit of energy in the diet decreases as an animal becomes larger. In practical broiler feeding, 2 to 3 feeds progressively lower in protein content may be used to match the ration to the nutrient needs of the broiler.

Recommendations for the protein content of rations for broiler chickens at various dietary energy levels are shown in Table 9–6. These requirements are listed for both a starting and a finishing period. Similar recommendations are shown in Table 9–7 for replacement pullets. Since replacement pullets are kept to maturity, the protein required per unit of diet changes markedly from hatching to the beginning of the laying period. In Table 9–7, recommended protein levels are given for 2 stages of growth.

Table 9–6.   Recommended Protein Levels in Rations for Broiler Chickens in Relation to Energy Content of Diet

| Metabolizable Energy | | Protein Required |
kcal/lb ration	kcal/kg ration	%
Starting diet (0–6 weeks of age)		
1,250	2,750	20.8
1,300	2,860	21.7
1,350	2,970	22.5
1,400	3,080	23.3
1,450	3,190	24.2
1,500	3,300	25.0
Finishing Diet (6 weeks to market)		
1,300	2,860	19.0
1,350	2,970	20.0
1,400	3,080	20.5
1,450	3,190	21.2
1,500	3,300	22.0
1,550	3,410	22.7

Table 9–7.   Recommended Protein Levels in Rations for Replacement Pullets at Different Stages of Growth

| Metabolizable Energy Content of Diet | | Protein Needed | |
| | | Starter 0–8 wk | Developer 8–20 wk |
kcal/lb	kcal/kg	%	%
1,200	2,640	19.0	13.5
1,250	2,750	19.7	14.0
1,300	2,860	20.5	14.5
1,350	2,970	21.3	15.0
1,400	3,080	22.0	15.5

In rearing laying stock, it is important to provide sufficient energy and protein to allow for normal development and feathering, but excessive fattening must be avoided. Restriction of energy intake by feeding low energy diets to growing pullets or by restricting the actual amount of a high energy ration has been beneficial in some studies. Pullets from broiler strains must be fed low energy diets or have energy intake restricted in some other way to prevent them from becoming too fat prior to sexual maturity. If the broiler breeders are allowed to get too fat, egg production will be depressed during the laying period.

Protein Requirements of Laying Hens

With each large egg laid, a hen produces about 6.7 grams of protein. This is equivalent to the amount of protein deposited daily by a growing broiler gaining at the rate of about 37 grams per day. Although hens do not always lay an egg every day, if the protein needs for maintenance are also considered, the daily protein needs for high-producing laying hens are fully as great as for a fast-growing broiler.

Average egg production, feed consumption, and body weight curves of a modern, high-producing strain of layers are shown in Figure 9–1. In a

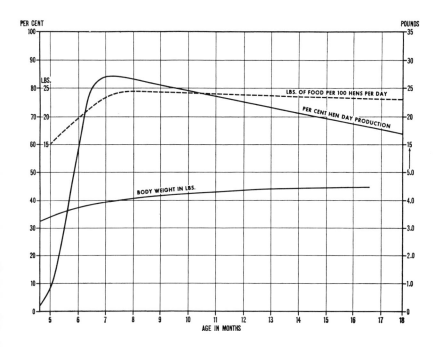

Fig. 9–1. Changes in rate of egg production, body weight, and feed consumption expected for high-producing laying hens during the production year. (Courtesy of Kimber Farms, Inc.)

typical flock, egg production would be expected to begin at 22 weeks of age when body weight is only 3.5 pounds. During the next few weeks, egg production rises rapidly to a maximum, while body weight continues to increase as the hen completes her body growth. As the production year advances and mature weight is reached, rate of egg production begins to fall gradually.

During the early stages of egg production, hens are gaining weight and depositing protein in their bodies as well as laying eggs. Later, protein needs for weight gain are reduced, but egg size is increased. To be able to produce large eggs at a maximum rate, hens must consume about 17 grams per day of a well balanced protein. The actual amount of protein required in the diet will depend on feed consumption.

The data in Table 9–8 show the percentages of protein that would be required in diets of laying hens consuming feed at different rates to achieve a protein intake of 17 grams per day. By making an assumption as to daily caloric intake, it is possible to make estimates of protein

Table 9–8.   Protein Requirements for Egg Production in White Leghorns

| Daily Feed Consumption | | Protein |
gm/hen	lb/100 hens	% of Diet
80	17.6	21.2
85	18.7	20.0
90	19.8	18.9
95	20.9	17.9
100	22.0	17.0
105	23.1	16.2
110	24.2	15.5
115	25.3	14.8
120	26.4	14.5

Table 9–9.   Energy and Protein Requirements of White Leghorn Hens

| Metabolizable Energy of Diet | | Cool Climate | | | Warm Climate | | |
kcal/lb	kcal/kg	Protein Required %	Feed/ hen/day gm	Feed/100 hens/day lb	Protein Required %	Feed/ hen/day gm	Feed/100 hens/day lb
1,181	2,600	15.0	117	25.7	16.5	105	23.1
1,250	2,750	15.5	111	24.4	17.0	100	22.0
1,318	2,900	16.5	105	23.1	18.0	95	20.9
1,386	3,050	17.0	100	22.0	19.0	90	19.8
1,454	3,200	18.0	95	20.9	20.0	86	18.9
1,523	3,350	19.0	90	19.8	21.0	82	18.0

requirements of hens receiving diets of varying energy levels. The suggested energy and protein relationships for white leghorn hens are shown in Table 9–9. These requirements are given for two climatic conditions, since environmental temperature affects energy intake and thus feed consumption.

Any statement of protein needs of laying hens must of course assume a proper amino acid balance of the dietary protein. A deficiency of an essential amino acid will result in poor egg production and reduced egg size just as will a deficiency of total protein. Amino acid requirements of layers are subject to similar variations as are requirements for total protein.

The determination of requirements for individual amino acids for laying hens is considerably more difficult than for growing chicks. Actual feeding experiments to test levels of each amino acid adequately are hard to perform because of the long feeding period necessary to evaluate properly the performance of laying hens. Purified diets containing crystalline amino acids have been successfully devised for laying hens, but their high cost makes long-term feeding experiments expensive. Estimates of the amino acid requirements of laying hens are based primarily on the amino acid composition of egg protein. The proportion of essential amino acids in dietary protein must closely follow the proportion of amino acids in the egg proteins synthesized. The estimated requirements for the essential amino acids for laying hens are given in Table 9–4.

VITAMIN AND MINERAL REQUIREMENTS

Most requirements of poultry for vitamins and minerals are precisely known, particularly for those vitamins and mineral elements likely to be deficient in practical rations. Except for a few of the vitamins or minerals that are not likely to be deficient under practical conditions, dietary levels can be recommended that will provide sufficient amounts to allow efficient growth and production.

Unlike protein, vitamins and trace mineral elements are usually supplied to poultry feeds in excess of their minimum requirements. Thus, requirements for these nutrients are usually not stated in terms of expected rate of feed consumption or energy content of the diet, since sufficient amounts over the minimum requirement are usually included in diets for poultry.

Estimates of the minimum requirements for vitamins and minerals for poultry are published by the National Research Council in *Nutrient Requirements of Poultry,* sixth edition, 1971. These are estimates of minimum levels required by poultry for growth, egg production, or reproduction. In practice, poultry rations are not formulated to minimum requirement levels because ingredients may vary in their nutrient content, and nutrients may be lost during processing and storage of the feed. The

Table 9–10.   Recommended Practical Levels of Nutrients in Feeds for Chickens (in % or units per lb)

	Starting Chicks and Broilers	Growing Chicks and Broilers	Laying Hens	Breeding Hens
Vitamins				
Vitamin A (IU)	5,000	3,000	4,000	5,000
D$_3$ (IU)	500	300	500	500
E (IU)	5	4	—	7.5
K$_1$(mg)	1	1	1	1
Thiamin, mg	1	1	1	1
Riboflavin, mg	2	2	2	2.5
Pantothenic acid, mg	6.5	6	2.5	7.5
Nicotinic acid, mg	15	15	12	15
Pyridoxine, mg	2	1.5	1.5	2
Biotin, mg	0.07	0.05	0.05	0.08
Folic acid, mg	0.6	0.18	0.18	0.4
Choline, mg	600	450	500	500
Vitamin B$_{12}$, mg	0.005	0.003	0.003	0.005
Linoleic acid, %	1.2	0.8	1.4	1.4
Inorganic Elements				
Calcium, %	1.0	0.8	3.7	3.7
Phosphorus (available), %	0.5	0.4	0.4	0.4
Sodium, %	0.15	0.12	0.12	0.12
Potassium, %	0.40	0.40	0.40	0.40
Chlorine, %	0.15	0.10	0.1	0.1
Manganese, mg	25	25	15	15
Magnesium, mg	250	250	250	250
Iron, mg	40	25	20	20
Copper, mg	5	5	5	5
Zinc, mg	20	15	30	30
Selenium, mg	0.07	0.07	0.07	0.07
Iodine, mg	0.17	0.17	0.15	0.15

These recommended levels may be converted to amounts per kilogram of diet by multiplying the requirements stated in IU or mg by 2.2.

recommended levels of vitamins and minerals shown in Table 9–10 are practical levels of these nutrients, which include margins of safety.

A critical test for the nutrient composition of a ration is its ability to support hatchability of eggs. The requirements of vitamins and trace elements for egg production are much less critical than are the requirements for hatchability. The quantity of vitamins and trace elements in an egg can be modified a great deal by the amount in the diet consumed by the hen. Rations for breeding hens normally are more liberally supplemented with vitamins, trace elements, and sources of possible unidentified nutritional factors than are rations for laying hens.

Calcium Requirements of Laying Hens

A major nutritional need in the diet of laying hens is calcium. For every large egg a hen lays she must use about 2 grams of calcium in the formation of the eggshell. A hen that lays 250 eggs per year deposits roughly 500 grams of calcium in her eggs, primarily in the form of calcium carbonate. This represents approximately 1,300 grams of calcium carbonate deposited by the hen in the shells of the eggs. Calcium is not efficiently used by the laying hen and probably only 50 to 60% of the calcium consumed is actually retained and deposited in the eggs. To produce the eggshells required, this hen would have to consume about 2,600 grams of calcium carbonate during a laying year, an amount considerably in excess of her body weight. This example illustrates the magnitude of the calcium metabolism that must go on in a laying hen. This is considerably greater than for any other species of animal.

The calcium requirement of laying hens is difficult to state in precise terms because egg production can be maintained at a high level with lower levels of calcium than are required to produce a satisfactory eggshell. Modern marketing and egg-handling conditions require a sturdy eggshell that will not crack easily during handling. When hens are near the end of their production year, the eggshells produced are normally thinner and of poorer quality than those produced by pullets in the early part of the production year. Hot weather will cause a thinner eggshell to be produced. Eggshell quality can also be influenced by respiratory diseases, which seem to affect the oviduct so that abnormal eggshells are produced. Not all these factors affecting eggshell quality can be corrected by feeding more dietary calcium.

Feed consumption is also important in determining calcium requirements when expressed as a percentage of the diet, for the same reasons discussed previously for protein requirements. It is possible for young pullets in the early stages of production to make good use of their dietary calcium and manufacture satisfactory eggshells when the calcium content of the diet is less than 3%. Under other conditions, particularly for rations for old hens in hot weather, the calcium content of a laying mash may be raised to as high as 4 to 4.5% in an effort to improve eggshell quality.

EVALUATION OF FEEDING PROGRAMS

The best estimate of the value of a ration for the production of poultry meat or eggs is the efficiency with which the conversion of food to product is made. A balanced ration may be defined as a combination of feeds furnishing nutrients in such proportions, amounts, and form as to properly nourish without waste a given group of birds for a particular purpose. The nutrient requirements for poultry discussed earlier in this chapter must be met with the feed ingredients available so that the final formula provides a balanced ration.

For economical poultry and egg production the cost of the ration must also be considered. The most economical feed is one that produces the most product at least cost. This is not necessarily the feed costing the least per pound.

Many poultry producers do not have complete knowledge of the nutrient composition of the feed they are using. They use a commercially produced feed and have no way to estimate the metabolizable energy content or some of the important nutrients. Therefore it is essential for a poultry farmer to know the efficiency of his feeding program.

Feed efficiency, measured in terms of amount of feed required to produce a pound of broiler or a dozen eggs, can be affected by a number of factors as seen in previous discussions. The most important of these are (1) rate of growth or egg production, (2) metabolizable energy content of a feed, (3) body size of laying hens, (4) nutrient adequacy of the ration, (5) environmental temperature, and (6) health of the flock.

When the feed efficiency of a healthy flock of laying hens in high production and housed in a comfortable environment is poor, the feeding program should be evaluated to determine if improvements in feed efficiency can be made economically. Adequate records of production and feed consumption are essential in evaluating a feeding program. Such records make it possible for a good poultry producer to know the pounds of feed required to produce a pound of broiler or a dozen eggs.

Palatability

Chickens have the ability to taste and appear to prefer certain flavors over others. If two feeds are offered to a group of chickens, one containing a preferred flavor compound and one not, the feed containing the desirable flavor will be consumed to a greater extent than the unflavored one. However, if no choice is given, both feeds will usually be consumed in about the same amount. Palatability, as such, is probably much less important in affecting feed consumption than the nutritional adequacy of the diet.

Rapid changes in rations for laying hens should be avoided, since occasionally a hen will refuse to consume a new ration with a consistency and appearance different from the one she has been previously fed. Mixing the new feed with the old for a few days will usually suffice to make the change smoothly.

Effect on Product

The composition of the feed can in some ways affect the composition of the product. Probably the yellow color of broiler skin and shanks or of the egg yolk (Plate III) is the most important characteristic that can be influenced by feeding. Some markets require different degrees of yolk color or skin color in broilers from others. There are special markets in food industries for deeply colored egg yolks. The color of the skin or shank of a broiler or of the yolk of an egg is primarily due to carotenoid pigments consumed in the feed. The amount of feed ingredients that are

PLATE III

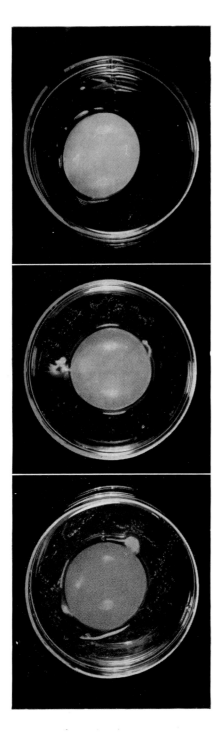

**Yolk Color Is Directly
Influenced by Feed**

—

Extremely Pale Yolk

Produced by hens fed a mixture
of—
    Oats 50%
    Bran 50%
    Occasional table scraps
    No green forage

—

Medium-Colored Yolk

Produced by hens fed a ration
of—
    Yellow corn 50%
    Wheat 25%
    Oats 25%
    No green forage

—

Deep Orange Yolk

Produced by hens fed a mixture
of—
    Corn 52%
    Wheat 24%
    Oats 14%
    Dried milk and soy
      bean meal 10%
    Green grass pasture

—

These three examples of the influence of feed on yolk color
were observed in three flocks
near Urbana, Illinois. The spots
appearing on the yolks are merely
light reflections.

Courtesy of the Illinois
Agricultural Experiment Station.

high in these pigments will greatly affect the pigmentation of these products. Corn, alfalfa meal, and corn gluten meal are the primary feedstuffs used to contribute these pigments. Many synthetic pigment compounds and other feed sources of pigments have been studied for their usefulness in feeding poultry. Pimento peppers, marigold petals, and algae meal are other feed sources containing high levels of carotenoid pigments useful in producing pigmentation desirable in poultry products.

Feed Formulation

Rations fed to poultry are combinations of available ingredients that supply the amounts of energy, protein, vitamins, and minerals that have been discussed earlier. The processes of ration formulation can be carried out by an experienced nutritionist rather easily with the aid of feed composition tables and a hand calculator. By combining various ingredients and adjusting the amounts used, the required nutrient levels can be

Table 9–11.   Examples of Broiler Starter and Finisher Rations

Ingredients	Starter Ration lb/ton	Finisher Ration lb/ton
Corn, yellow	793	1,300
Milo	300	—
Stabilized grease	70	50
Soybean meal, dehulled	630	260
Corn gluten meal, 60% protein	50	100
Fish solubles, dried	10	—
Fish meal, 60% protein	—	50
Poultry by-product meal	—	100
Corn distillers' solubles	50	50
Alfalfa meal, 17% protein	25	40
Dicalcium phosphate	40	25
Limestone	15	10
Salt, iodized	5	5
DL-Methionine or methionine hydroxy analog equivalent	1.6	—
Vitamin and trace mineral premix	10	10
Protein, %	23.5	20.5
Metabolizable energy, kcal/lb	1,410	1,480
kcal/kg	3,100	3,260
Calcium, %	0.93	0.81
Available phosphorus, %	0.55	0.52
Fat, %	6.1	6.1
Fiber, %	2.6	2.6
Linoleic acid, %	1.6	1.9
Xanthophyll, mg/lb	9.5	16.8
mg/kg	20.9	37.0
Methionine, % of protein	2.0	2.0
Methionine + cystine, % of protein	3.6	3.7
Lysine, % of protein	5.2	5.0

achieved. In commercial practice, formulation is often done by computers by a procedure termed "linear programming." Data on ration specifications, ingredient costs, and nutrient composition are given to the computer, which is programmed to calculate the combination of ingredients that meets the nutritional specifications at least cost. Computer formulation is rapid and enables a feed manufacturer to change formulas frequently as ingredient costs change.

Examples of modern rations, typical of those fed in commercial practice, are shown in Tables 9–11, 9–12, and 9–13. These rations, although typical, represent only one set of solutions to formulation problems. Depending on prices of ingredients, many other combinations can be used to make up poultry rations adequate in nutrients required by poultry.

For example, corn and milo have been used as energy sources in the broiler starter in Table 9–11, and soybean meal is the major protein supplement used. In the finisher ration, corn is the only grain used, but fish meal and poultry by-product meal are used as protein sources in addition to soybean meal. The corn gluten meal used in the broiler formula is used primarily to raise the xanthophyll level to ensure good pigmentation of broilers fed these rations. When yellow-skinned broilers

Table 9–12.   Examples of Pullet Starting and Rearing Rations

Ingredients	Starter 0–8 wk lb/ton	Developer 8–20 wk lb/ton
Barley	400	—
Corn, yellow	925	1,360
Oats	—	300
Standard middlings	—	—
Soybean meal, 50% protein	400	150
Meat and bone scrap, 50% protein	160	100
Corn distillers' solubles	50	—
Alfalfa meal	50	50
Dicalcium phosphate	—	15
Limestone	—	10
Salt, iodized	5	5
DL-Methionine or methionine hydroxy analog	1.5	0.80
Vitamin and trace mineral mix	10	10
Protein, %	21.5	14.4
Metabolizable energy, kcal/lb	1,325	1,390
kcal/kg	2,915	3,060
Calcium, %	0.97	0.90
Available phosphorus, %	0.58	0.50
Fat, %	3.5	4.1
Fiber, %	3.5	3.9
Linoleic acid, %	1.3	1.6
Methionine, % of protein	1.95	2.0
Methionine + cystine, % of prot.	3.60	3.8
Lysine, % of protein	5.0	4.4

are not required for marketing, pigmentation would not be a factor in formulation.

Various other ingredient combinations have been used in the rearing and laying rations shown in Tables 9–12 and 9–13, although they are based largely on corn and soybean meal. These two ingredients form the "backbone" of most poultry rations in the United States today.

A breeder ration is shown in Table 9–13. This ration contains fish meal and a large amount of corn distillers' solubles as sources of "unidentified" factors. The vitamin and trace mineral premix should contain higher levels of vitamin fortification than the one used for the layer. Breeder rations are usually more complex than layer rations to make sure that all nutrients needed by the embryo are put into the egg by the breeder hen.

The individual vitamin and trace element levels have not been calculated in these formulas. The vitamin and trace mineral premix would be formulated to add those nutrients that may be lacking in the ingredients used to make up the diet. Sample premixes for the rations given as examples are shown in Table 9–14. These are typical of the mixes used to supplement poultry rations in practice.

Table 9–13.   Examples of Layer and Breeder Rations

Ingredients	Layer lb/ton	Breeder lb/ton
Corn, yellow	1,330	1,265
Wheat shorts	—	—
Stabilized grease	20	30
Soybean meal, 50% protein	250	260
Fish meal, 60% protein	25	80
Meat and bone scrap, 50% prot.	130	50
Corn distillers' solubles	50	100
Alfalfa meal	30	50
Dicalcium phosphate	10	20
Limestone	130	130
Salt, iodized	5	5
DL-Methionine or methionine hydroxy analog equivalent	0.80	0.60
Vitamin and trace mineral premix	10	10
Protein, %	17.0	17.4
Metabolizable energy, kcal/lb	1,330	1,346
kcal/kg	2,925	2,960
Calcium, %	3.3	3.1
Available phosphorus, %	0.58	0.58
Fat, %	5.7	5.2
Fiber, %	2.3	2.6
Linoleic acid, %	1.5	1.7
Xanthophyll, mg/lb	9.0	9.7
mg/kg	19.8	21.3
Methionine, % of protein	2.0	2.0
Methionine + cystine, % of protein	3.7	3.6
Lysine, % of protein	5.1	4.9

Table 9–14. Typical Vitamin and Trace Mineral Premixes Used in Poultry Rations

Constituent	Broiler		Pullet		Layer	Breeder
	Starter	Finisher	Starter	Grower & Developer		
			Amounts for ton of diet (2000 lb)			
Stabilized vitamin A (IU)	10,000,000	5,000,000	6,000,000	2,000,000	2,000,000	10,000,000
Vitamin D$_3$ (IU)	1,000,000	550,000	500,000	500,000	1,000,000	1,000,000
Vitamin E (IU)	5,000	5,000	5,000	—	—	6,000
Synthetic vitamin K (gm)	2	2	2	2	2	2
Riboflavin (gm)	3	3	3	3	3	3
Nicotinic acid (gm)	30	20	20	15	—	20
d-Calcium pantothenate (gm)	10	4	4	2	—	5
Vitamin B$_{12}$ (mg)	6	6	5	2	2	6
Choline chloride (gm)	200	—	200	—	—	—
Antioxidant (ethoxyquin or butylated hydroxytoluene, BHT), (gm)	110	110	110	—	—	110
Coccidiostat	+	+	+	—	—	—
Antibiotic (gm)	5–10	5–10	5–10	—	—	—
Zinc oxide (gm)	100	100	100	100	100	100
Manganese sulfate, feed grade (gm) .	200	200	200	200	200	200
Corn meal to make total (lb)	10	10	10	10	10	10

Chapter 10

Diseases and Parasites

The best fed, housed, and genetically ideal chicken will not grow or lay eggs up to its potential if diseased or infested with parasites. Since massive numbers of broilers or laying hens are concentrated in a confined area in modern production systems, potential losses from a severe disease outbreak are great. The prevention of outbreak of disease is the key to minimizing losses. With few exceptions, treatment after a disease outbreak has occurred is costly and often unsuccessful, and the recovered flock does not return to peak performance. Management of broiler flocks, the production of replacement pullets, and the management of layers must be done with disease control and prevention clearly in mind.

Diseases can cause severe losses to production efficiency. An increase in the time required for a broiler to reach market weight or a decrease in rate of egg production will result in poorer efficiency in converting feed to product.

Agents of Disease

Any departure of an animal from a state of good health can be called a disease. This may be caused by specific pathogenic agents, nutritional deficiencies, or an environment to which the animal cannot readily adapt. The diseases to consider in this chapter are those caused by bacteria, viruses, fungi, protozoans, environmental poisons, behavior abnormalities, and external parasites such as lice, mites, and worms residing in the gastrointestinal tract.

With such an imposing army arrayed against the good health of a flock, we might despair at maintaining losses at a minimum. However, animals have many defense mechanisms against attack by disease-producing agents. Much of the strategy in disease control uses these natural defenses of the animal by methods such as stimulating antibody production against specific disease agents through immunization, or decreasing the intensity of the exposure to disease-causing agents through sanitation, quarantine, and good ventilation so that the odds against the animal are improved.

Diseases may be spread from one animal to another by two basic routes. Horizontal spread of disease occurs between one infected animal and another. This may involve contact with infected animals, contact with contaminated litter, airborne dust particles containing disease organisms, feed or water that has been in contact with infected animals, or vectors or carriers of disease such as insects, wild birds, or parasites that can pass the pathogenic agent from one animal to other. Vertical spread of disease is the passage of the disease-producing agent from parent to offspring through the egg. Horizontal spread of disease is most common, but some diseases such as pullorum disease, lymphoid leukosis, and mycoplasmosis can be spread by vertical transmission. Control of diseases spread horizontally often can be achieved by isolation and quarantine; vertical spread may be controlled by elimination of infected parent stock. Obviously, strategy aimed at control of a disease must be based on a thorough knowledge of its mode of spread.

How to Recognize Disease

Successful poultry managers can recognize signs of disease early before a flock is in serious trouble. When disease is recognized early some measure of control may be achieved by such measures as immunization of the rest of the flock, isolation, elimination of infected individuals, or administration of medication.

Sick animals may be dull and inactive and isolate themselves from the rest of the flock. They usually eat less and subsequently grow slowly or lay fewer eggs. Fertility and hatchability of eggs from a breeder flock may decline. Specific signs of disease may be evident, such as diarrhea, paralysis, coughing, wheezing, sneezing, inflammatory exudates on the skin, blood in the droppings, or other signs that distinguish them from healthy birds. Often a decrease in feed and water consumption is one of the first signs that something is wrong. If the flock manager can monitor the food intake, he may obtain an early indication of trouble developing because of disease. Once disease is suspected, prompt diagnosis of the disease is important so that measures can be taken to minimize loss.

Few poultry managers can have sufficient expertise to diagnose and treat all the disease problems they may encounter. Many states have diagnostic laboratories with trained poultry pathologists who will assist in diagnosis of disease problems. Feed manufacturers, integrated production companies, or breeders may have staff veterinarians who will assist in diagnosing disease problems in flocks they serve. Some veterinarians in private practice specialize in poultry diseases. These sources may all be used to obtain help when diseases cause problems in flock performance.

Often it will be necessary to bring affected animals to a diagnostic laboratory to determine the nature of a disease problem. When this is to be done, make sure the chickens selected represent the condition causing concern.

Several live birds showing symptoms are most useful for making diagnosis of disease. Partially decomposed, dead birds are useless to the pathologist. Dead birds should be kept in good condition by refrigeration or by packing in ice to prevent postmortem decomposition.

Be prepared to supply accurate information about the flock, such as number and age of birds, the number affected, the length of time symptoms have been observed, the number that have died, specific symptoms you have seen, descriptions of housing, feeding, and management methods used, and vaccinations given. This information can be very helpful in making an accurate diagnosis.

What Are the Problem Diseases?

If you ask a poultryman to name his most serious disease problem, he will undoubtedly say it is the one his flock has at that moment. There are a host of diseases that potentially can cause problems. The November issue of the *Journal of Avian Diseases* annually publishes reports from diagnostic laboratories in several regions of the United States that summarize the diseases diagnosed at these laboratories the previous year. Up to 80 separate conditions involving infectious agents, nutritional diseases, parasites, or mismanagement are listed in these reports. Although some idea of the relative importance of a specific disease can be obtained from examining these reports, a complete picture cannot be gained. Some diseases are so common and readily recognized that cases are not brought to diagnostic laboratories in proportion to the incidence encountered. Thus a true picture of the field problems met may not be obtained.

The annual report of the USDA Poultry Inspection Branch also lists problems associated with certain diseases. The amazing total of 335 million pounds of poultry was rejected for human consumption by inspectors in the United States in 1975. This represents about 2.1% of the total weight of poultry inspected. The most important causes of rejection were leukosis, airsacculitis, and septicemia, with no other cause of condemnation approaching the significance of the first three. Septicemia is a rather nonspecific term, since it includes birds that were rejected because of anemia, edema, dehydration, inflammatory lesions, cyanosis, hyperemia, or other causes that may be an indication of disease, but it does not specify what the disease might be. The loss through condemnations is only part of the loss to the poultry industry from disease. Mortality and loss of production efficiency from disease on the farm represent a still greater total loss to the poultry industry than the condemnation figures show.

Losses from some diseases have been cut to low levels because effective control procedures have been developed. Thus infectious bronchitis and Newcastle disease do not show up as major causes of loss primarily because of control measures now available. Relaxation of these control measures, however, would quickly restore these diseases to the forefront of causes of economic loss.

With a successful laying flock, the death rate may average about 1% a month or 10 to 12% over a production year. In broiler flocks an average mortality may be about 4%, but as low as 1 to 2% deaths up to market age can be obtained. These losses may be from a variety of causes, some of which may be due to specific diseases such as leukosis or Marek's disease, but often no one cause predominates. This low level of mortality is responsible for considerable economic loss to the poultry industry, but it is difficult to attack the problem because of the variety of causes of death making up the "nonspecific" losses.

DISEASES OF THE RESPIRATORY TRACT

Respiratory diseases as a group are among the most troublesome encountered in raising poultry. Newcastle disease, infectious bronchitis, and laryngotracheitis are caused by viruses, chronic respiratory disease (mycoplasmosis) and infectious coryza by bacteria, and aspergillosis is caused by a fungus. A flock with a respiratory disease shows signs of respiratory distress, such as gasping, wheezing, nasal discharge, and coughing.

The term *airsacculitis* is often used to characterize the clinical findings of respiratory infection, especially as encountered by inspectors in broiler- and turkey-processing plants. The accumulation of exudative material and thickening and discoloration of the air sac wall are signs of infection of the air sacs. Poultry meat inspectors condemn such carcasses as unwholesome for human consumption unless it is possible to remove diseased tissues. Airsacculitis has been one of the major causes of broiler carcass condemnations for many years in the United States. Most of the common respiratory diseases of poultry can result in airsacculitis so the term is not descriptive of a specific disease.

Although control measures for these diseases have been developed, problems with respiratory diseases in poultry still plague the industry. They are responsible for several millions of dollars' loss in carcass condemnations in processing plants, and even greater losses due to reduced performance and mortality in growing broilers and laying hens.

Mycoplasmosis (Chronic Respiratory Disease or CRD)

This is a complex respiratory disease caused by the organism, *Mycoplasma gallisepticum*, in association with bacterial infection, primarily from *Escherichia coli* and the viruses responsible for infectious bronchitis and Newcastle disease. The mycoplasma organism is a primitive type of bacterium, very small, with no rigid cell wall.

The disease affects the air sacs primarily. They become thickened and filled with exudates, and the lungs become hard. It is an expensive disease, since the mortality rate can be fairly high, growth rate can be reduced, and infected broilers may be condemned by inspectors in the processing plant.

The disease is spread both vertically and horizontally. The organism can be incorporated into eggs by infected breeders, and chicks can be hatched carrying the mycoplasmal infection. Transmission also occurs from contact with infected birds and will spread throughout a flock in this way.

The disease has been brought under much better control by the establishment of mycoplasma-free breeding flocks that will produce broiler chicks that start life free of the disease. Mycoplasma-free breeding flocks can be established by treating infected hatching eggs with the antibiotic tylosin to kill the organism contained in the egg. Chicks hatched from treated eggs will then be free of the organism. The chicks must be raised and maintained in isolation from possible exposure to the disease by contact with infected birds or by indirect contact with any person or piece of equipment that may have been in contact with infected birds. Testing programs must be maintained to be sure that the flock is kept free of *Mycoplasma gallisepticum*. Breeders and hatcheries have gone to great lengths in isolation and sanitation programs aimed at maintaining mycoplasma-free flocks. Such practices have included:

(1) complete fencing and restriction of access to breeding farms and sufficient isolation to prevent airborne infection from infected flocks.

(2) construction of houses that can be locked and screened against wild birds, with concrete floors that can be thoroughly cleaned and disinfected and keeping no other domestic fowl on the farm.

(3) prohibiting visitors, salesmen, servicemen, or other poultrymen from entering any of the houses.

(4) requiring workmen entering the farm to change clothing and shower before coming in contact with the flocks.

(5) allowing no equipment into the breeding farm that may have been in contact with other poultry. Bulk feed trucks must fill bulk feeders from outside the houses or in some instances first pass through fumigated buildings. Other delivery trucks are not allowed on the premises.

(6) using vaccines that are free of contamination with *Mycoplasma gallisepticum*.

(7) disposing of dead birds by incineration, deep burial, or by means of special disposal pits.

(8) closing hatcheries to all visitors and following rigid isolation and sanitation precautions.

Although such practices are costly and time-consuming, the benefits from mycoplasma-free breeding stock compensate for the care that must be taken. At the present time, probably well over 90% of the broiler breeding flocks in the United States are free of *Mycoplasma gallisepticum,* and the problems of chronic respiratory disease in broiler flocks have been greatly reduced.

Infectious Bronchitis

This is a highly contagious viral disease of poultry which produces infection in the lining of the trachea, bronchi, and air sacs of the respiratory system. Coughing, wheezing, acute respiratory distress, and death are observed in young birds; low egg production and poor egg quality are consequences of the disease in adults. Eggs laid by hens that suffer from bronchitis or have recently recovered from infectious bronchitis will have thin shells, often misshapen, with bumps of calcium deposits. The internal quality of the eggs will also be reduced. The disease is spread horizontally by contact with affected birds, air currents, and workmen or visitors who may move from infected to noninfected houses. There is no treatment for the disease once it is in progress, and the control of this disease is ordinarily through vaccination. A common procedure is to vaccinate young chickens at 4 days, 4 weeks, and 4 months of age and then once every 6 months after hens are in lay. The vaccine can be administered on a mass basis by mixing it in the drinking water.

Some temporary immunity to the disease is transmitted through the egg to chicks from dams immunized against infectious bronchitis.

Newcastle Disease

This viral respiratory disease has been known for many years in various parts of the world, but not until the middle 1940's did it become of major importance in the United States. It was first encountered in England near Newcastle-on-Tyne, from which it derives its name. In the United Kingdom today, however, the disease is usually called fowl pest. Newcastle disease is a highly infectious respiratory disease characterized by coughing, sneezing, rattling, and signs of severe respiratory distress. In a small percentage of the affected birds, nervous symptoms are observed, including varying degrees of muscular incoordination and partial paralysis (Fig. 10–1). Mortality can be severe, depending upon the virulence of the particular strain of virus responsible for the outbreak.

Four separate forms of Newcastle disease are known which are caused by four very similar viruses. These virus forms, known as Beach's, Beaudette's, Doyle's, and Hitchner's, cause slightly different forms of the disease. The Doyle's form causes particularly high mortality in adult birds and was responsible for some severe losses in many parts of the world in

Fig. 10–1.   This hen shows a typical posture observed in the small percentage of individuals in a flock with Newcastle disease that show nervous symptoms. (Courtesy of Dr. M. C. Peckham, Cornell University.)

the early 1970's. This form was found in southern California in laying flocks, but a successful eradication program was carried out by slaughtering infected flocks.

In laying hens it is common to observe 100% cessation of egg production, and eggs that are laid after an outbreak of Newcastle disease will have poor external and internal quality for some time. Egg production and egg quality will often recover to normal levels following an outbreak of Newcastle disease. Control of Newcastle disease is achieved primarily with vaccines prepared from killed virus or modified live virus preparations. Most vaccinations in the United States are done with live virus vaccines. These may be administered by wingweb inoculation, intranasal, or eyedrop methods, in the drinking water, or by spraying or dusting an entire flock. The immunity produced by the vaccines is not permanent and must be reinforced by periodic revaccination. The schedule often suggested is vaccination at 4 days, 4 weeks and 4 months of age, and then once every 6 months after hens are in lay. Newcastle disease and bronchitis vaccination can be given at the same time for protection against both diseases. Newcastle disease is spread horizontally by contact with infected birds, although it is not spread as rapidly or as widely as the bronchitis disease virus.

Laryngotracheitis

The symptoms observed in chickens suffering from laryngotracheitis are quite characteristic and often spectacular. The outstanding and most characteristic symptom is gasping. When inhaling, the bird may extend its head and neck upward with the mouth wide open, and when exhaling, the head is drawn back and lowered with the mouth closed (Fig. 10–2). Coughing, rattling, wheezing, and occasionally loud cries are heard as affected birds attempt to dislodge accumulations of mucus from the air passages. Laryngotracheitis is caused by a virus which causes an inflammation of the larynx and trachea. The spread of this disease is horizontal and relatively slow, through contact with affected birds or equipment or other material that has been in contact with affected birds. When the disease affects laying hens, egg production drops, but after the disease has

Fig. 10–2. Laryngotracheitis. Characteristic position during inspiration. (Courtesy of California Agricultural Experiment Station.)

run its course affected animals recover and seem normal. A portion of the recovered birds will remain carriers of the virus and are potential sources of infection to new susceptible stock that may be introduced into the house. Therefore, it is usually recommended that recovered birds be disposed of, or new stock should be vaccinated until all of the birds that have suffered from the disease have been discarded.

Since laryngotracheitis usually occurs in sporadic outbreaks, routine vaccination for this disease is not recommended. Very often the disease has been spread by introduction of ready-to-lay pullets transported in contaminated trucks and crates. The disease can be controlled by a vaccine prepared from a modified live virus which can be administered by an eyedrop vaccination method. When several flocks are housed on a single farm and the disease occurs in one of them, the remaining flocks may be protected by prompt vaccination.

Infectious Coryza

This disease is often considered to be the fowl equivalent of the common cold, although it is caused by the bacterium *Hemophilus gallinarum*. Infected birds have discharges from the nostrils and eyes and infection or swelling of the wattles and sinuses. Transmission is horizontal, by contact with infected birds. The spread of the disease is rather slow but can be enhanced by contact with drinking water that contains nasal discharge from infected birds. The organism does not live long outside of the chicken. Isolation rearing, disposal of old hens at the end of the laying year, and separation of chickens of various ages are effective control measures for the disease. Since birds that have recovered from the disease are carriers, they should not be kept in flocks or allowed to come into contact with young susceptible pullets.

The disease will respond to treatment with certain drugs such as sulfathiazole administered in the feed or to injections of streptomycin. Medication, however, is not the solution to effective long-term control.

Aspergillosis

This is a respiratory disease caused by the fungus, *Aspergillus fumigatus*, or by related fungi. Chickens with aspergillosis show typical signs of respiratory disease, such as gasping and rapid breathing. They may have increased thirst, loss of appetite, emaciation, and some nervous symptoms. Large masses or plaques of a cream-colored material may be found in the air sacs, syrinx, lungs, and bronchi. The fungus can be cultured from these plaques to confirm diagnosis (Fig. 10–3). *Aspergillus fumigatus* is a rather ubiquitous organism that is often present in the environment. When conditions in litter and feed support good growth of molds, the spores may be breathed in by chickens and result in aspergillosis. There is

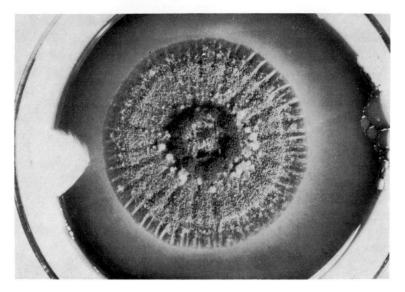

Fig. 10–3. A mold *(Aspergillus)* can be cultured to confirm diagnosis of aspergillosis. (Courtesy of Dr. M. C. Peckham, Cornell University.)

no treatment for the disease. The best way to avoid problems is to prevent heavy mold concentrations. Feed should be low in moisture, and litter should not be allowed to become moldy.

AVIAN TUMOR DISEASES

Several disease conditions in poultry are caused by viruses that result in tumors in a variety of body tissues. Marek's disease is a specific disease whose etiology and control have now become understood. Another group of tumor diseases caused by viruses termed the leukosis/sarcoma group are somewhat less understood, and control of the diseases caused by these viruses has not been accomplished.

Since these diseases are characterized by tumors caused by viruses, they have been extensively studied by virologists interested in cancer research in other species. The control of Marek's disease by a vaccine was the first example of an effective cancer vaccine that has been found for any species and represents a major advance in medical science.

Marek's Disease

Marek's disease is primarily a disease of young, growing chickens. In its usual form it affects birds between 3 and 5 months of age, although it may be seen in older or younger birds.

An acute form of the disease has been a serious problem in broiler flocks. This form may affect younger birds and cause high mortality. Losses from Marek's disease may occur not only from death during broiler growing but also from condemnations in the processing plant. Broiler meat inspection regulations require that carcasses showing evidence of tumors be discarded. Losses from Marek's disease can be a major problem in the production of replacement pullets destined for egg production.

Paralysis, to varying degrees, is one of the major clinical signs of Marek's disease. Since the disease affects the nervous system, many parts of the body may be affected. Legs, wings, and neck may be paralyzed, muscles may atrophy, and blindness may be observed. The

Fig: 10–4. A tumor involving the nerves going to the wing in a chicken affected with Marek's disease. The enlargement of two of the three nerve trunks in the plexus on the right (arrow) can be seen compared with the three normal nerve trunks directly opposite them on the left side. (Courtesy of Dr. M. C. Peckham, Cornell University.)

paralytic nature of the disease led to the use of the name "range paralysis" for this disease several years ago.

On autopsy, affected nerves may be observed to be greatly enlarged and often have a tumor-like appearance (Fig. 10–4). Tumors may be observed in any organ or tissue, with the ovary the most frequent site in females. Grossly visible tumors seem more common in the acute form of Marek's disease than in the less virulent form. Eye lesions are often found. Skin lesions are usually associated with feather follicles and often may be seen only after chickens are processed. Processed broilers with this lesion may be condemned by the poultry inspector.

The disease is caused by a virus belonging to a class of viruses termed herpesviruses (Fig. 10–5). The virus, although similar in some respects to

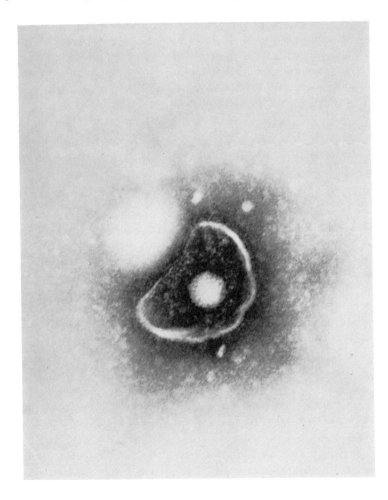

Fig. 10–5. An electron micrograph of a Marek's disease virus. The virus was obtained from a feather follicle of an infected chicken. (Courtesy of Dr. B. W. Calnek, Cornell University.)

herpesviruses that infect humans, has not been shown to infect man or to cause tumors in mammalian systems.The virus can be spread in chickens horizontally. There is little evidence that the agent can be transmitted through eggs. It can be spread by direct contact and through the air to chickens in close proximity but not in direct contact with infected birds. The virus is shed through feather follicles, and bits of feather and down may carry the agent. The virus can apparently live for some time in litter in houses containing infected birds and can infect newly introduced birds.

Control of Marek's disease has been accomplished by development of vaccines capable of protecting chickens from the virus. Three types of viruses can protect chickens against Marek's disease. A turkey herpesvirus can stimulate immunity to the Marek's disease virus in chickens while causing no pathology of its own. Marek's disease virus that has been attenuated or a nonvirulent strain of Marek's disease has also been used as the basis of vaccines. The turkey herpesvirus is most commonly used to produce vaccines against Marek's disease. This vaccine is easiest to use, since lyophilized vaccine that is easily stored and transported can be produced.

Marek's disease vaccine is usually given at hatching before chicks leave the hatchery. The vaccine is capable of providing 80 to 100% protection against Marek's disease and has been highly effective in reducing industry losses to this disease, which had been estimated as over 150 million dollars a year prior to discovery of the vaccine.

Genetic resistance to Marek's disease can also be developed in chickens. Progress in identifying resistant chickens can be rapid if chicks are tested for resistance by injections of Marek's disease virus. Breeding combinations can be selected that produce chicks resistant to the virus challenge.

Since Marek's disease is horizontally spread, reducing exposure to the virus to a minimum by isolation of young stock from adults and good isolation procedures to prevent introduction of the virus by visitors, equipment, or delivery trucks may be helpful as an adjunct to a vaccination program to reduce disease exposure until a good level of immunity develops.

Other Tumor Diseases

A variety of diseases characterized by tumors is caused by a group of viruses termed the leukosis/sarcoma group. The most common of these diseases is lymphoid leukosis, but other diseases termed erythroblastosis, myeloblastosis, myelocytosis, and osteopetrosis and several connective tissue tumors are the result of viruses from this group.

Lymphoid leukosis is the most common form observed under field conditions. In contrast to Marek's disease, lymphoid leukosis is primarily a disease of older chickens, 18 weeks of age or older. Younger chicks can

Fig. 10–6. A liver showing lesions typical of those seen in leukosis. (Courtesy of Dr. M. C. Peckham, Cornell University.)

be affected, however, and some evidence of viral infection in organs of young birds may be seen even though clinical signs of the disease are not visible.

This disease is seen most often in laying hens. Affected birds become thin and may die quickly. Tumors may be found in all tissues of the body except nerves. The liver is frequently affected, becoming large and very pale (Fig. 10–6). The term *big liver disease* has been used because of the appearance of the liver in hens affected with lymphoid leukosis. The bursa of Fabricius, an organ made up of lymphoid tissue, is invariably affected in lymphoid leukosis.

The lymphoid leukosis virus can be spread horizontally and vertically by transfer of the virus to eggs laid by infected hens. The disease apparently takes a long time to develop, since clinical signs may not be seen for several months. Horizontal transmission is slow and rather inefficient.

No vaccines have been produced that are effective against lymphoid leukosis virus. Since the disease can be spread by egg transmission, the best eventual control method may be to eliminate infected breeders from flocks. Hens carrying the virus can be identified by testing for virus and serum antibodies. If these are eliminated, young stock can only become infected by contact with infected birds. Thus systems designed to eliminate infected dams, as with *Mycoplasma gallisepticum* or pullorum disease, may eventually be the best way to control lymphoid leukosis.

COCCIDIOSIS

Although coccidiosis is controllable under most circumstances, the dollar cost spent for its control and the continuing research carried out to maintain control make this disease one of the most expensive encountered by the poultry industry. Coccidiosis is caused by protozoans belonging to the genus *Eimeria*. Some nine species of *Eimeria* affect poultry, of which six are pathogenic and can cause disease.

The coccidia do not spend their lives completely inside the chicken but have a life cycle with stages that are outside the body. A typical infection begins when a chicken ingests sporulated *oocysts* from the litter. These oocysts, in contact with trypsin and bile, release sporozoites. The sporozoites invade the mucosal cells lining the gastrointestinal tract where they grow and divide (schizogony) through several stages, increasing in number at each stage, and produce invading forms called *merozoites*. A process of sexual reproduction then occurs, and the fertilized gametes form oocysts which are discharged in droppings. More details of this process are shown in Figure 10–7.

These oocysts are noninfective until they have undergone a process of *sporulation* in the litter. This is a process that requires a warm temperature, moisture, and oxygen. Under ideal conditions, sporulation may occur in 24 to 48 hours for most species. Sporulated oocysts then may be ingested by chickens, and the life cycle begins anew.

The various species of *Eimeria* attack different locations in the gastrointestinal tract. *Eimeria tenella* attacks the cecal lining, producing cecal coccidiosis (Fig. 10–8). *E. necatrix* resides in the small intestine as does *E. maxima*. Some, such as *E. acervulina,* attack mainly the first sections of small intestine. In each case the coccidia cause destruction of the cells lining the intestine, bleeding, and ulceration of the intestine, and allow invasion of the damaged intestine by bacteria.

With *E. tenella* infections, blood in the droppings is usually observed. Infection by other species may be recognized by swollen intestine, white colonies of coccidia, and schizonts or necrotic lining of the intestine.

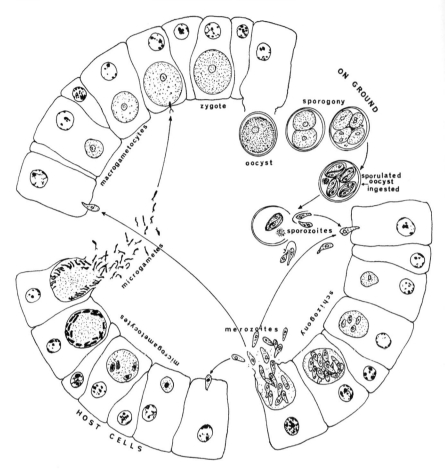

Fig. 10–7. The general life cycle of *Eimeria*, which shows various stages of development in the intestinal mucosal cells of the host. (From Noble, E. R., and Noble, G. A.: Parasitology: The Biology of Animal Parasites, 4th ed. Philadelphia, Lea & Febiger, 1976.)

Chickens with acute coccidiosis are obviously sick. They may be weak, droopy, and anemic, and mortality rates may be high.

Control of coccidiosis can take several paths. Since oocysts must have proper conditions to sporulate in litter, reducing litter moisture reduces sporulation. Wet litter is conducive to coccidiosis infection. The dose of oocysts taken in by the chicken may be kept low by avoiding high densities of birds or by using plenty of litter to dilute the oocysts. Since oocysts must be picked up from litter, housing in cages eliminates recycling of oocysts and effectively prevents the infection.

In broiler growing, the housing density and litter condition often cannot be ideal. Therefore control of coccidiosis has largely been accomplished

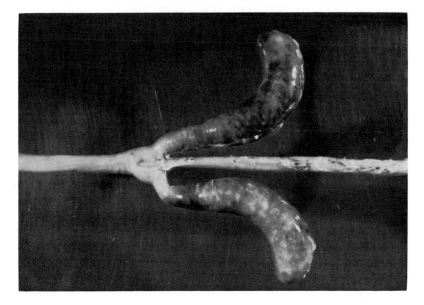

Fig. 10–8.   Ceca, showing swelling and discoloration caused by a coccidiosis infection. (Courtesy of Dr. M. C. Peckham, Cornell University.)

by the use of drugs administered in feed to kill or prevent the development of coccidia. These coccidiostats are included in virtually all rations for growing broilers.

The development of coccidiostatic drugs must be continuous because coccidia tend to develop resistance to those that were initially effective. A drug effective against the various species of coccidia when first marketed may lose its effectiveness as resistance is developed. "Breaks" may occur in its effectiveness and acute coccidiosis may cause losses. If chickens are exposed to small numbers of oocysts over a long period of time, they develop immunity to coccidiosis. This is important in raising pullets, especially if they are to be housed on the floor during the laying year. This controlled exposure may be natural, by controlling litter conditions and stocking density so that exposure is low. Flocks may be inoculated with small doses of mixed cultures to give controlled exposure. This procedure has the disadvantage that new species of coccidia may be introduced on a farm in the inoculum. Low doses of coccidiostatic drugs may also be used to help reduce infection but still allow immunity to be gained.

Cage-rearing and cage-laying systems have reduced coccidiosis problems greatly with laying hens. Cage growing of broilers is considered by many to be the ultimate solution of the coccidiosis problem. Since problems in raising broilers in this way have not yet been completely solved, this solution to coccidiosis problems awaits further developments.

SALMONELLOSES

Several diseases that potentially may cause severe losses in poultry are caused by organisms of the genus *Salmonella*. Pullorum disease and fowl typhoid are two specific manifestations of salmonellosis caused by nonmotile bacteria. A broad group of diseases called paratyphoid infections are also caused by salmonella organisms which are motile.

Pullorum Disease

This disease is caused by the organism *Salmonella pullorum*, a rod-shaped bacterium. At one time pullorum disease severely threatened the developing poultry industry because it caused severe losses in newly hatched chicks and was carried widely by adult chickens.

Pullorum disease is spread vertically from infected hens to chicks. Infected hens lay eggs containing the infectious organism, and newly hatched chicks will be infected with the disease. Chicks hatched from infected eggs have high mortality, are very weak and may have labored breathing or gasp for breath. Chicks hatched from noninfected eggs may become infected in the incubator by horizontal transmission from chicks that have hatched with the infection. The disease may not be manifested until a few days after hatching when chicks then show a tendency to huddle together, loss of appetite, and often a whitish diarrhea and high mortality. The organism causes lesions in many organs of the body,

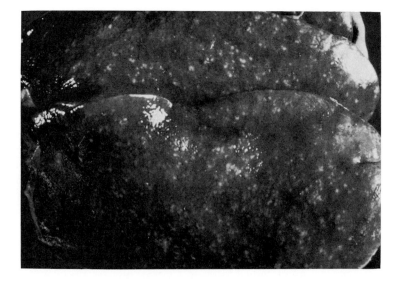

Fig. 10–9.   A liver showing focal necrosis typical of Salmonella infections. (Courtesy of Dr. M. C. Peckham, Cornell University.)

including the heart, spleen, liver (Fig. 10–9), kidney, and digestive tract, as well as the lungs.

Since the disease may be spread in the incubator, many of the current hatchery sanitation practices stem from measures introduced to control spread of pullorum infection. These include fumigation of eggs in the incubator with formaldehyde gas prior to hatching, as well as strict cleaning, use of disinfectants, and fumigation after a hatch has been removed from incubators.

Adults that carry the infection generally show no visible manifestations of disease, although there is some evidence that carriers may not be as good egg producers as noninfected hens. Lesions may be observed in several organs, particularly in the ovary, where misshapen and discolored ova may be found.

Since the major route of transmission and perpetuation of the disease is by transmission of the organism from infected hens through the egg to the chick, the method for control of this disease has been to eliminate infected breeders from flocks. Under the National Poultry Improvement Plan, breeders are tested each year by means of a blood test to detect antibodies of S. pullorum in carriers that could transmit Salmonella pullorum to their offspring. This program has been so successful that pullorum disease has been nearly eradicated from the United States. In 1975 only 0.0008% of the chickens tested had antibodies, and none of the turkeys tested were reactors. However, since occasional reactors are still found, the rigid testing programs cannot be relaxed without the risk of reappearance of the disease.

Fowl Typhoid

This disease is caused by the bacterium *Salmonella gallinarum*. The symptoms observed in affected chickens are similar to those of pullorum disease. Diarrhea, anemia, weakness, and death all may be observed with fowl typhoid. The liver, kidneys, and spleen may become enlarged and discolored. Since the organism is spread in the same way as *S. pullorum*, control measures for fowl typhoid are similar. Good hatchery sanitation and a vigorous program of detecting and eliminating reactors from breeding stock have been pursued under the National Poultry Improvement Plan. The drug furazolidone has been effective in reducing losses from chickens with fowl typhoid infection.

Paratyphoid Infection

This is a general term used to describe infections produced by several types of salmonella organisms other than *S. pullorum* and *S. gallinarum*. The symptoms are similar to those observed with pullorum and fowl typhoid. Droopiness, ruffled feathers, loss of appetite, profuse diarrhea, and pasting of the vent may all be observed.

Salmonella organisms responsible may be carried in the intestinal tract of recovered birds. Organisms of the *Salmonella* genus may affect several species of animal, including man, and control of salmonella organisms is a significant public health program affecting our food supply. Salmonella infections in man can result in severe intestinal disturbances and rarely even death.

Poultry products have been implicated as sources of infection in human cases of salmonellosis. Some feed ingredients are potential sources of salmonella infection, especially animal by-products such as meat meals, poultry by-product meal, fats, and fish meal. These ingredients must be processed properly to eliminate salmonella contamination, and feed mills must practice sanitation to prevent introduction of organisms into feeds.

Flocks with acute outbreaks of paratyphoid should not be used as sources of hatching eggs. Hatching eggs should be clean and fumigated soon after laying. Egg washers should contain clean solutions. Salmonella problems can be minimized if poultry are provided with a clean environment. This includes clean litter in recently cleaned and disinfected houses. Feed contamination by the organism should be eliminated. Potential introduction of infections from carriers such as rats and mice or wild birds should be prevented.

Nitrofuran drugs have been effective in preventing spread and losses from paratyphoid infections. Furazolidone has been particularly recommended for this purpose.

OTHER DISEASES

There is not sufficient space in this chapter to discuss all the diseases reported in chickens. For example, we will not discuss tuberculosis, fowl plague, fowl cholera, epidemic tremor, or bluecomb disease. These are all capable of causing serious problems, but their incidence in the United States is relatively low and may not constitute a serious problem at this time. Fowl pox, infectious synovitis, and infectious bursal disease are more common and are discussed briefly here.

Fowl Pox

This is a disease caused by a virus common in many parts of the world. Skin lesions or pocks that are black, raised scabs on the skin make the disease easy to recognize. The pocks are found on the comb, face, wattles, earlobes, shanks, and feet wherever there are no feathers (Fig. 10–10).

Although the disease has the features similar to small pox or chicken pox in humans, the fowl pox virus will not infect man.

Fig. 10-10. Appearance of fowl pox lesions on the comb and wattles about ten days after natural infection.

Chickens with fowl pox become very sick. Egg production, hatchability, and fertility in adults are reduced, and growth rate is severely retarded in young chicks. The disease is spread horizontally by contact with infected chickens. Mosquitoes carry the virus and make isolation of infected flocks difficult in some areas.

Inoculation with live virus vaccine can protect against fowl pox infection. Where the disease is endemic, vaccination may have to be routine in all flocks.

In areas where pox is not usually encountered, routine vaccination is not recommended. If an outbreak is encountered, affected birds should be isolated and the remaining birds in the flock vaccinated. Pigeon pox vaccine is milder and should be used if birds in lay must be vaccinated. The immunity induced by pigeon pox vaccine is short-lived while the immunity induced by the fowl pox vaccine is permanent.

Infectious Synovitis

This is an arthritic condition affecting the joints of chickens, especially the hock. It is caused by the organism *Mycoplasma synoviae,* a relative of the primary agent causing chronic respiratory disease. Infectious synovitis primarily affects growing broilers between 4 and 12 weeks of age, although it may appear in older chickens. High mortality has been reported, but in most cases mortality is low. Affected chickens are lame, grow slowly, and usually have pale combs and ruffled feathers. The joints swell, especially the hock joints and foot pads (Fig. 10-11). There is a viscous creamy exudate in the joints that can be seen at autopsy. The liver and kidney are usually enlarged and may be discolored.

Fig. 10–11. A swelling of joint and food pad of a chicken with infectious synovitis. (Courtesy of Dr. M. C. Peckham, Cornell University.)

Mycoplasma synoviae has been implicated in cases of airsacculitis in growing broilers. Even though more and more broilers are hatched from breeding flocks free of *Mycoplasma gallisepticum*, air sac problems are still observed which, as some pathologists have suggested, may be due to involvement of *Mycoplasma synoviae* organisms with viruses and other bacteria to cause a new type of airsacculitis. Broiler condemnations from synovitis are usually relatively low, only 2 to 3% of the total condemnations, but if the organism is involved in the production of airsacculitis, the losses due to this disease may be greater than previously recognized.

The production of *M. synoviae*-free breeding flocks probably is the best method for elimination of the disease, since it can be transmitted through the egg as well as horizontally. One difficulty is the production of *M. synoviae*-free breeders. Treatment of hatching eggs with antibiotics does not eliminate the organism from eggs. Heat treatment of hatching eggs under closely controlled conditions has been reported to kill the organism. This may provide a means for establishing *M. synoviae*-free breeding flocks.

The antibiotics oxytetracycline and chlortetracycline have been reported to be effective for control of synovitis if administered in the feed at levels of 50 to 100 grams per ton of feed.

Infectious Bursal Disease

This disease, recognized in 1962, affects young growing chickens. Outbreaks of the disease were first reported near Gumboro, Delaware, and "Gumboro disease" is often used as a synonym for infectious bursal disease.

The disease is caused by a virus that is persistent in the environment. Feed, water, and droppings from infected pens have been reported to be infectious for 52 days. Mealworms from houses in which outbreaks of the disease were observed were found to carry the virus.

Chicks with infectious bursal disease show a whitish diarrhea, soiled vent feathers, depression, loss of appetite, prostration, and in some cases death. Mortality rate may not be high but in some cases has reached 20 to 30%. The bursa of Fabricius becomes enlarged, cream-colored in appearance, with a yellowish fluid covering its surface. Kidneys are affected; chicks become dehydrated and may show darkening of the muscles and muscular hemorrhage. The clinical signs of the disease may last from 5 to 7 days.

Chicks between 3 and 6 weeks of age appear to be most susceptible to the disease. Because of the persistence of the virus, once it is observed on a farm it is difficult to prevent infection of subsequent flocks. Some immunity is passed to chicks by dams with antibodies to the virus. This seems to protect chicks for a few weeks after hatching when they are exposed to the virus.

POULTRY PARASITES

Parasites are organisms living on or within a host for the purpose of securing food. Thus nearly any of the bacteria or viruses causing disease could be considered parasites. However, for our purposes the term *parasite* is reserved for higher animal forms using fowls as sources of food. The most important ones are arthropods, the lice, mites, and ticks belonging to class Insecta or Arachnida, which are external parasites living on the surface of the skin, and the nematode and cestode worms that are internal parasites, living mainly in the gastrointestinal tract. Since parasites are all using the host as a source of food, they can cause irritation because of their feeding, loss of nutrients to the host, transmission of diseases as they move from one animal to another, and general reduction of the overall health of the host.

Pesticides

Generally, external parasites must be controlled by the use of insecticides. These pesticides are often toxic compounds that can be harmful both to the man applying them and to the chickens treated if they are used improperly. The safety of pesticides is constantly under surveillance by federal and state regulatory agencies. The residues of pesticides allowed in poultry meat and eggs are strictly regulated by the United States Food and Drug Administration. Eggs or poultry meat marketed with pesticide residues exceeding legal tolerances may be seized, and legal action may be taken against producers.

The benefits that pesticides can bring can be obtained only if they are used properly, observing all precautions for applications for which the specific pesticides have been found effective and safe. The pesticides registered for various agricultural applications have been under extensive review by state and federal regulatory agencies. Thus at the time of this writing it is difficult to give recommendations as to approved pesticides for control of external parasites that may be valid when the reader sees this section. Therefore recommendations for specific pesticides are not given here and should be obtained from local extension service sources.

Pesticides can be applied to poultry or to houses as dust, sprays, or mists, depending on the pesticides and the parasite to be controlled. Individual treatment of affected birds is effective, but usually impractical in commercial applications.

Poultry Lice

Lice are wingless, flattened insects from 1 to 6 mm in length. Some 40 species have been described on domesticated fowl of which 9 are found on chickens. A head louse, *Cuclotogaster heterographus* and the body lice *Menacanthus stramineus*, *M. cornutus*, and *M. pallidulus* are the most common lice encountered in poultry. Several species may infest the same

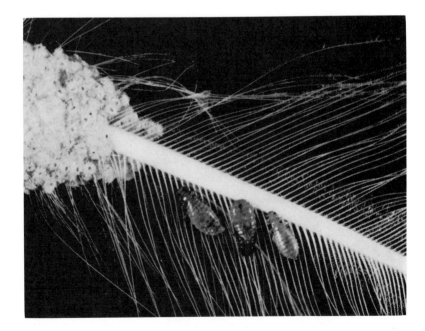

Fig. 10–12. Lice on a feather containing clusters of eggs at the base. (Courtesy of Dr. J. G. Matthysse, Cornell University.)

bird, but fortunately the control is similar for all species. Lice spend their entire life cycles on the host. They lay their eggs at the base of feathers and around the vent (Fig. 10–12). Newly hatched lice are small transparent versions of their parents and reach full size about 2 weeks after hatching.

Lice living on poultry are biting and chewing insects that consume scales, feathers, bits of skin, and feces that they find at the surface. Chickens with heavy louse infestations are likely to be inefficient, with generally lower levels of egg production or growth rate compared to uninfested birds.

Because lice are generally transferred from one infested bird to another, lice infestations are not likely to be encountered if chicks enter clean quarters, with no older birds.

Lice must be controlled by the use of insecticides to kill the lice on the body of the chicken and those in the houses. Thus the pesticide must be applied to the body of the bird as well as to roosts and houses for effective control. Several applications may be needed to kill lice hatched from eggs that may be present during the first application of the pesticide.

Mites

These are members of the class Arachnida. They are barely visible to the unaided eye, with broad unsegmented bodies with 4 pairs of legs. The

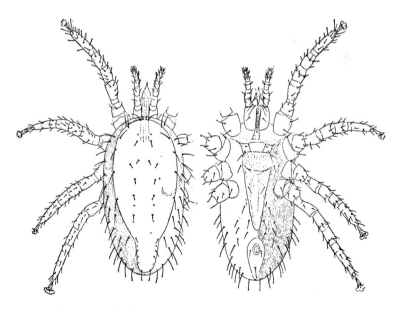

Fig. 10–13. The northern fowl mite, *Ornithonyssus sylviarum*. *Left,* dorsal view of female. *Right,* ventral view of female. (Courtesy of Dr. E. Baker, USDA, and the National Pest Control Association.)

red mite, *Dermanyssus gallinae*, and the northern fowl mite, *Ornithonyssus sylviarum* (Fig. 10–13), are the most common species found on chickens. Red mites do not spend their entire life cycles on the bird but live and breed in cracks and crevices of the house. Mites are sucking parasites that live primarily on blood and lymph. The red mite generally feeds only at night, leaving the host during the day to return to hideaways in the house. The northern fowl mite is present on birds and in the house at all times, during day and night. With cage housing of laying hens, the northern fowl mite is the most common external parasite encountered in caged hens in the United States.

Heavy mite infestations can cause considerable loss of blood with resulting anemia (Fig. 10–14). The fowl mite seems to find favorite locations on the chicken and may cause rejection of the carcass in the processing plant because of blemishes and damage to the skin.

Control of mites requires that both infested birds and their surroundings be treated with appropriate insecticides to get rid of mites on and off the birds.

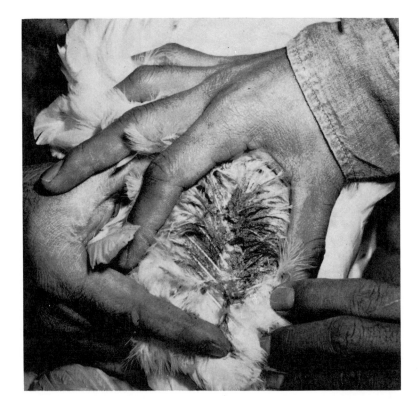

Fig. 10–14.   Mite infestations can at times be extremely severe. (Courtesy of Dr. J. G. Matthysse, Cornell University.)

Other mites that may cause problems are the scaly leg mite, *Knemidocoptes gallinae,* the depluming mite, *Knemidocoptes laevis,* and the air-sac mite, *Cytodites nudus.* Although not a serious problem in modern poultry production, they are troublesome when encountered and are difficult to control.

In addition to lice and mites, other external parasites sometimes can cause problems. These include chiggers (which are actually a larval stage of a mite), ticks, fleas, bedbugs, and some species of flies. In general, control of these parasites is similar to that needed to control mites, since they live both on and off the host.

Internal Parasites

Worms constitute the major internal parasites of poultry. The intestinal worms or helminths are primarily roundworms (nematodes) and tapeworms (cestodes). The most common roundworm found in poultry is the large roundworm, *Ascaridia galli.* This is a large white, round, unsegmented worm that may be about 2 to 5 inches long. Infection begins when chickens ingest eggs which hatch in the proventriculus or duodenum. The larvae enter the intestinal wall where they develop for a few days and then reenter the duodenum where they live until maturity (Fig. 10–15). Eggs passed out in the droppings develop to an infective stage in 10 to 12 days under good conditions of temperature and moisture.

Other roundworms of the genus *Capillaria,* a group of hairlike worms, also may inhabit the intestinal tract of chickens. The larvae and adults spend all their lives in the intestinal wall.

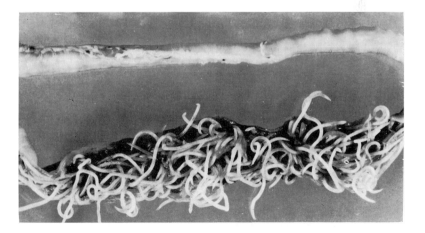

Fig. 10–15. The small intestine of a chicken that has been opened to reveal a severe infection with large roundworms, *Ascaridia galli.* (Courtesy of Dr. M. C. Peckham, Cornell University.)

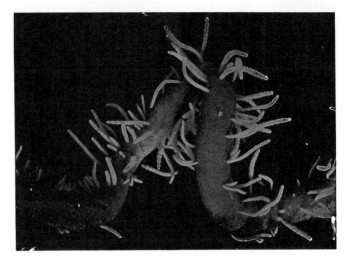

Fig. 10–16.   Inside of a hen's intestine showing attached tapeworms. (Courtesy of California Agricultural Experiment Station.)

The cecal worm, *Heterakis gallinarum,* is a small white roundworm that lives in the ceca. This worm has been a serious economic problem because it serves as a carrier for the protozoan *Histomona meleagridis*, which is the agent responsible for the disease blackhead, a particularly troublesome problem in raising turkeys.

Several species of tapeworm may live in the intestinal tract of chickens (Fig. 10–16). The life cycle of the tapeworm requires an intermediate host. Hosts are usually beetles, snails, slugs, crayfish, or flies. Thus control of the intermediate host often is important in control of the worm infestation.

Successful parasites rarely cause fatal harm to their hosts; this would also be fatal to the parasite. Chickens with heavy worm infestations generally are less productive, rather unhealthy in appearance. They may be inactive, with ruffled feathers and drooping wings. Capillaria infections have been implicated in poor absorption of vitamin A or pigmenting carotenoids so that pale shanks and skin or reduced egg yolk color has occasionally been blamed on Capillaria infection.

Control of internal parasites is largely a matter of sanitation. If chicks free of parasites are started in clean houses with clean litter, access to the worm eggs is prevented and infections do not become severe. Worm infections are more likely where ages of poultry are mixed and the cycle of infestation is not broken by repopulation and house cleaning. Poultry housed in cages do not have access to worm eggs in droppings and can be maintained free of worms.

Drugs termed *anthelmintics* are available to treat worm infections when necessary. Cecal worm infections can be treated with phenothiazine.

Piperazine compounds are useful against the large roundworm. Hygromycin, an antibiotic, can be used against the cecal worm, roundworm, and capillaria worms. Tapeworm infection can be treated with dibutyl tin dilaurate or dichlorophen. These drugs are available in various commercial forms and should be administered carefully according to the manufacturers' directions.

NONINFECTIOUS DISEASES

Disease is usually considered to be caused by infectious agents. However, we considered diseases caused by lack of nutrients in Chapter 8. Diseases also can be caused by toxic agents in the feed, litter, or water.

Mycotoxicoses are perhaps the most serious problems of this category that may be encountered. Toxins produced by the mold *Aspergillus flavus* are extremely toxic to animals. More than 100,000 turkey poults died in the United Kingdom several years ago when they were fed rations containing peanut meal contaminated with aflatoxins. These toxins, produced during growth of *A. flavus* on the peanut meal, can be very detrimental to poultry. Ducks and turkeys are much more susceptible to these toxins than are chickens. Levels as low as 1 μg of aflatoxin per gm of feed are lethal for ducks and turkeys, whereas chickens are only moderately affected by 4 μg of aflatoxin per gm of feed.

Mold growth is encouraged when grains, oil seeds, or complete feeds with high moisture are stored under conditions of high relative humidity. When grains and oil seeds contain over 11 to 13% moisture, mold growth can occur under proper circumstances. With peanut meals, no more than 7% moisture should be present for long storage. Under tropical conditions, molds in feeds may become a considerable problem, and some antifungal feed additives may be needed. Sodium propionate has been used extensively to retard mold growth.

The *Aspergillus flavus* is primarily a storage mold. Many other field fungi may infect crops during growth and maturation prior to harvest. Some of these molds may produce toxins or lower the nutritional value of corn. *Helminthosporium maydis* or southern leaf blight infection of corn in 1970 caused extensive damage to corn crops in many areas of the United States. The corn infested with *H. maydis* apparently was relatively nontoxic, although some reports suggested that growth of chicks fed blighted corn was not completely normal.

In general, it is good practice to avoid feeding moldy grains to animals if at all possible. If it is necessary to feed some mold-infected grain, feeding a sample to a small group of chickens for a short time is a good practice to determine if toxic molds may be present. It would also be wise to attempt to obtain an analysis for the presence of aflatoxins.

Toxic materials from other sources occasionally may get into feeds. In the mid-1950's thousands of broilers died when a toxic substance was present in fat incorporated into their diet. This fat was a by-product of a processing step that apparently caused the toxic substance to form. Weed seeds can contain toxic substances. Seeds of *Crotalaria* are quite toxic at levels of 0.05% of the seed in a feed.

Insecticides may be inadvertent contaminants in feeds. These are often relatively nontoxic to the chickens but may give residues of the insecticide in products that exceed legal tolerances for these materials in foods. The polychlorinated biphenyls (PCB's) are quite toxic, and instances of reduced egg production and impaired breeder performance from flocks fed contaminated feeds have been reported.

Feed additives must be used according to directions. Several arsenic compounds that are used as feed additives can cause toxicity if used in excess. Many coccidiostatic drugs may be growth-depressing if used in excess of recommended levels. Even nutrients such as selenium can be toxic if present at levels from 5 to 10 ppm in diets for chickens. One must not use the principle, "If a little is good, a lot may be better," in dealing with feed additives.

BEHAVIORAL PROBLEMS

Cannibalism can be a serious problem in raising poultry when large populations are kept in close confinement. Cannibalism can occur as toe picking in baby chicks or as feather pulling, vent picking, and head or tail picking in older flocks.

The causes of cannibalism are not well understood. One group of chickens may have considerable cannibalism, while others fed the same ration, housed, and managed similarly may have no difficulty whatsoever.

The lack of nutrients may result in cannibalism. When chicks are fed diets low in protein or deficient in an essential amino acid, some picking often occurs. Other nutritional deficiencies seem to cause irritability that may result in cannibalism. However, these deficiencies are usually produced under experimental conditions. Other factors implicated have been overcrowded housing conditions, insufficient feeding and water space, or too much light in the house. Properly controlled experiments to determine the causes are difficult to perform.

The best way to control cannibalism is to prevent it, because once started it may be difficult to stop. Proper debeaking is probably the simplest and most effective way to prevent chickens from picking each other (Fig. 10–17). Many broiler growers and some egg producers have their chickens debeaked at the hatchery. Debeaking at such an early age may not effectively control picking in adults. For replacement pullets, debeaking at 4 to 6 weeks of age has proven successful. Chickens at this age are easily handled, and the debeaking operation causes minimum stress.

Fig. 10–17. This hen was dubbed at hatching and debeaked at 6 weeks of age. The beak has not regrown and she cannot cause injury to other hens.

About two thirds of the beak is removed. Pullets can also be debeaked when they are moved to the laying house, but when they are debeaked at an earlier age they can recover from the stress prior to the onset of egg production.

Debeaking must be properly done. When chickens have too much of the beak removed they have trouble eating. Pelleted feed seems to be difficult for debeaked chickens to consume. Heavily debeaked chickens seem to have trouble consuming sufficient amounts of bulky feeds, very low in metabolizable energy value. Debeaking is commonly done with electric debeaking machines that are commercially available.

Hysteria

On some occasions, a condition of excessive fright has been observed in flocks of growing pullets or in layers. This may take the form of flight and piling up in corners of the house if floor housing is used, with the result that many birds may be suffocated. In caged layers, they may attempt to fly, resulting in injuries to wings and legs, or broken necks. The causes of outbreaks of hysteria are unknown, but care must be taken not to frighten birds needlessly by changing light intensity rapidly or bursting into a chicken house with much noise and quick movement.

Chapter 11

Marketing Eggs

The marketing of eggs involves buying and selling and the physical movement and distribution of eggs between the point of production and the point of consumption. To be effective, marketing must be concerned with those phases of production which influence egg quality, as well as with the preferences of consumers for certain characteristics of the retail product and for the type of package in which it is offered for sale. Between these two extremes come the many details of assembling, grading, standardization, processing, transportation, storage, financing, and merchandising. Obviously, the system of purchase, distribution, and sale is extensive and complicated, and the costs are considerable.

The ultimate objective of the marketing process is to put eggs in the hands of consumers with their original quality unimpaired. In practice this is seldom accomplished in a full and complete sense except when direct marketing from producer to consumer is involved. It will be the purpose of this chapter, however, to emphasize that objective and to point out the ways in which it may most nearly be attained.

THE GEOGRAPHICAL NATURE OF EGG PRODUCTION

The distribution of poultry flocks does not coincide with the geographical distribution of population. New York State, with about 9% of the population, produced less than 3% of the nation's eggs in 1976, while California, with about 10% of the population, produced nearly 14%, and Georgia with less than 2.5% of the population produced over 8% of the eggs.

Not all eggs produced in the United States are available for human consumption. Some are used for hatching, and many are used for a variety of other non-food purposes such as the production of therapeutic vaccines. The total of non-food uses amounts to nearly 7% of all eggs produced. If 1970 production totals by states are adjusted to allow for non-food uses, and if consumption in all states is assumed to be the same as the U. S. average of 316 eggs per capita, some states have a large surplus production, while others do not produce anywhere near enough to fill their own needs. In Table 11–1 are shown the ten states having the greatest surpluses in 1970 and the ten having the greatest deficits. Of the ten leading states in total population, only California produced a surplus of eggs.

Table 11–1.   Surplus and Deficit States in Egg Production, 1970

Surplus States*	Production exceeds consumption by: (million eggs)		Deficit States*	Consumption exceeds production by: (million eggs)	
		cumulative			cumulative
1. Georgia	3,438	total	1. New York	3,624	total
2. Arkansas	2,538	5,976	2. Illinois	1,754	5,378
3. Iowa	1,849	7,825	3. New Jersey	1,588	6,966
4. N. Carolina	1,736	9,561	4. Michigan	1,499	8,465
5. Mississippi	1,541	11,102	5. Ohio	1,467	9,932
6. Alabama	1,382	12,484	6. Massachusetts	1,310	11,242
7. California	1,312	13,796	7. Texas	1,062	12,304
8. Maine	1,007	14,803	8. Maryland	927	13,231
9. Indiana	967	15,770	9. Pennsylvania	693	13,924
10. Minnesota	831	16,601	10. Louisiana	434	14,358

Based on population as reported by the Bureau of the Census and production estimates by the U. S. Department of Agriculture.
* Calculated by assuming a uniform consumption of 316 eggs per capita, and adjusting total production downward by 10% because of eggs used for hatching and other non-food purposes.

Table 11–2.   Regional Patterns in Consumption and Supplies of Eggs, 1975

	New England	Middle Atlantic	East North Central	West North Central	South Atlantic	South Central	Mountain	Pacific
Total regional supply as % of total regional consumption	96	55	73	160	126	116	58	129
Shell eggs: Regional supply as % of regional consumption	104	53	72	137	134	120	64	129
Processed eggs: Regional production as % of regional consumption	31	74	82	343	69	86	18	130

Source: Poultry and Egg Situation, September, 1976.

Of the eight cities with a population of 800,000 or more in 1970, all but one were in the deficit states listed in Table 11–1. The exception was Los Angeles. The "egg stream" of the country continues to flow east just as it did 35 years ago, with the addition of a substantial northerly flow from the south central and south Atlantic states. Georgia, North Carolina, Mississippi, Alabama, and Maine are important surplus states east of the Mississippi River; Texas and Louisiana are the most important deficit states west of the river. The degree of self-sufficiency in production of shell and processed eggs by regions in 1975 is shown in Table 11–2.

MARKETING CHANNELS

Marketing channels for eggs have changed substantially during the past 20 years (Fig. 11–1). In the late 1950's 57% of eggs moved from producers to assembler packers who in turn supplied eggs to wholesale distributors, retailers, institutions, and egg-breaking plants. Thirty-five percent of eggs were sold directly to wholesale distributors while 7% were marketed by producers to retail outlets, institutions, and consumers directly. Only 1% of eggs moved directly from the farm to breaking plants.

The wholesale distributors' share of the market has dropped to 17% of the commercial egg supply. With increasing integration of the egg industry, more direct lines of marketing from the producer to the

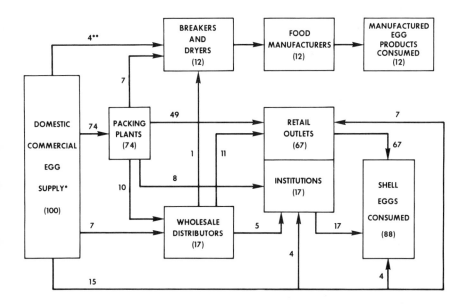

Fig. 11–1. Commercial marketing channels for eggs (1976). * Excludes exports, imports, eggs consumed on farms where produced, and eggs used for hatching. ** Percentages of domestic commercial egg supply. (U.S. Department of Agriculture.)

consumer have developed. In 1976, for example, 74% of the commercial egg supply moved directly to packing plants. Fifteen percent were sold to institutional or retail outlets and retailed directly to consumers. Approximately 12% of the commercial supplies of eggs were broken and ultimately used by food manufacturers.

THE MAINTENANCE OF EGG QUALITY

Because of the differences in geographical distribution of poultry and human population, the matter of maintaining the quality of poultry products during the time that elapses between their production and their delivery to the final consumer is of great importance. Its successful accomplishment requires that every individual who has anything to do with the marketing of eggs or poultry shall be "quality conscious" and interested in reducing the loss of original quality to a minimum. The advantage gained from strict attention to production factors that affect quality may be quickly lost if the products are not properly handled after they leave the farm.

Eggs are among the most delicate and perishable food products, are subject to rapid deterioration, and are easily affected by unfavorable surroundings. In food value, flavor, and general attractiveness, they are better when first laid than at any later time. Because consumers are quick to discriminate against poor eggs, it is important not only that the right kind of eggs be produced, but that they be so handled as to reach the consumer with the least possible loss of their original quality.

CONSUMER PREFERENCES

Consumers are the final judge of what constitutes quality in eggs and their measures or preferences do not always coincide with the measures used by the egg trade. Some consumers, for example, actually prefer eggs with medium or thin white over those with firm thick white. In general, consumers are not so much concerned with minor details representing egg quality as they are with size of the eggs and assurance of freshness.

Researchers in Wisconsin reported on a survey of purchasing habits of Wisconsin consumers. When a sample of 598 families was queried about their reasons for purchasing eggs from their current source, nearly two thirds of those satisfied with their present source cited freshness or quality as their primary concern; less than half as many indicated convenience of purchase was an important factor; and surprisingly less than 4.5% cited price as a primary consideration. Of approximately 28% of respondents who were not satisfied with their source, over four fifths cited freshness or quality as the major reasons for desiring an alternate source of eggs. Quality is clearly an important factor in the minds of consumers.

Per capita egg consumption in the United States has been on a generally downward trend during the past 25 years. Per capita consumption of eggs increased from 310 in 1938 to 402, the highest recorded, in 1945. Consumption was nearly constant from 1945 to 1952. Then it declined from 390 eggs in 1952, stabilizing at approximately 320 eggs during the late 1960's and early 1970's and finally decreasing to 276 eggs in 1976.

Many reasons have been put forward to explain the decline in per capita egg consumption. Although no one is certain of the exact causes, changes in eating habits have undoubtedly contributed to the decline. Eggs are traditionally a breakfast food. Recent surveys indicate that less time is taken in the preparation of breakfast, and that breakfast is not the significant family activity that it was in previous years. Convenience foods such as cereals and snack foods have assumed a greater share of the breakfast menu. The medical controversy over the role of cholesterol in heart disease may also have contributed to the decline in egg consumption.

NUTRIENT COMPOSITION OF EGGS

Eggs are richly endowed with nutrients. Perhaps this is not surprising, since the egg in its normal function in reproduction must supply all of the nutritional needs of the young chick embryo throughout its 21 days of development prior to hatching. Yolk is the richest portion of the egg in trace mineral and vitamin content. The high quality protein of eggs has been used for decades as a standard of high biological value, against which other foodstuffs are evaluated. The specific composition of eggs was recently determined through the cooperative efforts of researchers at the University of Missouri, Iowa State, and Ohio State universities. These data are shown in Table 11–3.

MEASURES OF EGG QUALITY

Quality in eggs, with reference to food value or market desirability, is measured (1) by external appearance; (2) by candling; and (3) by odor, flavor, and physical character of the opened egg. For the most part, these measures give only a gross picture that is sufficient for trade purposes. Exact measures of quality, in the scientific sense, have been almost totally lacking, though considerable progress in that direction has recently been made.

External Appearance

Under this heading may be mentioned size, shape, shell color and texture, cleanliness, and uniformity of eggs within a given sample or lot. Although small eggs of high interior quality may be worth more than large eggs of low quality, it is nevertheless true that size is a most important

Table 11-3. Nutrient Composition of Fresh Shell Eggs

Gross Composition*	Whole	White	Yolk
Solids (gm)	13.40	3.57	10.00
Protein (N. × 6.25) (gm)	6.38	3.13	3.18
Lipids (total) (gm)	6.52	—	6.71
Saturated	2.38	—	2.34
Monounsaturated	2.84	—	2.86
Polyunsaturated	0.92	—	0.88
Cholesterol	0.26	—	0.27
Ash (total) (gm)	0.52	0.23	0.32
Calories (C)			
Calorimetry	97.0	18.0	79.0
Calculated	87.0	14.0	74.0
Amino acids (gm)			
Alanine	0.339	0.193	0.156
Arginine	0.408	0.186	0.224
Aspartic acid	0.636	0.363	0.256
Cystine	0.143	0.100	0.052
Glutamic acid	0.790	0.439	0.358
Glycine	0.207	0.110	0.095
Histidine	0.148	0.072	0.079
Isoleucine	0.318	0.170	0.160
Leucine	0.529	0.276	0.274
Lysine	0.451	0.219	0.236
Methionine	0.207	0.129	0.075
Phenylalanine	0.302	0.183	0.122
Proline	0.291	0.150	0.128
Serine	0.488	0.212	0.254
Threonine	0.318	0.141	0.159
Tryptophan	0.092	0.049	0.046
Tyrosine	0.281	0.135	0.144
Valine	0.413	0.221	0.185
Vitamins			
A (IU)	117.0	—	157.0
D (IU)	19.2	—	33.5
E (mg)	0.54	—	0.77
B_{12} (μg)	0.57	tr	0.63
Biotin (μg)	9.70	1.68	8.03
Choline (mg)	437.0	0.42	218.0
Folic acid (mg)	0.016	tr	0.013
Inositol (mg)	8.19	1.24	6.70
Niacin (mg)	0.047	0.032	0.012
Pantothenic acid (mg)	0.729	0.042	0.966
Pyridoxine (mg)	0.073	0.002	0.069
Riboflavin (mg)	0.170	0.084	0.090
Thiamine (mg)	0.047	0.001	0.050
Minerals (mg)			
Calcium	31.1	2.9	26.9
Chlorine	91.1	58.4	31.9
Copper	0.033	0.007	0.026
Iodine	0.038	0.003	0.033
Magnesium	6.57	4.14	2.43
Manganese	0.021	0.002	0.022
Phosphorus	126.1	4.75	119.6
Potassium	73.1	49.0	21.7
Sodium	73.7	60.9	12.0
Sulfur	87.6	52.8	32.6
Zinc	0.79	0.003	0.74
Iron	1.19	0.004	1.17

By permission from Cotterill, O. J., Marion, W. W., and Naber, E. C.: A nutrient reevaluation of shell egg. Poult. Sci., 56:1927, 1977.

* For 60.8 gram egg.

factor in determining the price received for eggs in any market. The standard size is 2 ounces each, or 24 ounces to the dozen, and it has become customary to refer to 22-, 23-, 24-, or 26-ounce eggs when what is meant is the weight of a dozen. Eggs weighing up to 26 ounces to the dozen may sell at a premium over 24-ounce eggs, but extremely large eggs (30 ounces or more to the dozen) are not in great demand because of the greater danger of breakage when handled in ordinary containers and the extra expense in handling them in special packages. These objections do not, of course, apply to a strictly local market where extra size may occasionally be made the basis of extra premiums. Eggs weighing less than 24 ounces to the dozen will have to be sold at a discount in most, if not all markets, during a large part of the year.

Shape is not often of great importance, and in any event it is easily controlled by selection. It should be remembered, however, that short, round eggs do not make the best appearance in an ordinary case or carton and that long eggs are much more likely to be broken during shipment than are eggs of normal shape.

Shell color is, in the main, a breed characteristic, though there is often wide variation among individual hens in a particular flock when all are of the same breed and variety. If white eggs are to sell at a good price in a competitive market, they must be chalk white. A few tinted or creamy eggs in a case of white ones will cause buyers to turn to other shipments that are more nearly uniform. With brown eggs there is more tolerance because of the natural variation in brown shell color, but it is nevertheless true that of two cases that are equal in other respects, the one that is most nearly uniform in shade of brown color will be likely to sell first. All of this simply means that uniformity of shell color gives the seller a price advantage. Although there is no relation between shell color and interior quality, there is enough color preference in certain markets to warrant consideration by shippers. Thus New York City has long been known as a white-egg market. Boston, on the other hand, has long been regarded as a brown-egg market.

Eggs with rough, thin, or uneven shells are always discriminated against and should not be shipped to central markets. They should either be used at home or disposed of locally to customers who will appreciate the opportunity to get eggs of high interior quality at less than the regular market price. If the quantity of such eggs warrants, they may be broken out and sold as liquid eggs.

Uniformity helps to sell any product, and eggs are no exception to the rule. A case of eggs weighing 23 ounces to the dozen, if all eggs in it are alike, will be much easier to sell than a heavier case in which there is wide variation in size, shape, and color. It nearly always pays to sort eggs before sale or shipment in order to secure reasonable uniformity within each package.

Stained or dirty eggs are unattractive in appearance and must always be sold at a discount. Furthermore, dirty eggs will spoil more quickly than clean eggs, and careless washing makes matters worse because it increases the chance of spoilage. For these reasons it becomes important to do everything possible to prevent the production of dirty eggs.

Studies at the Missouri Station have shown that the percentage of dirty eggs can be materially reduced by following suitable management practices. When eggs from floor-housed hens were gathered only once daily, 31% were either dirty or slightly dirty, but when gathered four times daily the percentage dropped to 15. During a 6-month period 12.5% of eggs laid in trapnests were soiled, whereas 29.4% of those laid in open nests were dirty. In the Missouri tests white leghorns gave more than twice as many dirty eggs on a percentage basis as did all other breeds combined. Many more dirty eggs were found among those laid before nine o'clock than among those laid later in the day. Perhaps the most significant finding in these tests was that more than 99% of all eggs were clean at the moment of laying and before they came in contact with the nest. This is one of the reasons for the greatly increased use of laying cages for commercial egg production and the use of automatic egg collecting equipment.

Candling Quality

External appearance is not an accurate indication of what is to be found inside the shell, and it is therefore customary to make use of the practice known as candling in order to measure interior quality. Accurate candling can best be done in a darkened room with some arrangement for passing the light from a lamp or an electric light bulb through the eggs to the observer. Many of the important differences in interior quality can then be plainly seen. Candling equipment may range from a simple homemade affair costing but a few cents, to an elaborate mechanical device, with which is combined an automatic grader (according to egg weight). Regardless of the type of equipment, each egg must be individually examined.

The characters used in measuring quality on the basis of candling appearance are shell, air cell, yolk, white, and germ. Eggs that have thin, porous, or cracked shells are easily detected. None but sound shells should be passed when candling eggs for shipment.

The air space or air cell is usually at the large end of the egg, and can be plainly seen when the egg is candled. It develops between the two membranes that line the shell, and increases in size according to the amount of moisture evaporated from the egg. It should be fixed in position with no tendency to bubble or move about. A bubbly air cell is an indication of staleness and a weak shell membrane, or of rough handling, and an air cell that moves freely to any part of the egg is the result of a broken inner membrane.

When a strictly fresh egg is candled, the yolk cannot be seen except as a faint shadow. It should remain close to the center of the egg. In an egg of

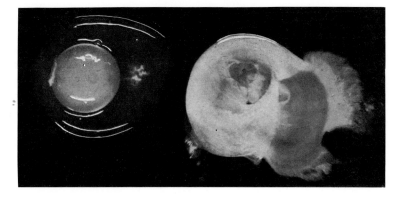

Fig. 11–2. These fertile eggs were held 4 days at 100° F. The egg on the left was thermostabilized by dipping in hot water to prevent embryonic development and normal breakdown of the thick white. (Courtesy of Missouri Agricultural Experiment Station.)

lower quality the yolk moves more freely and casts a darker shadow because it floats nearer to the shell. Much of this difference in appearance is really due to changes in the white, or albumen, rather than to changes in the yolk. In an egg of top quality the white is firm and clear and so thick or viscous that the yolk does not move freely in it. Under usual holding conditions the egg white gradually becomes thin, weak, and watery in appearance so that the yolk is permitted to move about as the egg is turned. As a result of this condition, the yolk floats close to the shell where it casts a dark shadow and is therefore more plainly seen in candling.

High-grade eggs must not show any visible germ development. Embryonic development can be prevented by dipping fertilized eggs in hot water (Fig. 11–2). This practice is not used, however, in commercial egg production, since fertile eggs are simply not produced for commercial sale.

Although most eggs are of excellent interior quality when first laid, there are some faults that occasionally appear in eggs from flocks that are receiving the best of care in every way. Blood spots, bloody eggs, meat spots, and body checks may be mentioned as examples. A blood spot is due to the rupture of a small blood vessel while the yolk is being formed. The result is that a small clot of blood is enclosed within the egg, usually on the surface of the yolk. Less frequently the clot may be so large as to color most of the white and give it a pink appearance before the candle. It is then referred to as a bloody egg and is unfit for food. Small blood spots can easily be removed after the egg is opened, so that the egg may be used, but such eggs should not be marketed (Table 11–4). Large processing plants today use electronic candling equipment that is capable of detecting very small blood spots that would normally escape the notice of experienced candlers (Fig. 11–3).

Table 11–4.   Incidence, Size, Location, and Color of Blood and Meat Spots in 2,761 Eggs from 36 Crossbred Hens

	Meat Spots %	Blood Spots %	Clear Eggs %
Incidence	38.1	9.3	52.6
Size of spots:			
Pinpoint	13.9	33.9	
Up to ⅛ inch	76.9	45.2	
⅛ to ⅜ inch	8.9	12.8	
Over ⅜ inch	0.3	8.1	
Location of spots:			
Albumen	58.6	Nearly	
Chalazae	29.1	100%	
Yolk	12.3	on yolk	
Color of spots:			
Dark	17.7		
Intermediate	26.8	All red	
Light	55.5		

Data of Helbacka and Swanson, 1958.

Fig. 11–3. Commercial egg processing plants are making increasing use of electronic equipment to detect eggs containing blood spots. (Courtesy of Poultry Tribune.)

Table 11–5. Summary of United States Standards for Quality of Individual Shell Eggs

Quality Factor	Specifications for Each Quality Factor			
	AA Quality	A Quality	B Quality	C Quality
Shell	Clean Unbroken Practically normal	Clean Unbroken Practically normal	Clean; to very slightly stained Unbroken. May be slightly abnormal	Clean; to moderately stained Unbroken. May be abnormal
Air cell	⅛ inch or less in depth Practically regular	³/₁₆ inch or less in depth Practically regular	⅜ inch or less in depth. May be free or bubbly	May be over ⅜ inch in depth May be free or bubbly
White	Clear Firm (72 Haugh units or higher)	Clear. May be reasonably firm (60 to 72 Haugh units)	Clear. May be slightly weak (31 to 60 Haugh units)	May be weak and watery. May have small blood spots* (Less than 31 Haugh units)
Yolk	Outline slightly defined Practically free from defects	Outline fairly well defined Practically free from defects	Outline well defined May be slightly enlarged and flattened May show definite but not serious defects	Outline plainly visible May be enlarged and flattened May show clearly visible germ development but no blood May show other serious defects

For eggs with dirty or broken shells, the standards of quality provide three additional qualities:

	Dirty	Check	Leaker
	Unbroken May be dirty	Checked or cracked but not leaking	Broken so contents are leaking

* If they are small (aggregating not more than ⅛ inch in diameter).

Table 11–6.   Summary of U. S. Consumer Grades for Shell Eggs

U.S. Consumer Grade	Quality	Tolerance Permitted %	Quality
(Origin)	*At least 85% must be:*		
Grade AA or Fresh Fancy	AA	Up to 15	A
		Not over 5	B, C, or Check
Grade A	A or better	Up to 15	B
		Not over 5	C or Check
Grade B	B or better	Up to 15	C
		Not over 10	Checks
(Destination)	*At least 80% must be:*		
Grade AA or Fresh Fancy	AA	Up to 20	A
		Not over 5	B, C, or Check
		Not over 0.5	Leakers or Dirties
Grade A	A or better	Up to 20	B
		Not over 5	C or Check
		Not over 0.5	Leakers or Dirties
Grade B	B or better	Up to 20	C
		Not over 10	Checks
		Not over 0.5	Leakers or Dirties

Table 11–7.   Tolerance for an Individual Case or Carton Within a Lot of U. S. Consumer Grades of Eggs as Specified

U.S. Consumer Grade		Case—Minimum Quality—% Origin	Destination	Carton—Minimum Quality Number of eggs (Origin and Destination)
Grade AA or Fresh Fancy	AA	75	70	8 eggs AA
Quality	A	15	20	2 eggs A
	B, C, or Check	10	10	2 eggs B, C, or Check
Grade A	A	75	70	8 eggs A
	B	15	20	2 eggs B
	C or Check	10	10	2 eggs C or Check
Grade B	B	75	70	8 eggs B
	C	5	10	2 eggs C
	Check	20	20	2 eggs Check

Note: Individual states often specify lower tolerances than are permitted under U.S. minimums.

Table 11-8. U. S. Weight Classes for Consumer Grades for Shell Eggs

Size of weight class	Minimum net weight per dozen oz	Minimum net weight per 30 dozen lb	Minimum weight for individual eggs at rate per dozen oz
Jumbo	30	56	29
Extra Large	27	50½	26
Large	24	45	23
Medium	21	39½	20
Small	18	34	17
Peewee	15	28	—

A lot average tolerance of 3.3% for individual eggs in the next lower weight class is permitted as long as no individual case within the lot exceeds 5%.

A "body check" is an egg in which the shell appears to have been cracked while in the uterus or shell gland, presumably before all the shell material was formed. The break is then sealed by the deposition of additional shell material, so that after being laid it appears normal when given but casual inspection. The weak shell is easily detected by candling. Such eggs should not be shipped because of the greater likelihood of breakage.

The official United States standards for quality of individual eggs with clean unbroken shells are summarized in Table 11–5. Other standards are given in Tables 11–6, 11–7, and 11–8.

Detailed definitions of terms used in describing eggs which conform to the various standards and grades may be obtained from the U. S. Department of Agriculture, Washington, D.C. 20250.

Egg Breakage

Since eggs are easily broken during gathering, transportation, and processing, it is important for both producers and processors to be alert to the problem in order to keep such losses at a minimum.

A North Carolina study of 18 processing plants revealed overall breakage of 7.3%, with about half of this occurring between farm and plant. And there is additional breakage before eggs leave the farm. Total breakage was 2.7% for hens in the first month of lay, but increased steadily with age until it reached 13.5% for those in the fifteenth month of lay. This is one reason that commercial egg producers prefer pullets to older hens and often force molt pullets after they complete a normal laying year.

In a recent survey of 24 fully mechanized cage layer operations in the Northeast, the average shell damage from the laying cage to the point of packing was slightly more than 12% of eggs laid. The distribution of breakage at specific points in production is shown below.

	Breakage
Situation A	
Farm-run eggs (cage to cooler)	4.98%
Situation B	
Total production and processing	
(point of lay)	4.60%
(cage to point of processing)	1.79%
(processing)	5.76%
Total damage	12.15%

Eggs from the fourteen flocks in situation A were packed in cases on the farm and shipped to an egg processing plant. Total shell damage averaged 4.98%, with a high of 8.30% and a low of 1.07% in the flocks studied.

In situation B, where farms were also involved in washing and packing, slightly more than half of the total breakage of 12.15% occurred from the point of lay to the point of processing. Most, 4.60%, occurred at the point of lay. Considerable variation existed among farms in total breakage. The lowest values were about 4%, and the highest, 24%.

As part of the above study, workers at Cornell University and Rutgers University determined the damage to eggs occurring through retail as well as production channels. In studies of 8 farms and 20 retail outlets, 57% of the total shell damage had occurred during egg production, gathering, and processing. Eighteen percent occurred in handling between the farm and the holding rooms at the retail outlets, 7% occurred in the transfer of eggs to display cases, and another 18% of the breakage took place due to consumers' handling of eggs in the display case. Eggs are a particularly fragile commodity. Any unnecessary step in the handling of eggs between the producer and the consumer is likely to increase the losses from shell damage.

Egg breakage and shell characteristics such as poor texture have been estimated to account for losses of 170 to 250 million dollars annually in the market value of eggs in the United States. Surveys such as these will be helpful to producers, packers, and retailers in identifying specific processes in egg handling where breakage is a potential problem.

Similar tests have been used to find critical points in egg processing machinery where breakage occurs most frequently, thus leading to improved design of such equipment.

Improvement in shell strength can sometimes be achieved by substituting cracked oyster shell for part of the pulverized calcium carbonate included in the usual layer ration. Two-thirds oyster shell and one-third pulverized limestone seem to be about right. Flakes of oyster shell remain in the gizzard long enough to provide a continuous supply of calcium that is nutritionally available throughout the long period of shell formation.

A study made at the Agricultural Research Center in Edinburgh, Scotland, showed a wide variation among strains of layers in the number of cracked eggs for hens in cages. Strains A and B had 64% and 59% cracked egs, while Strain G had only 12%. This, together with variation among individual hens ranging from a low of 2% to a high of 99%, suggests that selection against breakage could be highly effective.

Quality of Opened Eggs

Some characteristics of eggs cannot be observed until the eggs are opened. These include odor, flavor, and color of yolk. Since eggs will quickly absorb odors of various sorts, it is important that they be handled at all times in such a way as to prevent contact with any materials that might cause an undesirable odor or flavor.

The differences, seen in candling, between an egg with a firm white and a well-centered, dimly visible yolk, and an egg with a watery white and prominent yolk, are even more pronounced when the eggs are opened (Figs. 11–4, 11–5). The yolk of the first egg will appear well rounded, but that of the second will be flattened and spread out. The white of the first egg will stand up well, suggesting the original shape of the unopened egg, but that of the second will be watery in appearance and quite without shape. Attempts to influence this condition by feeding have, as a rule, been unsuccessful. Although it has been shown that holding conditions affect the rate of change in viscosity of the white, it appears that the individual hen is also an important factor. The most promising means of bringing about improvement in this respect are selection and breeding.

One other measurement has found its way into the description of official standards of quality in the sense that specific numerical values have been assigned and recognized, namely, the measurement of egg white or

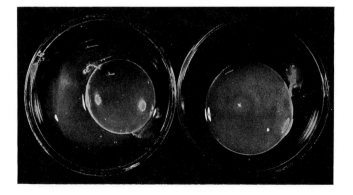

Fig. 11–4. Heat is the principal cause of loss in egg quality. A firm yolk and a dense white (left) are quickly changed by heat. The egg shown at the right has been incubated for three days.

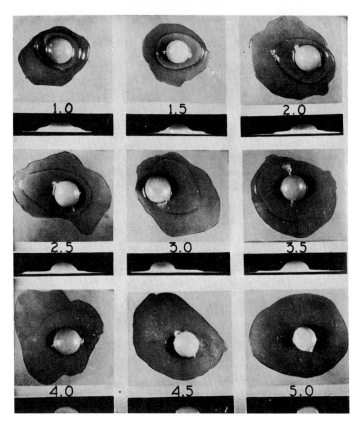

Fig. 11–5. Successive stages in the "broken out" appearance of eggs. No. 1 is approximately equivalent to U.S. AA quality, No. 2 to U.S. A quality, No. 3 to U.S. B quality, and No. 4 to U.S. C quality. (Courtesy of Institute of American Poultry Industries.)

albumen quality in Haugh units (Fig. 11–6). It is a precise measurement, and one that is too refined for widespread use, but students who may have an interest in becoming official inspectors or graders should be familiar with it.

Curiously enough, it is not feasible to define a single Haugh unit because the scale of values is always used in a multiple sense with values ranging from 100 down to a practical minimum of 20 or slightly lower. Haugh units are found by determining the logarithm of albumen height, corrected to a standard egg weight of 2 ounces (24 ounces per dozen). The log values are then expressed in convenient whole numbers by multiplying by 100. Since albumen height is influenced by the pull of gravity, the gravitational constant 32.2 is introduced into the calculation. The original Haugh formula is:

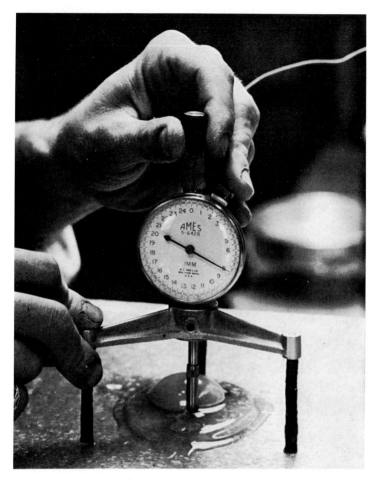

Fig. 11-6. Using a micrometer to measure albumen height in order to determine Haugh units. (Courtesy of Babcock Poultry Farm, Ithaca, New York.)

$$HU = 100 \log \left[H - \frac{\sqrt{G(30W^{.37} - 100)}}{100} + 1.9 \right]$$

HU = Haugh units
H = observed albumen height in millimeters
G = the gravitational constant, 32.2
W = observed weight of the egg in grams

For ease of calculation this can be simplified to:

$$HU = 100 \log (H + 7.57 - 1.7W^{.37})$$

Table 11–9.   Relationship Between Haugh Units and Albumen Height

Measure	49.6 grams (21 ounces per dozen)	53.2 grams (22.5 ounces per dozen)	56.7 grams (24 ounces per dozen)	60.2 grams (25.5 ounces per dozen)	63.8 grams (27 ounces per dozen)
Albumen Height (millimeters)		*Haugh Units for Eggs of Indicated Weights*			
10	102	101	100	99	98
9	97	96	95	95	94
8	92	91	90	89	88
7	87	86	84	83	82
6	80	79	78	77	75
5	73	71	70	68	67
4	64	62	60	58	56
3	53	50	48	45	42
2	37	34	30	26	22
Haugh Units		*Albumen Height for Eggs of Indicated Weights*			
100	9.6	9.8	10.0	10.2	10.3
90	7.6	7.8	7.9	8.1	8.3
80	5.9	6.1	6.5	6.5	6.7
70	4.6	4.8	5.0	5.2	5.4
60	3.6	3.8	4.0	4.2	4.3
50	2.8	3.0	3.2	3.3	3.5
40	2.2	2.3	2.5	2.7	2.8
30	1.6	1.8	2.0	2.2	2.3
20	1.2	1.4	1.6	1.8	1.9

Calculated Haugh unit values are shown in Table 11–9 for eggs of five different indicated weights from 21 to 27 ounces per dozen, and for albumen heights ranging from 10 to 2. The table also includes Haugh unit values of 100 to 20, by 10-unit intervals, with the corresponding albumen height measurements of eggs of the same five indicated weights. The relationship of Haugh units and of USDA Quality Scores to U.S. Standards of Quality of Individual Eggs is shown graphically in Figure 11–7. Note that each value in the scale of USDA Quality Scores covers a range of 8 Haugh units. This means that for most purposes, eggs differing by no more than 8 Haugh units are considered to be in good agreement. It is apparent also from a study of Table 11–9 that for eggs weighing from 1.75 to 2.25 ounces each (21 to 27 ounces per dozen), albumen height alone provides an adequate measure of egg white quality in trade channels.

The age of the laying hen influences albumen quality, measured in Haugh units. This is illustrated in Table 11-10 showing the results of a 1975 survey of heavy egg-type chickens carried through two cycles of production. Molting appears to have little benefit in improving albumen quality or shell strength.

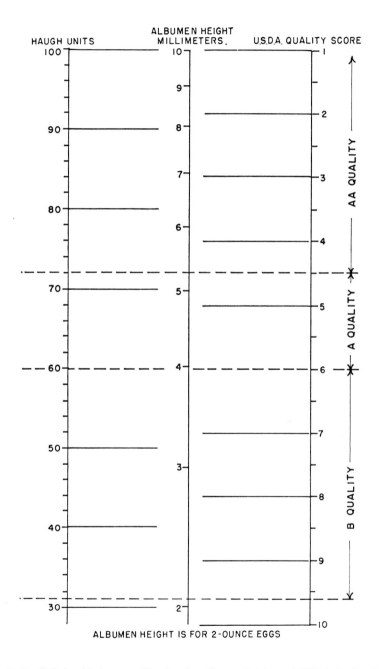

Fig. 11–7. Relationship between Haugh units, albumen height, and USDA Quality Score for 2-ounce eggs.

Table 11–10.   Average Haugh Scores of Eggs from Heavy Market-
egg Hens through Two Cycles of Production

1st Production Cycle		2nd Production Cycle	
Days*	Haugh score	Days*	Haugh score
28	94.0	420	75.8
56	88.2	448	69.8
112	80.8	476	71.6
140	76.9	504	69.1
224	74.8	532	68.6
252	74.4	588	63.6
308	73.9	616	65.5
336	70.5		
364	77.3		
(molt, June 1972)			

* Days after start of production.

Other Measures of Quality

Various attempts have been made to devise more exact measures of egg quality in order that careful scientific study can be undertaken of the facts that influence quality. The yolk index is a measure of the standing-up quality of the yolk. It is obtained by dividing the height of the yolk by its average diameter. The measurements are made after the egg is broken out into a small plate. Average values for fresh eggs usually fall between 0.42 and 0.40. As the yolk becomes flattened, the yolk index is lowered. When the value of the index is 0.25 or lower, the yolk is so weak that it is extremely difficult to handle it for measurement without breaking.

Deterioration in the eggs of individual hens has been measured by recording the percentage of thick and thin egg white. As the yolk increased in weight due to absorption of water from the white, the percentage of thick white decreased. The rate of change in percentage of thick white, under uniform holding conditions, was a characteristic of individual hens, and there was considerable variation among hens in this respect. The concentration of water in thick white remained exactly equal to that in the associated thin white, regardless of losses to the yolk and to the atmosphere.

Albumen score has been used by workers at Cornell and is in many respects the simplest of all measures to apply. The scale of scores is illustrated in Figure 11–5.

Workers at the California Station have described a method for the study of eggshell porosity, and have suggested a set of standards of comparison to be used with the method. The standards are shown in Figure 11–8. These workers found that the initial porosity in fresh eggs was normally

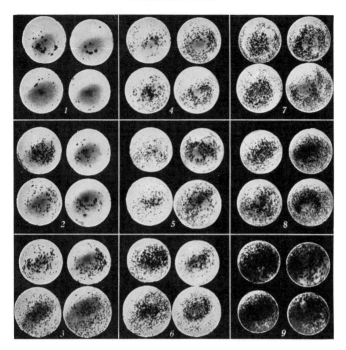

Fig. 11–8. Variation in shell porosity. The numbers *1* to *9* represent increasing shell porosity as shown by the increasing number of small spots on the interior of the shells. Both halves of each shell are shown, with air-space ends to the left. (Courtesy of California Agricultural Experiment Station.)

low, that it was uniformly distributed over the egg surface, and that it increased with holding time, more rapidly at higher temperatures. In eggs held for 25 days at room temperature the porosity increased from about Score 4 or 5 to Score 8 or 9.

DETERIORATION OF EGG QUALITY

Deterioration of eggs comes about in several ways, some of which have been mentioned briefly in connection with measures of egg quality. It will be profitable to inquire more fully into the specific processes by which deterioration is brought about.

Shrinkage. Shrinkage is caused by the evaporation of moisture from within the egg. The amount of shrinkage is usually measured by the size of the air cell as seen in candling. The rapidity with which it progresses depends upon the temperature at which the egg is kept, the humidity of the surrounding air, the rate of ventilation, and the porosity of the shell. In actual practice, temperature is the most important controlling factor. The vapor tension of water is about one fifth as much at 30° F as at 80° F, so that the lower the temperature of storage, at least down to near the freezing point of eggs, the better will be the quality of the eggs at the end of the storage period. The favorable effect of low temperature is, of course, not due entirely to the reduced evaporation, but the fact remains that low temperatures constitute the most important practical means of controlling egg quality during the marketing process.

The increase in porosity of the shell which occurs in held eggs, a change that is more rapid at high than at low temperatures, is also an important factor in shrinkage. Since the increasing porosity leads to an increasing rate of evaporation, it is evident that eggs should be placed under conditions of low temperature at the earliest possible moment after being laid.

The overall importance of low temperatures in maintaining egg quality is readily shown by the fact that infertile eggs of AA quality will drop to C quality by the end of 3 days if held at 99° F. If held at 75° they drop to C quality in about 9 days, at 60° in about 25 days, and at 45° in 65 days. But if held at 37° they can be kept for 100 days before dropping to C quality.

Liquefaction. Reference has been made to the increased visibility of yolk which results from a lowered viscosity of the white, permitting the yolk to float nearer to the shell and thus cast a darker shadow before the candle. The reasons for this liquefaction of the white, as it occurs under different sorts of conditions, are not yet fully explained, but some of the related facts are being brought to light. It has been shown, for example, that under the influence of osmotic pressure there is an actual passage of water from the white into the yolk. This may amount to as much as 2 grams per egg within a 10-day period with eggs held at 86° F. The vitelline membrane is compelled to stretch in order to make room for this incoming water and is thereby weakened and the substance of the yolk is made more fluid in character. These facts, together with the loss of mechanical support as a result of the disappearance of the thick white, explain the flattening of the yolk when such an egg is opened.

The chemical basis for thinning of egg white is not completely understood. Recent research, however, has implicated the egg-white proteins ovomucin and lysozyme in the gel structure of thick white. Ovomucin is a heterogeneous protein with at least one major peptide that is high in carbohydrate and sialic acid and a second that contains lower concentrations of carbohydrate. During the thinning process, these two fractions may dissociate, with the high carbohydrate fraction entering the soluble phase of the gel. These changes in ovomucin composition or in the interaction between ovomucin and lysozyme may be responsible for thinning of egg-white gel.

Shrinkage and liquefaction can be made to occur independently by imposing the right experimental conditions. If eggs are held in a desiccator over calcium chloride in an atmosphere maintained at 5% carbon dioxide, water will be removed from the eggs at a rapid rate by the calcium chloride. But if eggs are stored in a desiccator over a 5% solution of sodium hydroxide, a high humidity is maintained while carbon dioxide is rapidly removed from the air and, consequently, from the eggs. After 26 days all eggs subjected to the first treatment had air spaces from 0.25 to 0.5 inch in depth, showing extensive shrinkage, yet the interior quality as shown by white viscosity was excellent. Thick white made up 52% of the total white. In the second lot there was little shrinkage, but the eggs were badly liquefied, only 30% of the white being thick white. In this case the watery eggs actually contained more water than did the eggs with viscous whites. In practice, on the other hand, it is usually true that the eggs with "watery" whites are those that have undergone considerable shrinkage, i.e., an egg becomes more "watery" as it loses water by evaporation. The explanation is found in the fact that there is no necessary relation between these two processes. They simply happen to occur together. The loss of water so evident when a shrunken egg is candled is, after all, a relatively minor type of deterioration.

Gaseous Exchange. Loss of carbon dioxide is not only something that can be made to occur under experimental conditions, but a process which occurs normally under usual holding conditions. Carbon dioxide is liberated from an infertile egg at a rate which decreases from the time the egg is laid, at first rapidly, and then more and more slowly over a period of at least 100 days. Even afer 100 days at $10°$ C ($50°$ F) there is still an appreciable output amounting to 0.1 to 0.2 mg of carbon dioxide per egg per day.

Hydrogen Ion Concentration. The hydrogen ion concentration of fresh egg white, expressed as pH, has been variously reported as from 7.6 to 8.2, whereas that of eggs held for some time may be low enough to give a pH value of 9.5, especially if they have been held in a well-ventilated room at a fairly high temperature. This results directly from the loss of carbon dioxide, and it makes egg white under these conditions one of the most alkaline of natural biological fluids. Such a change means an increase in alkalinity (hydroxyl ion concentration) of about 80 times. It is significant that this change takes place less rapidly at low temperatures, which is another reason for holding market eggs at low temperatures from the time they are laid until they are ready to be consumed.

If eggs are held at room temperature, it takes approximately 10 to 12% carbon dioxide in the atmosphere to hold the pH of the egg white down to 7.6, whereas at temperatures near freezing 3% carbon dioxide will have the same effect. If sufficient carbon dioxide is introduced to hold the pH down to near that of the fresh egg, the thick white becomes turbid, but this turbidity quickly disappears with the escape of carbon dioxide after the eggs are removed from the storage room.

The point of interest seems to be that the carbon dioxide tends to reach an equilibrium between the concentration in the egg white and that in the air in which the eggs are kept. If newly laid eggs are stored in a confined

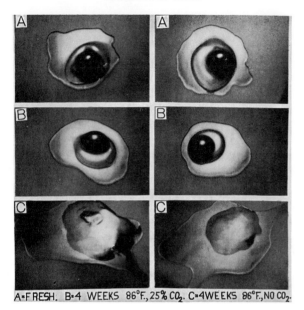

A=FRESH. B=4 WEEKS 86°F., 25% CO₂. C=4WEEKS 86°F., NO CO₂.

Fig. 11–9.   Showing the effect of carbon dioxide in preserving interior egg quality. A, the broken-out appearance of fresh eggs; B, eggs held four weeks at 86° F, in an atmosphere of 25% CO_2, C, eggs held four weeks at 86° F, but without added CO_2. (Courtesy of P. F. Sharp.)

space, that is, in a room or other container that is full of eggs, and unventilated, the carbon dioxide concentration of the air surrounding them will soon be higher than that of normal outdoor air, and the equilibrium point will be reached at a pH value for the egg white that is intermediate between the 7.6 and 9.5 values previously mentioned. If more carbon dioxide is introduced into the surrounding air, some of it will be taken up by the egg white and the pH will fall. Hence it may be said that the pH of the white of the egg is one of the controllable factors in the storage of eggs. Considerable practical use has already been made of this knowledge through the introduction of carbon dioxide into egg-storage rooms (Fig. 11–9).

   Bacterial Decomposition. The contents of normal fresh eggs are, as a rule, sterile. As long as the shells are kept clean and dry, there is little danger of bacterial invasion. The soiling of shells, especially with fecal matter, favors the entrance of bacteria, as does the presence of moisture. The increase in shell porosity with age has already been mentioned, and this undoubtedly makes conditions more favorable for bacterial infection. Once bacteria are inside the shell, increased temperature will hasten decomposition.

Fig. 11–10. The so-called "black-lamp" candler does an excellent job of detecting certain low-quality eggs. (Courtesy of Poultry Processing and Marketing.)

Much of the bacterial spoilage in storage eggs is of the sour egg type caused by *Pseudomonas* organisms. These bacteria produce not only some of the substances that are responsible for the sour odor, but also a pigment that spreads through the white of the egg and has greenish fluorescence when illuminated with ultraviolet light. Workers at the California station found that ultraviolet light of the right wavelength and intensity will penetrate the shell of white eggs and cause those which are infected with *Pseudomonas* to fluoresce with a bright green glow. Commercial candling equipment using this long-wave ultraviolet or "black" light has been widely used in the industry for the examination of eggs coming out of cold storage (Fig. 11–10).

It is also important that the water used for egg washing contain no more than 3 ppm of iron. Even as much as 5 ppm can cause a serious egg spoilage problem because iron favors the development of *Pseudomonas* organisms.

Certain other microorganisms, including molds, are found in eggs at times, and some of them develop at cold-storage temperatures. Certain of these organisms may also be involved in the breakdown or liquefaction of egg white during storage.

PRODUCER CONTROL OF EGG QUALITY

It has been stated that eggs are highly perishable. A fact of equal significance is that no process has yet been found for improving an egg of poor quality. It is rather obvious, then, that in any successful marketing plan emphasis must be placed on practices that will ensure the production of high-quality eggs and on handling methods that will preserve their original quality as long as possible. The importance of selection and breeding for desired egg characterisitcs and of feeding and management looking toward high-quality eggs has been discussed in previous chapters. Care and handling of eggs before they leave the farm are also important.

Some of the equipment and materials available to prepare eggs for the market are illustrated in Figures 11–11 through 11–17.

Deterioration in egg quality is a time- and temperature-dependent process (Figs. 11–18, 11–19). The internal quality of newly laid eggs from modern commercial lines is almost always AA or A grade except for low grades attributable to blood or meat spots. Lower grades are more frequent at the end of the production cycle.

Decline in internal quality can be minimized by the frequent gathering of eggs and by holding eggs at 50 to 60° F and a relative humidity of 70 to

Fig. 11–11.   Automatic in-line egg cooler which handles up to 35 cases (1,050 dozen) per hour. (Courtesy of Seymour Foods, Inc.)

Fig. 11–12. Egg-packing table in the FMC Egg Handling System. (Courtesy of FMC Corporation, Riverside, California.)

Fig. 11–13. An automatic egg-packing machine which receives eggs in random fashion from a conveyor belt and automatically places them large end up in either cartons or filler flats. (Courtesy of Egomatic.)

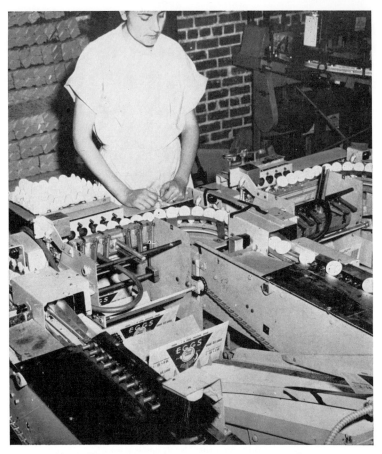

Fig. 11–14. This equipment grades and cartons eggs at a rate of 7,200 eggs an hour. (Courtesy of Poultry Tribune.)

Fig. 11–15. Weighing, shell-protecting and packaging are automatic in this plant at Modesto, California. (Courtesy of Poultry Processing and Marketing.)

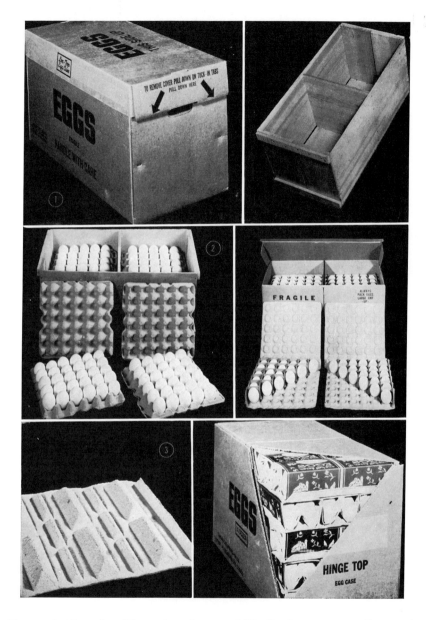

Fig. 11–16. Examples of fiber and wood cases and filler flats in common use. Shown at the bottom, left, is a molded pulp flat designed to reduce breakage in cartoned eggs. (Courtesy of Poultry Processing and Marketing.)

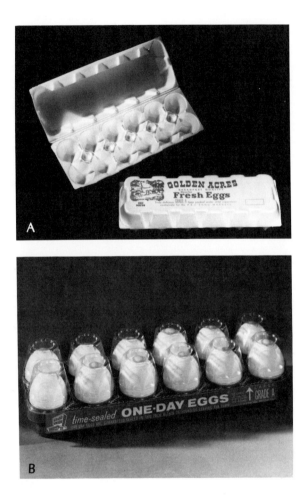

Fig. 11–17. A, Lightweight carton with special locking feature is being used successfully in store sales of eggs in New York. (Courtesy of New York State College of Agriculture at Cornell University.) B, Egg carton with transparent plastic cover has consumer appeal.

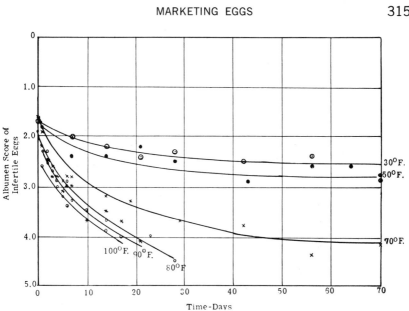

Fig. 11–18. Showing the effect of temperature on change in egg quality as measured by the albumen score. (Courtesy of Missouri Agricultural Experiment Station.)

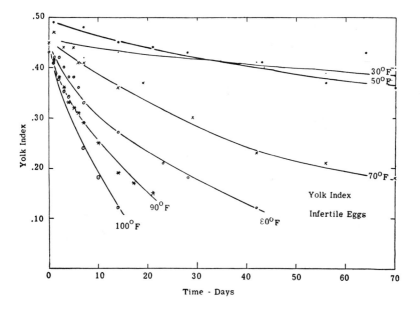

Fig. 11–19. Showing the effect of temperature on change in egg quality as measured by the yolk index. (Courtesy of Missouri Agricultural Experiment Station.)

80%. Holding that provides these environmental conditions is satisfactory for short-term storage of eggs during production and processing (Fig. 11–20).

Eggs must be clean in order to achieve a consumer grade. Several types of mechanical egg washers are available (Fig. 11–21). The smaller ones depend on swirling wash water containing a detergent-sanitizer and maintained at a temperature which is 30° to 35° F higher than the temperature of the eggs. Safe washing temperatures are in the range of 110° to 125° F. If the temperature of the wash water is lower than that of the egg, microorganisms and foreign substances may be drawn into the egg through the pores in the shell when the egg contents contract. Larger installations include an in-line cooler through which the newly collected eggs are conveyed before going to the washer. From the spray-type washer, eggs pass to a drying unit before going to the candler and grader. Prompt drying after washing is important to prevent growth of organisms and aspiration of organisms into the egg contents during cooling.

Fig. 11–20. A walk-in cooler for holding eggs. (Courtesy of Poultry Tribune.)

Eggs containing blood spots are particularly repulsive to consumers. All eggs that receive consumer grades have been scanned using candling lamps. Unfortunately, detection of blood spots by use of mass scanners is not 100% effective. In a recent study published by the Massachusetts Experiment Station, eggs were (1) washed and scanned prior to cooling, (2) washed, then precooled for 24 hours before scanning, and (3) precooled for 24 hours, washed, and then scanned. Approximately 4,320 eggs per treatment were scanned, then broken out for detection of blood spots. The results are shown in Figure 11–22. None of the 146 eggs containing blood spots of aggregated diameter less than 1/8 inch were detected using the mass scanner. Only 8 of 40 eggs containing blood spots of more than 1/8 inch aggregated diameter were detected in the sample from treatment 1. Fourteen of 27 such eggs in treatment 2, and 21 of 33 eggs in treatment 3 were detected. These and similar studies at other experiment stations

Fig. 11–21. A conveyor egg washer which spray washes and dries the eggs. Note the hand-operated vacuum lift. (Courtesy of Kuhl Poultry Equipment Company.)

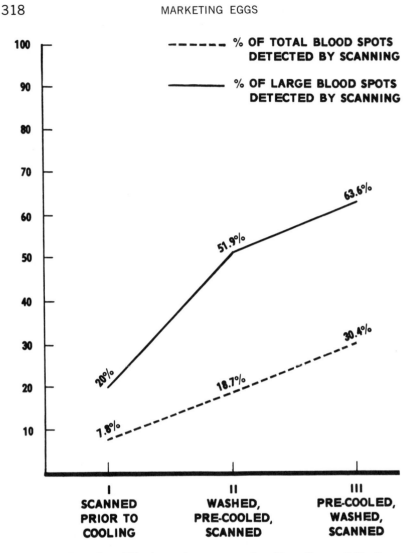

Fig. 11–22.   Detection of blood spots by mass scanning. (From Grover, R.M., Bezpa, J., Johndrew, F., Jr., and Tolman, W.J.: An Evaluation of Commercial Shell Egg Processing Methods. Publication No. 34, Cooperative Extension Service, University of Massachusetts, 1969.)

support the view that eggs should be held for a minimum of 24 hours prior to candling. Efficiency of blood spot detection may be increased further by use of electronic blood spot detectors.

Preservation and Cold Storage

The uneven seasonal production of eggs results in a surplus during the spring months and a scarcity during the fall and winter months. For many years cold storage was about the only means of bringing about a balance

Table 11–11.   Cold Storage Holdings of Eggs on August 1, by 5-Year Periods, 1916–1970, and Percentage of Total Holdings in Form of Frozen Eggs

| | Shell Eggs, cases* | Frozen Eggs | | Total case equivalent* | % frozen |
		Pounds*	Case equivalent*		
1916–1920	6.8	15	0.4	7.2	6
1921–1925	9.5	34	1.0	10.5	10
1926–1930	10.3	84	2.3	12.6	18
1931–1935	8.5	112	3.0	11.5	26
1936–1940	7.5	143	3.8	11.1	34
1941–1945	7.8	295	7.9	15.7	50
1946–1950	4.9	221	5.9	10.8	55
1951–1955	2.0	176	4.6	6.6	70
1956–1960	1.1	162	4.2	5.3	80
1961–1965	0.3	111	2.8	3.1	90
1966–1970	0.2	78	2.0	2.2	90

* Millions

between the seasonal changes in production and the much more nearly uniform rate of consumption. Now that seasonal variations in egg production have been greatly reduced by improved breeding and management methods, fewer eggs have to be stored. Total holdings on August 1 are about one fifth of what they were 25 years ago.

Cold Storage. The normal movement of eggs into storage begins in March, is most active during April and May, and reaches a peak, in terms of total holdings, about August 1. Prior to 1920, storage holdings consisted almost entirely of shell eggs, but the percentage of frozen eggs has increased steadily from 10% in 1921–1925 to 90% in 1966–1970 (Table 11–11). If this trend continues, as seems probable, storage holdings of shell eggs will soon become so small that they may not even be reported. Total into-storage movement of eggs, both shell and frozen, represented about 15% of concurrent shell egg production during the storage season in 1945–1946, but by 1975 the figure had dropped to less than 1%. Liquid eggs are being produced on a year-round basis, and there is much less need for them to accumulate in storage.

Shell Protection. Various methods of shell treatment designed to preserve interior quality have been tried from time to time. Some of these have been intended only for home use, and others have been used commercially. Most "shell-protected" eggs are placed in cold storage if they are to be held for any length of time, the process of shell treatment being used to prevent evaporation rather than as a substitute for cold storage.

Large quantities of eggs have been treated by dipping in light-weight mineral oils which are colorless, odorless, and tasteless. Evaporation is retarded, and much of the original carbon dioxide is retained inside the eggs so treated.

Now that egg production is nearly uniform throughout the year, with few shell eggs going into storage, there is much less need for any type of shell protection.

Tests at the Missouri Station have shown that quality can be stabilized effectively by dipping eggs for 10 to 15 minutes in water heated to 130° to 140° F. Eggs treated by this process retain their fresh broken-out appearance, and therefore their commercial grade, much longer than untreated eggs. Embryonic development in fertile eggs is completely arrested.

The only disadvantages were that the whites from thermostabilized eggs required more time for whipping and the volume of foam was reduced. The incidence of stuck yolks during storage was increased, especially when lower grade eggs were thermostabilized.

Liquid Egg Production. In 1949 there were nearly 500 egg-breaking plants in the United States, about 60% of them in the north central states. Currently the number of plants is about 250, and more than half of them are still in the north central region, although there has been a substantial increase recently in south Atlantic states.

All the larger plants use mechanical equipment for automatic egg breaking and for separation of yolks and whites (Fig. 11–23). A typical

Fig. 11–23. High-speed machines installed at collection stations break as many as 18,000 eggs per hour and separate yolks from whites. (Courtesy of Seymour Foods, Inc., in whose Machine Division the equipment was developed.)

plant in the west north central region may produce five million pounds of liquid egg annually. Total U. S. production of liquid eggs in some recent years has exceeded 800 million pounds, representing about 12% of annual farm egg production.

About 50% of the total production is in the form of whole eggs, including some that have been fortified by the addition of egg yolk. The remaining 50%, on a weight basis, is divided about 30% albumen and 20% yolk. Liquid yolks are further divided into plain yolk and special blends such as sugared yolk and salted yolk (Fig. 11–24). All three products are normally frozen and held in this form until used (Fig. 11–25). Liquid eggs are shipped in bulk to drying and processing plants in refrigerated trucks (Fig. 11–26).

Bakeries as a group are the largest users of frozen whole egg and albumen. Manufacturers of mayonnaise and salad dressings use large quantities of frozen salted yolks; ice cream makers use sugared yolks; and both noodle makers and processors of baby foods use plain yolks.

As of June 1, 1966, both federal legislation and laws in some states required that all liquid eggs be pasteurized at 140° F for three and one-half minutes. Prior to that date pasteurization was voluntary. The chief reason for the pasteurization requirement is the increased contamination of egg products by organisms of the *Salmonella* group. More than 100 different types or strains of *Salmonella* organisms have been found at various times

Fig. 11–24. Large vats used in blending egg products in a commercial breaking plant. (Courtesy of U. S. Department of Agriculture.)

Fig. 11–25. Containers of whole eggs, whites, yolks, and various blends are frozen rapidly in an air-blast freezer. (Courtesy of the U.S. Department of Agriculture.)

Fig. 11–26. Insulated stainless steel transport—5,500-gallon capacity—used to truck liquid eggs from breaking plants to the Topeka, Kansas, drying and processing plant. (Courtesy of Seymour Foods, Inc.)

in poultry and poultry products. Growth of these organisms can be inhibited during storage by freezing liquid eggs and holding them at low temperatures, but the organisms can multiply rapidly after the eggs are removed from storage. Pasteurization is the only known method of control to prevent the organisms from becoming a serious health hazard.

Dried Eggs. Prior to 1941, less than 1% of the eggs produced in the United States went to drying plants. Government purchases stimulated drying operations to such an extent that 45 million pounds were produced in 1941, 236 million in 1942, 262 million in 1943, and 321 million in 1944. The annual volume has since declined to less than 60 million pounds. A 30-dozen case of shell eggs will yield about 39.5 pounds of liquid whole egg or 10 pounds of a dried product containing 2.5% moisture.

The handling of shell eggs prior to drying is no different from the handling of eggs that are to be frozen. The liquid egg material is put through a clarifier to remove any bits of shell and is then screened to remove the chalazae and vitelline membranes. Pasteurization is important, not only to control *Salmonella* infection, but also to preheat the liquid so as to ensure a low-moisture powder that will not show any scorching.

Approximately 35% of broken-out eggs are dried. Liquid and frozen eggs constitute about 25 and 40% of the products from egg-breaking plants.

The liquid egg is then pumped under pressure of 2,500 to 5,000 pounds per square inch to nozzles through which it is released into a large chamber where it comes immediately into contact with a stream of air that has been heated to temperatures of 250° to 350° F. This causes instantaneous evaporation of most of the moisture from the egg material, which falls to the floor as a fine powder while the moist air passes on out of the drying chamber at a temperature of 150° to 160° F.

Modern driers produce a powder in which the moisture content does not exceed 2%. The temperature of the powder as it leaves the drier may be 150° F or higher, and this must be reduced quickly to less than 85° F if the product is to have good keeping qualities. Since the powder is extremely hygroscopic, the temperature must be reduced by contact cooling rather than by exposure to cold air. The powdered eggs are then packed immediately in sealed containers. Many of them are packed in carbon dioxide to remove the oxygen and lower the pH value in order to improve the keeping quality of the product.

Chief users of dried egg products are cake mix manufacturers, candy makers, and manufacturers of meringue powders. Some 5 million pounds are exported annually, chiefly to West Germany.

METHODS OF MARKETING

The route traveled by eggs from producer to consumer is, for the most part, completely different from what it was 30 years ago, and in some respects, different from even 10 years ago. (See Fig. 11–1.) Eggs are no longer sold by a farmer to a country store, picked up by a huckster, and taken to a local assembly plant, candled, packed in wooden cases, shipped to a city wholesale receiver, and sold to jobbers for grading and delivery to retail stores. Most of these intermediate handlers no longer exist. Eggs make the trip in much less time, and the consumer therefore has a better chance of getting high-quality eggs in every purchase.

If shell eggs only are considered, omitting those used for hatching and other non-food purposes, as well as those consumed on farms or used in the processing of liquid eggs and egg solids, it is probable that 9 out of 10 eggs go through chain-store warehouses on their way to supermarkets. The trend for several years has been for more and more eggs to make only this one stop on their way to the retail store. More than ever before, the establishment of a new egg farm must be predicated on finding a market and making suitable arrangements for disposing of the expected volume of eggs to be produced. Inevitably, this will involve consideration of a pricing agreement acceptable to both buyer and seller.

Some producers have built up a good local egg business by making regular deliveries to one or more independent retail stores. Others have found it profitable to set up small drive-in salesrooms, either adjacent to their farms or in small cities, but convenient for the motoring public.

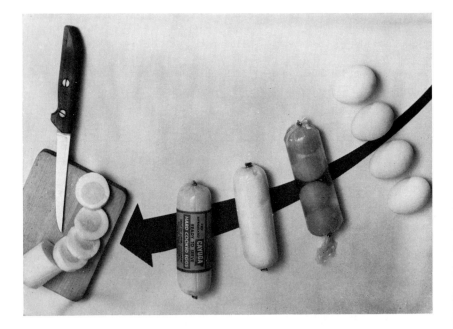

Fig. 11–27. Hard-cooked egg roll proved acceptable in both retail and institutional sales in New York State. (Courtesy of New York State College of Agriculture at Cornell University.)

NEW PRODUCTS

Egg consumption per capita reached a high of 402 in 1945 and has been declining since—to 276 in 1976, a decrease of 31%. In the same period of time, total egg production in the United States has increased by 15%, while population has increased 50%. If people were eating eggs today at the same rate they did in 1945, the nation's egg farms would have had to produce nearly a third more eggs than they actually did in 1976.

Consumption of broiler meat, by contrast, has increased from about 5 pounds per person (ready-to-cook basis) in 1945 to 37 pounds in 1970. Total chicken meat consumption was 22 pounds per person in 1945 and 41 pounds in 1970. This obviously meant a decrease in consumption of

Fig. 11–28. New products (omelet and egg and apple drink) from processed eggs. (Courtesy of N.Y.S. College of Agriculture and Life Science, Cornell University).

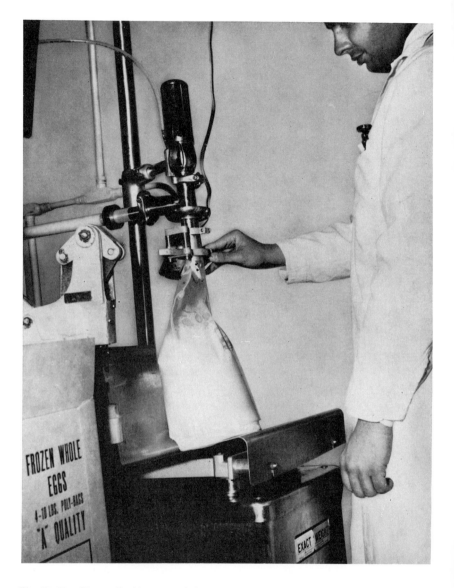

Fig. 11–29. Frozen liquid eggs are being marketed in 10-pound plastic bags. In a period of two years, more than 4 million pounds of homogenized, whole frozen eggs were sold to state institutions in New York. (Courtesy of Poultry Tribune.)

chicken other than broilers—mostly stewing hens—from 17 pounds per person in 1945 to about 4 pounds in 1970. Clearly, the housewife has accepted broilers as an economical and desirable food, but has used fewer and fewer eggs as well as much less stewing chicken. Since most of the nation's layers are replaced every 12 to 14 months, the industry is faced with the problem of disposing of some 300 million hens annually at low prices. Many of them are used in the manufacture of chicken soup.

Research workers have been cooperating with industry in developing, market testing, and promoting new egg and poultry products (Figs. 11–27, 11–28). Much of the research has been done at Cornell University and at the University of Connecticut. Among the new products finding their way into the market are chicken franks, bake-and-serve chicken loaf, baked chicken fillet, chicken hash, chicken burgers, hardboiled egg roll, kidspak of small eggs, and liquid egg for scrambled eggs and omelet. Turkey products include frozen turkey roll, turkey sausage, chopped turkey steak, turkey and waffles, freeze-dried turkey, and a turkey dinner in a disposable bag. Frozen turkey and chicken dinners have been on the market for several years.

Frozen eggs for the restaurant and bakery trade have been packed for many years in 30-pound cans. Now, as a result of a new packaging system developed by the New York State Department of Agriculture in cooperation with the U. S. Department of Agriculture's Consumer and Marketing Service, they are available in 10-pound disposable polyethylene plastic bags (Fig. 11–29). The 10-pound bag is equivalent to 100 shell eggs. Tests of the product for institutional use have shown that instead of taking an hour and 45 minutes to scramble 1,800 shell eggs, the time can be cut to 13 minutes by using the new package. In two years the program has marketed more than four million pounds of homogenized, whole frozen eggs, mostly to state institutions. Smaller packages have been developed for the retail trade.

EGG PRICING SYSTEMS

The egg pricing system in use today is still operating largely on the basis of wholesale trading in terminal markets, in spite of the fact that wholesalers who formerly handled most of the country's eggs have been to a great extent displaced by assembler-packers. Wholesale or base price quotations therefore no longer represent conditions across the country and do not facilitate orderly marketing. The price spreads for Grade A eggs sold in cartons are listed in Table 11–12.

The volume of eggs traded on the New York Mercantile Exchange in 1967, for example, was only 86,168 cases—about 17% above the average for the preceding 10 years, but less than one-half of 1% of total U. S. production. Two thirds of the eggs were purchased by the three largest buyers, and 71% were sold by the three largest sellers. This tends to make

Table 11-12.   Price Spreads and Costs for Grade A Large Cartoned Eggs

Item	1970	1974	1977[a]
		Cents per dozen	
Market basket series[b]			
Assembly	0.8	1.1	1.2
Packing	6.9	8.7	10.3
Long-distance transportation	1.3	1.4	1.6
Wholesaling	2.7	3.2	3.6
Retailing[c]	11.2	10.7	12.7
Total	22.9	25.1	29.4
10-city price spread[d]			
Farm to retailer	13.6	13.8	17.0
Retail	9.9	12.5	13.9
Total	23.5	26.3	30.9

Source: Poultry and Egg Situation #295. August 1977.
[a] Preliminary. Jan.-June only.
[b] U.S. average. Components estimated.
[c] In store only.
[d] For major cities.

exchange quotations unrepresentative and increasingly unsatisfactory in a rapidly changing industry.

Mercantile exchange trading in both New York and Chicago has been criticized for too frequent and too wide fluctuations in price while egg production, country wide, has become increasingly uniform. Also, since exchange trading lies outside the mainstream of commercial egg marketing, it has been criticized as being used primarily as a means of changing prices rather than for the purpose of buying and selling eggs.

Such criticisms led to a Congressional directive for an extended study of the problem by the U. S. Department of Agriculture, in cooperation with 13 state agricultural experiment stations. There are no easy solutions, but some of the possibilities are:

1. Computerized buying and selling through an existing or new organization of traders who would agree to conduct transactions according to prescribed trading rules. The results of trading could be used directly, or they could furnish a major indicator for the determination of base price quotations.

2. Using base prices at the delivered-to-retailer level of trading. Price-determining mechanisms at the Los Angeles and San Francisco markets have already moved in this direction.

3. Committee pricing, probably carried out under specific legislation. Such an approach might result in more stable prices than exist at present. A committee could quickly adapt to changing industry structure and practices.

4. Decentralized pricing, such as is practiced on live meat animals or in discrete "milksheds." An objection to this method is that eggs are more homogeneous in quality than are live animals, so that lots from various areas are readily substituted as necessary, making the market basically national in scope.

5. Administered pricing, operated almost entirely by private industry. Presumably this would require stricter industry determination and scheduling of quantities produced than exist at present.

6. Futures-oriented pricing in which cash market prices would be calculated from values for the nearest futures option. Active future markets would be required throughout the year and on several grades of eggs. At present, futures trading is operative only in Chicago, and only for large eggs. Futures prices are generally more stable than cash prices, but there would be numerous problems in making the necessary translations to cash market prices.

These and other possibilities are analyzed in detail in a 65-page publication entitled *Pricing Systems for Eggs* and issued as Marketing Research Report No. 850 by the Economic Research Service, U. S. Department of Agriculture, Washington, D. C. 20250 in May, 1969.

Chapter 12

Marketing Poultry

Until about 1950, most of the poultry marketed in this country came from farm flocks—essentially as a by-product of egg production, but with the great increase in commercial broiler growing and substantial increase in turkey production this is no longer true. Commercial broiler production has developed most extensively in the southern and eastern states, and many millions of pounds of processed broilers are trucked long distances to market. Georgia, Arkansas, and Alabama, the three leading states in broiler production in 1976, had only 5% of the population, but produced 43% of the commercial broilers.

Commercial broiler production, the major segment of the poultry industry, has grown 100-fold during the past 40 years. Whereas 34 million broilers were grown in 1935, over 3.2 billion birds were produced in 1976. Add to this the 140 million turkeys, approximately 225 million fowl, and 13 million ducks, and the per capita production of poultry meat exceeds 55 pounds annually.

Poultry certified as wholesome in federally inspected plants, on a ready-to-cook basis, in 1977, totaled 11.7 billion pounds, as follows:

	Million Pounds
Young chickens, mostly broilers	9,227
Mature chickens	512
All turkeys	1,892
Ducks	59
Other poultry	7

Twenty-five years ago over 40% of total shipments of dressed poultry to the four principal markets—New York, Chicago, Philadelphia, and Boston—were received during the three months of October, November, and December. Today, the slaughter of young chickens—about 80% of total poultry slaughter—is fairly well distributed throughout the year.

The marketing patterns of other species of poultry still are distinctly seasonal, although the seasonal trends have diminished somewhat in recent years. In 1966, 70% of turkeys were marketed during the months of August to December, and 60% of all ducks were processed during the months of May through September. In 1977 these figures declined to 60% and 51%, respectively, of the total annual production. Changes in seasonal trends of chicken, turkey, and duck production are illustrated in the following data on processed ready-to-cook poultry gathered by the U.S. Agricultural Marketing Service.

	Young Chicken		Turkey		Duck	
	1966	*1977*	*1966*	*1977*	*1966*	*1977*
			lb (millions)			
January	407	714	36	70	1.0	3.4
February	398	659	18	59	0.7	3.2
March	439	783	17	80	2.2	3.9
April	450	745	22	79	4.3	4.5
May	469	810	36	110	5.8	5.4
June	514	844	80	176	6.6	6.5
July	465	746	114	190	5.3	5.6
August	541	870	196	244	5.7	6.4
September	515	808	240	238	5.1	6.0
October	497	776	218	250	4.7	5.2
November	435	720	275	247	3.8	4.8
December	473	753	174	148	2.7	4.5
Total	5,603	9,227	1,425	1,892	48	59

PROCESSING

Read-to-cook poultry is available for purchase in supermarkets throughout the country, but only because there has been developed a highly commercialized operation for killing, dressing, eviscerating, cutting up, and packaging chickens and transporting them over long distances. Poultry processing is no longer a farm operation but a highly specialized business.

In 1975 the number of firms processing young chickens under federal inspection totaled 154. Fifty percent of these accounted for 80% of the volume. The 20 largest firms accounted for 55% of the volume. The eight largest processed 30% of the total volume, or 2.39 billion pounds of ready-to-cook poultry.

The number of functions performed varies considerably among firms. The results of a survey of firms having broiler packing plants are shown below. Nearly all firms were involved in the slaughter and evisceration of poultry. Two of the west coast firms specialized in processing poultry slaughtered elsewhere. Eighty-seven percent of the firms prepared poultry in cut-up form, whereas 31% were involved in further processing. A number of firms participated in receiving, long distance transport, and delivery to retail outlets.

Plants surveyed	38
Plants which:	
Buy live or ready-to-cook	9
Assemble live poultry	25
Slaughter, eviscerate	36
Cut up	33
Further process	12
Receive, warehouse, store	19
Long distance hauling	16
Deliver to retailers and institutions	29
Plants which are part of firms having:	
Hatcheries	28
Feed mills	29
Own production	19
Contract production	34

(U.S. Department of Agriculture)

Consistent with the high level of integration in the industry, most firms were involved in other phases of production such as hatching, feed milling, and broiler production.

The layout of a typical processing plant is shown in Figure 12–1. The plant is divided into two major processing areas: one for receiving, killing, and defeathering; the second for evisceration, final processing, and packaging. Separation of the two areas is intended to facilitate sanitation by separating the inherently dirtier phases of processing from those involved in preparation of the final product. Other aspects of plant design provide for accessory operations, office space, and the needs of plant personnel.

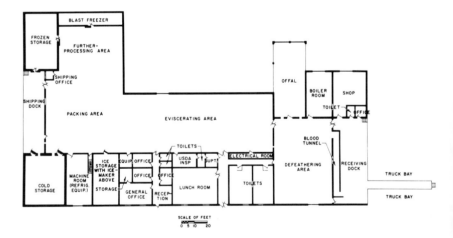

Fig. 12–1. Layout of the major areas of a plant that can process 9,600 broilers per hour. (Courtesy of U. S. Department of Agriculture.)

Most processing plants are located in production areas, thus minimizing shrinkage and other losses that accompany hauling of live poultry over long distances. Poultry received at the plant will have been fasted for 4 to 10 hours. This will allow time for the crop to become empty and for the intestinal contents to be reduced to a satisfactory point. About 60% of the 24-hour fasting loss of intestinal contents occurs in the first 3 or 4 hours. Fasting reduces crop and gastrointestinal contents which may contaminate carcasses during evisceration.

The degree of automation and the specific steps in processing vary somewhat among poultry plants. The sequence of processing events for a

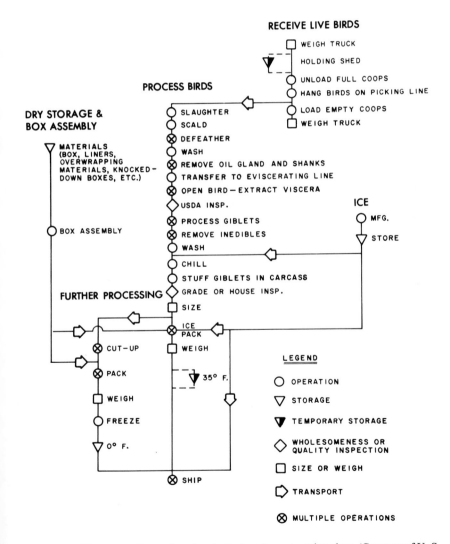

Fig. 12–2. Sequences of operations in a typical poultry processing plant. (Courtesy of U. S. Department of Agriculture.)

typical processing plant is shown in Figure 12–2, and the major events are described in the following paragraphs.

Receiving. Crated poultry arrive at the plant, and are transported in crates by conveyers to the shackling area (Fig. 12–3), where they are shackled by their feet. This is the starting point for continuously moving lines of shackles which transport the poultry about the killing, dressing, and eviscerating operations (Fig. 12–4).

Killing. Slaughtering is usually performed manually by severing the jugular vein at the ventrolateral base of the head. This is sometimes called the modified kosher method. When kosher killing is employed, the trachea and jugular veins are severed in a single stroke, and the severed trachea must be visible to the individual authorized to perform the kosher slaughter. Many plants employ electric stunning prior to killing. This serves to reduce struggling and also relaxes the feather papillae, thereby facilitating feather removal.

Bleeding. A bleedout time of approximately 1.5 minutes is required. Incomplete bleedout can cause discoloration of the carcass and consequent downgrading.

Fig. 12–3. Poultry are transferred from coops to shackles in a commercial processing plant. (Courtesy of the U. S. Department of Agriculture.)

Scalding. Although several scalding temperatures may be used, the semiscald at approximately 123 to 128° F at 1.5 to 2 minutes is most common. This is a relatively mild scald that is sufficient to allow feather removal, yet the outer layer of skin on the carcass remains intact. Finished carcasses scalded in this manner have an attractive natural appearance. Underscalding causes incomplete feather removal by the automated pickers. Overscalding may lead to irregular removal of the outer layer of the skin, causing an unattractive splotchy appearance, or a carcass with a pinkish cast if the outer layer of skin is completely removed. Loss of this protective layer of skin is correlated with shortened shelf life of the product.

Defeathering. Feathers are stripped off the carcasses by rotating drums or wheels containing long rubber projections ("fingers") (Fig. 12–5). As the carcass is brought in contact with the rubber fingers, the feathers, loosened by scalding, are stripped away with little damage to the skin. When semiscalds are used, feather pickers specifically designed to remove feathers from the hock region are often employed. The wax

Fig. 12–4.   Broilers in transit to the slaughtering room. (Courtesy of the U. S. Department of Agriculture.)

Fig. 12–5. An efficient mechanical picking machine called a Torq Featherator. Feathers are removed by spinning action of the small circular groups of rubber fingers. (Courtesy of Gordon Johnson Company.)

Fig. 12–6. Geese being plucked by the wax method. (Courtesy of Institute of American Poultry Industries.)

method, which gives a clean, smooth appearance to the finished carcass, is frequently used for ducks and geese (Fig. 12–6).

Singeing. All poultry contain some hairlike feathers called filoplumes. In the singeing process these are removed by passing the carcass quickly through a flame.

Washing. This spray washing step removes feathers, singed feathers, and other foreign material from the surface of the carcass (Fig. 12–7).

Pinning. Often, the carcass will contain developing feathers that have just pierced the skin. These feathers, which have the appearance of a quill with no plume, are unattractive and cause downgrading when present on the finished carcass. They are removed manually by grasping the protruding pinfeather between the thumb and the edge of a knife and giving a strong tugging motion.

Transfer to Eviscerating Room. The oil gland and feet are removed prior to transfer to the shackles leading to the eviscerating room. Carcasses are usually shackled at this point via the hocks and the neck or the neck alone.

Fig. 12–7. Defeathered chickens pass through washer on the way to the eviscerating area. (Courtesy of the U. S. Department of Agriculture.)

Fig. 12–8. Postmortem inspection. (Courtesy of the U. S. Department of Agriculture.)

Evisceration. In the first step of this operation, a vertical cut is made from the tip of the sternum to the vent, and with the vent still attached the viscera are drawn out, but remain attached to the bird for the postmortem inspection. After inspection (Fig. 12–8), the liver and gizzard are removed, and the remaining viscera are discarded. The gizzard is sliced open, and the inner lining and contents are removed.

Removal of Lungs and Kidney. This step is usually accomplished mechanically or by use of a strong vacuum aspirator. The tip of the aspirator is thrust into the thoracic cavity and the dorsal abdominal cavity to remove the lung and kidney tissue.

Removal of Head. The head is removed manually or automatically by allowing the head to drag through a V-shaped knife as the carcass moves along on shackles. Afterwards, the skin is slit along the dorsal surface of the neck to the shoulders.

Removal of Neck, Esophagus, and Crop. The skin is cut on the dorsal side to the shoulder and the neck is cut or broken off at the shoulders. The esophagus and crop are manually stripped from the neck region.

Washing. Carcasses are spray-washed with cold water inside and out to remove traces of blood, loosely attached tissue, or foreign material. The combined water use for all steps in processing totals 8 gallons per chicken.

Chilling. This step is designed to complete the removal of body heat. Rapid cooling prevents buildup of microbial population and will allow maximal shelf life of the final product. Most chillers rely on slush ice or ice water as the coolant. Agitation of the cooling solution is achieved mechanically. With mechanical in-line chillers, poultry can be cooled to less than 40°F in 30 minutes (Figs. 12–9, 12–10).

Weighing. Carcasses are transferred to a sizing shackle which automatically drops the carcass into the appropriate holding bin, according to carcass weight.

Cutting. Some poultry are halved or cut into parts at the processing plant. Others are cut up at retail outlets. In 1976, 35% of all young,

Fig. 12–9. Mechanical chilling equipment in a modern poultry processing plant. (Courtesy of Poultry Processing and Marketing.)

Fig. 12–10.   Ice chilling vats in a poultry processing plant. (Courtesy of Poultry Processing and Marketing.)

Fig. 12–11.   This automatic cut-up machine can cut pre-sized broilers into eight pieces as fast as the operator can feed them in. (Courtesy of Gainesville Machine Co., Gainesville, Ga.)

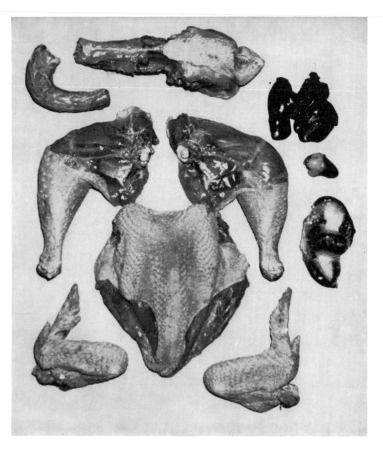

Fig. 12–12. Cut-up chicken parts ready for wrapping. (Courtesy of Beacon Milling Company, a Division of Textron, Inc.)

Fig. 12–13. Chicken parts packaged for sale at retail. (Courtesy of Poultry Processing and Marketing.)

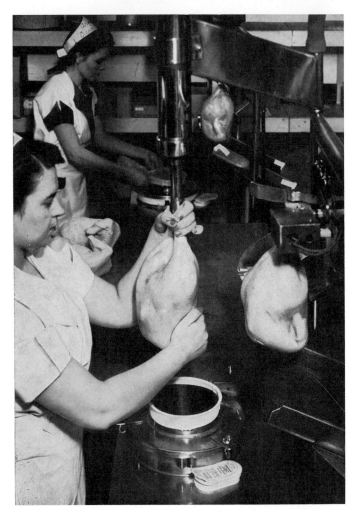

Fig. 12–14. Carcasses of roasting chickens are commonly wrapped in plastic before freezing, for better preservation of quality. (Courtesy of U. S. Egg and Poultry Magazine.)

ready-to-cook chickens were cut up in processing plants under federal inspection. Fifty-eight percent were sold as whole birds, many of which were cut up by retailers.

The automatic cut-up machine shown in Figure 12–11 saves much of the hand labor formerly required in processing cut-up broilers. Broilers are cut in half by hand and fed into the machine which cuts the front half of the carcass into two wings and two pieces of breast, and the back half into two drumsticks and two thighs. It can easily handle 40 to 50 birds a minute, and make a more uniform cut than can be done by hand, provided

Fig. 12–15. Refrigerated truck-trailer for long-distance hauling of processed poultry. (Courtesy of Poultry Processing and Marketing.)

the broilers are first properly sized to within a 4-ounce range in weight. Pieces of chicken ready for packing are shown in Figure 12–12.

Packing. In 1976, 92% of young ready-to-cook chickens were packed in chilled form. Unwrapped whole or cut-up chicken packed in ice is the most common product of broiler processing. This method of packing accounted for 55% of all poultry packed under federal inspection in 1975. Twenty-five percent were air-chilled, and another 14% were packed in carbon dioxide. Those that were air-chilled were typically wrapped at the processing plant. Final packaging is completed at retail outlets. Approximately 8% of ready-to-cook chickens were sold in frozen form by processing plants (Fig. 12–13). Roasting chickens are encased in plastic before freezing for better preservation of quality (Fig. 12–14). To prevent spoilage during shipment to distributors and retail outlets, processed poultry is shipped in refrigerated tractor-trailers (Fig. 12–15).

Killing, Dressing, and Eviscerating Losses

Weight losses represented by inedible parts of the chicken are important to both producer and processor, because they are the basis upon which maximum paying prices should be adjusted in relation to the market price of the final product. They are also related to feeding practices just prior to killing.

Table 12–1. Expected Yield in Pounds of Dressed Weight, Eviscerated Weight, and Edible Meat Weight as Related to Live Weight

Average Live Weight (lb)	From 100-pounds live weight						From 100-pounds dressed weight	
	Dressed Weight		Eviscerated (with giblets)		Edible Meat (with giblets)		Eviscerated (with giblets)	Edible Meat (with giblets)
	(a)	(b)	(a)	(b)	(a)		(a)	(a)
2.0	83.2	87.8	65.6	71.7	55.7		78.9	67.0
2.5	84.4	88.4	67.1	72.0	56.7		79.5	67.2
3.0	85.2	88.9	68.1	72.0	57.4		80.0	67.4
3.5	85.7	89.3	68.8	72.1	57.9		80.3	67.5
4.0	86.2	89.5	69.4	72.2	58.2		80.5	67.5
4.5	86.5	89.8	69.8	72.3	58.5		80.6	67.6
5.0	86.8	89.9*	70.1	72.3*	58.7		80.7	67.6
5.5	87.1	90.0*	70.4	72.4*	58.9		80.8	67.6
6.0	87.2	90.1*	70.6	72.4*	59.0		80.9	67.7

Calculated from data published by the U. S. Department of Agriculture and Ohio State University.
(a) McNally and Spicknall, 1949 (chilled weight basis) battery-raised R. I. Red males slaughtered in groups of 25 at biweekly intervals.
(b) Jaap, Renard, and Buckingham, 1950 (fresh dressed weight basis) over 1,600 males from 44 strains, all slaughtered at 12 weeks of age.
*These values are extrapolations beyond the 4.5-pound maximum live weight attained at 12 weeks of age by chickens used in the Ohio tests.

Killing and dressing losses consist of feathers and blood. The amount of blood lost is close to 4% of the live weight. This means a tenth of a pound for a 2.5-pound broiler and up to a fourth of a pound for a large roaster. The weight loss represented by feathers is more variable, but will average about 5% of the live weight. It is higher for females than for males, and lower for short-feathered chickens such as Cornish hen than for the more heavily feathered breeds.

Records for twenty lots of 300 chickens each in the 1951 Maine Broiler Production Test, when all were killed and dressed at the same time, showed an average killing loss of 8.8%. The average live weight of these chickens at time of slaughter was 4.94 pounds (cockerels and pullets combined). The lowest shrink for any lot was 6.0%, and the highest 12.4%. The yield of ready-to-cook poultry has averaged slightly greater than 72% of live weight since 1973. The 1975 yield of 72.8% is the highest on record.

Killing and dressing losses are sometimes complicated by the amount of feed remaining in the crops, but under ordinary conditions, when soft feed (as opposed to whole grain) is being fed, a fasting period of 4 hours prior to slaughter is sufficient.

Eviscerating losses are influenced by the plumpness and degree of finish of the carcasses and, like dressing losses, they tend to be greater with small chickens than with large. Losses will be lower for chickens that are grown to market weight on rations high enough in energy to produce a good covering of fat than for chickens that are somewhat thin or poorly finished.

Not too many reports have been published showing actual yields in terms of eviscerated weights or edible meat. Data from two tests—one at Beltsville, Maryland, and another at Columbus, Ohio—are summarized in Table 12–1. More information of this sort is needed, especially as related to different degrees of finish.

Average percentage yields for cut-up parts from fryers, based on chilled, ready-to-cook weight, including giblets, are approximately as follows: breast, 24%; legs (drumsticks), 15%; thighs, 16%; wings, 13%; back, 17%; neck, 7.5% and giblets, 7.5%.

Official Grading and Inspection

For many years the U. S. Department of Agriculture has offered the poultry industry official grading and inspection services on a voluntary basis. These services have been carried on under authority of Congressional acts which have provided that fees shall be charged users of the services to cover costs. Grading services are still permissive and are provided by the Department of Agriculture on a cost basis, but inspection service became compulsory with the enactment on August 28, 1957, of Public Law 85-172, known as the Poultry Products Inspection Act. It requires that all domesticated poultry slaughtered for human food and moving in interstate commerce be inspected for wholesomeness. The cost of such inspection service, except for necessary overtime and holiday work, is borne by the government. The regional distribution of slaughter plants operating under federal inspection in 1970 is shown in Table 12–2.

The sanitary provisions of the regulations are considered as the minimum requirements necessary to produce clean and sanitary poultry food products. They are adaptable to small as well as large poultry-processing operations. They require that processing operations be conducted in buildings that can be kept clean and free from rodents, other vermin, dust, and other conditions that would contaminate food products. Floors and walls in processing rooms must be impervious to moisture and be smooth and suitable for easy and thorough cleaning. The drainage and plumbing systems must be adequate to dispose of water and other wastes resulting from processing operations, be properly installed, and be equipped with approved traps to prevent the development of health hazards.

The equipment used in processing operations must be of metal or other impervious material and be constructed and placed so as to permit thorough cleaning. The operating procedures are designed so that they

Table 12–2.   Number and Distribution of Poultry Slaughter Plants under Federal Inspection, and Total Slaughter, 1970

	Plants by Size (Millions of Pounds)				
Region	Under 5.2	5.2 to 15.6	15.6 to 52.0	52.0 and over	Total
North Atlantic	19	6	14	6	45
East North Central	16	14	12	—	42
West North Central	11	20	28	a	59
South Atlantic	6	6	53	35	100
South Central	10	9	69	33	121
Western	8	16	21	11	45
48-State Total	70	71	197	74	412
	Total Slaughter (Millions of pounds, live weight)				
North Atlantic	34	55	371	408	868
East North Central	19	138	317	—	474
West North Central	16	249	806	a	1,071
South Atlantic	6	55	1,902	2,804	4,767
South Central	13	92	2,359	2,488	4,952
Western	8	180	634	a	822
48-State Total[b]	96	769	6,389	5,700	12,954

Data from the U. S. Department of Agriculture.

[a] Combined with next smaller group to avoid disclosing individual plants.

[b] Young chickens 10 million pounds; turkeys 2 million; other poultry less than 1 million.

will be practicable and at the same time capable of producing clean, sanitary poultry under conditions that will conserve quality and prevent deterioration and contamination of the product.

The inspection procedures provide for both antemortem and postmortem inspection of the birds and for disposal of birds or parts that are not acceptable for food. The inspector is responsible for the maintenance of sanitation throughout the official establishment. The preparation of food products which contain poultry and which are eligible to bear the inspection mark must be done under the supervision of the inspector.

Over 90% of all poultry meat sold by producers is federally inspected. Ninety-eight percent of all broilers are processed under federal inspection. The percentage of condemnations is normally under 3%, less than 0.3% from antemortem inspection. Diseases accounted for most of the condemnations among the 12.4 billion pounds of young chickens inspected in 1976. The most common causes of condemnations were leukosis, septicemia, airsacculitis, synovitis, and tumors. Fewer losses were attributable to bruises, overscalding, or other conditions resulting from improper handling and processing methods. Condemnations vary considerably from flock to flock. It is not unusual to find flocks with condemnation rates of 10% or more. Good management is important in maintaining a low condemnation rate.

MARKET CLASSES OF POULTRY

The U. S. Department of Agriculture has set up specifications for classes and grades of live poultry, dressed poultry, and ready-to-cook poultry. The following classes of chickens are specified:

Rock Cornish Game Hen or Cornish Game Hen. A Rock Cornish game hen or Cornish game hen is a young immature chicken (usually 5 to 7 weeks of age) weighing not more than 2 pounds ready-to-cook weight, which was prepared from a Cornish chicken or the progeny of a Cornish chicken crossed with another breed of chicken.

Broiler or Fryer. A broiler or fryer is a young chicken (usually 9 to 12 weeks of age), of either sex, that is tender-meated with soft, pliable, smooth-textured skin and flexible breastbone cartilage.

Roaster. A roaster is a young chicken (usually 3 to 5 months of age), of either sex, that is tender-meated, with soft, pliable, smooth-textured skin and breastbone cartilage that may be somewhat less flexible than that of a broiler or fryer.

Capon. A capon is a surgically unsexed male chicken (usually under 8 months of age) that is tender-meated with soft, pliable, smooth-textured skin.

Stag. A stag is a male chicken (usually under 10 months of age) with coarse skin, somewhat toughened and darkened flesh, and considerable hardening of the breastbone cartilage. Stags show a condition of fleshing

Table 12–3. Summary of Specifications for Standards of Quality for Individual Carcasses of Ready-to-cook Poultry and Parts Therefrom

Factor	Minimum Requirements and Maximum Defects Permitted		
	A Quality	*B Quality*	*C Quality*
Conformation:			
Breastbone	Normal Slight curve or dent	Moderate deformities Moderately dented, curved, or crooked	Abnormal Seriously curved or crooked
Back	Normal (except slight curve)	Moderately crooked	Seriously crooked
Legs and wings	Normal	Moderately misshapen	Misshapen
Fleshing:	Well fleshed, moderately long, deep and rounded breast	Moderately fleshed, considering kind, class, and part	Poorly fleshed
Fat covering:	Well covered—especially between heavy feather tracts on breast and considering kind, class, and part	Sufficient fat on breast and legs to prevent distinct appearance of flesh through the skin	Lacking in fat covering over all parts of carcass
Pinfeathers:			
Nonprotruding pins, and hair	Free	Few scattered	Scattering
Protruding pins	Free	Free	Free

Exposed flesh:[a]

Carcass Weight		*A Quality*			*B Quality*			*C Quality*
Minimum	*Maximum*	*Breast and Legs*	*Elsewhere*	*Part*	*Breast and Legs*[b]	*Elsewhere*	*Part*	
None	1½ lb	None	¾"	Slight trim on edge	¾"	1½"	Moderate amount of flesh normally covered	No limit
Over 1½ lb	6 lb	None	1½"		1½"	3"		
Over 6 lb	16 lb	None	2"		2"	4"		
Over 16 lb	None	None	3"		3"	5"		

Discolorations:[c]							
None	1½ lb	½"	¼"	1"	2"	½"	No limit[d]
Over 1½ lb	6 lb	1"	¼"	2"	3"	1"	No limit
Over 6 lb	16 lb	1½"	½"	2½"	4"	1½"	No limit
Over 16 lb	None	2"	½"	3"	5"	1½"	No limit
Disjointed bones		1		2 disjointed and no broken, or			No limit
Broken bones		None		1 disjointed and 1 nonprotruding			No limit
Missing parts		Wing tips and tail[e]		Wing tips, 2nd wing joint, and tail			Wing tips, wings, and tail
Freezing defects: (when consumer packaged)		Slight darkening over the back and drumsticks. Few small ⅛" pockmarks for poultry weighing 6 lb or less and ¼" pockmarks for poultry weighing more than 6 lbs. Occasional small area showing layer of clear or pinkish ice		Moderate dried areas not in excess of ½" in diameter. May lack brightness. Moderate areas showing layer of clear, pinkish or colored ice			Numerous pockmarks and large dried areas

From USDA Handbook No. 31, 1972.

a Total aggregate area of flesh exposed by all cuts and tears and missing skin.

b A carcass meeting the requirements of A quality for fleshing may be trimmed to remove skin and flesh defects, provided no more than one third of the flesh is exposed on any part and that meat yield is not appreciably affected.

c Flesh bruises and discolorations such as "blue back" are not permitted on breast and legs of A quality birds. Not more than one half of total aggregate area of discolorations may be due to flesh bruises or "blue back" (when permitted) and skin bruises in any combination.

d No limit on size and number of areas of discolorations and flesh bruises if such areas do not render any part of the carcass unfit for food.

e In geese, the parts of the wing beyond the second joint may be removed, if removed at the joint and both wings are so treated.

and a degree of maturity intermediate between that of a roaster and a cock or rooster.

Hen or Stewing Chicken or Fowl. A hen or stewing chicken or fowl is a mature female chicken (usually more than 10 months old) with meat less tender than that of a roaster, and nonflexible breastbone tip.

Cock or Rooster. A cock or rooster is a mature male chicken with coarse skin, toughened and darkened meat, and hardened breastbone tip.

Standards of quality for individual carcasses of ready-to-cook poultry and parts therefrom are summarized in Table 12–3. Detailed specifications for the various grades are based on these standards of quality, and copies may be obtained from the U. S. Department of Agriculture, Washington, D. C. 20250.

GRADES

The United States consumer grades for ready-to-cook poultry are applicable to chickens, turkeys, ducks, geese, guineas, and pigeons conforming to the several classes such as Broiler or Fryer, Young Tom Turkey, when each carcass or part has been graded by a grader on an individual basis. U. S. Grades A, B, and C are described as follows:

Grade A. A lot of ready-to-cook poultry or parts consisting of one or more ready-to-cook carcasses or parts of the same kind and class, each of which conforms to the requirements for A Quality, may be designated as U. S. Grade A.

Grade B. A lot of ready-to-cook poultry or parts consisting of one or more ready-to-cook carcasses or parts of the same kind and class, each of which conforms to the requirments for B Quality or better, may be designated as U. S. Grade B.

Grade C. A lot of ready-to-cook poultry or parts consisting of one or more ready-to-cook carcasses or parts of the same kind and class, each of which conforms to the requirements for C Quality or better, may be designated as U. S. Grade C.

MARKETING CHANNELS

Marketing channels vary greatly depending on the kind of poultry slaughtered. Over 90% of the broiler output from processing plants reaches the consumer as whole or cut-up birds without further processing. Over 47% of these are provided to retail or institutional outlets through the services of wholesale distributors. Less than 7% of broilers are further processed. The major marketing channels for ready-to-cook broilers are illustrated in Figure 12–16.

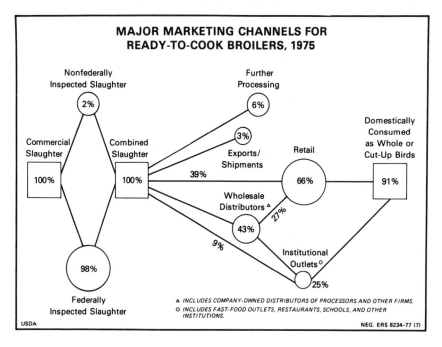

MAJOR MARKETING CHANNELS FOR READY-TO-COOK BROILERS, 1975

Fig. 12–16. (Source: U. S. Dept. of Agriculture, Agricultural Marketing Service, Poultry Division, Marketing News Bureau.)

Only 19% of mature ready-to-cook whole or cut-up chickens (mainly fowl from egg-producing flocks) reach the consumer directly via institutional or retail outlets. Over 80% of the slaughter is further processed.

Further processing is performed on more than half of the federally inspected ready-to-cook turkeys. Approximately three fourths of this processing is done by the slaughtering firm. Eighty-four percent of turkeys and turkey products are marketed to the consumer through retail outlets. Institutional outlets and exports account for 14 and 2%, respectively.

FURTHER PROCESSING

A substantial proportion of processed poultry is further processed for use in such products as precooked frozen parts, soups, poultry loaves (Fig. 12–17), cold cuts, frozen dinners (Fig. 12–18), pot pies and other specialized products too numerous to mention. Minced meat from mechanically deboned poultry (Fig. 12–19) is used in many of these products (Fig. 12–20). Approximately 7% of all certified ready-to-cook

Fig. 12–17. "Bake and Serve" chicken loaf is another new product developed at Cornell University and favorably received in market tests. (Courtesy of New York State College of Agriculture at Cornell University.)

Fig. 12–18. Frozen "turkey dinners" are being placed in cartons for shipment from this C. A. Swanson and Sons plant. (Courtesy of Poultry Processing and Marketing.)

Fig. 12–19. Deboning equipment is used in the preparation of poultry meat for many further processed items. (Courtesy of Stephen Paoli International Corporation).

Fig. 12–20. Frozen chicken sticks developed at Cornell University were favorably received by customers at central New York supermarkets. Boned poultry meat was dipped in a batter containing corn-flakes crumbs. (Courtesy of New York State College of Agriculture at Cornell University.)

young chicken in 1976 was further processed. Over 85% of all fowl and 35% of turkeys certified under federal inspection were used in further processing.

With improved processing and marketing technology, the proportion of poultry subjected to further processing will undoubtedly continue to increase. The trend is illustrated in data adapted from reports of the USDA Economic Research Service (Table 12–4).

Table 12–4.   End Use of Young Chickens Certified under Federal Inspection in Commercial Slaughtering Plants

Year	Total million lb	Whole %	Cut-up %	Further Processing %
1962	4,361	83	15	2
1967	5,876	74	22	4
1972	7,823	65	29	6
1976	8,987	58	35	7

Chapter 13

The Business of Poultry Keeping

Throughout the national economy it has become increasingly more profitable to employ capital than to employ labor. In the poultry business this has resulted in widespread use of such devices as bulk feed tanks, mechanical feeding and watering systems, medication by way of the water supply, egg collection belts, mechanical methods of cleaning houses, and manure disposal systems to haul the material away in liquid form. Processors use automatic picking machines, mechanical chilling equipment, machines to grade, wash, and package eggs mechanically, and high-capacity egg-breaking equipment. Liquid egg products are pasteurized by equipment that maintains automatic control of time and temperature.

These changes have accompanied the trend toward larger laying flocks and broiler plants, partly because only the larger operators can afford to install expensive equipment, but also because increasing labor costs of hand operations make it nearly impossible for small flock owners to compete successfully in poultry meat and egg production. The once common farm flock of poultry has virtually disappeared in most sections of the country, along with the country store and the local produce plant as outlets for eggs and chickens, and rail shipment of eggs and live poultry from local assembling plants to wholesale markets in a few large cities.

The trend in poultry and egg prices was downward until about 1973, as shown in Table 13–1. In 1973, owing to reduced supplies of eggs and broilers, prices increased to a new level and have remained high for several years. Despite increased prices for poultry products, feed prices have also risen dramatically, and the price relationships between poultry and eggs and feeds have continued to narrow. Production has had to become increasingly efficient both in terms of feed conversion and in terms of management practices. If it takes 6 pounds of feed to produce a dozen eggs, there is little margin for profit if that dozen eggs can be ex-

Table 13-1.   Prices of Eggs, Broilers, and Poultry Feed, by Alternate Years, 1951 to 1977, as Reported by the U. S. Department of Agriculture

Year	Eggs[a] (cents)	Broilers[b] (cents)	Laying feed[c]	Broiler grower[c]	Egg-feed ratio[d]	Broiler-feed ratio[e]
1951	47.7	28.5	$4.96	$5.36	9.6	5.3
1953	47.7	27.1	4.88	5.26	9.8	5.1
1955	39.5	25.2	4.58	5.00	8.6	5.0
1957	35.9	18.9	4.42	4.89	8.1	3.9
1959	31.4	16.1	4.44	4.84	7.1	3.3
1961	35.5	13.9	4.36	4.64	8.1	3.0
1963	34.4	14.6	4.48	4.80	7.7	3.0
1965	33.0	14.8	4.40	4.84	7.6	3.1
1967	31.2	13.3	4.29	4.65	7.3	2.9
1969	39.6	15.2	4.00	4.52	9.9	3.4
1971	31.1	13.8	4.34	4.88	7.2	2.8
1973	54.1	24.1	6.86	7.59	7.9	3.2
1975	52.8	26.2	7.35	8.15	7.2	3.2
1977	54.2	23.5	7.80	8.55	6.9	2.7

[a] Weighted average price per dozen.
[b] Weighted average price per pound.
[c] Average cost per 100 pounds.
[d] Pounds of laying feed one dozen eggs will buy.
[e] Pounds of broiler grower one pound of broiler will buy.

changed for no more than 7 pounds of feed. Consequently, poultrymen have been striving for higher and higher egg yields, which mean better feed conversion, as well as for more efficient use of labor and lower costs of housing.

COMMERCIAL EGG FARMING

Commercial egg production is a highly competitive business that involves a substantial investment of capital and a considerable element of risk. The demand for high-quality eggs is growing along with the increase in population, but the total demand at any one time is inelastic so that relatively small changes in total egg production can cause sharp declines in the prices that independent producers receive for eggs. Vertical integration has served to distribute the financial risk, and large volume has enabled such operations to make a profit in spite of narrow margins between production costs and market prices.

During the years from 1915 to 1940, economic studies of poultry farming were concerned with enterprises in which the number of layers was usually under 1,000, and the total capital investment was around $10,000 or $12,000. Successful commercial poultry farms today are likely to have from 10,000 to 50,000 layers, and individual specialized farms often have 100,000 or more.

The Capital Investment

A farm flock of 400 to 500 hens may be kept in a relatively low-cost building, but when 10 to 50 times that number of layers are kept, a more expensive building is necessary (Figs. 13–1, 13–2). Furthermore, there must be much more equipment such as an efficient water system, bulk feed tanks, automatic feeders, and egg collection belts, as well as egg washing and grading equipment and the like (Fig. 13–3). And if the enterprise is to consist of 50,000 to 100,000 hens, the capital investment rises to a really substantial total.

Not too many records of actual plant investment have been published, and it is probably best to approach the problem from the hypothetical point of view, estimating the actual costs involved in setting up plants of

Fig. 13–1. A flock of 15,000 layers in one half of this 400′ × 52′ four-story house in Middlesex, New York, averaged 262 eggs each in 12 months beginning July 1, 1959. Mortality rate was 11%, and feed conversion 4.15 pounds of feed for each dozen eggs.

Fig. 13–2. In an effort to reduce depreciation charges to a minimum, some poultrymen have turned to aluminum for construction of laying houses. This one is 500 feet long, 42 feet wide. (Courtesy of Poultry Tribune.)

Fig. 13–3.   Bulk tanks are an aid to keeping feed and labor costs low. Park Leghorn Farm, Warrensburg, Illinois. (J.C. Allen and Son Photo.)

varying capacity. This has been done by Dr. J. C. Headley for floor-managed flocks in Illinois, and some of his estimates will be used for illustration.

Total capital investment in house and equipment varied from $4.14 per bird capacity for the 1,000-layer plant to $3.25 for the 100,000-layer establishment, but the division between house and equipment remained almost constant from 10,000 to 100,000—63% house and 37% equipment. The total house investment ranged from just under $3,000 for the 1,000-layer plant to $205,000 for the plant for 100,000 layers. Corresponding totals for equipment were $1,154 and $119,639. Converted to an annual basis, the non-feed costs for plants from 5,000 to 100,000 capacity are shown in Table 13–2.

It is significant that the percentage distribution of non-feed costs among various items—stock, labor, housing and equipment, and so forth—was almost identical for all plants from 10,000 to 100,000 capacity. This indicates that a 10,000-layer plant, large enough to warrant installation of an egg collection belt, can be efficient in terms of direct labor used in caring for the hens. The calculations also make clear the importance of operating any plant at full capacity. The annual non-feed costs per layer amounted to $2.54 for a 25,000-layer plant, but jumped to $2.85 in a 50,000-layer plant operated at half capacity.

Table 13–2.   Synthesized Annual Non-Feed Costs in Relation to Size of Plant

	House Capacity (Number of Layers)				
	5,000	10,000	25,000	50,000	100,000
Depreciation:					
Housing (15-year life)	$773	$1,500	$3,467	$6,880	$13,667
Equipment (8-year life)	625	1,636	3,907	7,592	14,955
Interest (6% on average investment)	498	1,068	2,498	4,918	9,739
Manure removal (custom basis)	250	500	1,250	2,500	5,000
Utilities	90	280	600	1,200	2,400
Taxes	215	446	1,064	2,000	4,163
Supplies	700	1,400	3,000	6,000	12,000
Subtotal	$3,151	$6,830	$15,786	$31,189	$61,924
Stock depreciation (15% mortality)	8,515	16,630	41,075	81,150	161,300
Interest on stock investment	281	555	1,373	2,715	5,400
Labor ($1.50/hour)	3,285	2,190	5,213	9,600	18,600
Total non-feed costs	$15,232	$26,205	$63,447	$124,654	$247,224
Annual non-feed costs per layer	$3.04	$2.62	$2.54	$2.49	$2.47
	Percentage Distribution				
Stock charges	58	66	67	67	67
Labor	22	8	8	8	8
House and Equipment	12	16	16	16	16
Utilities, Taxes, Supplies	6	8	7	7	7
Manure removal	2	2	2	2	2
	100	100	100	100	100

From University of Illinois, Department of Agricultural Economics Publication AERR-68, January, 1964.

Costs and Returns

Cost of production includes both cash and non-cash items, and although cash costs in the production of eggs are rather high when compared with the cash costs in some other enterprises, they make up only about two thirds of the total cost. Feed purchased is by far the largest item in cash cost. Among the non-cash costs are the labor of the operator and that of members of his family, together with interest and depreciation that may be charged against the business. (Refer to Tables 13–3 and 13–4.)

Major Cost Items. The largest item of cost in the production of eggs is feed. It will normally make up from 65 to 70% of the total cost. With increased specialization, as on poultry breeding farms, many extra costs are introduced so that the relative importance of feed becomes less.

Table 13–3. Costs and Efficiencies of Egg Production by Regions, 1973–74

Item	Northeast	South	Midwest	California
Sample characteristics:				
Farms (number)	67	103	51	22
Layers per farm (thousands)	24.2	28.2	19.2	60
Eggs sold per farm (thousand cases)	15.1	17.9	12.2	37.8
Rate of lay (% hen-housed production)	62.6	63.5	62.5	62.0
Feed conversion (lbs/doz)	4.18	4.24	4.18	4.70
Mortality (%)	10.7	15.1	12.9	16
Costs, cents per dozen				
Feed	30.17	27.56	28.00	28.25
Replacement pullets	8.97	8.15	8.33	7.25
Hired labor	.47	.92	.80	2.15
Utilities	.70	.28	.55	.50
Other variables	.27	.69	.37	.40
Total variable costs	40.58	37.60	38.05	38.55
Depreciation	1.13	1.18	1.55	1.20
Repairs, maintenance	.20	.28	.20	.20
Taxes, interest	.80	.94	.88	1.40
Insurance	.17	.14	.18	.20
Total fixed costs	2.30	2.54	2.81	3.00
Total costs	42.88	40.14	40.86	41.55

Reported by U. S. Department of Agriculture, Agricultural Marketing Service.

Table 13–4. San Diego County, California, Egg Cost Study, 1974, 1975, 1976

	Average Costs ¢/dozen		
	1974	1975	1976
Feed cost	29.6	29.5	28.4
Net replacement cost	8.6	6.9	6.6
Labor cost	2.0	1.9	2.0
Miscellaneous costs	1.3	1.3	2.0
Depreciation (15%)	1.3	1.3	1.3
Interest (8%)	1.5	1.5	1.5
Management	1.0	1.0	1.0
Total net cost	45.3	43.2	41.9
Wholesale income	41.0	42.0	49.0
Profit, or loss per dozen	−4.3	−1.1	+7.1

Reported by Robert H. Adolph, Farm Advisor, California Agricultural Extension Service.

During periods of extremely high or very low feed prices, the normal relationship may be temporarily disturbed. Feed is also the principal item of cost in raising pullets for flock replacement, about twice the cost of the chicks to be raised.

If flock size is below 10,000 layers, labor will usually be the second largest item of cost, but with larger flocks and fully automated equipment, labor cost per layer is much reduced and stock charges—pullet replacement and depreciation of layers—will move into second place.

Sources of Income. Just as feed accounts for the largest share of expense, so market eggs form the chief source of income on commercial egg farms. Hatching eggs, cull hens, and young chickens sold for meat are of varying importance as sources of income on individual farms, but in the aggregate they are of only minor significance. This is quite in contrast to the situation on general farms in earlier years, when the income from poultry meat often approached and occasionally exceeded that from market eggs. When a poultry business is being expanded, the increase in inventory value of the flock may represent a significant percentage of total yearly receipts.

Major Factors Influencing Profits

Profits in egg production are influenced by many things, but the most important factors seem to be (1) size of business, (2) egg yield per hen, and (3) efficiency in the use of labor. The third factor is directly related to the first in that small flocks can rarely be handled as efficiently as large ones. On the other hand, labor is not always efficiently utilized on large flocks.

Under certain conditions the rate of mortality and depreciation of flocks may outweigh everything else. The price received for market eggs, though not often under the control of the operator, also may have much to do with the profit on the enterprise.

Size of Business. Many poultry businesses are less profitable than they might be because they are too small. A small flock can never make a large profit, nor can it ever cause the owner a large loss. One who is trying to make a living from poultry must keep a rather large flock and must assume the risk of a possible large loss in order to have the opportunity of making a reasonably large total net income. Economic studies of poultry farming have shown, without exception, that net income increases almost in direction proportion to the increase in size of flock. Within the limits of flock size that have come under careful study and observation, there has been little evidence of the application of the law of diminishing returns. It seems clear that if one intends to stay in the business of producing market eggs he should plan to maintain a flock that is larger than the average in most, if not all, sections of the country.

Not many recent records are available from which to show the effect of flock size on costs and returns, but when the 29 farms included in Table

Table 13–5.   Cost Control Measures and Other Data for 29 New York Poultry Farms, 1970

	19 Farms with Poultry only	10 Farms with Poultry & Grain
Number of hens	17,140	13,300
Man equivalent (Number of men).........	3.5	3.0
Number of hens per man	4,897	4,433
Eggs produced per hen	223	213
Layer feed bought per hen	$ 3.33	$ 2.79
Feed bought per dozen eggs produced	17.9¢	15.7¢
Pounds of feed per dozen eggs produced ..	4.6	4.3
Total labor cost per hen, including operator's labor	$ 1.35	$ 1.58
Total labor cost per dozen eggs produced .	7.3¢	8.9¢
Net power and machinery cost per hen ...	$ 0.75	$ 1.29
Building repairs, electricity, taxes, and insurance per hen....................	$ 0.35	$ 0.38
Total expenses per $100 of receipts	$ 90	$ 81
Total investment per hen	$ 7.39	$12.26
Average price received per dozen eggs	41.9¢	40.4¢

Agricultural Economics Extension Report 597, July, 1971.

13–5 are combined, and grouped according to number of hens per man, the effect on labor income is clear.

Hens per Man	Number of Farms	Labor Income per Operator
Under 4,000...................	15	$ 8,800
4,000 to 6,000	7	$12,535
Over 6,000	7	$19,150
All farms	29	$12,200

Eggs sold per hen on these farms in 1970 ranged from 169 to 259. The effect of this factor on labor income is also clear.

Eggs Sold per Hen	Number of Farms	Average Number of Hens	Labor Income per Operator
Under 210	5	14,802	$ 7,197
210 to 230.........	18	16,179	$13,047
More than 230.....	6	15,598	$15,559
All farms	29	15,816	$12,200

An analysis of 25 poultry farms in New York State (Table 13–6) demonstrates a close relationship between size and efficiency of production. As the size of the layer farm increased from 5,400 to 63,000 layers so did several important factors that affect profitability of the enterprise. The largest producers obtained the largest egg yields, highest efficiency of feed conversion, and the highest prices for their eggs. These farms had the lowest feed costs and were the most efficient in utilization of labor.

Egg Yield. Productive livestock has long been recognized as one of the essentials of good farming, and poultry farming is no exception to the rule.

Table 13–6. Relationship between Flock Size and Several Factors Affecting Profitability of the Enterprise for 25 New York Poultry Farms, 1975

Average Number of Layers	Eggs Sold per Layer	Av. Price Paid per Cwt Feed	Av. Price Received/ Doz. Eggs	Lb Feed per Doz Eggs	Hens per Man
63,000	275	$5.89	72.6¢	3.8	11,274
60,100	265	5.91	65.0	3.9	10,000
50,686	261	6.20	60.0	4.0	9,821
45,095	260	6.57	59.9	4.2	9,540
30,000	244	6.59	59.5	4.3	9,000
30,000	243	6.65	59.4	4.3	7,917
27,500	241	6.81	58.4	4.4	7,143
23,750	236	6.83	57.8	4.4	7,040
21,500	234	6.91	56.3	4.5	6,632
20,917	233	6.98	55.2	4.5	6,380
19,699	229	7.00	54.9	4.6	6,312
19,141	228	7.10	54.7	4.7	5,455
19,000	228	7.14	54.0	4.7	5,000
18,000	226	7.26	53.8	4.8	4,750
16,524	226	7.26	53.7	4.8	4,588
16,059	225	7.34	53.4	4.8	4,358
14,100	223	7.58	52.4	4.9	4,333
14,000	222	7.64	50.0	4.9	4,029
12,500	222	8.00	49.6	4.9	3,906
12,431	219	8.03	47.1	5.0	3,788
11,361	218	8.14	45.2	5.0	3,667
6,613	212	9.00	43.3	5.2	3,453
6,500	198	9.00	42.6	5.4	2,645
5,500	195	9.00		5.8	2,118
5,434	195				1,430

Agricultural Experiment Station, Cornell University.

High egg yields nearly always mean high costs per hen, but they usually result in low costs per dozen eggs, and of course they mean high gross returns per hen when comparison is made with low-producing flocks. The net result is that egg yield is one of the most important factors in determining the profits to be realized from a poultry farm business.

Data for 135 New York farms in 1946–47, given in Table 13–7, show the relation of egg yield to costs and returns at that time. Because of better breeding, feeding, and management, most commercial flocks today are laying as well as the best flocks of a few years ago, and the net effect of a small increase in average egg yield is not so apparent as it was formerly, but the differences are still important.

The effect of egg yield on profitability for contract egg producers is shown in data gathered by the Georgia Experiment Station for farms varying in method of housing (Table 13–8).

Table 13–7.   Relation of Eggs per Layer to Costs and Returns per Dozen Eggs on 135 Farms in New York State, 1946–47

	Light Breeds			Heavy Breeds		
	Low	Medium	High	Low	Medium	High
Number of farms	28	27	27	18	18	17
Average number of layers	1,252	1,022	1,006	604	609	629
Eggs per layer................	152	178	203	137	188	218
Percent mortality	13	17	15	21	13	15
Labor per dozen eggs (minutes)	9.3	8.1	7.2	6.8	7.8	9.0
Feed per dozen eggs (pounds)...	8.3	7.2	6.8	9.6	7.6	6.7
Cost per dozen eggs (cents):						
Feed	34.8	29.9	28.3	39.8	31.3	27.3
Labor	9.2	8.9	7.7	11.9	8.4	9.1
Buildings and equipment	3.8	3.6	2.8	3.6	4.2	3.5
Depreciation	6.9	6.1	6.9	2.3	2.9	2.3
Other.....................	2.8	2.9	2.6	4.2	3.6	3.5
Total	57.5	51.4	48.3	61.8	50.4	45.7
Returns per dozen eggs (cents):						
Eggs	54.7	54.4	55.7	51.1	51.4	51.2
Other.....................	0.2	0.4	0.3	0.6	0.6	0.5
Total	54.9	54.8	56.0	51.9	52.0	51.7
Profit per dozen eggs	−2.6	3.4	7.7	−10.1	1.6	6.0

Cornell Agr. Exp. Sta. Bulletin 864.

Table 13–8   Average Returns per Hen for Selected Contract Producers in Georgia, 1965–1970

	Average Returns per Hen (¢/hen)						
	Production (doz. per hen)						
	Below 15.0	15.0– 15.9	16.0– 16.9	17.0– 17.9	18.0– 18.9	19.0– 19.9	Above 20
Conventional floor	13.37	17.93	23.61	24.84	24.89	31.17	37.24
Manual cage	22.73	27.74	31.48	33.31	36.63	40.19	45.64
Mechanical cage	12.28	17.05	20.55	21.74	24.79	28.29	33.12
Average for all systems	16.13	20.91	25.21	26.63	28.77	33.22	38.67

Reported by Georgia Experiment Station.

The contract arrangement guaranteed the producers 5¢ per dozen for grade A eggs and 2¢ per dozen for undergrades. The contract producer was responsible for the following costs: labor, buildings, equipment, electricity, litter, and water. The contractor supplied the hens, feed, medication, egg packing materials, and technical service.

Under this contract arrangement, the return to the producer for his management and labor input was greatly affected by egg yield. A 30% increase in yield from 15 dozen eggs per hen to 20 dozen eggs per hen increased the return to the producer by slightly more than twofold. At the highest level of egg yield, for those producers with manual cage operations, the return averaged $13,700 for a flock of 30,000 laying hens.

One important reason why high egg yields are profitable is that the feed required for maintenance is constant for hens of any given weight and bears no relation to the number of eggs laid. The amount of feed consumed for each dozen eggs produced is therefore much less in the case of high-producing hens or flocks than it is for low producers. With the high-energy rations currently in use, a 5-pound hen laying 4 eggs every 10 days will eat 6.7 pounds of total feed for each dozen eggs, whereas a hen of the same size laying 7 eggs every 10 days will eat only 4.3 pounds of feed for each dozen. A 4-pound hen, because of her lower maintenance requirement, will do even better, eating 5.8 pounds and 3.8 pounds of feed for each dozen eggs, respectively, at the two rates of production. At 8 cents a pound for feed, the respective feed costs of a dozen eggs would be 54 and 34 cents for the 5-pound hen, and 46 and 30 cents for the 4-pound hen.

Labor Efficiency. Efficient use of labor is important on poultry farms because, as has already been stated, the number of hens kept has a great deal to do with the size of the farm income. For maximum labor efficiency it is necessary also to have good stock, because a high egg yield per hen makes possible the production of a large number of eggs per man. Eggs produced per hour of man labor, or per man employed per year, can be used as an index of labor efficiency.

In a study of labor saving on Pennsylvania poultry farms it was found that installation of automatic watering systems saved nearly one-half of chore time daily per 1,000 layers. Substantial savings in chore time and travel were effected by such changes as removing partitions and rearranging nests.

In a 1957 Illinois report the time required for hand feeding 1,000 hens averaged 25 to 30 minutes a day, compared with 10 to 12 minutes a day when self-feeders were used, and 6 minutes a day with mechanical feeders.

Competition has forced poultrymen to find ways of caring for more layers per man, or selling more dozens of eggs per man, or both, in order to get the cost per dozen low enough to leave a margin of profit with current egg prices.

Large commercial egg operations use bulk delivery of feed, automatic feeders to distribute feed to the laying pens, automatic egg washing and grading equipment, and in many cases mechanical belts for gathering eggs—all with the primary objective of saving labor and reducing the cost of each dozen eggs.

Table 13-9 shows the range of experience of commercial poultry farmers in New York State with respect to several factors related to size of business, production rates, and labor efficiency. The figure at the top of each column is the median of the highest 10% of the farms in that factor. For example, the figure 250 at the top of the column headed "Eggs Sold per Hen" is the median of the 10% of poultry farms with the highest

Table 13-9. New York Poultry Farms Ranked by Several Economic Factors

Rank by 10% Groups	Number of Hens	Eggs Sold per Hen	Hens per Man	Dozens of Eggs Sold per Man	Pounds of Feed per Dozen Eggs
1	55,000	250	12,000	240,000	4.0
2	30,000	235	9,500	175,000	4.3
3	20,000	225	7,500	125,000	4.6
4	16,000	220	6,000	100,000	4.7
5	12,000	217	5,000	85,000	4.8
6	9,500	214	4,000	75,000	4.9
7	7,000	210	3,500	65,000	5.0
8	5,200	205	3,000	55,000	5.2
9	4,000	200	2,500	45,000	5.4
10	3,000	185	2,000	35,000	5.8

From a chart prepared in the Department of Agricultural Economics, New York State College of Agriculture, for farms in New York State. Each column is independent of the others.

Table 13-10. Investment and Annual Operating Expenses Excluding Labor for 30,000-Bird Laying Flocks Housed under Various Conditions in Georgia, 1975

Housing	Feeding*	Collection*	Investment per Hen dollars per hen	Operating Costs excluding Labor dollars per hen	Labor Requirement hens/man hr/day
Floor, litter	mechan.	manual	3.72	0.713	1,100
Open house, cage	manual	manual	2.17	0.475	2,500
Open house, cage	mechan.	manual	2.80	0.575	2,750
Semicontrolled environment, cage	mechan.	manual	3.50	0.742	2,750
Controlled environment High rise, flat deck cage	mechan.	mechan.	3.80	0.777	3,000
Controlled environment 4-tier cage	mechan.	mechan.	2.80	0.633	3,000
Open high rise, wire floor	mechan.	mechan.	3.50	0.691	3,000

Adapted from the data of G.C. Lance: Poult. Sci., 57:835, 1978.
* Mechanized or manual.

number of eggs sold per hen. The other figures in that column are the medians for the second highest 10%, the third highest 10%, and so on. The nearer the top a given farm falls in respect to all five measures, the more successful it will be. A study by the Georgia Experiment Station demonstrates the greater labor efficiency of fully mechanized layer operations over those employing labor instead of capital for feeding and egg collection (Table 13–10).

Mortality and Flock Depreciation. One of the most serious problems confronting poultrymen in many sections of the country is the mortality rate among laying pullets, and to a less extent among older hens. Methods of sanitation, as previously pointed out, have enabled flock owners to bring the mortality rate of young growing chickens reasonably well under control, but the problem of reducing or preventing excessive mortality of laying stock is not yet completely solved. It appears that the most promising method of attack is through breeding and selection for highly resistant strains, but until the vital significance of the problem is fully appreciated, progress is likely to be rather slow.

Mortality among laying flocks not only causes a direct monetary loss amounting to the value of the birds that die, but it results in further indirect losses that may be even more costly in spite of the fact that they are less apparent. If no replacements are made, houses, equipment, and labor will be used with decreasing efficiency as the death loss mounts during the year. This is partly obscured by the common practice of making calculations, such as average egg yield, on the basis of the average number of layers in the flock during the year, or on the hen-day basis. A flock that has lost 50% of the original number by death may thus show an average yield well above 200 eggs. If all such calculations were made on the basis of the number of hens and pullets at the beginning of the laying year, the picture would often be quite different.

The mortality among commercial flocks observed in some of the economic studies of poultry farming made during the last 45 years was 7% in New Jersey in 1915–1916; 13% in Oregon in 1926–1928; 17% in New Hampshire in 1929–1930; 20% in Utah in 1929–1931; 25% in New York in 1940–1941, and 13% in California in 1956–57–58.

Fortunately there has been substantial improvement in this respect in recent years. Vaccination against Marek's disease has been a major factor in the reduction of laying hen mortality. Many commercial farms now experience a death loss of no more than 10%. If this is distributed uniformly through the year, the effect on the cost of producing eggs is small, especially with leghorns or other light breeds with relatively small market value when sold for meat. The difference between the inevitable depreciation and total loss by death is not very great.

Even if the pullets all lived through the first 12 months in the laying house, they would be worth less after a year of producing than at the beginning. As potential egg-producers they are worth more when about 6 months old and ready to lay than at any other time. The normal expectation is that they will continue to be worth less and less as they get older until their egg-laying value is equal to their meat value.

The difference between the value of a pullet at the beginning of the year and the value of the same individual at the end of the year is depreciation and is one of the important costs in commercial egg production. If a pullet is worth $2.00 at the beginning of the year and will bring but 50 cents after 12 months of laying, it has clearly cost the poultryman $1.50 just to own her for a year, without considering any expense for feed, labor, housing, interest, and the like. Whether one likes it or not, depreciation is just as much a part of the cost of producing eggs as it is a part of the cost of owning an automobile.

Price of Market Eggs. Although price is less completely under the control of the farm operator than the other factors that have been discussed, it is nevertheless true that the average price received for eggs is one of the most important factors in determining the labor income on a poultry farm. A high average price is the result of securing a large proportion of the yearly egg production during the high-price months, or of marketing eggs at premium prices, or both. If one can obtain a premium of one cent a dozen on market eggs when selling 20 dozen eggs per layer annually, the difference in income will amount to $800 a year on a flock of 4,000 layers. Going after a price premium may be a very profitable way for a poultryman to spend part of his time.

The Replacement Cycle

On most large commercial egg farms today chicks to be grown out as replacement pullets are started 2 to 4 times a year instead of only once in the spring. This makes it possible to maintain a fairly uniform output of eggs throughout the year. It also simplifies the problem of labor distribution and keeps brooding and rearing equipment, as well as layer houses, in use at near capacity most of the year.

It is usually more profitable to replace layers when they are 17 to 20 months of age than to keep them longer. Young birds lay at a higher rate and produce eggs of better shell quality than do older hens. California egg costs studies have shown, however, that feed and replacement costs per dozen eggs tend to balance out over a range of 12 to 24 months of production. As replacement cost goes down by keeping pullets longer, rate of lay goes down and feed cost per dozen goes up. Assuming a net cost of $1.60 per replacement pullet (after deducting a credit for salvage value of surviving hens) and a feed cost of $7.00 per 100 pounds, with a feed intake of 90 pounds per hen per year, the comparative costs work out as follows:

	Month of Lay		
	12	18	24
Dozens of eggs per hen...............	20	25	30
Replacement cost per dozen (cents)....	8.0	6.4	5.3
Feed per layer housed (pounds)	80	113	143
Feed per dozen eggs (pounds).........	4.0	4.5	4.8
Feed cost per dozen (cents)..........	28.0	31.5	33.6
Sum of feed and replacement cost per dozen eggs (cents)	36.0	37.9	38.9

An alternative procedure followed by many producers in some parts of the country is to buy started pullets from a dependable source instead of raising their own. In any event, as each group of layers approaches 17 months of age, both their performance and the current market situation should be studied before deciding on the exact age at which to sell them. Since brooding and rearing are on a year-round basis in today's operations, it may sometimes be better to skip a hatch and carry a good flock of layers for an extra 3 to 6 months than to replace them at an arbitrary age.

Hens that have gone through a molt will produce at a higher rate than at the end of the previous production year. They do not peak as well as young pullets, and the decline in production after the peak is more rapid than during the first year of production. It is possible, however, to obtain several months of good production using forced molting, and since the birds are of maximum size, large eggs will be produced rather than the high numbers of pullet and unmarketable eggs produced during the first cycle of production. Eggshell quality and internal quality of eggs decline steadily throughout the first production year. Poorer quality, in addition to the low egg production, contributes to the declining value of the production flock. Quality and production are considerably lower during the second cycle of production.

Various procedures are used to induce molting. In general they include cessation of stimulatory lighting and short-term restriction of water and longer term restriction of feed. One such program is shown below:

Days	
1,2	discontinue stimulatory lighting, remove feed and water.
3–7	provide water ad libitum, but continue to withhold feed.
8–29	provide water and feed ad libitum.
30	reinstate stimulatory lighting. Provide feed and water ad libitum.

Forced molting of layers to be retained beyond one year has become sufficiently common that the U. S. Department of Agriculture now reports

Table 13–11.   Summary of Average Labor Returns for Independent (Family Farm) Egg Producers in Georgia, 1965–1970

Type of Housing[a]	Cycle of Production	Size No. of Hens	Capital Investment $	Av.[b] Production doz/hen	Labor[c] Returns $/hr
Floor	first	10,975	38,852	18.07	1.56
Manual cage	first	12,128	36,505	17.25	2.15
Mechanical cage	first	23,607	85,457	17.25	3.51
Floor	second	10,975	25,462	10.12	1.66
Manual cage	second	12,128	21,709	10.12	2.12
Mechanical cage	second	23,607	56,657	10.12	3.46

Adapted from a report of the Georgia Agricultural Experiment Station.
[a]Floor: automatic feeders, manual egg gathering. Manual cage: hand feeding and egg gathering. Mechanical cage: mechanized feeding and egg collection.
[b] Length of production period. First cycle: 377 days, floor; 382 days, cages. Second cycle: 295 days.
[c] Returns to labor and management for labor required to care for the flock.

each month for 17 states both the percentage of laying stock being molted and the percentage of molt completed. The figures for California were 10 and 40%, respectively, in November, 1977, with all 17 states averaging 3.8 and 14.7%.

Table 13–11 summarizes the average labor returns for independent egg producers in Georgia using hens in the first and second cycles of production.

Poultry Farm Organization

Perhaps the most significant, and at the same time the most encouraging, fact growing out of the various analyses that have been made of poultry farm records is that whether the labor income is high or low depends almost exclusively on the operator himself. The possibilities seem to be limited only by the extent to which he will adopt profitable practices and a profitable farm organization.

Aside from the necessary physical qualifications, the operator of a specialized commercial egg enterprise should have a more or less natural aptitude for attention to details. Permanent success in specialized poultry farming is, to a considerable degree, a matter of constant and sharp attention to a great many details, the neglect of any one of which may lead to serious losses. Men who do not like to bother with too much detail are not naturally well fitted for success in specialized poultry farming. Persistent attention and genuine interest in details are necessary qualifications for the poultry business.

The accumulation of a reserve fund for tiding over an occasional bad year is a prime essential of permanent success in any type of specialized farming. Every enterprise has a bad year occasionally, sometimes owing to circumstances beyond the operator's control. The large cash expenditures required for feed make it especially necessary for the specialized poultry farm to have a reserve fund.

From a dollars viewpoint, the requirements for a successful egg-farming business can be simply stated.

1. Have productive stock. This means hens with the genetic makeup and the physical stamina necessary for high annual egg production. High production is essential if the feed cost of each dozen eggs is to be kept at a profitable level.
2. Keep enough hens—as many as one can care for. This is necessary in order to make possible a reasonably large gross income and to be able to reduce the man labor requirement.
3. Provide comfortable housing so as to permit year-round production. This means protection from extremes of both heat and cold, along with the necessary safeguards to flock health.
4. Feed a well-balanced ration. A close corollary is found in doing everything possible to encourage maximum feed consumption.
5. Practice quantity buying of feed and other supplies so as to permit maximum savings in costs. Bulk delivery of feed is an example.
6. Find and maintain a market outlet that pays a premium price for high-quality eggs.

BROILER PRODUCTION

The proportion of the total chicken meat supply furnished by commercial broilers has risen steadily from about 5% in 1935 to nearly 50% in 1951

Table 13–12.   Chick Production by Commerical Hatcheries, 1976, with Comparisons for 1939

| | Millions of Chicks, 1976 | | % of Yearly Total | |
	Broiler Type	Egg Type	1976	1939
January	279	38	8.0	4.5
February	268	40	7.7	9.4
March	310	54	8.9	20.3
April	311	60	8.9	26.5
May	321	60	9.2	21.9
June	309	47	8.8	7.8
July	304	40	8.8	2.1
August	296	38	8.5	1.5
September	272	40	7.8	1.6
October	268	40	7.7	1.5
November	268	34	7.7	1.4
December	283	39	8.1	1.5
U.S. Total	3,488	530	100	100

Based on data reported by the U. S. Department of Agriculture.

Table 13-13.   Commercial Broiler Production in the 10 Leading
Broiler States, 1976

	Number Produced (millions)
Arkansas	540
Georgia	452
Alabama	430
North Carolina	316
Mississippi	257
Maryland	199
Texas	191
Delaware	160
California	105
Virginia	89
10-State Total	2,739
U.S. Total	3,280
10-State Share of U.S. Total (%)	84

As reported by the U. S. Department of Agriculture.

and then to 80% in 1977. There are well-defined broiler-producing areas in Delmarva, northern Georgia, northwest Arkansas, Texas, North Carolina, Alabama, Mississippi, and in parts of New England, and similar if less extensive areas in several other states. Since most commercial producers depend on hatcheries for their supply of chicks, and since they can change sources promptly if performance is not satisfactory, there are many hatcheries and breeding farms that specialize in the production and sale of broiler chicks (Table 13-12). The total placement of broiler-type chicks in 21 commercial broiler producing states in 1976 was 3,293 million. The production for the ten leading states is given in Table 13-13.

The Broiler Business

Many broiler farms have lost money—sometimes because of disease, more often because of inefficient management, and at times simply because the market price of broilers at the time of sale was too low in proportion to the cost of feed which had gone into their production. The total production of broilers is enormous, and the business is well established in many areas, but it is nevertheless true that only the more efficient operators are in a position to make substantial profits.

The costs of broiler production for the period 1972–1974 were summarized by the U.S. Department of Agriculture based on the records of over 1,000 flocks in the South and Northeast. The data presented in Table 13-14 are separated into grower and contractor costs. Contract arrangements varied among farms, and production costs vary with seasonal unit prices of the items. The data do not necessarily represent current production costs on broiler farms.

Table 13-14.   Production Costs for Contract Broiler Production in
Three Regions[a]

Item	South[b] 1972-74	Northeast[c] 1972-74	West Coast 1974-76
Sample characteristics:			
Farms (no.)	108	118	88
Flocks sold (no.)	415	592	396
Average live weight			
(lb/bird)	3.77	3.96	3.98
Feed conversion			
(lb feed/lb broiler)	2.17	2.14	2.2
	Average Cents per Pound, Salable Live Weight		
Production costs:			
Grower			
Fuel	0.14	0.09[d]	0.06
Electricity	.07	.10	.11
Litter	.10	.03	.02
Hired labor	.15	.19[e]	.10
Miscellaneous	.19[f]	.02[g]	.03
Total variable	.65	.43	.32
Depreciation	.43	.43[h]	.47
Interest	.32	.21	.45
Insurance	.08	.08	.15
Repairs, maintenance	.11	.15	.13
Taxes	.05	.09	.15
Total fixed	.99	.96	1.35
Total grower	1.64	1.39	1.67
Contractor			
Feed	16.85	16.25	18.43
Chicks	2.80	2.77	4.13
Grower payment	2.30	2.63	2.15
Medication and vaccination	.24	.34[i]	.20
Fuel	.14	.32	.39
Litter	.02	.10	.05
Other	.32[j]	.11[k]	.24
Total contractor	22.47	22.52	25.59

[a] U. S. Department of Agriculture. Economic Research Service. Agricultural Economic Report 381. Data collected by the Georgia, Pennsylvania, and Missouri Agricultural Experiment Stations under cooperative agreement with Econ. Res. Serv., U.S. Dept. of Agr. Records from mid-1972 to mid-1976. [b] Includes Alabama, Georgia, North Carolina, Arkansas, Mississippi, Texas. [c] Includes Pennsylvania, Maine, Delaware, Maryland, Virginia. [d] Includes fuel use for manure and other waste disposal and fuel for heat. See also [e]. [e] Unadjusted for payment in kind frequently associated with manure disposal. [f] Includes water disposal, water, dues, and other costs. [g] Includes sanitation, dues, and other miscellaneous costs. [h] Includes rent. [i] Includes services for sexing, debeaking. [j] Includes administration, field supervision, insurance, and miscellaneous. Not all cost items included. [k] Includes sanitation, electricity, dues, and other miscellaneous costs. May not completely include some small items.

According to most contract arrangements, the grower provides the capital investment in buildings and equipment and supplies the labor and management. Total fixed costs vary from 60 to 80% of the growers' production costs, the largest share from depreciation of buildings and equipment and interest on the investment. Energy input (fuel and electricity and hired labor) represented 10 to 14% and 6 to 14% of the growers' total costs. The average returns above production costs for the grower varied with region from 0.5 to 1.25¢ per pound live weight of salable broiler.

Feed is by far the largest item in the cost of broiler production. It represented 72 to 75% of production costs in the three regions. Chick costs ranged from 12.3 to 16.1% and grower payments from 8.4 to 11.7% of total costs. Fuel costs were borne by grower or contractor depending on the contract agreement. Fuel plus electricity constituted 1.6 to 2.3% of production costs.

The broiler business requires a relatively large investment in short-term capital. From 40 to 50% of the total capital may be invested in chicks, feed, fuel, labor, and other cash costs. Furthermore, the amount of such capital increases rapidly as each lot of broilers approaches market age or weight. This is because feed represents about 60% of the total cost of production. It takes about 40 tons of feed to raise a lot of 10,000 broilers to market weight. They may eat only three fourths of a ton during the first week, but will require 7 to 8 tons during the final week, depending on the type of ration used, how well they have grown, and the weight at which they are sold.

Fig. 13–4. Automatic feeders save labor and reduce feed wastage, especially in broiler plants. A 40-foot house requires two loops to provide ample feeding capacity. (Courtesy of U.S. Egg and Poultry Magazine.)

Fig. 13–5. Exterior of a 300-foot broiler house. (Courtesy of Till M. Houston.)

Efficiency of feed utilization in the production of broilers has been increasing steadily for a number of years, partly because of the selection and breeding of chickens capable of rapid growth, and partly because of improved rations. Better management and improved housing, which have resulted in lower mortality, are also responsible for part of the improvement (Figs. 13–4, 13–5). The following data for selected years of the Maine Broiler Test are typical. The test was discontinued in 1966.

Year	Days Required to Reach 3.5 Pounds	Pounds of Feed for Each Pound of Gain
1952	74	3.13
1955	65	2.66
1958	60	2.18
1961	53	2.07
1964	49	1.87

Commercial broiler growers have made similar progress in improving feed conversion and in marketing broilers at young ages. The following data, made available through the courtesy of Lipman Research Center, Augusta, Maine, provide an excellent example.

Year	Market Age (days)	Market Weight (pounds)	Feed Conversion (pounds of feed per pound of weight)
1952	80	3.35	3.17
1953	78	3.20	3.12
1954	76	3.30	3.06
1955	74	3.35	2.87
1956	71	3.40	2.71
1957	71	3.45	2.56
1958	68	3.44	2.37
1959	70	3.65	2.43
1960	66	3.66	2.27
1961	67	3.80	2.24
1962	65	3.76	2.15
1963	63	3.85	2.15
1964	60	3.81	2.07
1965*	58	3.75	2.05

* Averages through July.

Since feed consumption increases with a decrease in environmental temperature, broiler growers are faced with the practical question of whether it is cheaper to provide some artificial heat in order to keep feed consumption at a minimum or to keep the broilers in unheated houses where they are certain to consume more feed. Workers at the University of Connecticut undertook to find an answer to this question. They found that with 2-pound broilers, as temperature dropped below 75° F, feed consumption increased by 0.6 pound of feed per 1,000 broilers per day for each drop of 1 degree of temperature. Simultaneously, feed conversion became less efficient at the rate of 0.1 pound of feed per pound of gain, with each decrease of 1 degree in environmental temperature. The

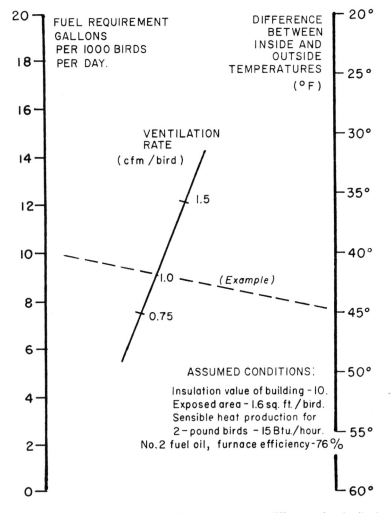

Fig. 13–6. Fuel required to maintain indicated temperature differences in a broiler house, with three different specified ventilation rates. (Based on data of Prince, Irish, and Potter, University of Connecticut.)

nomogram shown in Figure 13–6 was constructed from their data. It shows for the specified conditions the fuel requirement in gallons per 1,000 broilers per day to maintain any desired difference in temperature between inside and outside air for three different ventilation rates expressed as cubic feet of air per minute per bird.

Rate of Feed Conversion

Since feed is the largest single item of cost in broiler production, it follows that the rate at which feed is converted into poultry meat is an important measure of efficiency. Many factors affect the efficiency of feed utilization: environmental temperature, genetic potential for growth, nutritional adequacy of the starter, grower and finisher diets, and dietary energy concentration. Other environmental factors have an impact on efficiency. Uncomfortable temperatures, disease, and limited access to feed and water decrease the efficiency of feed conversion.

Energy consumption reflects the energy needs for growth, activity, and regulation of body temperature. Feed intake varies inversely with the concentration of energy in the diet. Australian researchers investigated the relationship between dietary energy level and food consumed to market weight for commercial strains of broilers. There were small differences between experiments, but the results of one experiment will be used as an example. In the range of 2.26 to 3.63 kcal of metabolizable energy per gram of feed, the relationship between feed intake and metabolizable energy for males and females to 1,500 and 1,800 grams body weight, respectively, was described by the following equations:

$$y = 8.64 - 1.59x \text{ (females)}$$
$$y = 9.64 - 1.76x \text{ (males)}$$
where y = total feed consumed per chick (kg) and
x = metabolizable energy content of the diet.

Using these relationships, the effect of dietary energy on food conversion is estimated as shown below:

Metabolizable Energy (kcal/lb)	Female[a] Feed Consumed (lb)	Feed Conversion[b] Ratio	Male[a] Feed Consumed (lb)	Feed Conversion[b] Ratio
1,000	11.3	3.42	12.7	3.18
1,090	10.6	3.21	11.9	2.98
1,180	9.9	3.00	11.1	2.78
1,270	9.2	2.79	10.4	2.60
1,360	8.5	2.58	9.6	2.40
1,450	7.8	2.36	8.8	2.20
1,540	7.1	2.36	8.0	2.00

[a] Males and females to 4.0 and 3.3 lb market weight.
[b] Feed conversion (lb)/lb of body weight.

The efficiency of feed utilization increases as the energy density of the diet increases. High energy feeds, however, are usually more expensive then low energy feeds.The broiler producer, therefore, must select the diet that optimizes feed costs per broiler.

Broiler growers must decide the age or weight at which to sell their flocks. Table 13–15 illustrates the effect of age on feed costs in commercial broiler production, based on data from the National Research Council on growth and efficiency of feed utilization of broiler chicks.

It can be seen from Table 13–15 that feed costs increase as a percentage of the market value of broilers as the age at marketing increases from 5 to 10 weeks. The increasing feed costs are a reflection of higher maintenance

Table 13–15.   Relationship between Age and Feed Costs in Broiler Production

Age wk	Body Weight lb	Feed Consumed lb	Feed Cost per lb Live Weight[a] ¢	Feed Costs, % of Market Value[b]
		Broiler Males		
5	2.20	3.72	14.88	62.2
6	3.05	5.34	14.88	64.4
7	3.90	5.34	15.58	67.4
8	4.62	9.25	17.02	73.7
9	5.35	11.40	18.11	78.4
10	5.99	13.77	19.54	84.6
		Broiler Females		
5	1.98	3.32	14.25	61.7
6	2.62	4.79	15.54	67.3
7	3.31	6.40	16.44	71.2
8	3.87	7.93	17.42	75.4
9	4.20	9.30	18.82	81.5
10	4.38	10.46	20.30	87.9

[a] Assuming 8.50¢ per lb of commercial feed—based on 1976 broiler grower feed prices.
[b] Based on U.S. annual average of 23.1¢/lb live weight in 1976.

Table 13–16.   Returns above Feed costs. Estimated from Values in Table 13–15

	Returns above Feed Costs	
Age wk	Male	Female
	¢/broiler	
5	19.20	17.52
6	25.06	19.81
7	29.32	22.06
8	28.09	21.99
9	26.68	17.97
10	21.32	12.27

requirements in older birds. Because females grow more slowly than males, a higher proportion of feed is used for maintenance of females than of males. Most broilers are marketed at approximately 8 weeks. At this age, feed costs represent 74% of market value for males.

Table 13–16 illustrates the return per broiler above feed costs. In this example the optimum return was obtained for males and females marketed at 7 weeks. These relations will vary depending on feed costs, market prices, and actual growth rates obtained under commercial conditions. The relationship of feed price and feed costs is shown below.

Feed Costs (¢) per lb of Broiler[a]

Feed Price ¢/lb	Weeks					
	5	6	7	8	9	10
7.0	11.83	12.25	12.83	14.02	14.91	16.09
7.5	12.68	13.13	13.75	15.02	15.98	17.24
8.0	13.52	14.00	14.66	16.02	17.04	18.39
8.5	14.37	14.88	15.58	17.02	18.11	19.54
9.0	15.22	15.76	16.50	18.02	19.18	20.69

[a] Males only.

These factors must be carefully monitored if broiler producers are to obtain maximum return on their investment. Many broiler producers have found that separate rearing of the sexes offers advantages in optimizing production costs and supplying a more uniform product at the time of marketing.

The demand for what have been called prescription-size broilers has been increasing. Cooking equipment, as well as cooking time, in food take-out stores is usually set for a uniform size of broiler and cannot be efficiently operated on any other basis. There is the further advantage that each customer is assured of the same size of serving. This is one reason for the increase in the practice of raising broilers "sex separate" instead of straight run.

Since male chicks reach a specified weight at an earlier age than do females, a broiler grower can more easily supply his market by separating the sexes when chicks are placed in the brooder house. At market time, a flock of males 49 days of age, for example, can be combined with a flock of females a week older so that perhaps three fourths of the entire lot will fall close to the desired weight. Color sexing of day-old chicks is a prerequisite to this type of operation. Some growers have even found it profitable to use a different feed formula for each sex to increase the total percentage that reach a desired market weight on a given date.

Sex separation may be worthwhile even if the grower is not concerned about meeting an exact weight specification at time of sale. Since pullets are less efficient feed converters than cockerels, maximum margins over cost can often be obtained by selling pullets as much as a week earlier than cockerels, when both are bought at the same price as baby chicks.

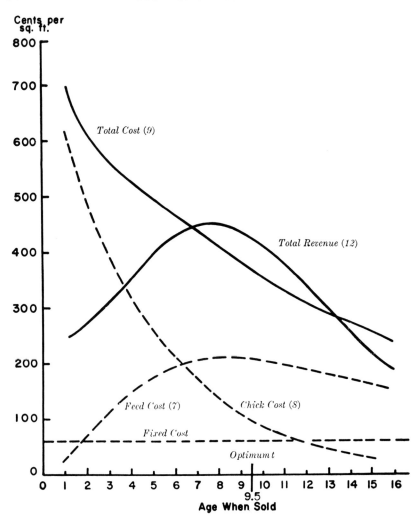

Fig. 13–7. Relationship between broiler costs, returns, and age (weeks) at sale, when calculated per square foot of available broiler house space. (After Hoepner and Freund in Virginia Agricultural Experiment Station Technical Bulletin 170.)

Some details of processing can also be adjusted more precisely under such conditions when mixed sexes and weights are handled at the same time. These would include scald water time and temperature, height adjustment of mechanical pickers, chill time in a continuous chiller, mechanical sizing of parts, and ease of uniform packaging.

The best time to market the flock depends on many factors: the requirement of the market, market price, feed costs, and fixed costs. The optimum represents a balance between all of these. Although the data in

Figure 13–7 are not recent, they illustrate the relationships between cost and returns in broiler production.

The higher the cost of feed, the earlier broilers must be sold if the grower is to obtain the maximum margin over feed cost. This is illustrated in the following calculations from the data in Table 13–15.

Returns above Feed Costs[a]

Age wk	Feed Price ¢/lb				
	7.0	7.5	8.0	8.5	9.0
	¢/broiler				
5	24.79	22.92	21.08	19.20	17.34
6	33.09	30.41	27.76	25.06	22.39
7	40.05	36.46	32.92	29.32	25.74
8	41.95	37.33	32.71	28.09	23.46
9	43.82	38.09	32.42	26.68	20.97
10	41.99	35.10	28.21	21.32	14.44

[a] Males only

On the other hand, high fixed or initial costs, such as a high price paid for chicks, may make it advantageous to sell at a later time in order to distribute these costs over more pounds of broiler and thus obtain a maximum margin. One set of costs increases, and the other decreases, the longer the chickens are kept, and the broiler grower is faced with the nice problem of deciding for each lot he raises when the combination of the two is at a minimum. The whole problem is further complicated by the prospect of a declining market.

Labor Efficiency

Efficient use of labor is an important means of increasing profits in the broiler business because more broilers raised per man mean more total dollar income per man. Size of business is therefore the most important contributing factor in labor efficiency. If only a few broilers are grown, one cannot afford to install expensive labor-saving equipment, but if the flock size warrants, there are many devices that will simplify work and reduce the number of hours required for each 1,000 broilers raised. Automatic watering systems alone may cut the chore labor in half, and the use of feed carriers or automatic feeding equipment will produce additional savings.

A recent development for handling live broilers between farm and processing plant is a bird suction system designated ChickenVeyor by the manufacturer. (See Fig. 13–8.) The self-contained equipment is truck mounted and is readily positioned outside a commercial broiler house, with the 7-inch diameter conveyor tube extending inside the house.

A

Fig. 13–8. Kice ChickenVeyor uses air-flow system to load 4,000 or more broilers an hour. *A,* Truck-mounted lift tower, showing horizontal tube from broiler house, and discharge spout for depositing chickens in racks or coops. *B,* Inlet hopper into which chickens are fed by catchers. *C,* Section of specially designed rack truck for easy loading of chickens as they leave the discharge spout. (Courtesy of Kice Metal Products Co., Inc., Wichita, Kansas.)

Chickens are dropped into a rubber-cushioned hopper that can be moved as loading progresses by extending the sectional tubing as necessary.

Labor is saved because catchers carry chickens only a few feet to the hopper, into which they are dropped one at a time, at a maximum rate of 120 a minute. Normal operating capacity is about half that, or 3,500 to 4,000 broilers an hour. Chickens move gently along the tube by suction, and eventually land on their feet in racks or cages for trucking to the processing plant, where they may be unloaded by air if desired. This method of handling keeps bruising at a minimum.

The same manufacturer can supply rack trucks under the trade name of ChickenVan. The racks have a side-opening door for each cage, and hinged tray-type bottoms for easy loading and unloading. Normal maximum capacity is twenty-five 4-pound broilers per cage.

Maximizing Annual Returns

The foregoing discussion has emphasized returns per pound of broiler for a single lot. Assuming that there is no appreciable price discount for broilers sold at the heavier weights, it has been shown that, as the price of feed decreases or the price of broilers increases, flocks should be carried to heavier weights. Many growers are tempted to do just the opposite— sell at lighter weights in order to take advantage of a good market. More and more growers are selling to buyers who want broilers that come as close as possible to a specified weight. As pointed out earlier, this often leads to the practice of growing males and females separately so that each can be sold at the desired weight instead of at some arbitrary age.

Table 13–17.   Effect of Various Factors on the Return per 1,000 Broilers in a Continuous Operation

Age at Market (weeks)	Av. Weight (pounds)	Av. Feed Consumption (pounds)	2-cent Change in Price of Chicks		½-cent Change in Cost of Feed per Pound		1-cent Change in Selling Price of Broilers	
			(a)	(b)	(a)	(b)	(a)	(b)
6	3.10	5.40	$149	$130	$204	$178	$187	$211
7	3.80	7.03	130	116	236	210	208	231
8	4.60	9.00	118	104	263	236	227	250
9	5.45	11.34	104	95	298	266	245	267
10	6.20	13.79	95	87	317	290	255	276
11	6.90	16.46	87	80	333	311	257	277
12	7.40	18.98	80	75	357	331	254	272

Growth and feed consumption from Maine Broiler Test results.
Calculations based on cockerels only.
(a) One-week interval between lots.
(b) Two-week interval between lots.

Table 13–18.   Effect of Time Allowed for Cleanup Between Lots in a Continuous Broiler Operation—10,000 Broilers per Lot

Age at market (weeks)	Time Allowed Between Lots				Av. weight* (pounds)
	7 days	10 days	14 days	21 days	
	Number of lots per year				
6	7.43	7.02	6.50	5.78	3.10
7	6.50	6.19	5.78	5.20	3.80
8	5.78	5.53	5.20	4.73	4.60
9	5.20	5.00	4.73	4.33	5.45
10	4.73	4.56	4.33	4.00	6.20
11	4.33	4.20	4.00	3.71	6.90
12	4.00	3.88	3.71	3.47	7.40
					Effect of one day
	Annual Gross Income When All Sales Are @ 21¢ a Pound				
6	$48,370	$45,744	$42,315	$37,628	$767
7	51,870	49,396	46,124	41,496	741
8	55,769	53,420	50,232	45,692	720
9	59,509	57,225	54,135	49,557	711
10	61,585	59,371	56,377	52,080	679
11	62,741	60,858	57,960	53,757	642
12	62,160	60,295	57,653	53,924	588

* Cockerels only, based on Maine Broiler Test results.

The specific dollar effect of changes in the cost of chicks or feed, or in the selling price of broilers, is shown in Table 13–17. The effect of varying the interval or cleanup time between lots is shown in Table 13–18.

In a completely integrated operation there are other variables to consider, such as costs in producing hatching eggs or in the hatching of the required number of chicks, the costs in feed milling, and the costs in processing the finished broilers. Under some conditions it may be more important to relate costs and returns to available space in broiler houses. In such cases it is convenient to reduce all figures to "cents per square foot" as shown in Figure 13–7. Note particularly the shape of the Feed Cost, Chick Cost, and Fixed Cost lines, and the curve of Total Revenue. The Total Cost curve is simply the sum of the other three cost curves.

Noles and Dendy, in Research Report 34 of the Georgia Station, summarized the results obtained by 78 Georgia broiler growers in 1967. These growers averaged 4.54 lots a year, with 17,443 broilers started per lot. Average final weight of broilers was 3.52 pounds, with a feed conversion ratio of 2.30 pounds of feed per pound of broiler delivered to the processing plant. Mortality rate was 3.13% and condemnation rate 3.10%. Net labor and management income per 1,000 broilers started averaged $24.88 for all farms in the study. Some of the detailed results are given in Tables 13–19, 13–20, 13–21 and 13–22.

Table 13-19.   Annual Costs and Returns of 78 Broiler Growers, 1967

	Average per Farm	Per 1,000 Broilers Delivered to Plant	Per Pound Delivered (cents)
Fixed Costs:			
Land, buildings, and equipment	$1995	$25.75	0.73
Variable Costs:			
Feed, litter, hired labor, electricity, and miscellaneous	$1846	$23.84	0.68
Total	$3841	$49.59	1.41
Income:			
Contract payment	$5434	$70.16	1.99
Manure	333	4.31	0.12
Total	$5767	$74.47	2.11
Labor and management income	$1926	$24.88	0.70

Georgia Agr. Exp. Station Research Report 34, December, 1968.

Table 13-20.   Relation of Flock Size to Labor Used—78 Georgia Broiler Growers, 1967

Birds Started per lot (1,000)	Average Number Started	Hours per Week per 1,000 Started		
		Family Labor	Hired Labor	Total
Less than 10.0	7,235	3.81	.22	4.03
10.0 to 14.9	12,019	2.75	.35	3.10
15.0 to 19.9	17,919	2.05	.27	2.32
20.0 to 24.9	22,450	1.40	.56	1.96
25.0 to 29.9	27,796	1.68	.31	1.99
30.0 and over	35,418	.94	.72	1.66

Georgia Agr. Exp. Station Research Report 34, December, 1968.

Table 13-21.   Effect of Mortality on Labor and Management Income—78 Georgia Broiler Growers, 1967

Mortality (%)	Number of Farms	Average Number Started per Year	Returns to Labor and Management per 1,000 Broilers Started
Under 2.00	17	81,958	$32.17
2.00 to 2.99	23	66,050	25.99
3.00 to 3.99	15	82,283	20.25
4.00 to 4.99	16	95,300	20.70
5.00 and over	7	81,676	15.71

Georgia Agr. Exp. Station Research Report 34, December, 1968.

Table 13–22.   Relationship of Final Body Weight, Feed Conversion Ratio, and Point Spread to Labor and Management Income of 78 Georgia Broiler Growers, 1967

	Number of Farms	Average Number Started per Year	Returns to Labor and Management per 1,000 Broilers Started
Final Body Weight (pounds)			
Under 3.40	13	59,156	$15.46
3.40 to 3.49	21	96,240	25.93
3.50 to 3.59	26	68,080	20.07
3.60 and over	18	93,504	34.58
Feed Conversion Ratio (Pounds of feed per pound of broiler)			
Under 2.20	13	68.527	$29.90
2.20 to 2.24	18	86,719	28.31
2.25 to 2.29	15	80,734	19.71
2.30 to 2.34	10	85,938	18.04
2.35 and over	22	78,228	23.42
Point Spread (Body weight divided by feed conversion ratio)			
Under 1.45	12	86,546	$18.04
1.45 to 1.49	15	75,070	19.41
1.50 to 1.54	16	73,168	19.62
1.55 to 1.59	13	79,914	29.60
1.60 to 1.64	15	76,190	27.09
1.65 and over	7	103,686	39.54

Georgia Agr. Exp. Station Research Report 34, December, 1968.

Since July, 1963, research workers in West Virginia have been studying another method designed to increase total annual returns in a continuous broiler operation. They used a windowless, insulated broiler house 32 × 72 feet in size, divided into three pens—a starting pen 32 × 12 feet, an intermediate pen 32 × 20 feet, and a finishing pen 32 × 40 feet. These pens provide 0.3, 0.5, and 1 square foot per broiler, respectively, when each lot contains 1,200 birds. Broilers are shifted from the starting pen to the intermediate pen at the end of 3 weeks, and to the finishing pen at the end of 6 weeks. At the end of 9 weeks they are sold.

As each pen is emptied, it is cleaned, washed thoroughly, and left idle for one week. Airtight partitions separate the pens, and the entrance to each pen is from the outside only, except when chicks are transferred from one pen to another through a panel opening.

With 3 weeks in each pen and a one-week interval between lots, 13 lots a year can be grown in a continuous operation, for a total of 15,600 broilers. Under the conventional system, the house would accommodate 2,304 broilers at 1 square foot per bird and, assuming the same one-week interval between lots, 5.2 lots could be grown in a year, for a total of 11,980 broilers. The difference works out as an increase of 30% for the new system. In the first year, the gain would be only 10% because it would take 8 weeks to fill the house to capacity.

The new system makes more efficient use of brooding equipment, as only two thirds as much is necessary, and fuel costs would be less per lot because a smaller volume of space would have to be heated. In northern parts of the country some heat would be needed in the entire house even under the new system. Annual fuel costs would of course be greater because more chicks would be brooded. With a lot of broilers going to market every 28 days, work loads would be evened out; chickens, feed, and supplies would arrive at shorter intervals, and the grower would be receiving a regular income every 28 days.

FUTURE OF THE POULTRY BUSINESS

Whenever there is temporary overproduction of poultry and eggs, the question of the future prospects for the business comes uppermost in the minds of many producers. In a business that is nationwide, every producer comes into more or less direct competition with producers in many other sections of the country. Certain sections have a price advantage in the selling of eggs and poultry, and others have an advantage in the way of low costs of production.

In the long run, the producer who will best be able to meet competition, and to survive recurring periods of depression in the industry, will be the one whose cost of production is lower than that of his competitors, and who is able, through individual initiative or collective organization, to receive a premium price for high-quality products.

The poultry business has become firmly established as a part of the agricultural production of this country. If it is to maintain and improve its position in the national economy, continued improvement in the quality of poultry and eggs that reach the consumer's table is essential.

Index

389